LAW AND DISAGREEMENT

Law and Disagreement

Jeremy Waldron

OXFORD
UNIVERSITY PRESS

OXFORD

UNIVERSITY PRESS

Great Clarendon Street, Oxford OX2 6DP

Oxford University Press is a department of the University of Oxford.
It furthers the University's objective of excellence in research, scholarship,
and education by publishing worldwide in

Oxford New York

Auckland Bangkok Buenos Aires Cape Town Chennai
Dar es Salaam Delhi Hong Kong Istanbul Karachi Kolkata
Kuala Lumpur Madrid Melbourne Mexico City Mumbai Nairobi
São Paulo Shanghai Singapore Taipei Tokyo Toronto

with an associated company in Berlin

Oxford is a registered trade mark of Oxford University Press
in the UK and in certain other countries

Published in the United States
by Oxford University Press Inc., New York

© Jeremy Waldron 1999

British Library Cataloguing in Publication Data
Data available

Library of Congress Cataloging in Publication Data
Data available

ISBN 0-19-826213-2
ISBN 0-19-924303-4 (pbk)

3 5 7 9 10 8 6 4 2

Typeset by Hope Services (Abingdon) Ltd.
Printed in Great Britain
on acid-free paper by
Bookcraft Ltd., Midsomer Norton, Somerset

And when men that think themselves wiser than all others, clamor and demand right Reason for judge; yet seek no more, but that things should be determined, by no other mens reason but their own, it is as intolerable in the society of men, as it is in play after trump is turned, to use for trump on every occasion, that suite whereof they have most in their hand.

Thomas Hobbes, *Leviathan* (1651), Chapter V

Acknowledgements

This book began life as a collection of my recent essays on jurisprudence. But in the course of working them up for publication, I found myself doing much more rewriting than I had expected, in several cases dividing up articles so as to make the argument more consecutive and in other cases writing entirely new pieces. I hope that the overall result is more like a book than a collection of essays.

To the extent that *Law and Disagreement* reproduces previously published work, I am grateful to publishers and editors for permission to use and modify that work here. Chapters Two, Three, and Four embody material originally presented as the 1994 Gerber Lecture at the University of Maryland Law School and published as 'The Dignity of Legislation' in the *Maryland Law Review*, 54 (1995). Chapter Five was published in the *Georgetown Law Review*, 84 (1996). Chapter Six appeared first in Hebrew in the *Tel Aviv University Law Review*, 18 (1994); it was published subsequently in a collection entitled *Law and Interpretation: Essays in Legal Philosophy*, edited by Andrei Marmor (Oxford: Oxford University Press, 1995). Chapter Seven appeared in a special issue of *Pacific Philosophical Quarterly* in 1995 devoted to John Rawls's book *Political Liberalism*. Chapter Eight was published in a collection edited by Robert George, entitled *Natural Law Theory: Contemporary Essays* (Oxford: Clarendon Press, 1992). Chapter Nine appeared first in the journal *Legal Theory*, 3 (1997). Chapter Ten reproduces the first half of an article entitled 'A Right-Based Critique of Constitutional Rights', which appeared originally in the *Oxford Journal of Legal Studies*, 13 (1993). Bits and pieces of the second half of that article have been scattered throughout Chapters Eleven, Twelve, and Thirteen. A version of Chapter Eleven appears in the *Aristotlean Society Proceedings* for 1998. A version of Chapter Twelve appears in a book entitled *Constitutionalism: Philosophical Foundations*, edited by Larry Alexander (New York: Cambridge University Press, 1998); Chapter Twelve also embodies portions of a short piece originally published as 'Freeman's Defense of Judicial Review' in *Law and Philosophy*, 13 (1994). A shorter version of Chapter Thirteen appears in the *Journal of Political Philosophy* (1998).

The present book does not include all the work that I have done recently on themes of disagreement, legislation, and rights. It will be followed shortly by another book, entitled *The Dignity of Legislation*, comprising the Seeley Lectures I gave at the University of Cambridge in 1996. There is a certain amount of overlap. Both books pursue a central agenda of mine, which is to enrich jurisprudence with the resources of political theory.

Both books attempt to recover and highlight ways of thinking about legislation that present it as a dignified mode of governance and a respectable source of law. The division of labour between the two volumes is as follows. *The Dignity of Legislation* is concerned mainly to explore the resources we have in our tradition of political thought for sustaining and elaborating the view of legislation I have just mentioned. It looks particularly at the work of Aristotle, John Locke, and Immanuel Kant – to see what we can learn from them in regard to the standing of this philosophically under-theorized form of law-making. The present volume – *Law and Disagreement* – is more analytic in its approach. It focuses more on lines of argument than particular thinkers. Rather than pursuing at length issues in the interpretation of (say) Locke or Kant, it consists more of argument and reflection about legislation, disagreement, and rights, peppered with haphazard references back to the canonical tradition of legal and political philosophy.

I have been pursuing this project for several years. It stretches back to a presentation I gave to the Columbia Legal Theory Workshop in 1993 and, in the case of my worries about the judicial review of legislation, to a paper I published in a Nomos Volume (XXXII) on *Majorities and Minorities* in 1990. Over the years, I have benefited enormously from the hospitality of various workshops and forums and from the comments, criticisms, and suggestions of friends and colleagues. They include Larry Alexander, Charles Black, Tom Campbell, Jean Cohen, Jules Coleman, Meir Dan-Cohen, Michael Dorf, John Dunn, Ronald Dworkin, David Estlund, George Fletcher, Jim Flynn, Jill Frank, Robert George, Les Green, Kent Greenawalt, Amy Gutmann, Bob Hargrave, David Heyd, David Johnston, Sanford Kadish, Victoria Kamsler, George Kateb, David Lieberman, Stephen Macedo, John Manning, Andrei Marmor, Frank Michelman, Michael Moore, Sidney Morgenbesser, Thomas Nagel, Philippe Nonet, Pasquale Pasquino, Stephen Perry, Thomas Pogge, Robert Post, Eric Rakowski, Joseph Raz, Ed Rubin, Alan Ryan, Carol Sanger, Sam Scheffler, Philip Selznick, Ian Shapiro, Scott Shapiro, Henry Shue, Paul Sigmund, Quentin Skinner, Peter Strauss, Cass Sunstein, Gwen Taylor, Richard Tuck, Maurizio Viroli, Will Waluchow, Bernard Williams, Iris Young, and Ben Zipursky. I am most grateful to all of them for their help.

I would also like to thank the institutions that have made this work possible. The Boalt Hall Fund at the University of California, Berkeley supported the project with summer stipends in 1993 and 1995. The Dean and Faculty of Columbia Law School provided a collegial environment in which to work in 1995 and a summer stipend to complete the remaining chapters in 1997. I am grateful also to the Department of Politics and the University Center for Human Values at Princeton for providing the time and resources I needed in the 1996–7 academic year, to Andrew Roberts, my research assistant at Princeton, and to Phil Christian and Mary Sue Daniels, my secretarial assistants at Columbia.

*   *   *

This book is dedicated – with my greetings and thanks – to George Kateb, whose work has been an inspiration to so many political theorists in the United States, and whose courtesy, integrity, and collegiality furnished a delightful atmosphere in which to work at Princeton. I have profited from many discussions with him on these themes and the book is better as a result. Having said that, I should add that I think George disagrees with almost everything that follows. But *that* – as we shall see – is the point!

Contents

Chapter One

Introduction

There are many of us, and we disagree about justice. That is, we not only disagree about the existence of God and the meaning of life; we disagree also about what count as fair terms of co-operation among people who disagree about the existence of God and the meaning of life. We disagree about what we owe each other in the way of tolerance, forbearance, respect, co-operation, and mutual aid. Liberals disagree with conservatives; socialists disagree with market economists; the party of freedom disagrees with the party of community and both disagree with the party of equality; feminists disagree with those who want the government to stand up for 'family values'; last-ditch defenders of the welfare state disagree with triumphant opponents of taxation; and pragmatists and utilitarians disagree with those who think the task of law is to vindicate the claims of order, retribution, and desert.

Since the publication in 1971 of John Rawls's book *A Theory of Justice*,[1] political philosophers have concentrated their energies on contributing to, rather than pondering the significance of, these disagreements about justice. Each has offered her (or, more usually, his)[2] own view of what justice consists in, what rights we have, what fair terms of social co-operation would be, and what all of this is based on. And though each is acutely aware of rivals and alternatives – we see them every day, down the hall, in the seminar room, and at academic conferences – it is rare to find a

[1] See Laslett and Fishkin (eds.), *Philosophy, Politics and Society*, 1–2, for the significance of Rawls's book in revitalizing anglophone political philosophy.

[2] I shall use the masculine form of the pronoun, here and throughout, but not to indicate that only men do or ought to do political philosophy – that would ignore the substantial contributions of philosophers like Annette Baier, Seyla Benhabib, Jean Elshtain, Martha Fineman, Carol Gould, Amy Gutmann, Jean Hampton, Virginia Held, Bonnie Honig, Frances Kamm, Christine Korsgaard, Martha Minow, Martha Nussbaum, Susan Okin, Carol Pateman, Hanna Pitkin, Deborah Rhode, Nancy Rosenblum, Judith Shklar, Yael Tamir, Judith Thompson, Patricia Williams, Iris Young, and many others. I use the masculine form to avoid what Susan Okin calls 'false gender neutrality', i.e. the misleading impression, which neutral or feminine forms might convey, that there is now a satisfactory balance between the work of men and women in this (or any other) part of the profession. (See Okin, *Justice, Gender and the Family*, 10–13.) The lamentable fact is that most work in political philosophy – especially work along the lines of 'I-expect-you'd-all-like-to-know-what-I-would-do-if-I-ruled-the-world' – is still done by men.

philosopher attempting to come to terms with disagreements about justice within the framework of his own political theory.

Perhaps that is as it should be: after all, the point of a theory of justice is to offer a coherent and persuasive vision of a society well-ordered by principles of justice and right. We ask each thinker to say what those principles are, how they are to be defended, and what are their implications. We do not expect anyone to dilute or compromise his vision by taking into account other and rival theories of justice (theories which, after careful thought and on what he takes to be good grounds, he rejects as mistaken). We think that if a theorist of justice does take a rival theory into account, he should do so mainly by way of 'product-differentiation' or in order to ponder possible weaknesses in his own theory, possible objections that might occur to his audience. But once he is convinced that the objections have been answered, he should offer his own theory as a candidate for moral and political hegemony. A well-ordered society, he should say, will be one structured by *his* principles of justice, not by any others. And he should expect his claims about justice to be considered and evaluated on that basis.

The alternatives are there, of course, and our philosopher will be acutely aware that his rivals are presenting their own theories in exactly the same spirit, excluding his principles from their conceptions of a well-ordered society, just as he excludes their principles from his. If he thinks about these alternative presentations – other than to prepare a defence of his own view against possible objections – he will think of them as helping (together with his own theory) to define a menu of options, a list of alternative social visions – each of them well-worked-out philosophically, each offering to do in a different way all the work that there is for a theory of justice to do. *Selecting* from this menu is a matter for the audience, for the public, and eventually (through whatever circuitous processes these things involve) for those who have the power and the will to make a difference in society.

This last thought indicates, however, that there is another aspect of the matter which ought to engage us as philosophers. Surely we should ponder the philosophical significance not only of justice itself, but of the nature and principled basis of political *choice* on matters of justice and right. Different people in society hold differing and opposed theories of justice; yet social decisions are reached, and institutions and frameworks established, which then purport to command loyalty even in the face of those disagreements, even when such loyalty seems like moral betrayal to those who hold a contrary view. Surely this is worth philosophical attention; surely it is a topic on which the political philosopher ought to have something to say, something that goes beyond reiterating his own theory of justice and expressing indignation when the rulers or voters opt instead for some alternative.

Reflecting on the philosophical significance of our political disagreements is not just a matter of *meta-ethics* – it is not a matter of arguing about relativism or scepticism concerning justice, for example, or of elaborating and defending moral realism. A confident theorist of justice may announce, 'Well, of course there is disagreement about justice; but as the moral realists have shown, the existence of disagreement is quite compatible with one of the contestant views being true and the others false.' He can say that, but it is hardly sufficient, particularly if it is just a prelude to his saying, 'And of course the true view about justice is *my* view, which I shall now proceed to explain . . .'. For if he is at all self-aware, he knows very well that he will be followed, one by one, by his ideological rivals, each making a similar announcement in similarly self-assured tones. The vocation of the *political* philosopher is to examine philosophically, not just the metaphysics, but the morals and politics of disagreement – the implications for social life, social organization, and social action of the fact that even among those who accept the proposition that some views about justice are true and others false, disagreement will persist as to which is which.

So there are at least two tasks for political philosophy: (i) theorizing about justice (and rights and the common good etc.), and (ii) theorizing about politics. My general aim in this book is not to discredit or distract us from the first task. But I want to insist on the importance of the second sort of theorizing as a distinct agenda for political philosophy. I believe that philosophers of public affairs should spend less time with theorists of justice, and more time in the company of theorists of authority and theorists of democracy, reflecting on the purposes for which, and the procedures by which, communities settle on a single set of institutions even in the face of disagreement about so much that we rightly regard as so important. We need, as I said, to see that as a *distinct* agenda, not one to be engaged in simply as an upshot, consequence, or way of pursuing the procedural implications of a particular substantive view. That is, we should not be asking questions like, 'What are the implications of (for example) John Rawls's theory of justice so far as democratic and constitutional procedures are concerned?' Instead we must ask, 'What are we to think about democratic and constitutional procedures, given that such procedures have to accommodate a politics for those who differ fundamentally about whether theories like Rawls's are correct?' We need to think of ourselves as pursuing the second agenda in the company of philosophers like Thomas Hobbes and Immanuel Kant[3] – philosophers who made the existence of disagreement among individuals about rights and justice fundamental to

---

[3] Since this may be a startling claim so far as Kant is concerned, readers may want to refer to the arguments in Waldron, 'Kant's Legal Positivism'. They should look too at Kant, *The Metaphysics of Morals*, 124.

the problems that their theories of authority, procedure, and political obligation were intended to solve.

2. SPECIAL JURISPRUDENCE

There is an obvious connection between political philosophy and the philosophy of law. The latter is not the whole of the former, for law is not all there is to politics. But there is a very significant overlap; the philosophy of law may be regarded as a large sub-field of political philosophy. Now, I said that there are two main tasks in political philosophy: (i) theorizing about justice, rights, and the common good, and (ii) theorizing about the ways in which communities act when their members disagree. Where does the philosophy of law fit in, so far as these tasks are concerned?

Law has to do with justice, and there is bound to be a connection between theorizing about justice and figuring out what is the right shape and foundation for our laws to have. Much of what we call *special jurisprudence* – i.e. jurisprudence focused on specific topics in law such as tort liability or criminal attempts[4] – should be filed under heading (i). In discussing, for example, whether criminal attempts deserve to be punished as severely as completed criminal acts or whether tort liability should be replaced by a New Zealand-style system of accident compensation, we are asking, 'What would be the right or a just way to order our legal relations in this area?' The proposals of a particular jurist will amount to a fragment of a theory of justice, and may either be informed by or – if put together with his other proposals – add up to a more abstract or comprehensive theory of justice of the sort that political philosophers (performing the first task) are familiar with.[5]

Still, I hesitate to say that special jurisprudence is nothing more than partial or fragmentary participation in the task of building, or working out the implications of, a philosophical theory of justice. It *may* be nothing more than that if the jurist approaches his topic (e.g. tort liability or criminal justice) as though he could consider it afresh in a 'Year Zero' sort of way, as though his consideration of it would go best if uncontaminated by

---

[4] This contrast between general and special jurisprudence (i.e. the philosophy of law as such versus the philosophy of particular legal topics such as tort liability) differs from the distinction between general (or universal) and particular (or local) jurisprudence (i.e. the philosophy of law as such versus the philosophy relevant to the law of particular jurisdictions such as England or the US). Obviously much particular jurisprudence is also special jurisprudence; but it need not be. I am grateful to Michael Moore for this point. See also Austin, *The Province of Jurisprudence Determined*, 16.

[5] See Coleman, *Risks and Wrongs* and Rakowski, *Equal Justice* for examples of different ways in which theories of this type may be articulated.

existing legal doctrine or the past decisions of courts. Sometimes we proceed in that way, particularly if we think an area of the law is in need of radical revision. More often, however, jurists identify a number of fixed points of existing doctrine which a good account – even a good normative or reforming account – of the law must 'fit'. They proceed as though this consideration of fit were as important to the success of their enterprise as any consideration of the abstract justice or moral appeal of their normative proposals. For them, it may count against an otherwise attractive conception of corrective justice (say) that it does not make sense of the imposition of strict liability in cases like *Rylands* v. *Fletcher*, or that it fails to untangle the knots of necessity and justification in the *Lake Erie Transportation* decision.[6]

Some may understand this use of existing doctrine as a kind of 'reflective equilibrium': we argue for a new view by showing that it is both attractive in its own right and not incongruent with considered judgements that we are reluctant to give up. In jurisprudence, however, the standing of a previous decision as one of the fixed points that a legal theory ought to fit is seldom a matter of the individual theorist's being wedded to it as a 'considered judgment' of his own, something that he in particular is loath to abandon. Instead it is seen as something which he is not at liberty to give up, given that he is offering an account of *the law* (albeit a normative and reforming account), rather than simply an announcement of his own view.

I think this way of proceeding tells us that legal argument is to be understood as much under the auspices of what I called task (ii) of political philosophy as under the auspices of task (i). Let me explain.

The best account of the tension between a legal proposal appealing to us as just and its fitting existing doctrine is given by Ronald Dworkin in *Law's Empire*.[7] It is essential to Dworkin's account that the requirement of 'fit' is the tribute that political principles require a judge or a jurist to pay to other political decisions that have been made in our society, even those made on a basis that the individual judge or jurist does not find morally congenial. In a pluralistic society, 'different people hold different views about moral issues that they all treat as of great importance'.[8] Fair political procedures are likely at various times and in various settings to enfranchise and empower the proponents of quite radically different principles. So, if we consider all the political decisions currently in force in our society, we will see that some of them were made by conservative legislatures, others by their liberal predecessors, others by feminist judges, and so on. One could,

---

    [6] *Rylands* v. *Fletcher*, LR 3 HL 330 (1868) and *Vincent* v. *Lake Erie Transportation Co*, 1910, 100 Minn. 456, NW 221.

    [7] See Dworkin, *Law's Empire*. See also Ch. 9, below.

    [8] Dworkin, *Law's Empire*, 178.

in a spirit of crusading zeal, simply ignore all this, brushing aside any decision or legal authority that did not comport with one's own heartfelt convictions about justice. But it is not clear that one would be engaging then in *legal* analysis; as opposed to simply announcing what, in one's own view, the law on the matter ideally ought to be. The legal enterprise is not one 'in which each person tries to plant the flag of his convictions over as large a domain of power or rules as possible'.[9] It is instead, as Dworkin puts it, the enterprise of trying to make the best of the principles of justice already 'instinct in the standing political arrangements of [one's] community . . . whether or not [one] thinks these the best principles from a utopian standpoint'.[10] In law above all, with its respect for authority, its idea of doctrine, and the discipline it imposes on the free range of our individual ideas, each of us proceeds from start to finish in a spirit of sharing the social world with intelligences, consciences, and sources of normative ideation other than our own. Law, as I said, aspires to justice; but it represents the aspiration to justice *of a community*, which – as Aristotle emphasizes – is made up not of those who think similarly, but of those who think differently, about matters of common concern.[11]

3. GENERAL JURISPRUDENCE

I have argued that special jurisprudence has a foot in both camps, so far as the two tasks of political philosophy are concerned. It involves respect for existing doctrine – even when existing doctrine involves ideas that the particular theorist disagrees with – and to that extent it pursues ideas associated with the second task. But still its overall aim is to work out what would be a good or a just way of organizing our arrangements in some area of law, and to that extent it is part and parcel of our theorizing about justice.

I believe, however, that when we turn from special to *general* jurisprudence – that is, when we reflect on law as such, on legal authority, legal obligation, the rule of law, etc.[12] – we move decisively and unambiguously to what I called the second task of political philosophy.

---

[9] Dworkin, *Law's Empire*, 211.   [10] Ibid., 213.

[11] Aristotle, *The Politics*, 21–2 (Bk. II, Ch. 2, 1261a17–b10): 'Is it not obvious that a state may at length attain such a degree of unity as to be no longer a state? – since the nature of a state is to be a plurality, and in tending to greater unity, from being a state, it becomes a family, and from being a family, an individual . . . So that we ought not to attain this greatest unity even if we could, for it would be the destruction of the state. Again, a state is not made up only of so many men, but of different kinds of men. . . . Hence it is evident that a city is not by nature one in that sense which some persons affirm; and that what is said to be the greatest good of cities is in reality their destruction.' See also Waldron, 'The Wisdom of the Multitude'.

[12] There is an excellent account of the tasks of general jurisprudence in the 'Introduction' to Dworkin, *Taking Rights Seriously*, vii–ix.

The claims that law makes – on our attention, our respect and our compliance – are the claims of an existing (and developing) framework ordering our actions and interactions in circumstances in which we disagree with one another about how our actions and interactions should be ordered. I am not just referring to the disagreements (about alimony, accidents, overhanging boughs, etc.) that cause conflict among us and lead us to bring our competing claims to court for adjudication. I mean that law purports to adjudicate such conflicts (among its many other tasks) and claims authority for its adjudications on principles which are themselves controversial in society. And it does so in frank acknowledgement of that controversy about principle. That is why the peremptory tone of its claim upon us is not 'Here's a basis for dispute-resolution which you should accept if you agree with it.' It is rather: 'Here's a basis for dispute-resolution which you are to accept whether you agree with it or not.'

The ground of this authoritarian claim is not that there are lawmakers who know better than we do (nor even that there are officials who have more power or access to more lethal weapons than any of us). The authority of law rests on the fact that there is a recognizable need for us to act in concert on various issues or to co-ordinate our behaviour in various areas with reference to a common framework, and that this need is not obviated by the fact that we disagree among ourselves as to what our common course of action or our common framework ought to be.

Given *this* as a basis for legal authority, a person should not be surprised to find himself from time to time under a legal obligation to participate in a scheme that he himself regards as undesirable on grounds of justice (to pay taxes, for example, to provide welfare assistance to people he regards as undeserving). That is more or less bound to happen, given that it is the function of law to build frameworks and orchestrate collective action in circumstances of disagreement. In modern legal philosophy, we pay a lot of attention to issues about conscience and civil disobedience. We think the law is in crisis when it conflicts with the firm and conscientious moral convictions of the individual citizen. But the premise of this book – that the point of law is to enable us to act *in the face of disagreement* – indicates that cases like these should not be regarded as crises, exceptions, or limiting cases for law's authority. It is *normal* for law, in what I shall later refer to as 'the circumstances of politics', to make claims that are at odds with the sense of justice of some or many of those who are under its authority.[13]

---

[13] Cf. the slightly different position of Gutmann, 'Democracy and its Discontents', 263: 'On [the] deliberative conception of democracy, we should expect democracy continuously to generate discontent with political outcomes because the moral understanding of human beings is inadequate to the task of determining what is just once and for all. We should therefore expect widespread discontent even with legitimate or provisionally justifiable democratic decisions.'

No doubt it is possible to develop something like a general jurisprudence as a part or implication of a particular substantive theory of justice. One would say: 'Here's the role that law would have in a society well-ordered by the principles of justice for which I have argued.' John Rawls does something like this for his theory, explicating familiar rule-of-law precepts as desiderata for procedural justice and institutional design, and connecting the idea of legality with liberal principles of publicity, generality, and transparency.[14] But this sort of approach to general jurisprudence is too easy. Of course there is less of a problem for legal obligation and the rule of law in a society whose citizens share the same fundamental view about justice (especially if that view is the correct one). And of course there are fewer conundrums about judicial reasoning and legal interpretation if all the standing rules and institutions of the society are based on that single well-founded view. The laws with which *we* are familiar, however, display their charms, make their claims, and require to be understood and interpreted, in circumstances that are much more contentious than this.

4. ROBERTO UNGER'S 'DIRTY LITTLE SECRET'

In a recent book Roberto Mangabeira Unger suggests that one of the 'dirty little secrets of contemporary jurisprudence' is 'its discomfort with democracy'. It shows up, he says, in every area of contemporary legal culture: not just 'in the ceaseless identification of restraints upon majority rule as the overriding responsibility of judges and jurists; in the consequent hypertrophy of countermajoritarian practices and arrangements; . . . and in the single-minded focus upon the higher judges and their selection as the most important part of democratic politics', but also in the failure to develop and generalize ways of thinking in jurisprudence that are appropriate to law understood as the creation and property of a free and democratic people.[15]

A prominent symptom of this failure is what Unger calls the 'marginalization' of legislation. In modern jurisprudence, even in the Hart and Sachs Legal Process materials which purport to be oriented to 'the variety of forms of law-making that proliferated in the aftermath of the New Deal', legislation is seldom given credit in its own right as a basis for legal growth and progress. Instead it is treated as 'a subsidiary last-ditch source of legal evolution, to be tolerated when none of the more refined modes of legal resolution applies'.[16]

---

[14] Rawls, *A Theory of Justice*, 54–60 and 235–43.

[15] Unger, *What Should Legal Analysis Become?*, 72–3 and 115.

[16] Ibid., 73. Unger seems to have in mind passages like the following (from Hart and Sacks, *The Legal Process*,164: 'A legislature has a primary, first-line responsibility to establish the

I think Unger is right about this. Perhaps he underestimates the work being done on legislation by legal scholars who would not describe themselves as philosophers: the work of William Eskridge and others on 'dynamic statutory construction', for example.[17] But this does not affect his point about jurisprudence. The best that can be said about what is happening, so far as legislative studies are concerned, is that the annals of legal philosophy are being enriched by the contributions of those who study statutes, rather than the other way round. If one asks what analytic jurisprudence has offered in return to the judge, lawyer, or law professor interested in legislation, the answer is embarrassing. Even when they construct theories of interpretation, analytic legal philosophers have almost nothing to say about the structural features of legislation that distinguish the interpretation of a statute from the interpretation of a principle or a poem. The only structures that interest contemporary philosophers of law are the structures of judicial reasoning. They are intoxicated with courts and blinded to almost everything else by the delights of constitutional adjudication. The embarrassing thing is that they are in danger of prolonging this intoxication long after their non-philosophical colleagues have moved on to a more realistic understanding of the sources of law.

What would it be like to imagine a jurisprudence that was comfortable with democracy? Much of what follows may be seen as an attempt to rise to Unger's challenge. This book is an attempt to glimpse a genuinely democratic jurisprudence: a philosophy of law that pays something more than lip-service to the ideal of self-government; a philosophy of law which indeed puts that ideal to work – hard and detailed work – in its account of the nature of law, the basis of legitimacy, the task of interpretation, and the respective responsibilities of legislatures, citizens, and courts.

Thus the first part of *Law and Disagreement* is about *legislation*: statutes and the institutions that enact them. In some ways, legislation as a topic has been treated by jurists in a way that is quite congenial to the concerns about disagreement that I have been outlining. No one is in any doubt that legislatures are adversarial institutions, operating indeed in a context of cacophonous disagreement. Parties with opposing views about social justice compete for control of the legislature, and the statutes that result

---

institutions necessary or appropriate in the everyday operation of government. For example, it must create courts. . . . But in relation to the body of general directive arrangements which govern private activity in the society its responsibility is more accurately described as secondary in the sense of second-line. The legislature characteristically functions in this relation as an intermittently intervening, trouble-shooting, back-stopping agency. . . . The private lawmakers, the courts, and administrative agencies are . . . the regularly available continuously functioning agencies of growth in the legal system.' See also Waldron, 'Dirty Little Secret,' 520.

[17] See Eskridge, *Dynamic Statutory Interpretation*. See also the discussion in Ch. 2, s. 1, below.

represent the short- or medium-term ascendancy of one view over the others.

However, when and to the extent that philosophers of law focus on the authority of legislation or the interpretation of a particular statute, the plurality and diversity of our lawmakers tends to be put to one side. Once enacted, a bill is taken to represent a *particular* view – a view which, by reason of its having prevailed in the politics of the legislature, we can now regard as singular and as authoritative in its singularity. If we are uncertain about its application, we can ask what light 'the lawmaker's intention' casts on our interpretive difficulty, just as though we were talking about the purposes or intentions of a single individual. The authority of statute law on this account is the authority of the person or faction that drafted it, voted for it, and pushed it through its stages. One defers to it, therefore – or rather, one defers to him or them – to the extent that one thinks this lawmaker can be trusted to come up with good or just laws, or at least better laws than one is capable of making for oneself.[18]

In what follows, I shall propose a different understanding of legislation. I have emphasized already that there are many of us and that we disagree about social justice. I believe it is no accident that in almost every society in the world, statutes are enacted by an assembly comprising many persons (usually hundreds) who claim in their diversity to represent all the major disagreements about justice in their society, and whose enacted laws claim authority in the name of them all, not just in the name of the faction or majority who voted in their favour. Most jurisprudential theories of legislation make these features marginal or problematic: for example, they develop a theory of the authority of a single lawmaker putting forward a determinate view of his own, and then they scramble to adapt that model to the inconvenient reality that in most cases legislation is enacted by and in the name of a large bunch of people who do not share a view about anything except the procedures that for the time being allow them to deliberate together in the assembly. I believe we should make the large numbers and the facts of diversity and disagreement central to our philosophy of legislation. Statutes, we should say, are *essentially* – not just accidentally – the product of large and polyphonous assemblies. And this feature should be made key to our understanding of how to deal with them – how to interpret them and how to integrate them into the broader body of the law.

5. RIGHTS AND CONSTITUTIONALISM

So far I have emphasized the work of legislatures in relation to disagreements about justice and policy. But I also want to address some questions

---

[18] Cf. the account of authority offered in Raz, *The Morality of Freedom*, 53.

about courts and constitutions, and *their* relation to disagreements about rights. The two are clearly connected. One issue – perhaps the main issue – about the dignity and authority of legislation is how it stands in regard to the terms of a written constitution embodying a Bill of Rights. The concern most commonly expressed about legislation is that legislative procedures may give expression to the tyranny of the majority and that legislative majorities are constantly – and in the United Kingdom, for example, endemically and constitutionally – in danger of encroaching upon the rights of the individual or minorities. So widespread is this fear, so familiar an element is it in our political culture, that the need for constitutional constraints on legislative decisions has become more or less axiomatic. 'I think', says Brian Barry (normally the most rigorous and argumentative of political theorists) that

there is little need for any argument in favor of the general point that *ex ante* nobody could reasonably reject the proposition that rules governing the legal system and the political system should be constitutionally entrenched.[19]

The laboured syntax of Barry's sentence is perhaps evidence that defenders of constitutional entrenchment protest too much in favour of their position. At any rate, what I want to do, particularly in Part Three of the book, is to subject this position to some questioning, particularly in light of the fact that the members of the liberal societies to whom this entrenchment is recommended seem to disagree with one another every bit as much and as strenuously about rights as they do about social justice and public policy.

The disagreement is evident at several levels.[20] First, there is no agreement about what it means to call something a right. Does 'right' connote a moral absolute, a self-evident truth, a universal, or some combination of the above? Are rights agent-relative claims, claims about benefit or interest, claims about liberty, claims about waivable duty, or what? Philosophers disagree about these formal issues; and to the extent that their esoteric arguments are heard beyond the confines of academe, those formal disagreements are echoed in various rival understandings of rights in society at large. Secondly, and more substantively, people (whether philosophically trained or not) continue to disagree radically about what rights we have – what they are rights *to* – and what they are based on. Disagreements of this second sort are rooted in turn in wider disagreements about the nature of justice (something which is particularly evident in the case of the so-called social and economic rights). Thirdly, even if there is a rough or overlapping consensus on a set of basic rights or civil liberties such as those secured by the amendments to the US Constitution

---

[19] Barry, *Justice as Impartiality*, 95.   [20] See also the discussion in Ch. 10, s. 6, below.

or those enshrined in the European Convention on Human Rights (ECHR), there is ferocious disagreement about what this consensus entails so far as detailed applications are concerned. Does the US Bill of Rights imply a right to privacy which in turn generates a basis for striking down laws that restrict abortion? Does the Second Amendment require legislatures to permit private individuals as well as well-regulated state militias to carry assault weapons? Does the ECHR permit corporal punishment in schools? I do not particularly care whether we call these disputes 'disagreements about rights', or 'disagreements about interpretation'. What matters is that they divide us in fierce and intractable controversies. And like almost all political disagreements, they appear to implicate issues on which everyone acknowledges that we need as a society to take a common view.

I need hardly add that most of those who disagree about rights in any of these three ways do so in good faith. It is not a case of there being some of us who are in possession of *the truth* about rights – a truth which our opponents wilfully or irrationally fail to acknowledge because they are blinded by ignorance, prejudice or interest. The issues that rights implicate are much too complicated to permit or require that sort of explanation. They are simply hard questions – matters on which reasonable people differ. They are *important* questions, to be sure, and people are properly ferocious and indignant in defence of the answers they take to be correct. But it is a mistake to think that the more important the question, the more straightforward or obvious the answer.

It is puzzling therefore that some philosophers and jurists treat rights as though they were somehow beyond disagreement, as though they could be dealt with on a different plane in law – on the solemn plane of constitutional principle far from the hurly-burly of legislatures and political controversy and disreputable procedures like voting. The puzzle is posed, for example, by Ronald Dworkin's theory of rights as 'trumps'.[21] If we say that it is the function of rights to 'trump' majority-decisions, it is surely incumbent on us to add some acknowledgement that people disagree about what rights we have and to offer some basis whereby that disagreement might be resolved, so that there is something determinate to do the trumping. We cannot play trumps if we disagree about the suits. Or if we do, we are open to what I regard as the unanswerable cynicism of Thomas Hobbes in the motto of this book: for people to demand that we treat *their* theory of rights as the one that is to prevail is 'as intolerable in the society of men, as it is in play after trump is turned, to use for trump on every occasion, that suite whereof they have most in their hand'.[22]

---

[21] See Dworkin, *Taking Rights Seriously*.   [22] Hobbes, *Leviathan*, Ch. V, 33.

Something similar may be said about slogans like 'the tyranny of the majority'. The most commonly expressed misgiving about unrestrained legislative authority is that minorities or individuals may suffer oppression at the hands of a majority. That is an acute danger where the votes of those who compose the differing factions represent nothing more than the particular interests or satisfactions of the voters. On that assumption, allowing a majority to prevail means allowing the interests of the minority to be sacrificed to those of the larger group. But nothing similar need happen between majorities and minorities if we assume that the members of the society are addressing controversial issues about rights in good faith, for on this assumption a vote may represent, not an individual interest, but an individual opinion on a matter of common concern. The point to remember here is that nothing tyrannical happens to me merely by virtue of the fact that *my opinion* is not acted upon by a community of which I am a member. Provided that the opinion which is acted upon takes my interests, along with everyone else's, properly into account, the fact that it is not *my* opinion is not itself a threat to my freedom or well-being.

Of course, since there is disagreement between my opinion and the opinion which commands majority support, I will not think that all interests have been properly taken into account or that the general good is being correctly perceived. And I *may* think consequently that there is a serious threat to my interests. But, again, we must remember that my interests need not be the subject of the disagreement. If all parties are approaching the decision in a public-spirited way, then the issues on which they disagree will not necessarily reflect differential levels of concern for their own respective self-interests. It is true that A may differ from B and C about the proper regard that is due to A's interests; but A may also differ from B and C about the proper regard that is due to B's interests. He may think that B and C, the majority, are underestimating the importance of some interest they have but he lacks.[23]

The more important point though is this. Even if the issue on which A (the minority) differs from B and C *is* the proper level of respect due to

[23] An example may help. It is notorious that many women dissent from the feminist position on gender equality and independence, and that some men do not. Suppose those of both sexes who are sympathetic to the feminist position happen to be in a minority. Then some members of the minority (the 'feminist' men) may characterize the disagreement by saying that there are people in the majority group (non-feminist women) who are not paying proper or sufficient regard to their own interest in freedom and well-being.

Similarly, affirmative action in the US is opposed by some of those whose interests it is intended to advance, and supported by many of those whose unfair advantages it is intended to offset or remedy. So if a majority decides that the rights of racial minorities do not generate an entitlement to affirmative action, we are not in a position to assume that *that* is the very majority whose actions and interests the minority rights in question were intended to constrain.

A's interest, there is no reason to take A's view of the matter any more seriously or think it is any more likely to be correct than the opinion shared by B and C – again, if all are approaching the matter in good faith. The majority is not necessarily right, to be sure – but on a matter concerning the rights of minorities, it is not necessarily wrong either.

I presume that nobody wants to say that an individual has a right just because he thinks he does. Once this is accepted, we must be very careful in our analysis of moral and political disputes to distinguish between the individual or minority rights which are the subject of the disagreement and the opinions held by an individual or a minority about their rights or the rights of others. If we make that distinction, we will see that there is no rights-based case for allowing minority *opinions* to prevail, though minority (or majority) opinions may make a good case for allowing certain minority *interests* to prevail. There is, accordingly, no necessary connection between the idea of majority-decision about rights and the idea of the tyranny of the majority.

All of this assumes that people sometimes or often vote their considered and impartial opinions when they are addressing controversial issues of justice and rights; it assumes, as I said, that their votes and opinions are not always the reflex of their interests. The relation between opinions and interests is a complex one. I believe, however, that it is true empirically that citizens and representatives often do vote on the basis of good faith and relatively impartial opinions about justice, rights, and the common good. I believe too that often our reasons for doubting this are quite disreputable. One is tempted to say, 'These people disagree with me and my friends, so they *must* be voting out of self-interest' – as though that were the only explanation. Succumbing to this temptation is, I think, particularly disreputable in the case of a rights-theorist, for it is essential to the idea of rights that persons are moral agents who can be trusted with the responsibility to direct their own lives and to perceive the proper limits placed on their own freedom of action by respect for the similar efforts of others. As I argue in Chapters Ten and Eleven, it simply will not do for theorists of rights to talk about us as upright and responsible autonomous individuals when they are characterizing our need for protection against majorities, while describing the members of the majorities against whose tyranny such protection is necessary as irresponsible Hobbesian predators. They cannot have it both ways.

At any rate, I shall proceed throughout this book on the assumption that people sometimes or often do vote their considered and impartial opinions. It is by no means invariably true, but a normative theory of law and politics needs an aspirational quality, and this is mine. I shall assume that in order for law to claim authority along the lines that I think it can and should, those who participate in making it ought to do their best to address in good faith the issues on which they know they disagree with others. If they proceed on any other basis, to that extent the authority of legislation and its relation to the existence of disagreement will need to be rethought. And if they proceed on a mixed basis – sometimes voting their interests, sometimes their opinions, sometimes entangling the two – then we must face the fact that we have a mixed and indeterminate situation so far as legitimacy and authority are concerned. This of course should not surprise us. We are building normative models, and it is their task to illuminate complexity, not hide it.[24]

Much of the third part of this book (particularly Chapters Ten through Thirteen) is devoted to a discussion of constitutional rights and practices such as judicial review of legislation. Readers will quickly discern my opposition to American-style judicial review. When citizens or their representatives disagree about what rights we have or what those rights entail, it seems something of an insult to say that this is not something they are to be permitted to sort out by majoritarian processes, but that the issue is to be assigned instead for final determination to a small group of judges. It is particularly insulting when they discover that the judges disagree among themselves along exactly the same lines as the citizens and representatives do, and that the judges make their decisions, too, in the courtroom by majority-voting. The citizens may well feel that if disagreements on these matters are to be settled by counting heads, then it is their heads or those of their accountable representatives that should be counted.

Disagreement on matters of principle is, as I have emphasized, not the exception but the rule in politics. It follows that those who value popular participation in politics should not value it in a spirit that stops short at the threshold of disagreements about rights. Such curtailment, I believe, betrays the spirit of those who struggled for democracy and universal suffrage. The workers who braved cavalry charges at Peterloo in 1819, the women who chained themselves to the White House railings or threw themselves under the hooves of the King's horse at Epsom in turn-of-the-century suffrage campaigns, the African-Americans who faced batons, police-dogs, fire hoses, and worse in the Civil Rights movement in the 1950s and '60s, did these things to secure a voice on the matters of political principle that confronted their community. They did not do them simply for the sake of a vote on interstitial issues of policy that had no compelling moral dimension. They fought for the franchise because they believed that controversies about the fundamental ordering of their society – factory and hours legislation, property rights, free speech, police powers, temperance, campaign reform – were controversies for them to

---

[24] I discuss this further in s. 6 of Ch. 13, below.

sort out, respectfully and on a basis of equality, because *they* were the people who would be affected by the outcome. Moreover, they did not fight for the vote on the assumption that they would then all *agree* about the issues that they wanted the right to vote on. Every individual involved in these movements was well aware that there were others standing alongside him who believed that his political views on matters of substance were mistaken. But they fought for the vote anyway on the ground that the existence of such principled disagreements was the essence of politics, not that it should be regarded as a signal to transfer the important issues that they disagreed about to some other forum altogether, which would privilege the opinions and purses of a few.

It will be clear that I feel strongly about these issues. They are particularly pressing in the United Kingdom, where constitutional reform is now firmly on the political agenda and where the institution of a Bill of Rights (perhaps by the incorporation of the ECHR into municipal law) together with something akin to American-style judicial review is a distinct possibility. The issues are much less pressing in the United States, where for better or worse judicial review of legislation is firmly entrenched as a practice. Though there have been American misgivings about this practice since its inception,[25] and though there are continuing debates about how it is to be understood, it is quite clear that no amount of philosophical argument about democracy, disagreement, or anything else is going to dislodge it. To the extent, then, that there is a political edge to my comments about rights and judicial review, I intend them to be heard in the British debate, not to offend American constitutional pride or sensitivity.

But the practical politics of rights matter much less in a book of this kind than our philosophical grasp of the issues involved.[26] If there is to be judicial review of legislation in the name of individual rights, then we should understand all three elements – rights, courts, and legislation – in a way that respects the conditions of disagreement that lie at the heart of our politics. Rights are urgent issues that we disagree about. Legislation is the product of a complex deliberative process that takes disagreement seriously and that claims its authority without attempting to conceal the contention and division that surrounds its enactment. Courts are also a forum for making social decisions in a context of disagreement, but though they have many advantages, they are not necessarily the most representative or the most respectful of the contending voices in the community. If we bear

[25] See, for example, Lincoln, 'First Inaugural Address,' at 57–9. The passage is quoted in fn. 27 of Ch. 12, below. See also Hand, *The Bill of Rights* and Hand, *The Spirit of Liberty*.

[26] In other words, this book is not to be read as putting forward a political or constitutional proposal. Instead it is an attempt to enhance our understanding of the issues at stake in various practices, institutions, and proposals.

these things in mind, I think we will have a better understanding of law and constitutionalism than if we erect a theory of justice and a philosophy of politics on the assumption that ultimately the members of a well-ordered society should be expected to agree on all serious issues of principle.

I. A Jurisprudence of Legislation

Chapter Two
Legislatures in Legal Philosophy

1. ADVICE TO LEGISLATORS

I said at the end of Chapter One that there are three elements in our modern understanding of judicial review: rights, courts, and legislatures. Of those three elements, the third – *legislatures* – is the topic to which philosophers of law have devoted least attention. There are plenty of normative theories of rights, and we are up to our eyes in discussions of judicial decision-making. But there is much less philosophical work on the topic of legislatures.

Notice I say 'legislatures' rather than 'legislation.' There is a long tradition in political philosophy of normative theorizing about *legislation*: discussions of the difference between good laws and bad laws, attempts to determine the limits of legislation (what issues legislatures should address, what issues they should leave to positive morality), and accounts of the sorts of things that ought to be taken into account when one embarks on the process of law-making.[1] Claude-Adrien Helvetius said in 1759 that 'if philosophers would be of use to the world, they should survey objects from the same point of view as the legislator', adding that 'morality is evidently no more than a frivolous science, unless blended with policy and legislation'.[2] Jeremy Bentham's *Introduction to the Principles of Morals and Legislation* is perhaps the best- known example of a philosopher taking this advice to heart. And in the late twentieth century Helvetius' challenge still resonates; indeed, it captures the spirit of what is sometimes called 'practical' political philosophy (the spirit embodied for example in the modern 'Philosophy and Public Affairs' movement).[3] Certainly much of what is written in modern philosophy about the theory of justice, particularly social justice or justice in regard to social and economic goods, is in fact about legislation. In John Rawls's theory, for example, although the first principle of justice-as-fairness (equal liberty) is assigned to the constitution of a well-ordered society and to its courts, the application of the second principle (equal opportunity together with the difference principle) is regarded as the proper province of the legislature.[4] And since the whole

---

[1] For an example of this kind of work, see Winston, 'Toward a Liberal Conception of Legislation'.
[2] Quoted in Postema, *Bentham and the Common Law Tradition*, 263.
[3] See Waldron, 'What Plato Would Allow', esp. 164–71.
[4] Rawls, *A Theory of Justice*, 198 ff.

conception is oriented to the basic structure of society rather than to the actions of individuals, one can make the case that legislators are to be understood as the primary audience for Rawls's work, so far as the practical application of his normative thought on social justice is concerned.

Most of this work consists of philosophical advice to the legislature. We write, as though to an MP or a Congressman:

Since you are making the laws, you ought to consider the moral values and principles that are relevant to the issues you are addressing. Moreover, you should consider them systematically, rather than haphazardly. Here they are, then, set out in a clear and scientific way, with lucid definitions, valid arguments, and ordered priorities.

And we set out for him a scheme of values and principles, clearly stated, rigorously ordered, and defended with various model-theoretic devices. Of course, what we offer the legislator is quite challenging, by political standards. He is accustomed to thinking in terms of tax rates and workfare proposals; we give him the Difference Principle, the Original Position, and the idea of Chain Connection. Still, we think of ourselves as performing a public service by showing the lawmaker what a philosophically rigorous theory of justice would look like.

From the lawmaker's point of view, however, the most striking thing about this advice is not the analytical rigour of the philosopher's presentation. It is the fact that any one philosopher's advice is likely to conflict with the advice offered by other philosophers. One philosopher may say (following Rawls) that justice consists in equality, understood in terms of the Difference Principle; but others will say that justice requires careful attention to issues of moral desert. Some will attempt to convince the legislator that justice is less important than values associated with community; others will lay out a recursive Lockean theory of historical entitlement; still others will argue that the very idea of social justice is based on a deep confusion about the proper role of law in a free society. And it is not just controversy: after a while, it will begin to seem like familiar controversy. For, although our legislator will no doubt be impressed by the esoteric rigour with which the philosophers set out their arguments, if he listens long enough he will recognize them as versions of views that compete already in the politics with which he is familiar: liberal views, conservative views, new communitarian views, free market views, and so on. Politics, he will explain patiently to his philosophical advisors, is much more about which of these views is going to prevail, than about the abstract and analytical details of their precise formulation.

Now the philosopher is unlikely to leave the matter there. He will respond to the legislator that of course he is aware that there are competing philosophical accounts of justice (and that these are just tidied-up versions of views that compete in the political market place). But he will say to the legislator that he thinks he (the philosopher) can produce excellent arguments to refute the other philosophical theories (and, *a fortiori*, their crude political counterparts). And maybe he can. At any rate, each of the philosophers we are imagining clamouring for the legislator's attention will set out not only his own view of social justice, but also an elaborate account of why alternative views are mistaken. Helvetius said that the philosopher should orient his work towards legislation. The philosophers we are imagining will certainly think that the appropriate way to do that is to figure out *first* which of the competing theories of justice is correct, from a philosophical point of view, and then offer *that theory* to the legislator in a form that the legislator can use. And though there's unlikely to be any consensus at this level either, still each of the competing philosophers will understand the point of what the others are doing: each is trying to show that *his* method of figuring out which philosophical theory of justice is correct is the method that the legislator should rely on.

By now, if the lawmaker has not lost patience altogether with the exercise, he may say this to the philosopher:

Your efforts to arrive at a rigorous statement of your view about justice, and to defend it against all other such views, are no doubt laudable. But you may be under a misapprehension as to how legislatures work. We do not wait for disagreements about social justice to be settled *outside* the legislature before we begin our activities. Instead, we do our work by *internalizing* those disagreements, by building them into the institutional structure of our assembly (with arrangements like government benches and opposition benches, majority and minority parties, debates, rules of order, whips, and roll-calls), indeed by making them part of the process of our law-making. The modern legislature is not an individual looking for philosophical advice. The modern legislature is an assembly of the representatives of the main competing views in society, and it conducts its deliberations and makes its decisions in the midst of the competition and controversy among them.

This response will irritate the philosopher, but in fact it is very important for legal and political philosophy. Legislatures in the modern world are almost always large assemblies. They are structured in a way that represents (or claims to represent) the more serious and substantial disagreements that there are in society about the way the society should be organized. And they make their decisions in the heat of these disagreements, not by reaching what purports to be a final conclusion as to which of the rival positions is correct, but by determining which position has for the time being the greater support among their members.

Compare a legislature with a court. A court too is structured in a way that allows rival views to be represented: it is an adversarial institution. The difference lies in the distinction, which courts embody, between the parties and the decision-maker (the judge). The parties make their adversarial presentations. Each tries to show that the other is mistaken. The judge listens to these presentations, then he goes away and thinks about them, returning with a verdict that purports to represent an impartial response to the competing advice he has received. Now legislatures sometimes hold hearings too: the difference is that, however judicious its demeanour, a legislative committee never tries to conceal the fact that its members are as partisan as the individuals who come before them (often more so). Whereas the parties to a lawsuit are entitled to expect the judge to be impartial, the parties who come before a legislative committee are under no misapprehension, nor is there any pretence at all, about the partisan views and commitments of the committee members. And when either the committee or the whole legislative assembly makes its decisions, it will make them on an explicitly partisan basis – that is, explicitly on the basis of the members' well-advertised opposed and divisive views about the issues under consideration. Multi-member judicial tribunals such as the US Supreme Court may perhaps come close to this, in the sense that it is often 'well known' in advance which way many of the justices will vote on a particularly controversial issue. But it is not part of the self-image of the court that this should be so; whereas it really *is* part of the self-image of the legislature.

So: legislatures incorporate disagreement into their proceedings, and they make their decisions in the midst of it. They make law on the basis of the explicitly partisan views and votes of their members. Is this institutional or structural fact significant for jurisprudence? Is it significant for the authority that legislation claims or ought to claim? Should it make any difference to the citizen's willingness to obey an enacted bill that he disagrees with? Is it significant for the status and dignity that a statute has or ought to have in relation to other sources of law? And does it make any difference to the way in which legislation ought to be interpreted? These are questions which I think have been neglected in modern legal philosophy, and they are the questions that I shall address in Chapters Two through Six of this book.

2. THREE ISSUES

The structural features of legislatures that interest me are size, diversity and disagreement, together with the institutional arrangements that frame decision making in that context – party organization, deliberative structure, formal debate, rules of order, and voting. I want to ask about the implications of these structures and arrangements for issues about the nature of law, the basis of its authority, and the exigencies of interpretation. There are three areas of particular puzzlement in which attention to the distinctive structural characteristics of the modern legislature might be important: *textuality*, *intention*, and *voting*.

(a) *Textuality*. Modern legal theory is fascinated by the textual quality of law[5] – by the fact that legal conundrums can often be expressed as problems about the meanings of words. Legislation presents itself as written law, and problems about its meaning often begin with the idea of the 'letter' of the law. Actually I doubt that 'the letter of the law' is an idea associated only with legislation; custom has its 'letter' too, as it signifies its presence in well-worn, almost incantatory sayings.[6] But legislation is the legal form in which emphasis on the words themselves – *ipsissima verba* – is most prominent in modern jurisprudence. A statute consists of an enacted form of words, and the problem of interpreting and applying it is the semantic problem of bringing a form of words into relation with persons, things and events in the world.

P. S. Atiyah and Robert Summers have remarked that one could imagine a legal system according 'no particular respect to the verbal form in which legislative texts are cast, treating statutes simply as cases are treated in the common law system'.[7] In fact, however, that is not the way we treat statutes. Now there ought to be a reason why this is true.[8] It is not enough simply to say that the legislature is an authoritative source of law, and that is why its *ipsissima verba* must be respected. For we do not treat all authorities in this way – hanging, as it were, on their every word. I suspect the answer has to do with the sort of institution that a legislature is: a large gathering of disparate individuals who purport to act collectively in the name of the whole community, but who can never be sure exactly what it is they have settled on, as a collective body, except by reference to a given form of words in front of them. I shall develop this argument, below, in Chapter Four.

(b) *Legislative Intent*. A theory of legislative structure ought to cast some light on the troubled question of 'legislative intent' and in particular to the question of whether it is appropriate to resort to legislative history in order to establish legislative intent. Surely whether an appeal to legislative intent in the course of statutory interpretation is either possible or

---

[5] 'A rule of Law must be predicated of some assemblage of words – It never can be predicated of a bare assemblage of naked ideas. It is words only that can be spoken of as binding: because it is words alone that are producible with certainty when occasion comes for any individual to be bound.' – Jeremy Bentham quoted by Postema, *Bentham and the Common Law Tradition*, 291.

[6] See Kelly, *The Human Measure*, 11–12.

[7] Atiyah and Summers, *Form and Substance in Anglo-American Law*, 97.

[8] And my further hunch is that this reason may provide us with important clues as to how to approach the task of statutory interpretation. After all, how we interpret a given set of words is a problem that ought to be framed by a sense of why we are obsessed with exactly *this form of words* in the first place.

desirable depends in large part on the sort of institution a legislature is, and on the way it acts when it performs its law-making function. A theory which takes seriously the size and diversity of the collective bodies that actually enact statutes in the modern world ought to have considerable advantages in this regard over those which assume, for philosophical purposes, that legislative authority might as well be vested in a single individual.

Empirical considerations are no doubt relevant too. What evidence of intentions shared by legislators emerges from the congressional record or from other sources? To what extent do legislators actually pursue shared intentions when they legislate? Realistically, whose intentions get privileged (which legislator? which sub-group? insiders? freshmen? marginalized legislators? minor parties?) when appeals to legislative intent are made? These empirical questions are important. At the same time, we need to frame that empirical enquiry with a more theoretical sense of what law-making by a large and diverse body is supposed to be like, and what its authority is supposed to consist in. I shall address this issue in Chapter Six (though there is also some preliminary discussion towards the end of section 4 of the present chapter).[9]

(c) *Voting*. Legislation is enacted by voting, and voting has a bad name in jurisprudence.[10] It seems so mindless – counting heads and letting a single vote at the margin decide matters, when what is at stake is some great issue of principle or some complex matter of policy. It contrasts with the elaborate deliberative processes of courts, where the grounds and reasons for a decision are embodied in the argument that appears in a written judgment. A contrast of this kind is sometimes taken as a basis for justifying judicial review in the United States, and for arguing in favour of constitutional changes that would make legislation vulnerable to judicial review in the United Kingdom and elsewhere.

Admittedly such argument is usually conducted without much attention to the actual behaviour of courts. Someone worried by voting ought also to be exercised by the fact that the votes of five justices defeat four on the US Supreme Court, whatever the quality of the written arguments their clerks have concocted. Indeed, it seems plausible that a procedure such as voting will be necessary in *any* institution consisting of more than one person that attempts to settle disagreements about what the community's policy ought to be or what principles the community should adhere to.

A theory of legislative structure has a lot to offer in this regard. By emphasizing the composition of the legislature – modern legislatures

---

[9] See fnn. 52–8, below, and accompanying text.

[10] See the discussion in Postema, *Bentham and the Common Law Tradition*, 15–16. See also Ch. 5, below, particularly s. 1.

consist of a large number of persons who disagree about what is good for the community – it can present the fact that laws are enacted by voting as a matter of fairness, not as a matter of moral or philosophical embarrassment. The point of a legislative assembly is to represent the main factions in the society, and to make laws in a way that takes their differences seriously rather than in a way that pretends that their differences are not serious or do not exist. That such a body cannot usually proceed on the basis of deliberative consensus is thus not an embarrassment, but a tribute to this particular approach to the making of laws: the idea is that we will make our laws in full cognizance of our disagreements, not in a way that attempts to finesse them.[11] Also, by emphasizing that even deliberative bodies have to vote when their members disagree, it can rebut the presumption that bodies which decide matters by voting cannot possibly be regarded as deliberative. I will develop this argument in more detail in Chapter Five.

There are other jurisprudential issues about legislation, to which the structural considerations I have emphasized seem less relevant. These include issues about statutory obsolescence and issues about the ways in which government agencies undertake the detailed articulation and development of statutory schemes. There is a fine and flourishing literature on these topics,[12] although it is fair to say, I think, that virtually nothing has been contributed to it by scholars who specialize in legal philosophy. These discussions are often labelled 'jurisprudence', when they are pitched at a sufficiently high level of abstraction. But as I said in Chapter One,[13] what is really happening is that the annals of legal philosophy are being enriched by the contributions of law professors who study legislation and the interpretation of statutes, rather than the other way round. If one looks at what traditional positivist jurisprudence itself has to offer the judge, the lawyer, or the law professor interested in legislation, the cupboard is alarmingly bare. Sure, there is a philosophical literature on the general problem of statutory interpretation, which in a way comprises the first two of the topics I mentioned (textuality and intention).[14] But with one or two exceptions, this discussion has proceeded without reference to the structural features of legislatures. (The most prominent exception is Ronald Dworkin's discussion of statutory interpretation in *Law's*

[11] Compare Sunstein, *Legal Reasoning and Political Conflict*, for an account more favourable to the finessing of disagreement.
[12] See, e.g., Calabresi, *A Common Law for the Age of Statutes* and Eskridge, *Dynamic Statutory Interpretation*.
[13] See Ch. 1, fn. 16, below, and accompanying text.
[14] See, e.g., the extraordinarily valuable contribution made to Rule-of-Law jurisprudence by Rubin, *Law and Legislation in the Administrative State*.

Empire.)[15] For the most part, it remains true that legal philosophy has *taken* immeasurably more from the 'black-letter' study of statute law than it has contributed over the past fifty years.

My aim, then, in this part of the book is to begin to redeem this debt and, by focusing specifically on legislative structure, to ask what legal philosophy – in alliance with political theory – can contribute to the jurisprudential understanding of what it is for *a bill enacted by an assembly* to be taken seriously as a source of law. I want to spend the rest of this chapter, however, understanding why exactly modern jurisprudence – particularly modern positivist jurisprudence – has been so deficient in this regard.

3. STRUCTURE AND SCEPTICISM

When I say we have neglected the importance of legislative structure, I do not mean that it has been neglected throughout the academy. In empirical political science, the study of legislation is almost entirely a study of behaviour and interaction *within* the legislature. Political scientists would never dream of treating 'the legislature' as a single entity, or actor, or author of statutes. Statutes emerge from the legislature, but what is interesting to the political scientist are precisely the structures and patterns of interaction and influence within and around the legislature that determine that final unitary outcome. So the *focus* is right, so far as the enterprise of this book is concerned: plurality, disagreement, and the structure of collective action. Still, the mood is different. The theories and models produced by empirical political scientists, though skillfully constructed for their own comparative, explanatory, and predictive purposes, have a number of drawbacks so far as normative jurisprudence is concerned.

First, they are not focused specifically on the *law-making* process. Political scientists remind us, correctly, that law-making is just one of the functions performed by the institutions we call legislatures, and, from the point of view of political power, not necessarily the most important.[16] A political scientist's analysis of law-making behaviour in legislatures is likely to be continuous with his analysis of other functions performed by these bodies – functions such as the mobilization of support for the executive (in the UK the actual selection of the executive), the venting of grievances, the discussion of national policy, the processes of budgetary negotiation, the ratification of appointments, and so on. From an empirical point of view, it may be impossible to predict how a given set of legislators will behave in sessions devoted specifically to law-making

---

[15] Dworkin, *Law's Empire*, 313–54. See also the discussion of disagreement, as a theme in Dworkin's jurisprudence, in Ch. 9 below.

[16] See, e.g., Wheare, *Legislatures*, 1–3.

without understanding what is going on between them (and between them and their constituents and various interest groups) in other 'legislative' contexts that really have nothing to do with that task. (Legislator A may promise to support B's bill, but only in return, say, for B's support in blocking a judicial appointment.) This is bound to contrast with the jurisprudential point of view, which regards law-making as an activity whose character and significance are *sui generis*.

Secondly, political scientists will want to emphasize – again, quite properly from a descriptive and explanatory point of view – that the law-making power, though nominally vested in the legislature, is in reality located elsewhere in the political system. Certainly, this is what a sharp observer would have to say of the United Kingdom, whose 'legislature' seldom seriously considers any bill not proposed by the executive and seldom fails to enact any bill that the executive does propose.[17] It may be less true in the United States, for there the executive is not defined by its ability to control the legislature; but even in the US, there is a common view that the executive has become the 'aggressive spirit' in the legislative process and that Congress has become merely a place to 'amend and delay'.[18] Whatever its merits, this conclusion is likely to be of less interest to the jurist than to his colleague in political science. For what strikes some political scientists as mere honorific decoration – the executive's securing formal parliamentary or congressional approval of its legislative measures – is likely to seem to the jurist an indispensable aspect of a measure's legitimacy and authority as *law*.[19]

Thirdly, empirical models of legislative behaviour tend to be non-normative to the point of cynicism.[20] I do not mean that political science

[17] Thus Samuel Beer: 'As a model of what actually goes on, the notion of Parliament as chief law-maker . . . is a gross distortion – a common fate of models.' – Quoted in Norton, *Legislatures*, 74. See also Atiyah and Summers, *Form and Substance in Anglo-American Law*, 299–306.

[18] This is reported (though not endorsed) as a consensus view in mid-century political science, in Redman, *The Dance of Legislation*, 16–17. See also Polsby, *Congress and the Presidency*, 131.

[19] See also Luhmann, *A Sociological Theory of Law*, 159: '[L]egislative decision-making cannot be treated as the explanatory origin of the validity of the constituted meaning of the norms. Seen from a causal angle, there are always further origins and origins preceding them which are often more important than decision-making. Law does not originate from the quill of the legislator. The decision of the legislator . . . finds a multitude of norm projections from which he selects with greater or lesser decision-making freedom.' But the standpoint of causal explanation may not be the jurisprudential standpoint. As Luhmann goes on to point out (ibid., 160): 'The function of legislation does not lie in the creation or production of law, but in the selection from and in giving symbolic dignity to norms as binding law.' Legal positivism, as he puts it, is about 'attribution' not 'causality' (*idem*). I am grateful to Ed Rubin for this reference.

[20] Maybe I exaggerate in suggesting that political scientists are more cynical about the legislature than casual observers. There is an excellent and instructive response to a journalist's cynicism about legislatures by a distinguished political scientist in Polsby, 'Restoration Comedy', 1517–19.

makes fun of legislators in the spirit of P. J. O'Rourke.[21] Nor do I mean merely that such models offer little prescriptive guidance to legislators as to how their tasks should be performed – though that may be true (and understandable). I mean that empirical models do not present the process of legislation in a manner that advances our normative understanding of law: they do not present legislation in a particularly helpful light so far as the normative tasks of jurisprudence are concerned (tasks like constructing theories of interpretation, for example). Again, that is partly because political scientists do not find it necessary to distinguish in principle, in their account of legislators' behaviour, between the production of a law (which is something for courts to interpret, and thus something for courts to think hard about how they *ought* to interpret) and the production of a political deal on budget, policy, or appointments (which may need no elaborate interpretation, and thus no normative theory of interpretation, at all).

In fact, the situation may be even worse than this. Not only do students of legislative behaviour not produce the normative or normatively-relevant models of law-making that jurisprudence requires (and why should they?), but the models they do produce are often grist to the mill of jurisprudential theories which disparage and discredit legislation as a source of law. I will return to this point throughout the book, but I want to put it on the table at the outset. The theories of government that are used in American jurisprudence often present a rather unattractive image of ordinary legislating as deal-making, logrolling, interest-pandering, pork-barrelling, horse-trading, and Arrovian cycling – as anything, indeed, except principled political decision-making. Legal scholars draw on the work of interest group theorists in political science – theorists who view legislative outcomes simply as deal-making between the representatives of more or less powerful private interests, so that a given piece of legislation has little inherent dignity or authority of its own. They say, for example, that in interpreting statutes '[t]he courts do not enforce the moral law or ideals of neutrality, justice or fairness; they enforce the deals made by effective interest groups with earlier legislators.'[22] Others, in public choice theory, convinced by Condorcet's and Arrow's theorems about the possible incoherence of collective decision making, go even further. A large body such as a legislature, making its decisions by voting, may not have enough collective rationality even to settle on a stable deal, let alone articulate the public interest. What emerges from the legislative process may well be a matter of who controls the agenda or, even more arbitrarily, of where in the cycle of voting a 'decision' happens to pop out.[23]

---

[21] O'Rourke, *Parliament of Whores*, 49–65 (required reading, in my view).
[22] Landes and Posner, 'The Independent Judiciary in an Interest-Group Perspective', 894.
[23] See, e.g., Riker and Weingast, 'Constitutional Regulation of Legislative Choice', 373.

I shall not embark here on any extensive discussion of the modern literature of public choice. It is worth noting, however, that the cynical approaches just outlined are meeting with increasingly confident replies as jurists who self-identify as 'civic republicans' lay normative stress on the role of virtue and deliberation in public life while other scrupulous observers ponder the failure of legislatures to actually exhibit the arbitrariness and instability that Arrow's and Condorcet's results would predict.[24] Both these developments are congenial to the approach I want to take. Even so, it is worth bearing in mind, first, that many republicans remain sceptical about the prospects for virtuous civic deliberation *in legislatures* (as opposed to in coffee shops, in the courts, or in law reviews),[25] and, secondly, that a renewed focus on the way in which legislators deliberate about the public interest (as opposed to special interests or their own interests in re-election) has done little so far to abate the strategic enthusiasm among lawyers and philosophers for the judicial review of statutes they find morally or politically uncongenial.[26] Even though we are now willing to regard at least some of our legislators as public-spirited individuals, we have not evolved a theory of legislative outcomes that would give them the sort of dignity and standing in the political community that we associate with the final outputs of the judicial process.

Some have suggested that the model of legislation we use in constitutional jurisprudence is valued by legal scholars less for its descriptive verisimilitude, and more for the credibility it lends to the practice of judicial review of legislation by silencing misgivings about the 'counter-majoritarian difficulty' that judicial review is sometimes thought to involve.[27] If the legislative process is a discreditable mess anyway, no one should be too concerned when its products are disparaged by lawyers and reviewed and struck down by courts. Political scientists know better of course. Unlike law professors, they have the good grace to match a cynical model of legislating with an equally cynical model of appellate and Supreme Court adjudication. If legislators are rent seekers, what do judges maximize?[28] If voting can produce Arrovian cycles among legislators, can it not also produce such cycles among the members of an appellate panel?[29] Even if they support judicial review, most political scientists do

---

[24] A helpful and up-to-date overview is provided by Farber and Frickey, *Law and Public Choice*.

[25] See, e.g., Michelman, 'Law's Republic'.

[26] Cf. Gutmann and Thompson, *Democracy and Disagreement*.

[27] See, e.g., Unger, *What Should Legal Analysis Become?* and the discussion in s. 4 of Ch. 1, *supra*. See also Waldron, 'Dirty Little Secret'. The phrase 'counter-majoritarian difficulty' is taken from Bickel, *The Least Dangerous Branch*, 16.

[28] For an honourable attempt by a legal scholar to face up to this question, see Posner, *Overcoming Law*, 109 ff.

[29] As Farber and Frickey point out in *Law and Public Choice*, 6, if we think for Arrovian reasons that 'chaos and incoherence are the inevitable outcomes of majority voting, then

not base that support on any asymmetry in the motivations they ascribe to judges and legislators, respectively.[30]

What I want to do is apply the canon of symmetry in the other direction. I want to ask: What would it be like to develop a rosy picture of legislatures and their structures and processes that matched, in its normativity and perhaps in its naïvety, the picture of courts – 'forum of principle' etc.[31] – that we present in the more elevated moments of our constitutional jurisprudence?

Let me elaborate that point a little, for it will help explain what I have in mind when I talk of '*normative* jurisprudence'. There are plenty of books and articles in political science and constitutional law which cast legislation in a negative light – denigrating the process and disparaging the legitimacy of its results. These are implicitly normative theories, but their normative valence points in a direction opposite to the prescriptive force of the statutes to which they apply. Whereas statute law presents itself as prescriptive, mandatory, and authoritative, the common law and public choice accounts of legislation do their best to discredit those pretensions. By contrast, in this part of the book I would like to begin developing an account of legislatures and their processes which articulates democratic, pluralistic, and proceduralist values – values which point, more helpfully for jurisprudence, *in the very same direction* as the prescriptive force and the authoritative pretensions of statute law itself.

For many hardened observers of legislatures, particularly in the United States, any such aspiration is a sign of naïvety.[32] The conditions under which legislation is actually enacted, they say, point us not in the direction which the enactment prescribes, but in the opposite direction – in the direction of caution about its provisions. But even if this caution is understandable, a theory which expresses nothing but caution is inadequate for jurisprudence. Legislation exists not just as a political event – for us to denigrate or make jokes about – but as something which claims authority. Unless we propose to treat the authority claimed for legislation as pure superstition, eventually that claim requires philosophical explication. Or, even if we *are* convinced that the conditions under which it is enacted seriously discredit legislation as an authoritative source of law, it behoves us to ask: would this be true of all legislation, legislation enacted under any conditions, or only legislation enacted under conditions that fell seriously short of some ideal? If we take the latter approach, then it is incumbent on

appellate courts are equally bankrupt. . . . If we accept the thesis as to legislatures, we are left with nowhere to turn.' See also Ch. 5, s. 1, below.

[30] For a helpful and balanced discussion, see Dahl, *Democracy and its Critics*, 187–91.

[31] See Dworkin, *A Matter of Principle*, 33.

[32] See, e.g., Riker, *Liberalism Against Populism*, and Macey, 'Promoting Public- Regarding Legislation Through Statutory Interpretation'.

us to articulate a reasonable ideal, showing how the authority of legislation *could* be linked practically to certain conditions of legislating in the
circumstances of modern life. For only if we are in possession of such an
ideal, are we in a position to say how far existing legislatures fall short of
that ideal and what, exactly, it is that they fall short of.

4. LEGAL POSITIVISM

As one begins the task of elaborating such an ideal, one looks naturally to
jurisprudence of the positivist persuasion. Legal positivists are preoccupied
with positive law – that is, law deliberately posited as a basis for social
order. To the extent that their theories have had a normative edge, they have
traditionally preferred a legal system dominated by a legislature to one
organized around common law traditions. Historically this has been a particularly powerful strand in English legal theory, originating with Thomas
Hobbes and finding its fiercest and most sustained exposition in the work
of Jeremy Bentham. These early positivists regarded legislation as the paradigm of law – the paradigm of what law is and certainly the paradigm of
what law ought to be. Common law, by contrast, they saw as an unsystem-
atic and unpredictable mess, because it lacked precisely the explicit author-
ial attention that was associated with legislation at its best. This story is too
well known – or rather it is too well told in Gerald Postema's excellent book,
Bentham and the Common Law Tradition – to bear repetition here.[33]

And one would think this predilection had persisted, too, into the twentieth century, dominated (as twentieth century jurisprudence is often
taken to be dominated) by positivist legal theories. Many of the leading
works in recent Anglo-American jurisprudence continue to present themselves as positivist. Like their philosophical ancestors, they maintain that,
in theory, propositions are to be regarded as law on account of their institutional pedigree, and by virtue of the occurrence of certain contingent
law-making events. The institutions in question may no longer be
Hobbesian sovereigns, and the events no longer political commands. But
the fundamental insight remains: a norm is law, not by virtue of its content, but by virtue of its source. Legal validity is a matter of institutional
provenance. The two leading ideas of modern legal positivism – 'the
sources thesis' and 'the rule of recognition'[34] – appear to focus philosophical attention exactly on the decisions of bodies like legislatures as institutional sources of law.

---

[33] See Postema, *Bentham and the Common Law Tradition*, particularly 328–36 for a discussion
of normative positivism.

[34] For 'the sources thesis,' see Raz, *The Authority of Law*, 47. For 'rule of recognition', see
Hart, *The Concept of Law*, 94–5.

Appearances are deceptive. Like the members of other jurisprudential schools, modern legal positivists in fact turn out to be much more interested in adjudication than they are in the structures and proceedings of legislatures. Indeed, the sense I get from reading the work of mainstream positivists like Joseph Raz and H. L. A. Hart is that detailed consideration of the structural aspects of legislatures that I have been emphasizing – size, diversity, disagreement, decision-procedures – is simply not required in connection with any of the serious tasks that are posed in modern jurisprudence.

In some positivist theories, legislation is barely visible at all. Joseph Raz argues, for example, that it is a mistake to think of the legislature as key to the systematicity of a body of law.[35] What makes a legal system a *system*, he argues, is not the dominating position of a legislature, but the fact that there is an organized set of norm-applying institutions which recognize norms as valid in virtue of the same source-based criteria. On the traditional positivist understanding, a phrase like 'source-based criteria of validity' would refer us automatically to a legislator. But in principle, Raz says, there is no reason why courts need to orient themselves towards a legislature at all. The criteria of validity shared by a system of courts may refer simply to a heritage of earlier decisions by similar norm-applying institutions. Suppose the following two things are true of a legal system: (1) it is the task of the courts to apply pre-existing norms; and (2) any determination by a court as to what those pre-existing norms are is binding. A system of courts governed by these principles might develop a complex and evolving body of law, each constituent norm of which would be valid by virtue of its source (in a determination by a court as to what some pre-existing norm amounted to), without any institution thinking of itself or being perceived as a legislative body, that is, as a body whose function it was to change the law or to deliberately enact new law. Of course law in such a system would change, and new law would be created; but it would be created by virtue of mistakes by courts in the application of the task laid down in (1), mistakes which would nevertheless themselves acquire the status of existent legal norms by virtue of the doctrine of authority laid down in (2).[36] Such a system would satisfy Raz's own 'sources thesis'[37] and it would involve the operation of a rule (or rules) of recognition.[38] But it would not be oriented, as those ideas are often thought to be oriented, towards a sovereign legislature as source, and towards criteria of valid enactment as the basis on which law is distinguished from non-law. Hence, Raz concludes that 'the existence of norm-*creating* institutions,

[35] Raz, *Practical Reason and Norms*, 129–31.
[36] Ibid.,132–48; see also Raz, *The Authority of Law*, 105–11.
[37] Raz, *The Authority of Law*, 47.
[38] For Raz on rules of recognition, see *Practical Reason and Norms*, 146–8.

though characteristic of modern legal systems, is not a necessary feature of all legal systems . . .'.[39]

It is difficult to know what to make of this argument. It's a little like Raz's insistence that the idea of a *sanction* is not logically connected to the idea of law, and that the imagination need not baulk at the idea of a legal system without coercion or punishment.[40] In fact, in our experience, the association of law with sanctions is more or less universal, and (as Raz readily concedes[41]) the same is true of the association of at least modern law with the deliberate activity of a legislature. But universality in experience is not enough, Raz thinks, to command the attention of the legal philosopher, particularly if the experience is confined to particular social conditions: 'Since a legal theory must be true of all legal systems, the identifying features by which it characterizes them must of necessity be very general and abstract. . . . It must fasten only on those features of legal systems which they must possess regardless of the special circumstances of the societies in which they are in force. This is the difference between legal philosophy and sociology of law.'[42]

What about the dominant modern positivist conception – that of H. L. A. Hart? Legislation certainly *seems* to be at the centre of Hart's jurisprudence. Hart argued that the mark of a legal system is the capacity of a community to deliberately articulate and change its rules and practices. 'It is', he wrote, 'characteristic of a legal system that new legal rules can be introduced and old ones changed or repealed by deliberate enactment.'[43] The ability to change rules deliberately is a striking feature of the contrast in Hart's jurisprudence between 'pre-legal' societies and modern legal

---

[39] Raz, *The Authority of Law*, 105. See also the discussion ibid., 87–8.

[40] See Raz, *Practical Reason and Norms*, 157 ff.

[41] Raz, *The Authority of Law*, 87: '[L]aw-creating institutions are of the greatest importance in modern societies . . .'.

[42] Ibid., 104. There is reason to think Raz has now moved away from this position. In recent presentations, and in conversation, he has emphasized that neither the concept of law nor legal theory can be regarded as having a content or a set of interests unaffected by times and circumstances.

[43] Hart, *The Concept of Law*, 175. I take it that this is a contrast between legal rules, which can be changed deliberately, and rules of *positive* morality, which cannot. Thus, I read it as a contrast between two types of social phenomenon, not as a contrast between the positivity of law and the transcendent reality of morality. This reading is consonant with the fact that, according to Hart, traditions are also immune to deliberate change in exactly the way that morality is said to be (ibid., 176). However, there are also passages which support an interpretation contrasting the positivity of law with the transcendent existence of moral reality. At ibid., 176, Hart writes: 'Much moral philosophy is devoted to the explanation of this feature of morality, and to the elucidation of the sense that morality is something there to be recognized, not made by deliberate human choice.' See also the discussion at ibid., 230. Of course the two readings are not inconsistent. One explanation of the immutability of positive morality might be that it is essential to the mode of morality's positive existence that its practitioners think of its standard as transcendent and beyond their capacity to change. (And, of course, *this* could be true even if moral realism were false.)

systems. A 'pre-legal' society is one governed by a set of conventional customs or moral practices. Everyone knows the rules, for the rules exist only as practices whose normativity is 'internal' to the lives of those governed by them. The rules are the rules *of these people*, not just in the sense that these are the people to whose conduct they apply, but in the sense that these are the people in whose consciousness and interaction the rules consist. Legal change is not unthinkable for such a society, but it will involve a 'slow process of growth, whereby courses of conduct once thought optional become first habitual or usual, and then obligatory, and the converse process of decay, when deviations, once severely dealt with, are first tolerated and then pass unnoticed'. In such a society, there is no means 'of deliberately adapting the rules to changing circumstances, either by eliminating old rules or introducing new ones . . .'.[44] The transition to distinctively *legal* governance involves the gradual institution of practices of more deliberate legal change. It involves the establishment of secondary rules specifying the basis on which new rules are to be enacted, and a basis on which duly enacted rules can be recognized as such. It also involves, inevitably, the emergence of a corps of specialist law-detectors – professionals who know the marks of legislation, who know how to tell which (putative) rules have been given social authority and which have not.

This contrast between the legal and the pre-legal helps explain Hart's hesitation about regarding the rule of modern law as 'an unqualified human good'.[45] For Hart, the thesis that law is not necessarily moral and not necessarily just (a thesis long regarded as the essence of legal positivism) is something more than a conceptual point.[46] It involves, as Hart puts it, a sobering truth: 'the step from the simple form of society, where primary rules of obligation are the only means of social control, into the legal world with its centrally organized legislature, courts, officials, and sanctions brings its solid gains at a certain cost'.[47] Since 'a great proportion of ordinary citizens – perhaps a majority – have no general conception of the legal structure or of its criteria of validity',[48] the dominance in social life of *deliberately enacted* law means that those who make and can recognize such law may use that capacity and that specialist knowledge for their own benefit and to the detriment of the rest. The rest will find that they know less and less about the detailed basis on which their society is organized, certainly less than they or their ancestors did when it was organized solely on the basis of primary rules, and they will be less in a position to question or participate in the processes by which they are governed. The prospect of injustice thus accompanies the division of labour involved in

---

[44] Hart, *The Concept of Law*, 92–3.
[45] Adapting a phrase from Thompson, *Whigs and Hunters*, 266.
[46] *Pace* Coleman, 'Negative and Positive Positivism', 11.
[47] Hart, *The Concept of Law*, 202.   [48] Ibid., 114.

the growth of technical law.[49] 'In an extreme case,' Hart concluded, 'only officials might accept and use the system's criteria of legal validity. The society in which this was so might be deplorably sheeplike; and the sheep might end in the slaughter-house. But there is little reason for thinking that it could not exist or for denying it the title of a legal system.'[50]

Thus the prospect of legislation, or something like legislation, seems key to much of what is distinctive and interesting in Hart's jurisprudence and in his speculative legal sociology.

Admittedly much of this could be developed, if need be, without specific reference to legislatures as such. On Hart's account, the transformation from the pre-legal to the legal involves the institution of courts as well as rules of enactment. And the sort of legal system Joseph Raz asked us to imagine (a system of primary norm-*applying* institutions) would involve many of the same phenomena – professional specialization, differential power, and alienation from legal culture among the wider membership of the community – that worried Hart in connection with the emergence of written law. Indeed we can credit Raz with a broader social thesis: technicality in law emerges with the institutional development of any system of legal authority. Authority cannot exist, according to Raz, and legal authority (in whatever shape or form) cannot do its work, unless there is a basis for recognizing pronouncements as authoritative which stands apart from the content and merits of the issues that the authority addresses.[51] The systematization of that basis for recognizing pronouncements as authoritative will always seem esoteric and technical, and will always tend to become a domain of specialist knowledge, in comparison with a people's substantive engagement with the primary norms and practices of their pre-legal community. This will be so whether what emerges is a system of judicial authority, or a system of legislative authority, or both.

Even so: *if* one were to focus on the modern legislature, one might still expect some assistance and inspiration from H. L. A. Hart. For Hart's jurisprudence is well known for its capacity to explain and characterize the internal normative constitution of legislatures. A society has a legislative capacity, Hart argued, not (as Bentham and Austin thought) in virtue of the political emergence in that society of a habit of obedience to the commands of a sovereign; a society has a legislative capacity in virtue of the acceptance, among a corps of officials, of certain rules about rule-articulation, rule-making, and rule-change. These secondary rules explain how a legislature can be legally constituted, and how it can be governed

---

[49] Of course it is not the only source of injustice. The pre-legal society might have its own forms of oppression as well as its characteristic inefficiencies.

[50] Hart, *The Concept of Law*, 117. See also Green, 'The Concept of Law Revisited', and Waldron, 'All We Like Sheep'.

[51] Raz, *Ethics in the Public Domain*, 203. See also Ch. 5, s. 4, below.

as well as structured by rules. They help explain features like bicamerality, for example, and also legal constraints on legislation such as those imposed by the US Constitution. Hart sets out these resources in the early chapters of *The Concept of Law*, mainly as a basis for criticizing the ideas of sovereignty that dominated earlier positivist theories. He sets them out; and certainly they are promising for our purposes. But he does nothing with them.

Why not? And what could he have done? In the rest of this section I want to develop an argument which *might* have been built on the foundations Hart provides for us, but which was not. It's an argument about the relation between rules of recognition, the internal structuring of the legislature, and legislative intent. And it's an argument which does take legislative structure seriously as an integral concern of jurisprudence.

Consider for a moment the role of rules of recognition in a modern legal system. A rule of recognition, according to Hart, is a complex practice among judges and other officials whereby rules are identified as law by reference to certain criteria.[52] But identified as law as opposed to what? When one sorts among various putative norms or rules using the validity criteria embodied in a rule of recognition, what are valid rules being contrasted with? An obvious (because trivial) answer is: *non*-legal rules or *non*-legally-valid rules. But what are these? Are they moral rules (that is, *merely*-moral rules), with which valid law is typically contrasted on the positivist conception? As matter of fact, I do not think this is the contrast that the rule of recognition is supposed to address. As Hart sets out the problematic of recognition, it's a matter primarily of formulaic uncertainty: in a society without secondary rules, 'if doubts arise as to what the rules are or as to the precise scope of some given rule, there will be no procedure for settling this doubt'.[53] This problem of course is hardly likely to arise in Hart's paradigm pre-legal community, for there primary rules exist simply in the conduct and normative consciousness of the members of the community, and for this mode of existence it is not clear that there is anything to be uncertain *about*.[54] The problem is one that is likely to crop up as the society becomes more differentiated, and as it begins the business of formulating and perhaps deliberately changing its laws. Certainly, any community that experiments with secondary rules of change is quickly going to have to address problems of uncertainty and recognition. For given that laws exist now by means of enactment, and not just in

---

[52] Hart, *The Concept of Law*, 110.   [53] Ibid., 92.

[54] There are Wittgensteinian themes about implicit rule-following that need to be addressed here. My point is that in the most straightforward cases of Wittgensteinian rule-following, there is no place for articulate uncertainty (or for that matter certainty) about the precise formulation of the rule one is following. (Hart's connection to these Wittgensteinian themes is in part via Winch, *The Idea of a Social Science*. See also MacCormick, *H. L .A. Hart*, 29–30 and Hacker, 'Hart's Philosophy of Law'.

normative patterns of conduct, the precise content of particular laws becomes an intelligible object of knowledge,[55] uncertainty, and controversy.

Another way of putting this is to say that the rule of recognition performs important functions in relation to *disagreement* in society. Two types of disagreement are relevant. First, a society that enacts law will confront a variety of enactment-proposals put forward by individuals and factions within the society. Because the proposals may be at odds with one another, inevitably not all of them will be accepted. So some means must be found of distinguishing between successful and unsuccessful proposals for enacted laws. As Joseph Raz puts it, one of the essential functions of legal recognition is 'to mark the point at which a private view of members of the society, or of influential sections or powerful groups in it, ceases to be their private view and becomes (i.e. lays a claim to be) a view binding on all members notwithstanding their disagreement with it'.[56] Secondly, in addition to broad disagreements of principle, there may be disagreements in detail among rival proponents of what is more or less the same legislative proposal. If enacted law is to settle at least some cases at the level of particularity at which they present themselves, a rule of recognition will need to provide a basis for specifying not only which proposal, but *which version* of a given proposal, has been enacted.

It is instructive to see how the first of these points is highlighted in the legal philosophy of Thomas Hobbes. In Hobbes's conception, law is concerned with the problem of conflict and competition between rival views and interests. For example, different people are willing to fight for rival definitions of justice (whether because a particular definition advances their material interests or simply because they are, in some other fashion, attached to a particular definition). That is the context that makes legislation necessary; but also for Hobbes it is the context that makes secondary rules like rules of recognition necessary. We need a rule of recognition, on Hobbes's account, not just because there is uncertainty as to what the law is, but also because there is disagreement in the community as to what ought to be taken as law:

Nor is it enough the Law be written and published; but also that there be manifest signs, that it proceedeth from the will of the Soveraign. For private men, when they have or think they have force enough to secure their unjust designes, and convoy them safely to their ambitious ends, may publish for Lawes what they please without, or against the Legislative Authority. There is therefore requisite, not only a Declaration of the law, but also sufficient signes of the Author, and Authority.[57]

---

[55] Knowledge, in the sense, now, of knowing-that, not just knowing-how.
[56] Raz, *The Authority of Law*, 51.
[57] Hobbes, *Leviathan*, Ch. 26, 189. See also Hobbes, *De Cive*, 174–7.

Such signs, Hobbes says, will depend on accessible criteria of validity such as 'publique Registers, publique Counsels, publique Ministers, and publique Seals'.[58] On this account, the rule and apparatus of legal recognition is oriented to a compelling and substantive political end – viz., the end of ensuring that when someone faces what purports to be a legal demand, he knows that that demand really *is* playing the role which Hobbesian law and Hobbesian legal validity aspire to play so far as the promotion of peace and the diminution of conflict are concerned. He can know that only if he has some guarantee that the demand can be traced to a sovereign authority, which alone can provide a basis for social peace and order. Source-based criteria of validity, and the rules which recognize them, attempt to furnish that guarantee.

In the Hobbesian picture, we usually imagine a variety of legislative proposals put forward by individuals, one of which is adopted authoritatively by the sovereign-legislator and then promulgated with the marks of valid law. But as I emphasized at the very beginning of this chapter, modern legislative politics do not work quite like that. Modern legislatures do not just respond to disagreement; they internalize it. For us, it matters that legislation should emerge from a process that is *deliberative*, a process distinguished not just by its Hobbesian decisiveness, but also by the engagement with one another in parliamentary debate of all of the views that might reasonably be thought competitive with whatever legislative proposal is under consideration. Modern legislatures are structured to secure this, with rules about representation (of parties as well as interests and localities), rules about hearings, rules about debates, rules about amendments, and above all rules about voting.

These secondary rules are extremely important in giving us the type of enactment-process we want. But they also pose a version of the very problem that, as we have just seen, it is the task of a rule of recognition to address. In the sort of legislature that we have, it is important to maintain a distinction between *deliberation* (which we value for its diversity and adversarial character) and *enactment* (which we value for its determinacy and univocality). Deliberation is understood to involve an array of contributions which we expect to stand in a dialectical relation to whatever is eventually enacted. Some of the contributions in debate will be in direct opposition to the law; some will be expressions of lukewarm support, or rebuttal of particular objections; others may support the measure with an enthusiasm that goes somewhat beyond its terms. Concerning this array of contributions, our rule is that the only contributions which have legislative authority are those actually reflected *in the text* that has been voted on. Legal validity, in our jurisprudence, is traced to the event and moment

<hr />

[58] Hobbes, *Leviathan*, 189.

of enactment rather than to the parliamentary process as a whole, precisely because there is so much in the deliberation preceding the enactment that cannot possibly be regarded as part of the enacted law.[59]

Of course we – no less than Hobbes – suffer from the social malady of private persons trying to put their own particular spin on the laws that have been enacted. In our type of legislature, however, one can do this not just by the crude method (which Hobbes condemned) of simply misrepresenting what was enacted; one may do it also by citing contributions that were made in deliberation as though they too were part of what was enacted or as though they too might form an authoritative basis for interpreting, glossing, or spinning what the text of the enactment amounts to.

This of course is the issue of *legislative intent*. As I said in section 2 of this Chapter, one of the perennial issues in legislative interpretation has to do with the status of evidence about what the lawmakers had in mind that goes beyond the text of the bill they enacted. (Consider, for example, the claim that a particular deliberative contribution – which is perhaps more detailed than the legislative text – is in effect a part of the legislation on account of its being the contribution of the bill's sponsor.) I indicated in that earlier discussion that there may be reasons for being wary of such appeals to 'legislative intent' based on such evidence.[60] And now we can begin to see what those reasons might be. The existence of disagreement and its internalization (as deliberation) in legislative politics poses a problem of recognition – that is, a problem of exactly the sort that Hart and, before him, Hobbes saw it was the function of a rule of recognition to address. We value deliberation in our processes of legal change, but it is an obvious and necessary implication of that ideal that *not everything which is said in legislative debate can have legislative authority*. Accordingly, we value the integrity of a deliberative process that ends in *voting* so that there is a fair basis for determining which among the various contributions that have been made in debate are to count as law and which are not. If legislative deliberation is not to fall apart into chaos and indeterminacy, modern rules of enactment and modern rules of recognition have to work together to maintain that integrity and secure the distinction between deliberative contributions and enacted text. The problem then with interpretive doctrines which accord authority to parts of the deliberative record other than the enacted text is that they make it much more difficult to do this.

I embarked on this long digression because I wanted to give some flavour of the opportunity *missed* in *The Concept of Law* by H. L. A. Hart's failure to consider the deeper jurisprudential significance of legislative

---

[59] I am grateful for this point to Jules Coleman and the members of the New York Jurisprudence Discussion Group.

[60] I develop this argument in detail in Ch. 6.

structure and its relation to rules of recognition. (The context – patient readers will recall – was a more general discussion of the lack of interest shown by modern legal positivists in issues about legislatures and legislation.)

The argument I have just developed focuses particularly on the fact that a legislature is a place where many things are said but only some of them are enacted, and it emphasizes that it is one of the functions of a rule of recognition to tell us which is which. But the sad fact is that Hart seems simply uninterested in the sort of place the modern legislature is. He seems uninterested in the relation between its structural features and the substantive issues of recognition and interpretation that might crop up when judges or citizens confront a statute. For philosophical purposes, though he used the form of words 'the Queen-in-Parliament' as his legislative paradigm, the points he makes in the second half of *The Concept of Law* might as easily have been made – indeed many of them *were* made – with reference to the activities of a unitary legislator called 'Rex'.

5. THE UNITARY MODEL

Overall, one gets the impression from modern legal philosophy that it matters little for jurisprudence whether legislatures are thought of as single individuals or as structured bodies comprising hundreds of persons who disagree profoundly with one another about the matters on which they are legislating. Philosophers are, I think, most comfortable treating the legislature on the model of a single individual. The unitary model is the default position.[61] Thus a legislature is not only said to *act*, but to possess a *will* and to have *intentions*, which are treated (as they are in the case of persons) as states of mind not necessarily disclosed in what it does. Certainly, it is well known that this way of speaking founders on the fact

---

[61] Lytton Strachey (*Eminent Victorians*, 192–3) tells the following story about the influence of this default model on Florence Nightingale's proof of the existence of God. When Miss Nightingale wrote a book of philosophy:

One copy was sent to Mr. [John Stuart] Mill, who acknowledged it in an extremely polite letter. He felt himself obliged, however, to confess that he had not been altogether convinced by Miss Nightingale's proof of the existence of God. Miss Nightingale was surprised and mortified; she had thought better of Mr. Mill; for surely her proof of the existence of God could hardly be improved upon. 'A law,' she had pointed out, 'implies a lawgiver.' Now the Universe is full of laws – the law of gravitation, the law of the excluded middle, and many others; hence it follows that the Universe has a lawgiver – and what would Mr. Mill be satisfied with, if he was not satisfied with that?

Perhaps Mr. Mill might have asked why the argument had not been pushed to its logical conclusion. Clearly, if we are to trust the analogy of human institutions, we must remember that laws are, as a matter of fact, not dispensed by lawgivers, but passed by Act of Parliament. Miss Nightingale, however, with all her experience of public life, never stopped to consider the question whether God might not be a Limited Monarchy.

that a legislature comprises many people not just one person, and people with quite radically varying states of mind.[62] But jurists persist with it all the same, trying again and again to fit legislation into the Procrustean form of individual intentionality, either by attempting to minimize (preferably to *one*) the number of persons who are said to be 'really' engaged in a given legislative initiative,[63] or by constructing more and more arcane formulas for privileging some subset of like-minded representatives whose shared intentions can be called the intentions of the House.

There is nothing new about this default position. It has permeated legal positivism since the foundation of that school. True, in both Jeremy Bentham's work and John Austin's, we find a gesture towards the idea – which of course was the political reality in contemporary England – that the legislature might be a large and numerous body. Nevertheless the style and presentation of the idea of legislative sovereignty remained firmly individualistic in these theories. Thus Bentham began by saying neutrally that we identify a sovereign whenever we notice 'any person *or assemblage of persons* to whose will an entire political community are (no matter on what account) supposed to be in a disposition to pay obedience: and that in preference to the will of any other person'.[64] But that phrase – 'assemblage of persons' – was almost his only concession to the point. For the rest of his jurisprudence and in much of his political philosophy, the sovereign was almost always referred to as 'he' (and for once, refreshingly, it is the number not the gender of the pronoun that preoccupies us).[65] And this despite Bentham's insistence that he was talking about those who

[62] See Dworkin, *Law's Empire*, 313–54.

[63] For an early example, see Hobbes, *De Corpore Politico*, Ch. XXI, 120: 'In all democracies, though the right of sovereignty be in the assembly, . . . yet the use thereof is always in one, or a few particular men. For in such great assemblies . . ., there is no means any ways to deliberate and give counsel what to do, but by long and set orations . . . In a multitude of speakers therefore, where always either one is eminent alone, or a few being equal amongst themselves, are eminent above the rest, that one or few must of necessity sway the whole; insomuch that a democracy, in effect, is no more than an aristocracy of orators, interrupted sometimes with the temporary monarchy of one orator.'

[64] Bentham, *An Introduction to the Principles of Morals and Legislation*, 18, my emphasis. Austin's language is similar: 'every positive law, or every law simply and strictly so called, is set by a sovereign person, or a sovereign body of persons, to a member or members of the independent political society wherein that person or body is sovereign or supreme'. (Austin, *Lectures on Jurisprudence*, Lecture VI.)

[65] In Bentham, *An Introduction to the Principles of Morals and Legislation*, the implicit recipient of the philosopher's advice almost always appears in the text as 'the legislator' – as in: 'the happiness of the individuals, of whom a community is composed . . . is the end and the sole end which the legislator ought to have in view' (ibid., 34) – with scarcely a reference to the pluralistic possibility. The same is true of Bentham's more analytic discussion of juridical language. For example: 'Power and right, and the whole tribe of fictitious entities of this stamp, are all of them in the sense which belongs to them in a book of jurisprudence, the results of some manifestation or other of the legislator's will with respect to such and such an act' (ibid., 206). (But see also Bentham, *A Comment on the Commentaries*, 122, for some impatience with monarchical interpretations of British parliamentary legislation.)

actually make laws, not just the monarchs who sign them: 'I speak here of those who frame laws, not of those who touch them with a sceptre.'[66] I am not saying that Bentham was uninterested in legislative assemblies. On the contrary, he can claim to have founded the peculiar English obsession with the shape and furniture of legislative chambers – an obsession which surfaces again in the writings and speeches of Winston Churchill.[67] But he saw no consequences for jurisprudence in the assembly aspect of legislation.

One way to read this is to see it as indicative *sub rosa* of a definite bias in political philosophy in favour of monarchy – whether in the form of the philosopher-king, the unitary sovereign, or the enlightened despot. Certainly that is what one would conclude from associating the positivism of Bentham and Austin with that of Thomas Hobbes. For when Hobbes said 'the Legislator is *he* . . .',[68] the language was not at all neutral, but reflective of his personal conviction that monarchy was by far the best form of government, among other reasons because 'a Monarch cannot disagree with himselfe, out of envy, or interest; but an Assembly may; and that to such a height, as may produce a Civill Warre'.[69] All the same, since Hobbes had no choice but to acknowledge that this 'one thing alone I confess in this whole book not to be demonstrated but only probably stated',[70] the strict logic of his position required him to repeat from time to time that, in theory at least, sovereignty might be vested 'either in one Man, or in an Assembly of more than one'.[71]

But I do not think of modern legal positivists as closet monarchists. Their persistence with the image of legislation as analogous to one man's act of will stems rather from an implicit belief that the structure and character of a legislature is genuinely uninteresting from the point of view of legal philosophy. It is thought of as a matter of *pre*-legal structure and *pre*-legal reasoning,[72] not a matter of structure and reasoning in which jurisprudence as such should have any interest. Though, as I stated earlier, positivist jurisprudence defines law in terms of its sources, the property of *being a source of law* is for the positivist the most interesting thing that can be said about a person or institution. What matters is that *this* is where laws come from, *this* is the agency by which they are posited. That is the remarkable thing; and any *other* features that the body may possess – including the features that actually enable it to have this jurisgenerative quality – pale into philosophical insignificance by comparison.

---

[66] In Bentham, *An Introduction to the Principles of Morals and Legislation*, 238n.
[67] See Wheare, *Legislatures*, 7–13.   [68] Hobbes, *Leviathan*, 185.
[69] Ibid., 132. See also Hobbes's discussion in *De Cive*, Ch. X, ss. x–xv, 136–8.
[70] Hobbes, *De Cive*, Preface, 37.   [71] See, e.g., Hobbes, *Leviathan*, 120, 129, and 184.
[72] The phrase is Joseph Raz's, in conversation.

From this point of view, what matters about a legislature is that a reasonably determinate statute comes out, from time to time, as an act of the legislature. Its determinacy may be product of a single mind, or it may be the product of a bunch of people finding a way to combine their diverse views into something singular: *e pluribus unum*. But jurisprudence is interested in the *unum* and what we are to do with it; it is uninterested in whether it comes *e pluribus* or not. Who cares whether a Parliament has one House or two, 435 seats or a hundred? Legal philosophy can afford to treat the legislature as a black box and leave its unwrapping to the political scientists. In other words, representing the legislature, at least stylistically, as though it had the character of a single author of the texts we call statutes is a logical representation of the singularity of the source of law *qua* source. It is not, I think, intended as a politically-loaded or wishful representation of the ideal character of the source-institution itself.

The point is connected with what legal positivists *do* in modern analytical jurisprudence. They spend most of their time defending the general idea of the sources thesis against various forms of natural law opponent. In that debate, what matters is the possibility that a community might confer the status and authority of law on certain norms in virtue of their institutional provenance. What matters is not one account of the institutional details versus another, but rather the abstract idea of institutional provenance as the basis of law's authority rather than substantive criteria of morality or justice. Once that abstract idea is established, the institutional focus shifts very quickly to the courts. This is because the modern opponents of legal positivism are much less interested these days in defending the proposition *lex iniusta non est lex* against the sources thesis,[73] than they are in arguing that the sources thesis cannot give an adequate account of what goes on in the courtroom.[74]

6. THE PRETENSIONS OF GENERAL JURISPRUDENCE

Added to this is a sense that there are important philosophical tasks to be performed at the level of *general* jurisprudence[75] – that is, jurisprudence addressing the very ideas of *law* and *legal system*, apart from the institutional peculiarities of particular jurisdictions. From the point of general jurisprudence, the possibility that a legislature might consist of one person

[73] Cf. Finnis, *Natural Law and Natural Rights*, 23–49.
[74] See Dworkin, *Taking Rights Seriously*, 48–80.
[75] This is general in the sense of 'universal' (as opposed to 'local') jurisprudence – see Postema, *Bentham and the Common Law Tradition*, 306. This does not involve the distinction we were using in Ch. 1, between general and special jurisprudence, where 'special' referred to particular areas of law, such as torts or criminal law.

or many persons is simply beneath notice.[76] Since those who take this approach do not want general jurisprudence to confine itself to the study of democracies, for example, they hold that we should not build into our concept of legislation the premise that it is necessarily the product of the many acting in a representative assembly. We want our philosophy of law, they will say, to tell us what is in common between legislation by a prince in a Gulf Emirate and legislation in the American Congress or the German *Bundestag*.

I suspect this quest for institutional neutrality in legal theory is largely misguided. Of course, if we stipulate a sufficiently high level of abstraction, we will have no choice but to ignore the features that distinguish some sources of law from others. We might, for example, try to find a definition of positive law that blurred out the distinction between statute and custom, or a definition of 'source of law' that licensed no distinction between legislation by a parliament and judge-made law in a hard case. But after a while, the pay-offs would begin to evaporate in the heady realms of such abstraction, and we would be overwhelmed by the distortions introduced by a theory that insisted that one size fits all.

In fact, of course, the modern positivist notion of source-of-law is not institutionally neutral. One way of seeing this is to consider the difference that was made in jurisprudence when the paradigm of man-made law shifted from custom to legislation. Customs can be seen as immemorial, earthy, local, and conventional, inhabiting a region between habit, prescriptivity, and consent that is only partially captured by modern notions like the internal aspect of rules.[77] They need not be mindless artefacts of common behaviour. On the contrary, jurists have always talked of customs being held, remembered, and in that sense *posited* in a community: 'According to the ancients, a local custom is an establishment held and preserved in a country by the old wise men by agreement, and maintained according to the condition of the place as long as it is accepted and suffices.'[78] What is more, customs may even be worked up into an articulated system, capable of intellectual coherence and relatively conscious growth: we all know that as part of the historical ideology of common law (whether or not it corresponds to reality). For generations of jurists, particularly in Western Europe, custom was the soul of man-made law.

Now, there is a world of difference – marked by a century or two of savage disagreement among lawyers – between this jurisprudence of custom and a legal philosophy that identifies man-made law as typically the expression of a legislator's sovereign will. In a way that is difficult for us

[76] See Raz's comment on the difference between legal theory and legal sociology, *supra* fn. 42 and accompanying text.

[77] See Hart, *The Concept of Law* 55–7 and 88–91.

[78] Jean Boutellier, *Somme Rurale* (1603), cited in Kelley, *The Human Measure*, 104.

to grasp, the partisans of custom in the eighteenth and nineteenth century regarded legislation – by an enlightened despot, for example – as having much more in common with the scientistic 'Natural Law' of the philosophers and the theologians than with the humble sublunar reality of the norms which generations of ordinary folk had posited for themselves in various countries. Legislation tended to be associated with reason and rational thinking, with the ability of one enlightened mind to cut through the accreted layers of local usage. Where custom was inarticulate, legislation presented itself in shining formulas of principle. Where custom was irredeemably parochial, legislation might be the same everywhere – reason's common solution to common human problems. And where custom was consensual, legislation would be the coercive offspring of sovereignty – not inherently oppressive, of course, but something that might have to be imposed on an ignorant people by someone more enlightened than them.

There is no space here to pursue this contrast further.[79] But no one can have any doubt about which conception has triumphed in modern positivist jurisprudence – particularly legal positivism as it has developed out of the English school of Bentham and Austin. What I want to emphasize is the obvious point that there is a massive difference – in substance, ethos and rhetoric – between a positivist jurisprudence dominated by an image of customary law and a positivist jurisprudence dominated by an image of legislator's law.

It is true that the hegemony of the latter has retreated a little in anglophone jurisprudence in the last thirty years. We are well aware of the attempts that were made on behalf of the legislator model to subsume custom altogether – for example, in Bentham's definition of customary law as 'a miscellaneous branch of statute law ill-expressed and ill-defined'.[80] And we think we know (from Hart's work among others[81]) how to resist that assimilation. We are now not fooled by the alleged neutrality of the legislator model, into inferring from the fact that both custom and legislation count as positive law, that they must therefore both be the product of somebody's will.

In much the same way, I think we should be open to the possibility that there is a similar discrepancy, similarly relevant for jurisprudence but belied by the common term 'legislation', between the positing of laws by one enlightened legislator and the law-generating activity of a large-scale representative assembly. We should certainly be alert to the consequences of continuing to use the rhetoric and ethos of a single-legislator model to

[79] See Kelley, *The Human Measure*, esp. 89–108 and 165–208 for a detailed account of the role of custom in European jurisprudence, from the 12th to the 17th century.
[80] Bentham, *Of Laws in General*, 235.
[81] Hart, *The Concept of Law*, 44–8 and 77–96.

describe a practice which is essentially and structurally different from that (different, for example, because it involves more than one person, and thus necessarily involves relations among persons in a way that single legislator models do not). We should be particularly alert to this danger, since we know that the single-legislator model which some are using as their 'neutral' model of legislation is one that has already tried and failed to render reductively in its own image other diverse (and importantly diverse) sources of positive law.

Chapter Three
Legislation by Assembly

1. NUMBERS

The United States Supreme Court has nine members; the executive arm of the United States government is headed by one man (the President), working with a Vice President and a cabinet of around twenty members; and the two houses of the US Congress have between them 535 members. Now why does the legislative arm of the federal government have almost twenty times as many members as the other arms of government combined? In the United Kingdom, the House of Lords sitting as a court normally hears cases with a panel of five judges; the executive comprises the Queen, her Prime Minister and about twenty cabinet ministers; and the British legislature has almost two thousand members.[1] The House of Commons alone has more than twenty times as many members as the highest court and the cabinet combined. Why the disparity in scale between the various branches of government?

There is a similar difference between the size of the legislature and the size of the other branches of government in just about every country in the world. Almost everywhere, legislatures are assemblies rather than individuals, and assemblies of anything from fifty to almost three thousand members,[2] not assemblies of cabinet size. No doubt, we should qualify this by observing that subordinate legislation is often made by single individuals or by very small rule-making agencies. But this should not distract us: such individuals and agencies always derive their authority from a sovereign legislature that comprises hundreds of members. If we want to state the point more carefully, we can say this: almost everywhere *sovereign* legislatures are assemblies rather than individuals; in almost every legal system, legislation bases its *final* authority as law on the fact that it is the product of (or its production has been authorized by) a large popular assembly.

As I have said, this contrasts quite markedly with the other great institutions of government. The highest court in each system characteristically

---

[1] Provided we count not only the House of Commons (659 members) but also the Queen and the House of Lords (26 bishops and archbishops, more than 800 hereditary peers of England, a smaller number of Scottish peers, 200 or more life peers, and more than a dozen serving and retired Lords of Appeal).

[2] The Chinese People's Congress – officially that country's legislature – has a membership of 2,977.

comprises a very small number of judges (the nine justices of the US Supreme Court is a typical figure). The executive is often just one person with a small cabinet of twenty or so. Again, let's not be distracted by the fact that large numbers of people are organized hierarchically under these officials: inferior courts and their staffs; subordinate executive officers and agencies; and so on. What is remarkable about the legislature is that the apex or, if you like, the highest rung in its hierarchy is occupied by hundreds of persons, each of whom counts as the equal of each of the others so far as their final law-making authority is concerned. In the other branches of government, the highest slot is occupied by just one person or a handful. In legislation, particularly legislation at the highest level, we seem to think it important that authority be plural, and that the people be governed by *people* – large numbers of people – not just by one individual person.

As we saw in Chapter Two, empirical political scientists are likely to respond to all this by highlighting the efforts that are made in most legislatures to limit the number of members who participate actively in the drafting and consideration of a given measure. Legislative proposals may come ready drafted from the executive, as in Britain, or consideration of a bill may be concentrated under the much more manageable auspices of a specialist congressional committee, as in the United States. It may *look* like we prefer legislation by assembly, these scientists will say, but our *real* legislators are party bosses and committee managers.

As a matter of political theory, however, that response is unconvincing. Certainly the members of legislative assemblies participate in law-making to greater or lesser degrees, and it is part of the political scientist's job to record and explain this. And certainly there are power structures within parties and within legislative assemblies that belie the formal equality of their members. But though these practices are important, they do little to undermine the continuing association of the authority of a statute as law with its emergence from an institution comprising hundreds of representatives. Despite all the structures and hierarchies, despite the committees, cabals, and corridors, the constitutional requirement that a bill be deliberated upon and passed by (say) Congress or Parliament as a whole survives not merely as a 'dignified' charade (like Royal Assent in the United Kingdom),[3] but as something regarded as a matter of right by the representatives themselves and as crucial to the standing and authority of legislation in the community. As I said, hard-headed political scientists might locate the *real action* in the executive, in the corridors of Congress, or in the committee system. But I have no doubt that if they were advising constitution-framers in an Eastern European country on the appropriate body

---

[3] For the contrast between 'dignified' and 'effective' elements in a constitution, see Bagehot, *The English Constitution*, 4.

for making laws, they would urge the institution of something like a large parliamentary or congressional assembly. And that would not be seen as a quaint concession to anachronism, like restoring a Hohenzollern to the throne of Romania. It would seem a matter of real importance. Somewhere in our tacit theory of the authority of legislation is a sense – a sort of constitutional instinct – that discussion and enactment by a *large* assembly of representatives is indispensable to the recognition of a general measure of principle or policy, put forward by the powerful, as law.

The aim of this chapter is to run this instinct to ground, so to speak, to unearth its roots; and to see what it tells us about the distinctive image of law that is evoked when legislation is enacted by an assembly.

2. 'BLIND MULTITUDE'

The instinct for large legislative *assemblies* survives, remarkably, despite a clear consensus among theorists of politics in the modern era that the size of a legislative body is an obstacle rather than an advantage for rational law-making. (John Locke is about the only exception, with his insistence in the *Second Treatise* that the people 'could never be safe nor at rest, nor think themselves in Civil Society, till the Legislature was placed in collective Bodies of Men, call them Senate, Parliament, or what you please'.[4])

Part of that consensus is explained by a sense, originating no doubt in ancient prejudice but surfacing also in the Enlightenment, that the larger the legislative assembly the lower the average level of wisdom and knowledge among the lawmakers. The views of the Marquis de Condorcet are typical. Though he proved arithmetically that majority-decision can make a group more likely to give correct answers to some question than the average member of the group (provided the average individual competence is greater than 0.5), and that the bigger it is the more likely it is that the majority answer will be right,[5] he also maintained that average individual competence tends independently to *decline* as group size increases (and then of course the arithmetic of majority decision works in the other direction):

A very numerous assembly cannot be composed of very enlightened men. It is even probable that those comprising this assembly will on many matters combine great ignorance with many prejudices. Thus there will be a great number of questions on which the probability of the truth of each voter will be below ½. It follows

---

[4] Locke, *Two Treatises*, II, para. 94, 329–30. I guess Jean-Jacques Rousseau could be classed as an exception also. For Rousseau, however, the issue was direct democracy versus representation, whereas the phenomenon that interests me is the preference for a larger rather than a smaller assembly of representatives. (See also fn. 11, below, and accompanying text.)

[5] I discuss Condorcet's 'Jury Theorem' in Ch. 6, s. 4, below.

that the more numerous the assembly, the more it will be exposed to the risk of making false decisions.[6]

Even if the ignorance and stupidity of a large group of legislators is not a problem, there is still a concern, exhibited for example by James Madison in *The Federalist*, about the susceptibility of large numbers to passion and malign influence:

the more multitudinous a representative assembly may be rendered, the more it will partake of the infirmities incident to collective meetings of the people. Ignorance will be the dupe of cunning, and passion the slave of sophistry and declamation. The people can never err more than in supposing that by multiplying their representatives beyond a certain limit they strengthen the barrier against the government of a few. Experience will forever admonish them that, on the contrary, after securing a certain number for the purposes of safety, of local information, and of diffusive sympathy with the whole society, they will counteract their own views by every addition to their representatives. The countenance of the government may become more democratic, but the soul that animates it will be more oligarchic.[7]

No doubt some of this is due to 'the greater . . . proportion of members of limited information and weak capacities', over whom the eloquence of a few rhetoricians will hold sway. But Madison also seems to be suggesting that 'group-think' is likely to infect a numerous assembly, whatever the quality of the individuals who compose it. A large multitude is always liable to various forms of 'confusion and intemperance':

In all very numerous assemblies, of whatever characters composed, passion never fails to wrest the scepter from reason. Had every Athenian citizen been a Socrates, every Athenian assembly would still have been a mob.[8]

Above all, there is a concern among political theorists about large numbers of representatives co-ordinating sufficiently to produce a coherent body of laws. Partly this is a matter of an assembly's factiousness – the Hobbesian concern which we quoted in Chapter Two: 'a Monarch cannot disagree with himselfe . . . but an Assembly may; and that to such a height, as may produce a Civill Warre'.[9] But even if faction is not the problem, numerosity has been thought an obstacle in itself. William Blackstone described the task of extracting 'a system from the discordant opinions of more than five hundred counsellors' in a representative assembly as 'Herculean'.[10] Jean-

---

[6] See Condorcet, *Selected Writings*, 49. See also the discussion in Estlund et al., 'Democratic Theory and the Public Interest'.

[7] Madison et al., *The Federalist Papers*, Number LVIII, 351. I am grateful to Marshall Sanger for this reference. The whole discussion in *Federalist* LV–LVIII is worth reading in this connection.

[8] Madison et al., *The Federalist Papers*, LV, 336.   [9] Hobbes, *Leviathan*, Ch. 19, 132.

[10] Blackstone, *Commentaries*, cited in Lieberman, *The Province of Legislation Determined*, 62.

Jacques Rousseau asked, in *The Social Contract*, 'How can a blind multitude, which often does not know what it wills . . . carry out for itself so great and difficult an enterprise as a system of legislation?'[11] (It was in large measure this difficulty of co-ordination that he addressed with his image of 'the law-giver' a mythic figure distinguished as much by his singularity as by his 'superior intelligence'.) A hundred years later, John Stuart Mill worried about the prospects of coherent law emerging when bills were 'voted clause by clause in a miscellaneous assembly'.[12] He argued in general that '[n]o body of men, unless organized or under command, is fit for action';[13] and since legislative functions are as much matters of action as executive functions, he concluded that 'a numerous assembly is as little fitted for the direct business of legislation as for that of administration'.[14] Walter Bagehot wrote at about the same time and in similar fashion about the House of Commons: 'Here are 658 persons, collected from all parts of England [*sic*], different in nature, different in look and language.'[15] How is something coherent supposed to emerge from the babel of their cross-cutting proposals and counter-proposals? There is a saying in England, Bagehot added, ' "a big meeting never does anything"; and yet we are governed by the House of Commons – by "a big meeting" '.[16]

So our question remains: how could something which is so obviously a bad idea – in Bagehot's words law-making by a 'big meeting' – have become so entrenched as a principle of constitutional organization?

3. DEMOCRACY

The political value most naturally associated with the modern legislature and with the authority of its product – legislation as positive law – is *democratic legitimacy*. Not all jurists accept the association. Some disparage the democratic credentials of statutes, because they are doubtful about Parliament's or Congress's success in representing the people, or because they are bewitched by the formal difficulties of public choice theory, or because they simply do not regard democracy as anything other than a derivative or instrumental value. Still, most students of legislation figure that a claim of democratic legitimacy – if it could be sustained – would be the best one could say for the authority of a statute. The democratic and

---

[11] Rousseau, *The Social Contract*, II. vi, 193.

[12] Mill, *Considerations on Representative Government*, Ch. V, 109. Mill continued: 'The incongruity of such a mode of legislating would strike all minds, were it not that our laws are already, as to form and construction, such a chaos, that the confusion and contradiction seem incapable of being made greater by any addition to the mass.'

[13] Ibid., 102.   [14] Ibid., 109.   [15] Bagehot, *The English Constitution*, 122.

[16] Ibid., 123.

representative credentials of the legislature, such as they are, are supposed to be the best reason a court or a citizen can have for deferring to its decisions.

However, democratic credentials come in all shapes and sizes. A single elective ruler – an American President, for example – may have democratic credentials in virtue of having more popular support than any other candidate for his office. But these are not the sort of democratic credentials we associate with legislation. Instead, we almost instinctively associate the legislative function with the authority of a large *assembly*. By itself the democratic ideal does not explain this preference. That is, it does not explain why, in the case of a President, we focus respect for the will of the people onto the choice of a single individual, whereas in the case of legislation, respect for the popular will involves election to an assembly of several hundred men and women.

The same is true of our conception of representation. In theory a large population might be represented by a single person. Thomas Hobbes's theory of representation is the best known example: 'A multitude of men, are made One Person, when they are by one man, or one Person, Represented.'[17] In practice, however, we prefer a form of representation in law-making that matches the plurality of the represented with a plurality of representatives. By itself the idea of democratic representation cannot explain this preference.

Nor can the preference be explained as a matter of a commitment to popular participation. In fact, more people participate in Presidential elections in the US than in the (off-year) election of representatives to the legislature. Nor can we seriously regard the size of the legislature as a surrogate for popular participation. Someone might say that by insisting on a large legislature, we are attempting to maximize the number of citizens directly involved in the making of the laws. We accept that for practical reasons not everyone can participate directly. A quarter billion people cannot assemble in the mall in Washington to make their laws, and they would be unable to deliberate even if they did assemble. So – the argument might run – we have to limit the numbers involved, but still we try and keep the number as high as possible. That is why we have hundreds of legislators rather than just a few dozen. The argument will not wash. Though I have said we should be struck by the difference in scale between the size of the legislature and the size of the other branches of government, the fact is that the difference between them is trivial when compared to what would be required for direct democracy. The figures do not really matter – but roughly they are as follows: if the legislature comprised twenty members, 99.99999 per cent of the US population of voting age would be

---

[17] Hobbes, *Leviathan*, Ch. 16, 114.

non-participant (in the sense required by direct democracy); in fact, because it comprises about 500 members, only 99.9998 per cent are non-participant (in the sense required by direct democracy). One would have to have a pretty sensitive theory of direct democracy, to think that a tiny difference like this really mattered.

As it happens, the preference for large legislative assemblies is much older than democracy, at least much older than the forms of democracy with which we are familiar. As we will see in sections 4–6, it has much more to do with a particular conception of *law* – and of what it is for a set of norms to constitute the law *of the land* or the law *of a people*. Though in the modern world we associate the legislature's character as an *assembly* with the idea of democratic representation, in an older understanding – an understanding which may *enrich* democratic jurisprudence rather than simply being an elaboration of it – law-making was associated with a process that related a legislative proposal to the complexity and multiplicity of persons, regions, relations, and circumstances, with which the proposed law would have to deal.

4. LEGISLATION AND CUSTOM

At the end of Chapter Two, I referred to the difference between custom-oriented models of law and models of law organized around the idea of a sovereign legislator. I said we should not be fooled into inferring, from the fact that both custom and legislation count as positive law, that they must therefore both be the product of somebody's will. And I suggested that we should perhaps leave ourselves open to the possibility that there is a similar difference, similarly relevant for jurisprudence but belied by the common term 'legislation', between the positing of laws by one enlightened legislator and the law-generating activity of a large-scale representative assembly.

In fact, there are connections of substance, not just analogies, between the two differences – that is, between (1) sovereign legislator *versus* custom, and (2) monarchical legislator *versus* legislative assembly. The substantial similarity is between the second term in each antithesis: customary law and legislation by an assembly. On their face, custom and assembly-legislation look quite different as sources of law. But in the next two sections I shall explore some important connections between them. It turns out that there are surprising affinities in historical jurisprudence – in particular, medieval jurisprudence – between the idea of legislation by an assembly and the idea of customary law. The common denominator is *the people*. In each instance – custom and legislative assembly – one can say, 'The people are governing themselves.' In each case, we have what legal historian Walter Ullmann calls an 'ascending' rather than a 'descending' model of legal authority.[18] With both custom and legislation by popular assembly, law wells up from those who are subject to it, rather than being handed down to them from on high.

Like all historical explorations, the discussion that follows will be suggestive rather than demonstrative. But it is exciting none the less, for I think it provides us with better clues than we can glean from conventional jurisprudence, as to what explains our constitutional instinct for large legislative assemblies.

5. *'LEX TERRAE'*: THE LAW OF THE LAND

I begin with a rather obvious question. When English kings like Henry III or Edward I legislated in the thirteenth century, why did they think it important to assemble hundreds of their subjects in a parliament to ratify their law-making, as opposed to simply making law on their own regal authority? No doubt part of the answer has to do with sordid fiscal realities. Then as now the consent of parliamentary bodies was necessary (in practice, if not in principle) for taxation. But why also associate *law-making* with such an assemblage of subjects? After all, the only well worked out conception of legislative authority in contemporary legal philosophy was summed up in the Roman law adage *'Quod principi placuit, vigorem legis habet'*.[19] On this conception, law was given by the *voluntas principis*, the will of the prince. And that will was conceived (in Walter Ullmann's words) as 'autonomous, independent and, to use a modern term which seems quite legitimate to employ in this context, . . . sovereign.'[20]

The answer is that, while *'Quod principi placuit . . .'* may have been the dominant view in academic jurisprudence in Paris or Bologna, it was not the only conception of law with which people were familiar. Law has not always been thought of in terms of the paradigm of sovereignty, will, and power. An older and perhaps historically more important understanding conceives of it as the law of a people or the law of the land, rather than the law of a king or the will of a prince. On this older conception, law is originally something held in common, something essentially *ours*, something indeed which only exists to the extent that it is embedded in and part of a shared way of life. Such an understanding of law need not preclude legal change, though metaphors of organic growth rather than artificial innova-

---

[18] For the idea of 'ascending' and 'descending' models of government, see Ullman, *Principles of Government and Politics in the Middle Ages*, 19 ff.

[19] 'What pleases the prince has the force of law.'

[20] Ullmann, *Principles of Government and Politics in the Middle Ages*, 123.

tion are commonly appealed to. It need not even preclude deliberate legal change. But to the extent that deliberate legal change is understood as alteration in a way of life (not simply a change in the operation of a ruling apparatus, such as a king's household), it may seem intuitively, if not jurisprudentially, appropriate for those who embark on it to proceed in a way that pays tribute to law's status as something essentially common, something essentially shared.[21]

These are not just sentimental generalities. Law understood as something sociologically 'thicker' than the edicts of a prince, law understood as something instinct in existing social arrangements, law on the ground, so to speak, was a conception taken in deadly earnest in medieval society. Inasmuch as it embodied or symbolized the realities of social, military, and economic power, such a conception of law was guarded jealously by those whose political position might be undermined by a more imperious model of legislation.

Nowhere is this more evident than in the case of feudal law and in the resistance that surfaced in early thirteenth century England to the theocratic pretensions of the monarchy of King John. A king like John might flatter himself that he held sovereign authority *Dei gratia* and that he was entitled to rule the people given to him by God, using such laws 'as he makyth himself'.[22] And certainly a grasp of these ideas was indispensable for understanding the *theory* of medieval kingship. But the reality of the king's position was much more complicated than the theory of kingship indicated. His position was also compassed around with a set of feudal ideas that, in fact, starkly contradicted the theocratic theory, and placed the king firmly in a network of relations with other members of the community:

So far from standing outside and above the community entrusted to him, so far from forming an estate of his own, so far from his *voluntas* constituting the material force of law, the feudal side of his kingship meant that by virtue of the contractual character of the feudal nexus, he had rights and duties, just as the tenants in chief had them, that for purposes of government and the making of laws he had to proceed by consultation and agreement.[23]

The key notion in all of this – a notion we have already mentioned – was *lex terrae*, the law of the land, in the sense in which that phrase (and not John's own formulation, '*lex regni nostri*') was used in the Magna Carta:

[21] See ibid., 125–6, for some interesting etymological speculation on the difference between 'legis-*datio*' (which is the act of a superior to his subjects) and 'legis-*latio*' (which has more to do with *bearing* the law – *ferre, latum* – than with *giving* the law).

[22] The phrase is from Sir John Fortescue's *The Governance of England*, quoted by Ullmann, *Principles of Government and Politics in the Middle Ages*, 191. See also Ullmann's discussion of '*Dei gratia*' and of medieval coronation oaths, ibid., 117–37.

[23] Ullmann, *Jurisprudence in the Middle Ages*, 58.

No free man is to be taken and imprisoned, or disseised, or outlawed, or exiled, or by any means distrained, nor will we proceed against him, . . . except by the judgment of a court of his peers according to the law of the land (*per legem terrae*).[24]

Lex terrae meant, in the first instance, the law that constituted the feudal system. It meant the land law, and the body of tenurial rights and contractarian arrangements that bound together lord and vassal, from the relations between the king and his barons to those between the lowliest villein and his manor. Walter Ullmann argues that *lex terrae* was not customary law strictly speaking. But it was certainly law implicated in the most concrete manner with the actual social relations of the country. It was a system

of native growth, born out of the exigencies of time and place, man-made and adapted to contemporary needs. . . . For these reasons it stood in a somewhat stark contrast to the purely speculative theocracy of the king. It was a working arrangement of an intensely practical kind, very little burdened by the incubus of first principles, of dogmas, of Authority.[25]

I said that the law of the land comprised *in the first instance* the structural principles of feudalism. That was its stasis. But it also had a dynamic aspect, involving a certain view of the basis of the system's flexibility and a certain attitude to legal change in general. If the key to feudalism was the contractual bond between lord and tenant, the key to legal change in the feudal understanding was council and consultation. Inasmuch as law needed to be made or modified, it was to be made or modified on the very basis of co-operation between the king and his barons that was, in any case, its essence. The barons were the king's 'natural counsellors' in this regard; they were not simply those whom he might *choose* to consult. New law, on this conception, emerged from a plurality of persons in consultation rather than from the single will of the prince. This is not to say that, on the feudal understanding, the king had no authority of his own. But the sphere in which he could act on his own initiative – in his dealings with other monarchs, for example, or in ordering his household – was not regarded by his subjects as a sphere in which the *lex terrae* could be modified by his say-so. The *lex terrae* could be modified only in and by the *communitas regni* – the political community of the kingdom – an essentially pluralistic body comprising initially the king and those whose feudal relations with him constituted the fabric of the realm. (And when – much later

[24] Magna Carta, Ch. 39; I have translated '*nisi per legale judicium parium suorum vel per legem terrae*' along lines suggested by Ullmann 1961, 163–4. (For a different view, see Holt 1992, 328.)

[25] Ullmann, *Principles of Government and Politics in the Middle Ages*, 152. Ullmann also notes that, in effect, *lex terrae* was the thirteenth century term for what was later called the Common Law of England: see ibid., 170 and also Ullmann, *A History of Political Thought in the Middle Ages*, 150.

– legislative authority was associated with the democratic branch of government, it was not a matter of the people seizing sovereign legislative authority hitherto held by a monarch; it was rather a matter of their elected representatives coming to be regarded as indispensable members of the pluralistic *communitas regni* which had always been conceived to have this power.)[26]

In his account of all this, Walter Ullmann is at pains to stress that *lex terrae* not be regarded as popular custom, and that the legislative framework it encompassed not be understood as populist law-making. Certainly *communitas regni* had very little to do with civic republicanism:[27] Simon de Montfort was no Hannah Arendt! And neither the feudal arrangements nor the barons' claims were understood in terms of anything remotely approaching political equality or participatory democracy. Ullmann is equally emphatic, however, that the broader idea of representative government was in fact made possible by the feudal conceptions we have sketched here. It cannot be emphasized enough that the feudal was *essentially* pluralistic: feudal arrangements related the abstract authority of government jointly and severally to an array of power-holders, each with his own rights, status, territory and jurisdiction. Theoretically, there might be a considerable gap between the idea of legislation by the king and his barons and the idea that *any* distinct element or place or corporation in the land is entitled to be represented in law-making. But feudal arrangements were practical, not theoretical. And in practical terms, the two ideas do have a certain resonance: no significant *locus* of power in the land is to be excluded from the process by which the law of the land is modified. Similarly, the legislative authority of the *communitas regni* embodied the idea that what was in the interests of the kingdom could be determined only by those who were substantially affected, that is, only by *their own* insight into *their own* needs and wants. In the theocratic conception, it was the king's understanding of the interests of the community that was all important; a single individual's understanding of everyone's interest was both dominant and sufficient. In the feudal conception, by contrast, the idea took hold that in legislation the main elements of the kingdom – and there were many of them – were entitled to speak for themselves. Once that was accepted, then broader ideas of representation in law-making found, as Ullmann put it, an 'easy and unimpeded . . . inlet',[28] and the steady growth of the English tradition that eventually included the commons in parliamentary legislation begins to become intelligible.

[26] See Post, *Studies in Medieval Jurisprudence*, 163–238, for a discussion of the influence of the maxim '*Quod omnes tangit ab omnibus decidentur*' ('What affects all should be decided by all') in English law and politics.
[27] See also Ullmann, *Jurisprudence in the Middle Ages*, 59.   [28] Ibid., 190.

My aim in all of this is to understand what I have called our constitutional instinct for *law-making by assembly*, even in the face of a consensus among modern political theorists that 'big meetings' are the last things one should use for legislation. With this brief and sketchy account of law-making in medieval England, I think we can get a sense of why the theoretically tidy idea of projecting the determinacy of law back onto the univocality of a single legislator never really got a grip in political or constitutional reality. People may not always have had *our* sense of the plurality of the community. The feudal account is not our account, and hopefully its last vestiges will be swept away in the new British government's plans for reform of the House of Lords. Still, the idea that the community for which law is made is essentially plural, and in its essence incapable of representation by a single voice, was second nature to our feudal predecessors – as it is, I think, to us.

6. BARTOLUS AND '*PARIS POTENTIAE*'[29]

There is a second connection between legislation by assembly and customary law which I think is worth pursuing. This connection is found not on the margins of medieval jurisprudence in a damp feudal kingdom off the coast of France, but near its sunny centre, in the cities of Northern Italy. Like the case we have just discussed, it illustrates the dissonance between a jurisprudential theory of legislation organized around the idea of '*Quod principi placuit . . .*' and the social reality of ordinary law-making by the leaders (*plural*) of the community.

From the thirteenth century on, cities such as Pisa, Milan, Bologna, Ferrara, and Florence had quietly developed their own institutions of government. They prided themselves on the independence of their republican institutions, and they used those institutions as a matter of course to make laws to govern politics and commerce within their walls. By all accounts, their enactments were of very high quality. There was, however, a jurisprudential difficulty. Contemporary legal theory did not recognize the legislative sovereignty of such cities. Technically, the cities were subject to the Holy Roman Empire, and Roman law recognized no general legislative authority except the *merum imperium* of the Emperor. With regard to the kingdoms of Southern Italy and Northern Europe, jurists eventually developed theocratic conceptions of kingship which enabled them to say '*Rex in regno suo est Imperator*'.[30] (How useful such conceptions were is, as we saw in section 5, another matter.) But it was not clear how such

[29] I am greatly indebted to my Princeton colleague Maurizio Viroli for making me aware of the contribution to jurisprudence of Bartolus of Sasseferrato.

[30] Roughly: 'The king is Emperor in his own realm.'

doctrines could be applied to self-governing cities. Even in those cities which were ruled by single individuals, there was no question of the local tyrant regarding himself as the *princeps* of '*Quod principi placuit, vigorem legis habet*'; and certainly doctrines evolved for theocratic monarchy had little or no application to cities that retained republican forms of government.[31] How then were the evidently successful legislative capacities of these cities to be understood in juridical terms?

The problem was not just philosophical. The German Emperors periodically strove by military and political means to realize their historic claims to the *Regnum Italicum*. And the Italian cities, for their part, measured their *libertas* in terms of their ability to resist these efforts. But they had no means of investing these efforts with any legal respectability. As Quentin Skinner points out,

> ever since the study of Roman law had been revived at the universities of Ravenna and Bologna at the end of the eleventh century, . . . the cardinal principle of legal interpretation – and the defining characteristic of the so-called school of Glossators – had been that of following with absolute fidelity the words of Justinian's Code, applying the results as literally as possible to prevailing circumstances. Now there could be no doubt that the ancient law-books stated in so many words that the *princeps*, whom the jurists agreed in equating with the Holy Roman Emperor, had to be regarded as the *dominus mundi*, the sole ruler of the world. This meant that as long as the literal methods of the Glossators continued to be employed in the interpretation of Roman law, the cities had no possibility of vindicating any *de jure* independence from the Empire, while the Emperors were assured of the strongest possible legal support in their campaigns to subjugate the cities.[32]

This political dimension is important, for it ruled out one possible solution to the jurisprudential difficulty. In theory, a city might have the right to enact its own laws as a concession or delegation from the Emperor; but that could hardly be regarded as the basis of a sovereign independence that the Emperor was busy trying to suppress.

Other possible solutions were limited in their scope. No one denied that a corporation or a collegial body such as a university was entitled to legislate for its own internal affairs. But such legislation was limited in its application to those who were members of the body in question, whereas it was undeniable that the cities were exercising something more like territorial sovereignty – that is, the right to enact laws that would bind anyone who came within their walls or traded in their markets.

---

[31] The original basis of '*Quod principi placuit . . .*' in Roman law was that the Roman people had transferred their original law-making power to the emperor. See Tierney, *Religion, Law, and the Growth of Constitutional Thought*, 56. The transfer, however, was not understood to be reversible, and certainly not reversible to the people of a city other than Rome.

[32] Skinner, *The Foundations of Modern Political Thought*, Vol. I, 7–8. See also Canning, *The Political Thought of Baldus de Ubaldis*, 18–19.

The problem – to repeat – was one of *legal* theory. (Even the political problem that Skinner refers to is a matter of securing an element of *de jure* respectability for the cities' *de facto* independence.) To the extent that one can distinguish in this period between jurists and theorists of politics (which is not very much), the latter had much less difficulty with all this. The revival of Aristotelian theory – by such thinkers as Thomas Aquinas and Marsiglio of Padua – put the city (in the sense of *polis*) at centre stage; and even when they argued for kingship these thinkers did not regard civic legislation as inherently anomalous.[33] We need to remember, however, that Aristotle's authority was by no means secure in thirteenth century thought: his works on natural philosophy were banned in Paris in 1210, his *Politics* was not even available in Latin until 1250, and there were grave doubts about its respectability. (True, Thomas Aquinas took it as his mission to undertake a 'Great Synthesis' of Christian and Aristotelian thought. But we must not be misled by the *eventual* success of this enterprise, or by the prominence of Aristotle and Aquinas in *our* canon of legal and political thought, into thinking that everyone in this period regarded Aristotle as '*the* Philosopher' or that philosophy had already become what Hobbes later derided as 'Aristotelity'.[34] If anything, the jurists were as doubtful about Aristotle as the bishops, though Aristotle had less to say on matters they regarded as important. Certainly it was quite unclear at the time how the arguments of the *Politics* could be melded with the Glossators' literal adherence to the Justinian code: Aristotle was not a juristic authority and his jurisprudence, such as it was, sat rather uncomfortably with the principles of Roman Law. Even Bartolus of Sasseferrato,[35] who did more than any other jurist to open legal philosophy to the spirit of the new political science, always quoted Aristotle in a way that indicated that an audience of lawyers could not be expected to be familiar with his authority.[36]

It was Bartolus – in Skinner's view, 'perhaps the most original jurist of the Middle Ages'[37] – who came up with a solution to the difficulty about

[33] This is particularly true of Marsiglio of Padua, *Defensor Pacis*, 27–80. See also Marongiu, 'The Theory of Democracy and Consent in the Fourteenth Century', 406. For the passage in Aquinas most congenial to civic legislation, see Aquinas, *On Princely Government*, 2–5. For the prevalence of consent-based themes in medieval life and thought, see generally Tierney, *Religion, Law and the Growth of Constitutional Thought*, 40–2.

[34] Hobbes, *Leviathan*, Ch. 46, 462.

[35] Bartolus of Sasseferrato lived from 1314 to 1357. His works are not available in English translation, and I cite them here from secondary sources (mainly Sidney Woolf and Walter Ullmann).

[36] See Woolf, *Bartolus of Sassoferrato*, 175 and 386. Skinner takes a different view of Bartolus's reliance on Aristotle: Skinner, *The Foundations of Modern Political Thought*, Vol. I, 51–2. See also Viroli, *From Politics to Reason of State*, 58.

[37] Skinner, *The Foundations of Modern Political Thought*, Vol. I, 9. See also Ullmann, *Jurisprudence in the Middle Ages*, 266, for the reputation of Bartolus as '*princeps juristorum*'.

legislation. The key to Bartolus's contribution – what makes him a *Post*glossator – lay in his recognition that when legal doctrine appears to contradict stable and well-established facts, it is sometimes the legal doctrine not the facts that ought to be modified. The cities legislate; they legislate competently; they act as though they are sovereign; and their law-making appears to be accepted by those over whom they claim authority. If legal theory denies that such a legislative capacity is possible because only the Emperor is sovereign, then legal theory must be adapted to reality.

The adaptation proceeded by way of an analogy between statute and customary law. No jurist had ever denied that custom was a legitimate source of law or that customary law applied to everyone who lived in the locality where the custom was current with or without the imprimatur of a superior: 'No emperor, king or pope had any say in the people's own usages and customs.'[38] In the traditional view, customary law was based on ancient usage. However, Bartolus argued that usage itself – a mere mode of conduct – was not the essence of the matter. The binding force of custom as law was based on the *tacit consent* of those whose lives it structured and without whose acquiescence it could never have become established. As Ullmann puts it:

Usage is, in [Bartolus's] opinion, '*causa remota,*' the tacit consent of the people is '*causa proxima,*' of Customary law. '*Usus et mores sunt causa consuetudinis, dico causa remota, nam causa proxima est tacitus consensus, qui colligitur ex usu et moribus.*'[39] The binding force of customs was, therefore, ascribed to the tacit consent, which may be considered as the will of the people to impose obligations and confer rights. Certain modes of conduct as such did not produce force of law.[40]

True, the inference of consent from a pattern of behaviour is always problematic. But that problem was overcome by an emphasis on the frequency of the acts and transactions in question over a long period of time. A people who regularly oriented their activities to a norm that no one had imposed upon them, over a period of (say) ten years, may reliably be regarded as having agreed to be bound by that norm.

Once one accepted this consensual account of customary law, the next step was obvious enough. '[I]f the citizens . . . can by tacit consent create unwritten law, what [reason] is there for not ascribing to them the same law-creating ability in the shape of the written law?'[41] The difference was

---

38 Ullmann, *Principles of Government and Politics in the Middle Ages*, 283.

39 Roughly: 'Usage and mores are the cause of custom – i.e. the remote cause – but the proximate cause is tacit consent, which is inferred from usage and mores.'

40 Ullmann, *Jurisprudence in the Middle Ages*, 269.

41 Ullmann, *Principles of Government and Politics in the Middle Ages*, 283. I have modified the first sentence of this passage to correct a slight infelicity. Ullmann's original reads: 'if the citizens . . . can by tacit consent create unwritten law, what *obstacle* is there for not ascribing to them the same law-creating ability in the shape of the written law?'

simply the mode of expression of the popular will: tacit consent created customary law, whereas written or statutory law is created by consent voiced explicitly in a popular assembly. As Bartolus put it, '*tacitus et expressus consensus aequiparantur et sunt paris potentiae*': tacit and express consent are equivalent and of equal force, so far as the generation of law is concerned.

It's a remarkable conclusion and, philosophically, quite striking from our perspective. For not only does it establish an equivalence between custom and civic legislation, but it does so by way of an analogy between tacit and express consent that, from our perspective in modern liberal philosophy, seems to get the matter exactly the wrong way round. *We* privilege express consent, and we regard tacit consent as the poor cousin, to be resorted to by a theorist when there is no other basis of legitimacy. The Bartolist conclusion challenges not just that priority but the reasoning behind it, for it appeals to a notion of consent that is more substantial than linguistic. The Bartolist argues: an explicit performative expression of consent that takes place at a certain moment may not have the legitimating force of a long and established pattern of conduct. The *statement* 'I agree' may be the product of whim or an uninformed judgement. Indeed its only advantage seems to be its linguistic unambiguity, and that may be secured for tacit consent in other ways (by its frequency and longevity, for example).[42] Still, the Bartolist argues, under certain circumstances we may be persuaded to take the formal linguistic moment as the equivalent of a long and established practice, and that is the basis on which we may confer upon civic legislation something akin to the dignity and legitimacy of custom.

Why, in any case, was consent as such so important in Bartolus's argument? I think the hidden premise of his approach may have been this: it is only law in its *coercive* or *imperious* aspect that requires authorization from on high, according to traditional Roman law doctrine. We can do what we like consensually (just as two people can bind themselves in a contract without authorization) or we can do as we like collegially (as those who have bound themselves together into a corporation of some sort); but to issue orders that bind without consent is the exclusive prerogative of the Emperor. So, if tacit consent means that customs do not require the authorization of a superior, then by the same reasoning, express consent means that statutory enactments do not require the authorization of a superior. Admittedly, the argument is stretched a little thin, for as we saw this move is supposed to provide legitimacy for statutes that apply to *anyone* who comes into the city not just those who voted in the assembly to enact it; that is why the corporatist model did not provide a solution. But this is char-

---

[42] See Canning, *The Political Thought of Baldus de Ubaldis*, 100.

acteristic of the Postglossator movement: the terms of the Code and the Gloss are stretched to allow the doctrine effectively to change.

The result is that those whom Bartolus influenced were able to see their way clear to a juridically respectable understanding of civic legislation. Cities can legislate with the same authority with which they evolve and adapt their customs. Since they thus dispense with the imprimatur of a superior, they become in effect sovereign or self-governing entities – a proposition which Bartolus expressed in a striking phrase, *'civitas sibi princeps'*.[43] The city becomes its own prince for the purpose of the traditional doctrine of legislation and may enact laws as it pleases (*prout sibi placet*) on any matter affecting the common good.[44]

It is pretty clear that this argument presupposes a degree of republican organization within the cities to which it applies. If the consent of the people is to do the work for legislation that tacit consent does in regard to custom, it must be a consent rooted in the minds and lives of those who are going to have to live with the laws that it ratifies. Ultimately, the case for a city's legislative authority is that a free people wills its own form of life, rather than subjecting itself to the authority of another. That is the characteristic of customary law, and that, Bartolus is saying, is what is characteristic too of the enactments of civic assemblies. Evidently the will of a tyrant in charge of a city does not get the benefit of Bartolus's argument,[45] for the tyrant's will has exactly the sort of imperiousness *de haut en bas* that is supposed to be the prerogative of the Emperor.

There are also points to be made about the *process* by which the will of the people is ascertained. In the case of custom, the will of the people is manifested by frequent observance over a relatively long period of time. The passage of time provides an opportunity for people to experience the rule or practice in question, to become aware of its advantages and

[43] Canning (ibid., 96) calls this the 'juristic masterstroke' of the Bartolist approach, and he notes that it amounts, in the end, to a civic version of *'Rex in suo regno est imperator regni sui'*. Thus, as Canning puts it, 'the law-making activities of the people, whatever the de jure claims of the emperor, break through to sovereignty'.

[44] Ullmann, *Principles of Government and Politics in the Middle Ages*, 284. For some discussion of implicit limits, see Woolf, *Bartolus of Sassoferrato*, 147 ff.

[45] See Woolf, *Bartolus of Sassoferrato*, 162–9. Woolf notes, ibid., 162, the irony of Bartolus's achievement in this regard: 'We have repeatedly remarked that the political thought of Bartolus is eminently practical, that his theories at once reflect and interpret the actual Italian conditions of his time. But it might well be asked whether his thought, however praiseworthy, has not after all been out of touch with these conditions. It may be said that, while the whole trend of his thought has so far been to free these Civitates from an Empire which was a shadow, in reality they were fast falling under the power of tyrants, indeed were for the most part already fallen.' But he responds (ibid., 171–3), first, that Bartolus believed tyranny to be a passing episode in the history of the Italian cities, not their permanent destiny, and secondly, that Bartolus used his populist theory of statutory authority as a premise for the complex and indisputably practical task of assessing the authority of the enactments of tyrants of varying sorts – *tyrannus manifestus, tyrannis velatus, tyrannus ex parte exercitii*, etc. For that account, see ibid., 164–9.

disadvantages, and by their action – or rather by the emergence of a pattern of action – to manifest either acceptance, rejection, or modification of its terms. Bartolus was under no illusion that consensus for the purposes of customary law required unanimity: different people differently situated would have differing experiences of and different attitudes towards a given practice. Still, over time, one looked for the emergence of a stable view – the view of most, the view of the greater part. That is, one looked to ensure that any objections to or difficulties with the practice were not so widespread as to make it non-viable as a practice. For legislation to have the same legitimacy, there must be something roughly equivalent to all this in the process of giving express consent. Presumably the equivalent in the case of statute law is some form of deliberation, with *consensus majoris partis* (now defined rather less vaguely than in customary law) emerging from a discussion of the pros and cons of the legislative proposal. Deliberation is the equivalent of experience and voting is the equivalent of the manifestation of consent in the viability of the practice. Without some such political procedure in the process of enactment, the parity between custom and statute would be completely unconvincing.

And so we come back to our theme of legislation by assembly. In the case of both statute and custom, the basis of legal authority has to do with a process (formal or informal) that brings together the plural and disparate experiences and opinions of those who are going to have to live with the norm in question. So far as statutes are concerned, the process may involve a literal assembly of the people or (more commonly) some form of elected council. The point is that, on this approach, legislation could not possibly be conceived on the model of one man's action. Even if fewer than all the people were involved, even if in the interests of practicability one were to accept the Bartolist maxim '*Concilium representat mentem populi*',[46] still the practical manageability of a representative council was *a concession from the people*, in all the diversity of their opinion and experience, rather than an approximation to the univocality of a monarch. As Ullmann points out:

It was no longer the superior insight of the Ruler which determined what was in the interests of the people, but the people itself was recognized as perfectly capable of forming its own judgment on what was in its interests, for at all times the people retained control of the Council.[47]

If people thought significant experience was being slighted, or significant opinion overlooked, in the process of legislation, then it was perfectly appropriate on this model for them to complain and to do something about it, for the laws that were made in this assembly were *their* laws and the basis of the laws' legitimacy was supposed to be *their* understanding

---

[46] Roughly: 'The council represents the mind of the people.'
[47] Ullmann, *Principles of Government and Politics in the Middle Ages*, 216–17.

and *their* acceptance of the place the laws would occupy in *their* way of life.

7. LEGISLATION, ANCIENT AND MODERN

I find all this fascinating. I am sure though that there are some more analytically-minded readers whose patience has been sorely tested by 'the admixture . . . of feudalism and antiquarian lore with English jurisprudence' and who have been tempted to ask, 'Does law really need to be set off with this antique and Gothic tracery? Does jurisprudence have ends of its own so idle and unimportant to mankind, that it must stand indebted to such sources of interest as an antiquarian society can supply?'[48] Who cares, they may say, what Bartolus thought or what arrangements were satisfactory to King John and his barons? What has this to do with our modern understanding of Parliament or the United States Congress?

I am not a fan of the Cambridge history-of-ideas school of political theory,[49] but I make no apology for the historical exploration we have just undertaken. For I am convinced – as I argued in Chapter Two – that our understanding of legislation in modern analytical jurisprudence is impoverished, and that it needs, for its improvement and reconstruction, all the help it can get. At present, we legal philosophers talk about 'Rex, the legislator'. We develop models of authority that ask, 'Under what circumstances does *one man* have authority over another?' And the best we can make philosophically of the process of statutory interpretation is to present it as though it were insight into the intentions of a single lawgiver. We present all this as the best we can do in analytical jurisprudence (as, indeed, all that needs to be done) in the way of understanding institutions that *for centuries* have consisted of hundreds of individuals acting together. The fact is that modern legal philosophers in Britain and America are not really interested in legislatures and legislative structure at all. Those things, we tend to say, are for political science or public choice theory, not for philosophy. Tell a legal philosopher about legislative structure, and he will say, impatiently, 'When do we get to talk about the Supreme Court and how judges should decide cases?' And so we rest lazily content with an image of legislation – Rex's law – that was already being called in question six hundred years ago by jurists who took their vocation a little more seriously than we do.

Having vented that spleen, of course one acknowledges there are limits on the extent to which we should rely on either of the models discussed in

[48] Smith, *Remarks on Law Reform*, 8–9, quoted with enthusiastic approval by Mill, *Essays on Equality, Law and Education*, 84.
[49] See Waldron, *The Right to Private Property*, 132–6.

this chapter. I accept that. Once the legislative enterprise gets under way, it takes on a life of its own, and its intimate connection with community and plurality can easily be lost. Certainly, I am not suggesting that today the more or less universal practice of assembling large bodies of representatives to approve legislation indicates a delicacy about changing the *lex terrae* that might have been appropriate in the reign of Henry III, nor am I suggesting that it implies a twentieth century reception of the equivalence of custom and statute expounded by Bartolus of Sassoferrato in the 1340s and '50s. The stuff I have been talking about *is* all as foreign and unfamiliar as it looks.

What I do want to insist on, however, is that an understanding of the feudal stuff and the Bartolus stuff also points up the antiquity, the artificiality, the infertility, and certainly the philosophical dispensability of the models of legislation with which we *are* familiar. For if *communitas regni* and *paris potentiae* are antiquarian ideas, *still* the idea that legislation is best understood on the model of one man's intentional action is even more a matter of Gothic tracery: even those whom I have quoted in Latin thought that the conceptions connoted by '*Quod principi placuit . . .*' were really quite hopelessly out of date. In other words, a historical explanation can sometimes assist us to see how unhelpful our *current* models are. And if we are lucky, that exploration can point us towards alternatives. At the very least, it may open up a *space* in legal philosophy for new ways of thinking about legislatures and legislation – new ways that promise to make plurality, procedure, structure, and disagreement central features of our legal philosophy rather than marginal excrescences that have to be lopped off or relegated to some other discipline in order to fit a Procrustean jurisprudence that is politically as well as theoretically obsolete.

Chapter Four

Text and Polyphony

1. 'TALKING SHOPS'

Legislatures in the modern world do not just assemble and vote. They deliberate: that is, their members *talk* to one another about the measures they are considering. For this they are sometimes denigrated as mere 'talking shops' – a critique quite close to the spirit of Bagehot's concern about 'big meetings'.[1] But, as John Stuart Mill pointed out, we ought to treasure the deliberative capacities of our legislatures:

Representative assemblies are often taunted by their enemies with being places of mere talk and *bavardage*. There has seldom been more misplaced derision. I know not how a representative assembly can more usefully employ itself than in talk, when the subject of talk is the great public interests of the country, and every sentence of it represents the opinion either of some important body of persons in the nation, or of an individual in whom some such body have reposed their confidence. A place where every interest and shade of opinion in the country can have its cause even passionately pleaded, in the face of the government and of all other interests and opinions, can compel them to listen, and either comply, or state clearly why they do not, is in itself, if it answered no other purpose, one of the most important political institutions that can exist anywhere . . .[2]

In this chapter, I want to discuss the character and conditions of talk in the legislature, and its relation to the textual character of the law that is enacted as the upshot of such talk. The topic of talk – or more solemnly '*deliberation*' – is now a common theme in discussions of democratic institutions. There has been a renewed emphasis on *speech*, *discourse*, and *conversation* in recent political and legal theory, particularly in theory that has been influenced by the work of Jurgen Habermas.[3] Jurists influenced by Habermas have suggested, for example, that a commitment to the US Constitution is 'less a series of propositional utterances than a commitment to taking political conversation seriously. . . . [T]he Constitution is best understood as supportive of such conversations and requiring a government committed to their maintenance.'[4] They suggest too that the

---

[1] Bagehot, *The English Constitution*, 123.
[2] Mill, *Considerations on Representative Government*, Ch. V, 117.
[3] See especially Habermas, *Moral Consciousness and Communicative Action* and Habermas, *Between Facts and Norms*.
[4] Levinson, *Constitutional Faith*, 193.

authority of judicial decision-making is 'sustained less by the perceived correctness of the result than by the coherence of the result, for coherence permits conversation, and it is ultimately a faith in our ability to converse morally that holds us together'.[5]

Much of this is far-fetched in ways I cannot go into here – in its aestheticism, for example, or in its conception of discourse as an end in itself.[6] But one point is particularly important for our purposes. There is a constant temptation in modern discourse-jurisprudence to take as an implicit procedural ideal the model of an informal intimate conversation among friends. Tocqueville once remarked that an American cannot converse without falling into the mode of political formality: '[H]e speaks to you as if he was addressing a meeting; and if he should chance to warm in the course of the discussion, he will infallibly say Gentlemen, to the person with whom he is conversing.'[7] We are in danger of making the opposite error. So taken are we with models derived from ordinary conversation, we are inclined to ignore the formalities necessary for political discourse in a numerous and diverse society. Certainly, an informal conversation among friends has attractive features of equality, openness and mutual respect. But it also tends to be predicated upon the idea that participants share implicit understandings and that their interaction is oriented towards the avoidance of adversarial disagreement and the achievement of consensus. And these, I think, are qualities which are quite misleading so far as our models of political deliberation are concerned.

Instead I want to focus on some relatively formal characteristics of legislative talk. I want to focus on the formal characteristics that make what happens in the legislature more like *proceedings* than like conversation, and the results of legislative proceedings more like canon than consensus. I believe these formal characteristics are related inherently to the fact that it is the task of modern legislatures to gather together large numbers of people who are not necessarily on casual 'speaking terms' with one another, and who participate in legislative deliberations not as individual conversationalists but as representatives. In other words, I want to explore what legislative talk has to be like in the context of the account we want to give of the relation between number, structure, and diversity in the legislature (on the one hand) and the reception and authority of legislation as a source of law (on the other).

We may begin this inquiry by returning for a moment to John Stuart Mill. Mill thought that the virtues which made a parliament good at discussion made it a very poor place for what he called 'the direct business of

---

[5] Carter, *Contemporary Constitutional Law-making*, 143.

[6] See Elster, *Sour Grapes* for a critique of theories of political process that take discourse as an end in itself. See also the discussion in Ch. 11, below.

[7] Tocqueville, *Democracy in America*, Vol. I, Ch. xiv, 240.

legislation'.[8] He shared the view of the theorists we discussed in section 2 of Chapter Three: a big meeting is not a good basis for public action. The problem he saw was partly a matter of co-ordination – 'No body of men,' he said, 'unless organized and under command, is fit for action' – and partly a matter of expertise – 'There is hardly any kind of intellectual work which so much needs to be done not only by experienced and exercised minds, but by minds trained to the task through long and laborious study, as the business of making laws.'[9]

However, the solution which Mill recommended did not do away with the connection – which, as we saw in Chapter Three, is one of our constitutional instincts – between large-scale debate and legislative *authority*. Though we need an expert 'Commission of Legislation' to draft and, if need be, codify our laws, it was no part of Mill's proposal that such a commission should have legislative authority. As Rousseau said of his lawgiver, 'he who frames the laws . . . has not, or should not have, any rights of making law'.[10] Or, as Mill put it, 'the Commission would only embody the element of intelligence in their construction; Parliament would represent that of will.'[11] Actually, even this does not get the matter quite right. For if parliament engages in discussion in the process of enacting or refusing to enact one of the Commission's proposals, then it does not merely represent will as opposed to intelligence; it represents intelligence – collective intelligence emerging from discussion – in the service of will. Or, to put it another way, the intelligence of the parliament is practical intelligence; that of the Commission is theoretical intelligence, albeit theoretical intelligence with a view to a practical task.

This point, however, does not lessen the need for a notion of deliberation oriented specifically to the task and circumstances of legislation. An assembly debating whether to confer authority on the measure before it (whether the measure was drafted by a subset of its members or by an expert parliamentary counsel) is doing something different from sponsoring an open-ended conversation. It must pay attention to deadlines, whether these are features of its constitution or of the exigencies of the challenges which it faces. It must respect its responsibility, of the whole assembly to action and consequences, and of members to its constituents. It must deliberate at every stage and in every aspect of its proceedings, in a way that allows some articulation between stages and aspects – so that a procedure involving drafting, consultation, committee hearings, bicameralism, conference committees, first, second and third readings, and so on, can add up to a structured but unified legislative process.

---

[8] Mill, *Considerations on Representative Government*, Ch. V, 109.   [9] *Idem.*
[10] Rousseau, *The Social Contract*, Bk. II, Ch. 7, 195.
[11] Mill, *Considerations on Representative Government*, Ch. V, 112.

Above all, our conception of legislative deliberation must respect the fact that a representative assembly is characteristically a place where people assemble who are different from one another – in their backgrounds, experiences, and beliefs – and often opposed to one another – in their views about policy, social justice, and rights. What is more, these are not just features that an adequate conception of legislative deliberation must come to terms with. They are features that a good conception will make the best of – so that law is seen to emerge from the legislative process in a way that can answer citizens' concerns about partisanship, ignorance, and disagreement.

Aristotle, in Book III of the *Politics*, suggested that 'the many, of whom each individual is not a good man, when they meet together may be better than the few good, if regarded not individually but collectively'.[12] Elsewhere I have argued that behind this is the idea that a number of individuals may bring a diversity of perspectives to bear on issues under consideration, and they are capable of pooling these perspectives to come up with better decisions than any one of them could make on his own.[13] Just as Aristotle in the *Ethics* synthesizes a view about virtue out of the *endoxa*[14] – fragments of popular wisdom and diverse and opposed philosophical conceptions – so Aristotle imagines politics as a process by which each of a large number of people contributes through argument and confrontation to a practical intelligence that outstrips the intelligence of which any one of them is capable.

Of course the fact that a view was entertained by Aristotle (or, for that matter, John Stuart Mill) does not make it right. We may or may not subscribe to this speculation that, in a legislative context, the many can come up with better results than the few by pooling their insights and experience. But whether or not they guarantee better laws, the existence of diverse perspectives in the community and the necessity of bringing them to bear on proposed statutes are surely important features in any account of why the task of legislating is entrusted to assemblies. I believe that these features in turn can help frame the way we ought to think about the deliberative process itself. I shall argue in this chapter that, in particular, they help us to understand the relatively high level of formality associated with debate, enactment, and output in a legislative assembly.[15]

---

[12] Aristotle, *The Politics*, Bk. III, Ch. 11, 1281b. See the quotation in Ch. 6, s. 4, below (fn. 48 of Ch. 6, and accompanying text).

[13] Waldron, 'The Wisdom of the Multitude'.

[14] Aristotle, *Ethics*, Bk. VII, Ch. 1, 1145b1.

[15] In their discussion of 'the inherent formality of statute law', Atiyah and Summers neglect this aspect. (Atiyah and Summers, *Form and Substance in Anglo-American Law*, 96 ff.) They stress (i) its 'rank-formality' (i.e. priority over other forms of law); (ii) its 'content-formality' (i.e. tendency to embody arbitrary or conventional elements); (iii) its 'mandatory formality' (i.e. the application of standards embodied in a statute is non-optional; it cannot

2. DIVERSITY

A page or two ago, I said that the problem with discourse ethics is that it tends to assimilate political deliberation to the more cozy and informal features of conversation. So let's try a move in the opposite direction. Suppose that – instead of a conversation among friends – we take the following as our paradigm of legislative deliberation.

A large number of persons have assembled in a hall as representatives from different parts of a diverse society. Let us suppose that it is a radically diverse society – so that the members of the assembly represent not only different interests and regions, but come from completely different backgrounds, ethnic and cultural, as well as representing whatever political differences divide them. (Imagine, for example, that we are considering the national legislature in India or in some other vastly diverse modern state.) The representatives may belong to various religious traditions; they may be familiar with quite different social forms; they may have disparate senses of what gives meaning to life. They may not even speak the same language. Perhaps there is a state language stipulated for their proceedings in the legislature; if so, we may think of it as a second language for most of them, and one that they must use carefully and hesitantly.[16] Certainly, their presence together in the chamber attests to the fact that they share some sense of common purpose – though it may not be much more than a foreboding that any attempt to disentangle their diverse interests into more homogeneous 'nation' states, each with a legislature of its own whose members really *do* understand each other, would be fraught with the most frightful dangers and difficulties.[17]

To the extent that such a body seeks to legislate on common problems, it is necessary for the members to be able to talk to one another, so each can contribute insights and perspectives, including some that would

be 'distinguished' as case law can); and (iv) its 'interpretive or textual formality' (i.e. the identification of the law embodied in a statute with a canonical form of words). The aspect on which I am concentrating here may be regarded as a fifth dimension: (v) procedural formality. I shall argue later in this chapter that (v) contributes considerably to our understanding of (iv).

[16] For a discussion of languages of legislation, see Laundy, *Parliaments in the Modern World*, 63–5.

[17] Cf. Rushdie, *Imaginary Homelands*, 404: 'Secularism, for India, is not simply a point of view; it is a question of survival. If what Indians call communalism, sectarian religious politics, were to be allowed to take control of the polity, the results would be too horrifying to imagine. Many Indians fear that that moment may now be very near. I have fought against communal politics all my adult life. The Labour Party in Britain would do well to look at the consequences of Indian politicians' willingness to play the communalist card, and consider whether some Labour politicians' apparent willingness to do the same in Britain, for the same reason (votes) is entirely wise.' (I have discussed this in Waldron, 'Minority Cultures and the Cosmopolitan Alternative', 792–3.)

otherwise be quite outside the experience of the other legislators he is addressing. However, the very reasons that make this interaction desirable and necessary also make it quite unlikely that the members can proceed with their deliberations as though they were conducting an open-ended conversation among friends. They simply are not transparent to one another as friends are, and they do not have much common ground on which confidences could be shared, premises assumed, and nuances taken for granted.

Indeed, the prospects for mutual *mis*understanding and for talking at cross-purposes are greatly enhanced by the very features of their situation that make it important – on the Aristotelian grounds we mentioned at the end of the last section – for them to be talking to one another. These representatives cannot deal with one another like members of a tightly-knit *gemeinschaft* or an 'old-boy's network'. They share very little beyond an overlapping sense of common problems, and the rather stiff and formal language that they use in their debates about those problems. If any one says, in the rather cozy way that people have who share tacit understandings, 'Come on, you know what I mean', the answer is likely to be: 'No, I don't know what you mean. You had better spell it out for me.'

Of course this is an extreme example. The chambers of the British House of Commons are much more homogeneous than this, and the United States Congress more homogeneous still. There are reasons for dwelling on the more extreme model nonetheless.

First, as we have seen, the less diverse the body of representatives, the weaker the case (at least the Aristotelian case) for legislation by an *assembly* as opposed to legislation by a single representative individual.

Second, and more generally, exaggeration has advantages in ideal-type analysis. By highlighting the diversity associated with the sheer plurality of a modern legislature, the model I have introduced helps us to understand the challenges and techniques that come along with diversity so far as deliberation and decision-making are concerned. Maybe in a more homogeneous legislature, these concerns can be discounted *pro tanto*. There is nevertheless some theoretical advantage in using an exaggerated model to focus our attention on them, particularly when – as I shall argue – they offer us a plausible basis for understanding certain features of modern legislation which are otherwise somewhat bewildering: for example, the high degree of formality associated both with legislative deliberations and with legislative outputs.

Thirdly, there are philosophical reasons for taking this approach. We pride ourselves on having not only a diverse society, but a political philosophy – particularly liberal political philosophy – oriented specifically to the challenges and difficulties of that diversity. Jurisprudence should participate in that orientation. In its philosophical assumptions about the sources of law, it should not err on the side of social homogeneity. Of course it is true that actual diversity may be somewhat less extreme than our legal or political models can accommodate. Still, the liberal instinct is that we should not be counting on that. (Indeed, it is an important criticism of recent *communitarian* theories that they presuppose cultural and ethical homogeneity to an extent that is really quite reckless in the circumstances of the modern world.[18])

What I am saying, in other words, is that we should be careful to avoid building in any premise of ethnic and cultural homogeneity as a prerequisite in our models of politics and legislation. The narrow impulses of communitarianism, tribalism, and nationalism are wreaking enough havoc in the world as it is, without the encouragement of analytical jurisprudence. If there is a conception of law that makes no such assumption – or that celebrates diversity or, at any rate, comes to terms with it – we should try to state that conception clearly, and make it central in our jurisprudence if we can.

3. RULES OF ORDER

We left our diverse legislators in their chamber, a little unsure of each other and a little tongue-tied. We might imagine that from time to time one of them will stand up and make a proposal to his fellow representatives. My experience of faculty meetings is that this is likely to evoke a flurry of responses: some the original speaker will recognize as opposing his idea; some will appear to misunderstand it; some may put forward a different proposal or a counter-proposal, which in turn will evoke similarly confusing responses. Some members may stand up and make speeches on quite different matters; some will tell stories about their constituents of tenuous or indeterminate relevance; some will interrupt by chanting slogans, singing hymns, telling jokes, or shouting threats. Matters that various members conceive as having great urgency will cut across one another. Responses to one idea will be taken as responses to a different idea, and no one will be able to keep track of where they have got to on any particular front.

In circumstances of this kind we see the importance, not just of the sort of Legislative Commissions that Mill talked about, but also, when their work comes to be considered, of things like deliberative formality, parliamentary procedures, and Robert's Rules of Order. For it is clear from the scenario just outlined that an assembly like ours needs to *structure* and *order* its deliberations, if it is to achieve any of the advantages that the

---

[18] See Rushdie, *Imaginary Homelands*, 404.

Aristotelian theory suggests may accrue from legislation by the many. The members of our assembly need to establish rules and procedures that address issues like the following: How are debates initiated and how are they concluded? Who has the right to speak when, how often, and for how long? Who may interrupt, who may exact an answer to a question, who has a right of reply? How is a common sense of relevance maintained – or in other words, how are members assured that they are not talking at cross purposes? What issues, subjects, or details may be addressed at various stages in the proceedings? How are topics for debate selected, how are subject-matter priorities set, and how is an agenda determined? How is the conduct and conclusion of a deliberative session related to the assembly's powers of resolution and action?

Blandly stated, these matters might seem obvious and beneath notice in jurisprudence. It is tempting to regard procedural rules as arbitrary conventions, with no intrinsic philosophical significance of their own. I think that would be a mistake. Many political scientists have noted the remarkable similarity in parliamentary procedures around the world. There are no doubt historical reasons: the global influence of the Westminster tradition, for example, largely as a legacy of British imperialism. But the similarity can also be understood as a common human response to a similar set of problems: the circumstances of procedure, so to speak.[19] Wherever there is a felt need for common action as an upshot of deliberation in circumstances of diversity and disagreement, then needs of the kind outlined in the previous paragraph are bound to be felt.

The representatives in our model feel the need for what Hannah Arendt described as the 'in-between' of politics – a set of enduring rules and procedures that constitute a public space, a 'stable worldly structure to house, as it were, their combined power of action'.[20] Arendt has made more than almost any other modern theorist of the human appetite for politics and for 'the joys of discourse, of legislation, of transacting business' in the public realm – particularly in her imagery of Revolutionary America going 'to the town assemblies, as their representatives later were to go to the famous conventions, neither exclusively because of duty nor, and even less, to serve their own interests but most of all because they enjoyed the discussions, deliberations, and the making of decisions'.[21] Her more romantic interpreters attribute to her an unruly, agonistic, virtuoso conception of political action which might defy the need for anything as mundane as Robert's Rules of Order.[22] But if we say Arendt was unconcerned with the

[19] Cf. Rawls, *A Theory of Justice*, 126–30, on moderate scarcity, limited altruism, and ethical and religious diversity as 'the circumstances of justice'. See also the discussion at the beginning of Ch. 9, below.

[20] See Arendt, *On Revolution*, 86, 175, and 249.   [21] Ibid., 119 and 131.

[22] See Honig, *Political Theory and the Displacement of Politics*.

formalities of political order, we can make little sense of her preoccupation with foundations, with constitution-building, with the need for patience and discipline in politics, and with the hard task of constructing and sustaining a realm where human freedom can become powerful and not spend itself in the futility associated (in her work) with immediacy and the natural.[23] The imagery Arendt uses is the imagery of 'housing', and it is surely no accident that concerns about legislative procedure in the broadest sense often associate themselves with an interest in the shape and furnishings of the legislative chamber itself.[24]

To be sure, Arendt also emphasizes the spontaneity with which civic assemblies spring up whenever they are given the chance to do so. But part of what is intriguing in this is that everyone seems to know on these occasions that if you constitute a public meeting, no matter how local the basis, no matter how spontaneous the impulse, there are procedures to be followed, chairs elected, motions moved, questions asked, amendments put forward, speakers for and against, points of order, questions put, votes taken, and minutes recorded. If one listens for it, it is surprising how much this is 'second nature' in our political culture – as much a part of our political being, in Aristotle's sense, as the faculty of speech itself.[25]

4. THE RESULTING TEXT

I have focused so far on what the ideal-type of a diverse legislature contributes to our understanding of procedural formality. I want to turn now to the formality of legislation – i.e. statutes – considered as *products* of processes of this kind.

Here what is to be characterized and explained is the way we treat legislation as *text*: the way we feel ourselves bound by (and associate authority with) *the very words* that the legislature produces, to a much greater extent than we do in regard to other sources of law (or other sources of authority). Unlike common law principles, for example, the standards embodied in statutes have canonical formulations. A statute yields 'rules

---

[23] When Arendt uses agonistic imagery, it is the image of the actor with a mask in formal Greek drama, not the image of any transparently emoted performance in a Californian sense. We need formality precisely to the extent that we are not open or transparent to one another; and it is of course Arendt's main point in the early part of *On Revolution* that the attempt to unmask one another and reveal each other's 'true self' leads ultimately to madness and to terror. (Arendt, *On Revolution*, 88–109.)

[24] Wheare, *Legislatures*, 3–9. See also Arendt, *The Human Condition*, 194–5: 'Before men began to act, a definite space had to be secured and a structure built where all subsequent actions could take place, the space being the public realm of the *polis* and its structure the law; legislator and architect belonged in the same category.'

[25] For 'second nature,' see Kelley, *The Human Measure*, ix *et passim*.

in fixed verbal form':[26] the rule that has been posited by the legislature is the rule expressed by the very words that are used in the bill that the legislature has passed. I *think* this is what Hans Kelsen meant when he wrote in *The Pure Theory of Law*, that

[t]o say that acts, specially legislative acts, 'create' or 'posit' a norm, is merely a figure of speech for saying that the meaning or the significance of the act or acts that constitute the legislative process, is a norm. It is, however, necessary to distinguish the subjective and objective meaning of the act. 'Ought' is the subjective meaning of every act of will directed at the behavior of another. But not every such act has also objectively this meaning; and only if the act of will has also the objective meaning of an 'ought,' is this 'ought' called a 'norm.' . . . The legislative act, which subjectively has the meaning of *ought*, also has the objective meaning – that is, the meaning of valid norm – because the constitution has conferred this objective meaning upon the legislative act.[27]

In context Kelsen is trying to distinguish between the 'ought' implicit in the subjective prescriptions of a robber and of a tax inspector: 'The command of a gangster to turn over to him a certain amount of money has the same subjective meaning as the command of an income tax official, . . . [b]ut only the command of the official . . . has the meaning of a valid norm.'[28] But we may also see him as noticing the fact that in the case of a legislature, the criteria of validity make the content of the subjective norm and the content of the resulting objective norm *the same*. Because the legislature *says*, 'Everyone in circumstances C is to refrain from acts of type A' it becomes the law that everyone in circumstances C is to refrain from action A. This contrasts with the jurisgenerative activity of courts: a judge may say, 'Individual P_1 is to refrain from a particular action A_1 in a particular set of circumstances C_1' and it is up to *subsequent* judges and legal commentators to determine what general norm they take to have been established by this piece of particular-focused text.

This contrast between legislation and other sources of law should be treated carefully. Certainly, there is a textuality to all law. 'A rule of Law', wrote Bentham, 'must be predicated of some assemblage of words – It never can be predicated of a bare assemblage of naked ideas.'[29] Even in a pure common law system, there are authoritative renderings of the texts of judgments handed down by courts, including the statements of reasons etc. offered by each judge – official law reports, which effectively settle any

---

[26] Twining and Miers, *How to do Things With Rules*, 58–9, cited in MacCormick, *Legal Reasoning and Legal Theory*, 56.

[27] Kelsen, *The Pure Theory of Law*, 7–8.   [28] Ibid., 8.

[29] The passage continues: 'It is words only that can be spoken of as binding: because it is words alone that are producible with certainty when occasion comes for any individual to be bound.' – Jeremy Bentham in *A Comment on the Commentaries*, quoted by Postema, *Bentham and the Common Law Tradition*, 291. See also Bentham, *Of Laws in General*, 184 ff. for the 'incompleteness' of non-verbalized laws.

dispute about what was said in giving judgment. Still, in the common law tradition, *what the judge said* (in the sense of *the exact words that were used*) is not understood as essential to the identity of whatever standard was laid down. A different judge may be thought to be following the same principle even though he uses different words; and when he does, there is no sense that the original wording is canonical and his a revision or reinterpretation. The principle simply does not have a canonical expression.[30] Interpretation in common law is thus not oriented towards a given form of words as it is in the case of statutes.[31] To say this is not to deny that statutes need interpretation or that the words of the enactment (and their 'plain meaning') are often insufficient to determine the statute's application. The point is rather that, in the case of statutes, the problem of interpretation begins from a sense that there is 'a single, definitive, linguistic formulation'[32] of the standard being considered – there are *words there* which may (or may not) actually *have* a plain meaning – whereas in the case of other sources of law, hermeneutical difficulties get going on a somewhat different basis.

There are in addition important differences between legal systems in this regard. Atiyah and Summers note that English judges 'tend to adopt a more textual, literal approach, while American courts tend to take a more purposive and, therefore, substantive, approach' to statutes.[33] But it is possible to exaggerate these differences,[34] and in any case, the point is

[30] But see Greenawalt, *Law and Objectivity*, 66, for a discussion of the idea of 'overlapping' formulations.

[31] This is not to be read as implying that the distinction between canonically-worded and non-canonically-worded standards corresponds to the distinction between 'rules' and 'principles' in Ronald Dworkin's early jurisprudence: see Dworkin, *Taking Rights Seriously*, 22–31. Dworkin's distinction turns on the kind of normative force that different standards are conceived to have. Dworkin insists, moreover, that it is a mistake to suppose that even statutory rules have canonical formulations: 'it is a commonplace that lawyers will often misrepresent the rules that a statute enacted if they simply repeat the language that the statute used. Two lawyers might summarize the effect of a particular statute using different words . . .; they might still both be saying the same thing' (ibid., 76). Of course, even if this is true (about the way standards are constructed through interpretation), it may still be the case that the language used in the statute is canonical in regard to that problem of interpretation in a way that the language used by other sources of law is not. I doubt that Dworkin would deny this. His recent characterization of the judge's task in regard to legislation is as follows: 'He [i.e. Hercules, the ideal judge] tries to show a piece of social history – the story of a democratically elected legislature enacting *a particular text* in particular circumstances – in the best light overall . . .' – Dworkin, *Law's Empire*, 338 (my emphasis).

[32] See Summers, 'Statutes and Contracts as Founts of Formal Reasoning', 74.

[33] Atiyah and Summers, *Form and Substance in Anglo-American Law*, 100–1.

[34] Atiyah and Summers cite an observation by Posner, 'Statutory Interpretation – in the Classroom and in the Courtroom,' 807–8, to the effect that a judge 'rarely starts his inquiry with the words of the statute, and often if the truth be told, he does not look at the words at all'. Posner acknowledges that this is more accurate as a description of constitutional interpretation, and that it applies to legislation only in regard to statutes which have been around for a long time, which have accumulated a large body of case law around them, and which even in their original wording invoked common law concepts and traditions. (The example he gives is the Sherman Act.)

not that statutory language is treated with exactly the same respect the world over, but rather that it is treated, in every legal system, with somewhat more focused respect than the language used by or in other sources of law in that legal system (including other textual sources of law).[35]

My hunch is that this textual canonicity and the procedural formality discussed in the previous section are connected. At first glance, there is no obvious reason that procedural formality should necessarily issue in output-formality or interpretive-formality. We might imagine a proclamation made by a monarch with all sorts of formal pomp and ceremony, and yet it might be understood that the purpose of the occasion's formality was to impress upon subjects the personal authority of the ruler, not any commitment on his part to the particular linguistic expressions that were used. In these circumstances, one might want to say, with Hobbes, that 'it is not the Letter, but the Intendment, or Meaning . . . (which is the sense of the Legislator,) in which the nature of the Law consisteth'.[36] In other cases, however, a link between procedural formality and output formality might be more significant.

Think back to the predicament of the radically diverse legislature we imagined in sections 2 and 3. The members of that body found it necessary to order their deliberations with formal rules governing the setting of an agenda, the initiation and conclusion of discussion, the right to speak, the structure of debate, and the basis of voting and decision-making. Those familiar with parliamentary procedure, whether in national legislatures or small-scale public meetings, will know that debating rules are oriented towards and ordered by the idea that at any time there is *a specified proposition under discussion*. Even in the most basic forums, once a motion is moved and seconded, the deliberative body has a specific form of words on the table for discussion, and the organizing principle of debate becomes (roughly) that all and only contributions to the consideration of *that proposition* are to be heard, until either the time set for debate runs out or the question defined by that proposition has been resolved. This insistence that there be a formulated motion, and the concomitant rule that speakers observe norms of relevance in regard to that motion, are the primary basis on which parliamentary procedure seeks to avoid the nightmare of people talking endlessly at cross-purposes and failing to make the sort of contact with one another's contributions (synthetic or dialectic) that practical deliberation requires.

Occasionally in the course of discussion, someone may feel that it would be wiser for the assembly to be discussing a somewhat different proposition than the one specified, perhaps worded in a subtly or substantially

---

[35] See for example the comparison between statutes and contracts in American law, in Summers, 'Statutes and Contracts as Founts of Formal Reasoning'.

[36] Hobbes, *Leviathan*, Ch. XVI, 190.

different way. If they want to press this point, the parliamentary rule is that they must move an amendment, changing the wording of the motion under discussion in a specifically formulated way. Proceedings are then devoted to a discussion of the virtues of the amendment, *qua* amendment, and a vote is taken on that, before the substantive discussion is resumed. And again, we see the virtue of this way of doing things in a diverse assembly. In conversation among friends, the topic may shift in an open-ended way, and people familiar with one another have both the willing-ness and the ability to keep track. But in an assembly consisting of people who are largely strangers to one another, deliberation would be hopeless if there was a sense that the topic might or might not have shifted slightly after every contribution. So, although amendment processes exist, their formulaic character and the rules governing their proposal and adoption, provide a way of keeping track of where the discussion is, a way of keep-ing track that does not depend upon implicit understandings which some of the members may not share.

When discussion is exhausted, a vote may be called for, and – again if my experience of faculty meetings is any indication – someone will imme-diately leap to their feet and say, 'I'm all confused. What exactly are we voting on?' In a well-run assembly, the clerk or secretary will be in a posi-tion at that stage to read out the proposition (as amended) which now is the focus of the final vote. Once again, the determinacy of that proposition, as formulated and as amended, is important for establishing a sense that we are all orienting our actions in voting to the same object. It is important for me to know, for example, that what I take myself to be voting against is exactly what my opponent takes himself to be voting in favour of. Otherwise the idea that our votes, on a given occasion, are to be aggre-gated and weighed against one another becomes a nonsense.

What I have just described is, of course, rudimentary by comparison with the procedures employed in actual legislative assemblies such as the House of Commons or the US Congress. Bills are longer and more com-plex than the sort of motions one hears at a public meeting. They have usu-ally been drafted – more or less competently – in advance, and there are many stages of deliberation (including committee stages, whose proceed-ings may be much less formal) that they must go through before they are adopted. And this is to say nothing of the vicissitudes of bicamerality, con-ference committees, and so on. For the most part, however, these compli-cations enhance the need for a determinate text to focus and co-ordinate the various stages of the legislative process. Without a text to consider, mark up, amend, confer about, and vote upon, the process of law-making in a large and unwieldy assembly would have even a greater air of babel-like futility than that which is currently associated with Congress or the House of Commons.

Thus, whether we are talking about a small-scale meeting or a large-scale legislative process, the positing of a formulated text as *the resolution under discussion* provides a focus for the ordering of deliberation at every stage. The existence of a verbalized bill, motion, or resolution is key to norms of relevance, and key to the sense (which procedural rules are supposed to provide) that participants' contributions are relevant to one another and that they are not talking at cross purposes. Maybe a one-person deliberative body can do without this (though even there, many of us are familiar with the mnemonic virtues of a formulated proposition in our own solitary decision-making). And maybe decision-making in a small group or junta can do without this as well, if they can move towards consensus on the basis of conversational informality. But the sense of a determinate focus for discussion – something whose existence is distinct from the will or tacit understandings of particular members[37] – some such sense is indispensable for a large and diverse assembly of people whose knowledge and trust of one another is limited.

5. WORDS AND MEANINGS

I doubt that this argument will convince those whose main contribution to jurisprudence consists in stressing the indeterminacy of the meanings that are associated with the words one finds in legal texts. If words can mean anything at all – if every judge and every legislator is his own Humpty-Dumpty – then it would seem that textual determinacy as the focus of deliberative procedure adds absolutely nothing to quell the babel of diverse voices and diverse understandings with which my model began. Whereas before, the members of the assembly were talking at cross purposes because there was no formulated proposal on the table, now they are talking at cross purposes because they understand the formulations on the table to mean quite different things.

There is no knock-down reply to an objection of this kind,[38] and there is certainly no space here to give the matter the attention it deserves. But I think the appropriate tack to take is the following.

To the extent that law makes use of specific verbal formulations, it seeks to connect and associate itself as a social institution with another institu-

---

[37] Compare the characterization of the advantages of a written constitution in Arendt, *On Revolution*, 157: '. . . the Constitution, a written document, an endurable objective thing, which, to be sure, one could approach from many different angles and upon which one could impose many different interpretations, which one could change and amend in accordance with circumstances, but which nevertheless was never a subjective state of mind, like the will'.

[38] Though see Greenawalt, *Law and Objectivity*, 34–89. (Cf. Waldron, 'Assurances of Objectivity', 553.)

tion – the institution of natural language. In particular, it seeks to associate itself with *whatever interpersonal determinacy there may be in natural-language communication*. It does not do this gratuitously, out of some fetish for the word, say, or for literacy as such. It does so for a variety of excellent reasons, some of which I have attempted to outline in this chapter. I doubt very much that law as such (or jurisprudence) is committed to any particular theory of how or why natural languages have the interpersonal determinacy of meaning that they do – or even what it is for them to have such determinacy. These are intriguing issues for linguists and philosophers; but in most cases philosophers of law have neither the training nor the good philosophical sense to tell a plausible account from a bogus one. At any rate, from the point of view of jurisprudence, what matters is that natural language already appears to offer some assistance (though it is, as we all know, *limited* assistance)[39] in regard to things like deliberative determinacy. We may not be able to say why the specification of a given set of signs, identified as meaningful in a natural language, answers certain purposes that are associated ideally with the sharing of certain meanings; we may not even be able to say much about what sharing a meaning is. But it is indisputable that law makes an investment of exactly this sort in the determinacy-resources of natural language (such as they are, and however they are explained). What I have tried to show is the nature and importance of that investment in the context of the generation of law by large multi-member assemblies.

6. TEXT AND AUTHORITY

The account I gave in section 4 is not the only explanation of the textuality of statute law. Jurists often stress the need for people to know where they stand in relation to the law and it may be thought that textuality serves important functions in regard to *notice*. When Lon Fuller's hapless legislator, Rex, announced the contents of his codes would remain a state secret, his subjects to his surprise were deeply resentful: 'They declared it was very unpleasant to have one's case decided by rules when there was no way of knowing what the rules were.'[40]

It may be wrong, however, to associate this need for predictability with the specific characteristics of legislative textuality. First, to the extent that legislative textuality secures predictability it may do so only if the text is of a certain sort – specific rather than general, univocal rather than ambiguous, determinate rather than vague, and devoid of terms that would leave the citizen at the mercy of an interpreter's judgement or

[39] See Waldron, 'Vagueness in Law and Language'.
[40] Fuller, *The Morality of Law*, 35.

discretion. Textuality as such guarantees none of these.[41] Secondly, the existence of a canonical text will not serve the interests of predictability unless the text is relatively stable, intelligible, and learnable. Critics often charge that the sheer scale of modern legislation – the number of bills enacted, their size, and their complexity – militates against predictability. This helps us understand why F. A. Hayek, who in all his work has emphasized the importance of the predictability of law,[42] is in general an opponent of any image of law centred upon legislation.[43] Hayek suggests that people are more likely to have a sense of where they stand, and of the basis on which they can make plans, if they conceive themselves to be governed by broad principles implicit in a stable set of social practices (interpreted, upheld, and occasionally modified by judges), than if they conceive themselves to be governed by the constant output of formulaic rules from a legislature. The basis of legal predictability for Hayek is the stability of frameworks of property and contract not the textuality of statutes. Certainly if people are to be governed by legislation, it is better from Hayek's point of view that they be governed by an openly legible text than by secretly recorded commands. But this does not mean that the canonical textuality of legislation makes any particular contribution to predictability compared with other sources of law.

What I am suggesting, then, is that there is more to the textuality of statute law than can be explained on the basis of the citizen's need for predictability. If there is anything to the explanation I offered in section 4, then we might want to start thinking about the relation between legal authority and textual canonicity of legislation in a slightly different way. I will postpone most of what I want to say about respect for legal authority until Chapters Five and Six. Here I offer a few brief comments.

The conception of authority standardly accepted among legal philosophers at the moment is that of Joseph Raz. According to Raz, the point of recognizing someone or some institution as an authority in regard to a certain practical matter is that we do better, in regard to the reasons that apply to our actions in that matter, by trying to follow directives issued by the authority than by trying to figure out for ourselves what is to be done about the matter in question.[44] (I recognize the State of New Jersey as an

---

[41] Think for example of the textuality of the Eighth and Fourteenth Amendments to the US Constitution.

[42] See e.g. Hayek, *The Constitution of Liberty*, esp. 142–61.

[43] See Hayek, *Rules and Order*, esp. Chs. 4 and 6.

[44] See Raz, *The Authority of Law*, Chs. 1–2, and Raz, *Morality of Freedom*, Chs. 2–4. See especially ibid., 53 for what Raz calls *the normal justification thesis*: '[T]he normal way to establish that a person has authority over another person involves showing that the alleged subject is likely better to comply with reasons which apply to him (other than the alleged authoritative directives) if he accepts the directives as authoritatively binding and tries to follow them, rather than by trying to follow the reasons which apply to him directly.'

authority on traffic speed if I reckon I will drive more safely and efficiently on the Princeton Turnpike by following the State's instructions and speed limits than by trying to figure out the optimal mix of safety and efficiency in every locality for myself.) How does this conception of authority connect to what I have been arguing about statutory texts?

One reason for thinking that a modern legislature satisfies the Raz formula for authority is, as we have seen, the Aristotelian argument about the pooling of diverse perspectives and experiences.[45] A legislative assembly is likely to come up with better answers than I can because its membership makes available a broader range of experience and insight than I can accumulate on my own. However, we have also seen that the existence of orderly discussion is necessary in order to secure whatever Aristotelian advantages accrue from deliberation in a large and diverse group. Unless the diverse experiences and knowledge of the various legislators can connect and be synthesized, it is unlikely that their interaction will produce standards that are superior to those that any individual citizen could work out for himself, and thus unlikely that their output has authority in the Raz-ian sense. Orderly discussion requires among other things a focus on a determinate text as the motion under discussion: without that the discussants have no assurance that they are not talking at cross-purposes. The textuality of a legislative measure is thus connected to the conditions under which it may plausibly be regarded as authoritative: authority requires superior expertise; superior expertise comes from deliberation among those who are different from one another; deliberation among those who are different from one another is possible only on the basis of formal rules of order; an agreed text as the focus of discussion is key to formal rules of order.

In Chapter Five, I shall argue that Raz's conception is not the only conception of authority relevant in circumstances of disagreement.[46] Those who disagree about what reasons apply to them in some area of life often have a common interest in submitting to a single authoritative determination of what those reasons are. On this conception, respect for legislative authority is in part acknowledgment of the need for a common solution and respect for the conditions of fairness in which a common solution was arrived at among those who disagreed about what it ought to be.

It is tempting to associate this conception of legislative authority with democratic principles. I said in Chapter Three that one of the values most commonly associated in the modern world with legislation *qua* positive law is democratic legitimacy. The idea is that we should defer to statutes even when we disagree with them (and even when we think they fail the

---

[45] Aristotle, *Politics*, Bk. 3, Ch. 11. See also Waldron, 'Wisdom of the Multitude'.
[46] See, below, Ch. 5, s. 6.

test of Raz-ian authority) because they have been enacted by a democratically accountable entity. But we also saw in Chapter Three that the democratic principle, so stated, is insufficient to explain our preference for a legislative *assembly* rather than a single elected legislator.[47] I think it is also insufficient to explain the particular way in which authority is accorded to legislation – viz. by taking seriously the exact words that were used in the formulations that emerged from the legislative chamber. The moral of this is that if we are to answer the challenge of developing a genuinely democratic jurisprudence we have to proceed at the level of detail, and not simply at the level of broad gesture. We have to relate democratic principles to the complex texture of law. The argument I made in section 4 offers an explanation for the importance of textuality – the authority of the *ipsissima verba* – which is oriented primarily to the legislators' dealings among themselves, rather than directly to the issue of their collective authority *vis-à-vis* the people. It is oriented to the notion of legislation by the many, and it suggests that that notion may have consequences for how the legislative output of the many is to be regarded by its interpreters.

Let us return to the fairness dimension of respect for legislative authority. Respect for statute law is partly a matter of the importance we associate with the representative character of a legislature. I shall argue in Chapter Five that in the circumstances of politics, it is important that communities make decisions in forums and using procedures that are respectful of disagreement and allow contending voices to be heard in a debate about what the solution to a common problem should be. Respectfulness requires fair representation of diversity. But fair representation of diversity also requires attention to the conditions under which diverse representatives can deliberate together coherently. And again, this brings us to the importance of legislative texts as the focus of orderly deliberation. Thus, fairness-based respect for the legislature as a body may determine not only that we respect the standards which it posits, but also that we respect these more formal aspects of the way in which its posited standards are arrived at, – and thus that we respect them under the auspices of that (text-based) formality.[48]

These lines of argument help to make sense of the position in legislative studies sometimes described as 'textualism'. In the hands of jurists like Antonin Scalia,[49] textualism often seems simple-minded: legislative interpretation is about the construction of a text, so obviously the text is all that there is as a basis for legislative interpretation. Alternative approaches are

---

[47] See Ch. 3, s. 3, above.

[48] I have developed this here and in Ch. 5 as a matter of general civic obligation to the legislature. A more complete account would discuss how this affects the respect owed to the legislature specifically by the courts, in the context of democratic legitimacy and the separation of powers.

[49] Scalia, *A Matter of Interpretation*.

discredited and the emphasis on the text is fiercely defended, but the *point* of that emphasis is left largely unexplained. I doubt that the account I have given is a complete explanation, but it is a beginning. And the broader point is that attention to explanations of this sort is necessary if textualism is to be regarded as anything other than a way of lambasting more 'creative' or 'dynamic' approaches to statutory construction.

Chapter Five

Legislation, Authority, and Voting

1. IS VOTING ARBITRARY?

In Chapter Four, we talked about the importance of formulated propositions – motions under discussion – in structuring the deliberations of the
legislature. In the present Chapter, I want to focus on the next stage: enactment. I want to look at the process whereby a proposition ceases to be
merely an anchor for discussion and is given authority as a source of law.[1]

Bismarck is reputed to have observed that nobody who likes either law
or sausages should pay too much attention to the processes by which they
are produced.[2] Probably he had in mind the chaotic and ill-informed
histrionics of legislative debate. It has to be said, however, that the process
of enactment which follows is also not all that savoury. Motions put before
the legislature acquire legal authority as statutes by being *enacted*, that is,
through being approved by the various chambers of the legislature and
assented to by the head of state. That sounds all very solemn and dignified, until we recall that the particular mode of passage in a legislative

---

[1] Throughout this chapter, I shall use the phrase 'source of law' in John Chipman Gray's
sense: Gray, *The Nature and Sources of the Law*, 84–5, 123–5, and 152. This is not *quite* the same
usage as 'source of law' in Joseph Raz's 'Sources Thesis': 'A law has a source if its contents
and existence can be determined without using moral arguments . . . The sources of a law are
those facts by virtue of which it is valid and which identify its content.' – Raz, *The Authority
of Law*, 47–8. See also Raz, *The Concept of a Legal System*, 210 ff.

[2] This aphorism was attributed to Otto von Bismarck, by Justice (then Judge) Scalia in
Community Nutrition Institute v. *Block* 749 F 2d 50 (1984). Judge Scalia began his opinion by
saying, 'This case, involving legal requirements for the content and labeling of meat products
such as frankfurters, affords a rare opportunity to explore simultaneously both parts of
Bismarck's aphorism that "No man should see how laws or sausages are made" ' (ibid., 4).
(An earlier attribution to Bismarck is by Terrell CJ in *In Petition of Edward Graham*, 104 So. 2d
16 (1958), at 18.) However, the same quotation was attributed to Benjamin Disraeli by
Macfarland J in *Shields* v. *Shields* 224 Kan. 604, 584 P 2d 139 (1978) and to Winston Churchill
in Schwartz 'Curiouser and Curiouser', 600. There are many different versions of the aphorism also: 'The making of laws, like the making of sausages, is not a pretty sight', 'Laws are
like sausages. You should never watch them being made', 'Law and sausage are two things
you do not want to see being made', 'To retain respect for sausages and laws, one must not
watch them in the making', 'If you like laws and sausages, you should never watch either one
being made', and my favourite, 'The less people know about how sausages and laws are
made, the better they'll sleep at night.' No one seems to know when or on what occasion
Bismarck made this observation (if indeed it was Bismarck). Some years ago there were
rumours on the Internet that the quotation had been tracked down to its source; since then,
however, the trail seems to have been lost. I am grateful (?) to my Columbia colleague Peter
Strauss for starting me off down this road.

chamber is voting and majority-decision – a purely statistical determination of whether there are more members in favour of the bill than against it. Bills do not reason themselves into legal authority; they are thrust into authority with nothing more credible than numbers on their side.

In various activities, we settle things by tossing a coin: we toss a coin to determine which side is to defend which goal at the beginning of a soccer game. No one would think *that* an appropriate basis for determining which propositions should be accorded authority as sources of law. But counting votes seems much more like coin-tossing than like the exercises of reason and intellect that characterize the consecration of other sources of law – for example, the development of a new doctrine, principle, or exception in the deliberations of a court. How, then, can we be expected to take legislation seriously when it is determined in this apparently arbitrary way?

It is possible to make law-by-voting look even more arbitrary than this. Among students of 'public choice', Kenneth Arrow is commonly taken to have shown that neither majority-decision nor any other method of aggregation can guarantee that a coherent group preference can be constructed rationally out of a variety of coherent individual preferences. Under certain conditions, the aggregation method may yield the result that the group 'prefers' option X to option Y, Y to Z, and Z to X, leaving it completely arbitrary where in this cycle we take 'the view of the majority' to rest.[3]

Intriguing though it is, I do not intend to address this particular problem. There are two reasons. First, as I noted in Chapter Two, public choice scepticism is meeting with increasingly confident replies as empirically scrupulous observers ponder the failure of legislative assemblies to actually exhibit the arbitrariness and instability that Arrow's Theorem predicts.[4] Arrow's Theorem by no means guarantees that legislatures will face these difficulties. The conditions under which Arrovian cycling will not result in the context of majority-voting are well known. They turn out to be the conditions of much ordinary and constitutional politics. What is more, the procedural devices – like agenda-setting – which can produce a determinate outcome even when those conditions do not obtain cannot be assumed a priori to be arbitrary or unfair. Second, it is important not to be distracted from our present consideration of voting and majoritarianism. If majority-decision is an arbitrary basis for law even in the orderly cases *not* affected by Arrow's Theorem – for example, cases where legislators' preferences are uni-peaked or where there is an independently fair method of agenda-setting – then that is a much more serious problem for

[3] For a helpful recent summary, see Russell Hardin, 'Public Choice versus Democracy'.
[4] See Farber and Frickey, *Law and Public Choice*, esp. 47–62. See also Ch. 2, above, fn. 23–5, and accompanying text.

a theory of legislation. It is at any rate a problem that needs to be dealt with on its own terms, for it is clear that legislatures the world over are going to continue to use voting and majority-decision as central features of their decision-procedures, whatever the public choice theorists say.

Considered more broadly now, the charge of arbitrariness has a number of different aspects, so far as legislation is concerned. The most important aspect contrasts an arbitrary process with a reasoned one, in a context where reason is necessary because of the high stakes of policy, morality, and justice that are involved.[5] The issues that legislation addresses are issues where important individual interests are being balanced, and if great care is not taken, there is a danger that some will be oppressed or unjustly treated. Yet *voting* – counting heads – seems the very opposite of the sort of care that justice requires. Other aspects of arbitrariness have to do with the inconstancy of the law that results, as various parliamentary factions strive back and forth for numerical superiority,[6] and of course the possibility of incoherence that accompanies this.[7]

My intention in this part of the book is to present legislation in a better light than it usually appears in jurisprudence. As I said in Chapter Two it is worth asking what it would be like to develop a rosy picture of legislatures and their processes that matched, in its idealism, its normativity and perhaps its naïvety, the picture of courts that we present in our constitutional jurisprudence. I ask this, in part because in questions of constitutional design it is important to compare like with like. In modern constitutional law, the arbitrariness of majority-decision in a legislature is often cited as a way of enhancing the legitimacy of judicial review. In the end, of course, this is a hopeless strategy. Appellate courts are invariably multi- membered bodies whose members often disagree, even after delib-

---

[5] Cf. Postema, *Bentham and the Common Law Tradition*, 15–16: '[I]n the view of Common Law theory, legislation is inevitably the product of a temporary aggregate of arbitrary wills. Since it was thought legislation is the product of will, and not of rational reflection on an existing order independent of will, and since it is validated only by conformity to formal or procedural constraints, there is no guarantee that the individual laws will be reasonable or just.'

[6] There is a fine statement of this concern in Hobbes, *De Cive*, Ch. X, 137–8. In many cases 'the Votes are not so unequall, but that the conquered have hopes by the accession of some few of their own opinion at another sitting to make the stronger Party'. They try therefore to see 'that the same business may again be brought to agitation, that so what was confirmed before by the number of their then present adversaries, the same may now in some measure become of no effec t. . .'. Hobbes continued: 'It follows hence, that when the legislative power resides in such convents as these, the Laws must needs be inconstant, and change, not according to the alteration of the states of affaires, nor according to the changeablenesse of mens mindes, but as the major part, now of this, then of that *faction*, do *convene*; insomuch as the Laws do flote here, and there, as it were upon the waters.'

[7] Cf. Postema, *Bentham and the Common law Tradition*, 16: '[B]ecause the legislative body is a temporary and constantly changing aggregate of disparate wills, unconstrained by any systematic considerations, there is no reason to expect that the legislative product will add up to an internally coherent and reasonable system.'

eration. When the judges on a panel disagree, they too make their decisions by voting and majority-decision. The difference, when an issue is shifted from legislature to court, is a difference of constituency, not a difference of decision-method. So, if voting yields arbitrary decisions, then most of constitutional law is arbitrary. By the same token, as Farber and Frickey point out, if we think for Arrovian reasons that 'chaos and incoherence are the inevitable outcomes of majority voting, then appellate courts . . . are equally bankrupt. . . . If we accept the thesis as to legislatures, we are left with nowhere to turn.'[8]

However, as we saw in Chapter Two, the issue of judicial review is not the only reason we need a philosophical theory of legislating. And so whether courts use majority-decision or not, we still need to face the question squarely in regard to legislatures. What are we to make of the relation between legislating and voting, in an ideal model? How can we possibly present legislation as a dignified and respectable source of law, when we recall that a given statute might have had no legal standing at all if some individual had happened not to be present in the legislature when a particular vote was counted, or if a whim had moved him to vote the other way? How should that awareness bear on our interpretation of the provision, and on the spirit in which it is received and integrated into the law?

2. 'DELIBERATIVE DEMOCRACY'

I am looking to present legislation in a good light, but there is one dewy-eyed approach I will not follow.

Modern proponents of 'deliberative democracy' stress conversation and consensus as the key values. Ideally, they say, 'deliberation aims to arrive at a rationally motivated *consensus* – to find reasons that are persuasive to all who are committed to acting on the results of a free and reasoned assessment of alternatives by equals'.[9] Such an ideal is important in terms of the logic of deliberation: to argue in good faith is to present reasons that (one thinks) the other should accept, and for two or more people to persist in argument is for them to notice and pursue the possibility that in the end the same considerations will convince them all.

However, accepting consensus as the internal logic of deliberation is not the same as stipulating it as the appropriate political outcome. This is where deliberative theorists often go wrong. They assume that dissensus or disagreement is a sign of the incompleteness or politically unsatisfactory character of deliberation. Their approach implies that there must be

---

[8] Farber and Frickey, *Law and Public Choice*, 55.
[9] Cohen, 'Deliberation and Democratic Legitimacy', 23.

something wrong with the politics of deliberation if reason fails, if consensus eludes us, and if there is nothing to do but count heads. Indeed, some have even suggested that we can only be sure that a political process *is* deliberative if its outcome is unanimity. A deliberative politics, we are told,

seeks an answer to which we all can agree, since it is reached from a debate in which each is able, freely and fully, to offer his reasoned judgment under rules that treat no person as privileged and no answer as presumptively favored. . . . Since each is able to present his reasoned judgment, each is able to ensure that the mutual advantage realized in the answer embraces his own good. Since no one is privileged, each is able to ensure this only by equally embracing the good of his fellows, and so demonstrating his equal respect for them and their endeavors. A reasoned interchange, in which all seek an answer to which all must agree, results in unanimity. The procedure of deliberative politics is thus informed by the standards that its outcome must satisfy.[10]

On an account like this, any need for voting must seem like an admission of failure.

It is tempting therefore for the theorist of deliberative democracy to try and marginalize voting and the decision-procedures (such as majority-decision) that voting involves in his account of deliberation. This can be done in several ways. The deliberative ideal might be confined in its application to those who share common understandings (that is, those who are unlikely to disagree) and who regard politics as a way of ascertaining what those shared understandings are.[11] Or it might be confined to areas of politics – such as constitutional politics – that the theorist in question regards as more than usually consensual.[12] Or the theorist of deliberative democracy might infer that there is something wrong with the motivations of the participants when voting is found to be necessary. This third strategy is the most common and the most disturbing. Like Rousseau, deliberative theorists are always inclined to suspect that a division into majority and minority factions is a sign that some or all are voting on a narrow basis of self-interest, rather than addressing issues of the common good in the spirit that deliberative models presuppose.[13] They admit there is a second-best-theory problem of how to change people's motivations and inculcate the civic virtues and concern for the common good that deliberative politics presupposes. Still, they think that once we *get* a genuine deliberative democracy, the sordid business of counting votes will be largely unnecessary, at least on serious matters of principle. The authority

[10] Gauthier, 'Constituting Democracy', 320.
[11] See Walzer, *Spheres of Justice*. For a critique, see Dworkin, *A Matter of Principle*, 216 ff.
[12] This seems to be the strategy in Gauthier, 'Constituting Democracy', 322.
[13] Rousseau, *Social Contract*, Bk. IV, Chs. 1–2, 247–51. Concerns similar to mine are expressed by Young, 'Communication and the Other', at 125–6.

of legislation will consist in its deliberative provenance not its majoritarian credentials.

I will not take that approach. A good theory may make idealistic assumptions about people's motivations,[14] but even if it does, it should hold on to a sense that in the real world, even after deliberation, people will continue to disagree in good faith about the common good, and about the issues of policy, principle, justice, and right which we expect a legislature to deliberate upon.[15] The very best theories of deliberative democracy are characterized by their willingness to accept this point and incorporate it into their conception of deliberation.[16] And certainly, I think legal philosophy needs to put this prospect of disagreement in the core, not at the periphery, of its theory of legislation. To ignore it or wish it away, is like wishing away scarcity in the foundations of a theory of justice.[17]

3. LEGAL POSITIVISM

The worry about voting can be seen as part of a more general concern about positive law. The idea of positive law is the idea of a proposition that is arbitrarily law, a proposition that is treated as a source of law in virtue of some fact or action that has no intrinsic connection to the content, substance, or quality of the proposition itself. It happens to have been posited – that's the important thing – so *there it is*, and our duty as judges or scholars is to make something legal of *that*, rather than of anything else that might have been posited instead.

The idea of something's being law by fiat is troubling in ethics and theology. It is the familiar problem of Plato's *Euthypro*: can an action be pious and good simply because the gods happen to command it? And if law by command is a problem in heaven, it is certainly a problem for legal authority on earth. Remember Thomas Hobbes's definition of law –

CIVILL LAW, Is to every Subject, those Rules, which the Common-wealth hath Commanded him, by Word, Writing, or other sufficient Sign of the Will, to make use of, for the Distinction of Right and Wrong.[18]

– and the definition of command that went with it –

---

[14] See above Ch. 1, text accompanying fn. 24.

[15] See also Knight and Johnson, 'Aggregation and Deliberation', at 286–7.

[16] See Gutmann and Thompson, *Democracy and Disagreement*, esp. Ch. 2. The subtitle of Gutmann and Thompson's book is: 'Why moral conflict cannot be avoided in politics, and what should be done about it'.

[17] See the discussion of the circumstances of justice and, analogously, of the circumstances of politics in section 7 below.

[18] Hobbes, *Leviathan*, Ch. XXVI, 183.

COMMAND is, where a man saith, *Doe this*, or *Doe not this*, without expecting other reason than the Will of him that sayes it.[19]

Why, we want to ask, should the mere fact of someone's saying 'Do this!' provide any sort of reason for taking 'this' as a standard of right and wrong? There might be something about the 'this' that seems appealing as a criterion for action. But why should the fact that the words 'Do this!' have been spoken by a sovereign[20] trump our own deliberation on that issue of substance? After all, the tone or word of command might be associated with *anything*. One neuron fires in the sovereign's brain and X becomes the standard of right and wrong; a different neuron fires instead, and now right and wrong are governed by not-X. The same with voting: one member of the assembly wobbles drunkenly into the 'Yea' lobby, and we are all now subject to X; the same member stumbles in another direction, when the vote is close, and we are governed instead by the opposite.

Maybe there are other things associated with the fact of command that are worth bearing in mind. Hobbes says that if A has told B to 'Do this!' B may assume that his doing it will promote A's interests, '[f]or the reason of his Command is his own Will onely, and the proper object of every mans Will is some Good to himself'.[21] The fact that the 'this' would be good for A may indeed be some sort of reason to do it. Similarly, a majority vote may tell us that doing X would advance the interests of more legislators than it would frustrate; and if we are fond of our representatives, this too may be a reason for doing it. But these are weak and inconclusive reasons, and what lies behind them seems radically insufficient as an account of the authority of law.

Anyway, most of us think there is greater reason to respect a proposition as a source of law when its propounder is motivated to express a view on what is conducive to the common good, not just his own self-interest. But then the worry about positive law can be stated quite sharply. The common good is something about which each of us may have a view. And if anyone expresses a view about the common good, each of us is likely to have an opinion, also, about the substance of the view being expressed. So there will be argument and criticism, back and forth. Now, in the course of this opinionated process, why should any of us be additionally impressed (let alone conclusively impressed) by the fact that one of these views has secured expression or promulgation in the particular manner and in the particular array of social circumstances that amount to the positing of law? It is, after all, definitive of legal positivism that the facts about expression,

[19] Hobbes, *Leviathan*, Ch. XXV, 176 (emphasis in original).

[20] Ibid., Ch. XXVI, 184: '[t]he Common-wealth is the Legislator. But the Common-wealth is no Person, nor has the capacity to doe anything, but by the Representative, (that is, the Soveraign;) and therefore the Soveraign is the sole Legislator.'

[21] *Idem*.

promulgation, institutions, power, etc. which constitute *positing* are, for that very reason, not themselves considerations relevant to the debate about the merits of the view in question. Whether they amount to *being commanded by a person who is usually obeyed* or *being commonly practiced around here* or *having a larger number of supporters than any alternative view on the issue in question* – the social facts that make a proposition a source of law, on the positivist account, are not in themselves the sorts of things that make it more reasonable, respectable or attractive. It is as though we were being asked to respect or defer to a view, in an important debate, because it was propounded by the person with the loudest voice.

That's the shape of the general worry about positive law – of which the concern that interests me, about the majoritarian credentials of legislation, can be seen as a special case. Of the modern legal positivists, H. L. A. Hart has been most ready simply to bite the bullet on this issue. He met what I have called the general concern by denying that the fact that something was law, according to positive criteria, was any reason for respecting or deferring to it. The general concern about legal positivism, he said, is based on 'an enormous overvaluation of the importance of the bare fact that a rule may be said to be a valid rule of law'.[22] The implication of positivist jurisprudence, on Hart's account, is not that propositions are to be *respected* as law by virtue of some social fact about their provenance, but that they are to be *identified* as law on that basis, leaving it a further question – an independent *moral* question – what respect, if any, is due to them on that ground or any other.[23]

4. RAZ'S ARGUMENT

Joseph Raz offers a more complicated answer – one that makes a virtue (or at least a necessity) of the substantive arbitrariness of the positive criteria by which propositions are identified as sources of law. Still, he ends up in much the same position as Hart: an entitlement to respect is something a norm must earn; it is not part of what is said when we identify it as *legally valid*. The complicated route by which Raz reaches this conclusion is important for us, and I want briefly to explore it. Law, Raz argued, purports to be authoritative, and though it may not in fact *be* authoritative, it must surely be the sort of thing that in its form is *capable* of being authoritative. Now, according to Raz, the point of recognizing someone or some institution, A, as an authority in regard to a certain practical matter, M, is that we do better, in regard to the M-related reasons that apply to us, by

---

[22] Hart, 'Positivism and the Separation of Law and Morals', 75.
[23] See also Hart, *The Concept of Law*, 203–7.

trying to following directives issued by A than by trying to figure out for ourselves what is to be done about M.[24] This point would be defeated if we had to figure out for ourselves what was to be done about M in order to recognize something as A's directive in the matter; and that is what a substantive criterion of legal validity would require. It is thus important for law's aspiration to authority that recognizing and following something as law be seen as *an alternative to* trying to figure out for oneself what is to be done about the matter that the law addresses. It is important therefore that the criteria for recognizing something as law be unrelated to the merits of the issue which the law purports to address. In this sense, it is important that the criteria of legal validity seem arbitrary in regard to the issue of substance.[25]

I shall call this Raz's Argument. We will return to it later in this chapter,[26] for a version of it will play a part in the case I want to make about the respect (though not now the *authority*, in Raz's sense) to be accorded the results of majority-voting.

For now, notice how little of the apprehension about arbitrariness is actually dispelled (or intended to be dispelled) by Raz's Argument. Raz does not show that in order for law to be authoritative, the criteria for identifying it must be arbitrary *tout court*, as though any sort of arbitrariness would do. He shows, *negatively*, that if law is to be authoritative, the criteria one uses for identifying a directive as law must not include figuring out for oneself what is to be done about the substantive issue the directive addresses. The criteria must not be *non-arbitrary in that sense*. Both the commands of a unitary sovereign and the results of a majoritarian voting process pass this negative test. (So do the deliverances of an augury, a chimp at a typewriter, and the results of tossing a coin.)

On the affirmative side, a directive, D, cannot be regarded as authoritative (on Raz's conception) unless there is some way of identifying D as the sort of thing we would do better to follow than to trust our own judgement. Though (as Raz's Argument shows) this way of identifying it cannot be substantive, it may be procedural or institutional or having to do with the origin of the directive. There must be something about D's provenance or the procedure by which it was arrived at, that gives us greater confidence in our trying to follow D than in our trying to figure out for ourselves what is to be done about the matter that D addresses.

---

[24] Raz, *The Morality of Freedom*, 53.
[25] I draw here on Raz, *Ethics in the Public Domain*, 202–4 and 214–15.
[26] S. 10, below.

5. ASSEMBLY VERSUS SINGLE-LEGISLATOR MODELS

Raz's affirmative requirement may be more of a difficulty for legislation produced by an assembly than for other sources of law. The classic positivists – Thomas Hobbes, Jeremy Bentham, John Austin – characterized legislation in terms of the activity of a single person, *the sovereign*, who would turn his mind to legal problems and come up with clear and unambiguous answers.[27] Part of what they had in mind was a contrast between the authority of a legislator's enactments and the authority of common or customary law. As I said in Chapter Two, in late eighteenth- and nineteenth-century jurisprudence, legislation tended to be associated with reason and rational thinking, with the ability of one enlightened mind to cut through 'the cobweb of ancient barbarism',[28] to sift out rational solutions from the accreted layers of local usage, to replace the 'immense and unsorted heap' of common law rules[29] with coherent, rational principles. Indeed, the intellectual achievement of a single legislator seemed to have more in common with divine or natural law than with the humble sublunar reality of the norms which generations of ordinary folk had posited for themselves.[30]

In a contrast of this kind, however, legislation by *an assembly* as opposed to a single individual boded to make matters worse, not better than they already were under Common Law. Indeed, there were doubts among the early positivists as to whether an assembly could even get its act together sufficiently to produce a unequivocal piece of legislation. 'A Monarch', Hobbes said, 'cannot disagree with himselfe, out of envy, or interest; but an Assembly may; and that to such a height, as may produce a Civill Warre.'[31] Moreover, the activity of the unitary lawgiver was often conceived not merely as legislative but as codificatory. Clearly, any account of the authority of a law-making body must pay some attention to the effect of a statute on the overall coherence of the laws. People have had grave doubts about assemblies in this regard. John Stuart Mill's are typical:

[E]very provision of a law requires to be framed with the most accurate and long-sighted perception of its effect on all the other provisions; and the law when made should be capable of fitting into a consistent whole with the previously existing laws. It is impossible that these conditions should be in any degree fulfilled when laws are voted clause by clause in a miscellaneous assembly.[32]

---

[27] See Ch. 2, s. 5, above.
[28] A delightful phrase from a letter by Bentham to the *Gazeteer* (1770), quoted by Postema, *Bentham and the Common Law Tradition*, at 266.
[29] Bentham again, quoted by Postema, *idem*.
[30] See Kelley, *The Human Measure*, esp. 89–108 and 165–208.
[31] Hobbes, *Leviathan*, 132.
[32] Mill, *Considerations on Representative Government*, Ch. V, 109.

Different members will be enthusiastic for different parts of a bill under consideration, and different members too will be solicitous for its impact on different aspects of the existing law. Unless the legislature is a single individual capable of holding *the whole thing* in his mind, there will be nobody to look after the big picture, to consider the effect of this bill as a whole on the body of laws as a whole. However, Mill doubted whether in fact a representative legislature would make matters all that much worse: 'The incongruity of such a mode of legislating would strike all minds, were it not that our laws are already, as to form and construction, such a chaos, that the confusion and contradiction seem incapable of being made greater by any addition to the mass.'[33] But this is hardly reassuring if the basis of legislation's authority is supposed to be that it improves the *corpus juris*.

In modern discussions of legal authority, the contrast is less often between the enactments of a single legislator and the multi-authored hotchpotch of common law; it is, instead, between the legislator's enactment and the citizen's own individual view about what should be done in regard to the issue which the legislation addresses. In this comparison, the single-legislator model no longer has an obvious edge, for now like is being compared with like – the single intellect of the enlightened legislator with the single intellect of perhaps the equally enlightened citizen. But the assembly model is even worse off. In the ideal case, a legislative assembly comprises the enlightened representatives of an enlightened citizenry. The problem of a statute's authority is: why should an enlightened citizen prefer the legislature's view of some matter to his own (or, at least, why should he *act* on the legislature's view rather than his own) when he has thought things through as carefully as his representatives have. In the situation I have in mind, the citizen ends up holding a view which is exactly that of the members of one of the factions in the legislature. When they vote and the view which he supports loses, why should he concede any authority to the one that prevails?

In Chapter Four, we considered Aristotle's argument about the members of the assembly pooling their knowledge to come up with a better answer to the question before them than any one of them could come up with on his own. But in an enlightened society, where legislative deliberations are transparent to and continuous with the exercise of public reason generally, whatever advantages accrue from the Aristotelian process will inure also to the benefit of the interested and politically active citizen. So, once again, if two rival syntheses emerge – one of them his, and one of them more popular than his among the members of the legislative assembly – why should the citizen not act on his own view?

[33] Mill, *Considerations on Representative Government*, Ch. V, 109.

Anyway, it is not clear that the assembly model is even a plausible candidate for authority in the Raz-ian sense. Raz asserts that 'a directive can be authoritatively binding only if it is, or is at least presented as, someone's view of how its subjects ought to behave'[34] – an assertion glossed by Andrei Marmor as the idea that 'only an agent capable of communion with others can have authority over them'.[35] The directives of a single legislator who is also a natural person fit readily into this schema; but it is much more difficult, as Marmor notes, to present an assembly as 'an agent capable of communion with others' or its enactment as 'someone's view of how its subjects ought to behave'. Either we have to characterize the assembly as a fictitious or artificial person with a view of its own, or we must say that what is *really* being taken as authoritative is the view of (say) the bill's sponsor or a representative member of the legislative majority.[36]

As I said in section 2, it seems a mistake, even for conceptual or philosophical purposes, to abstract away from plurality and disagreement as features of the processes by which law is produced. Though we phrase our philosophical accounts of the respect due to law in the language of monarchy – How can *one* person have authority over others? How should *Hercules* reach his decisions? – very few of us are really prepared to embrace the idea of either a legislative or a judicial *monarch*. So perhaps we ought to turn things round a little bit, and explore the possibility that majority-decision commands our respect precisely because it is the one decision-procedure that does not, by some philosophical subterfuge, try to wish the facts of plurality and disagreement away.

6. AUTHORITY AND RESPECT

We are investigating the authority that a statute has (or ought to have) by virtue of its enactment. However, in what follows, I want to deploy a conception of the *authority* of law that differs somewhat from the standard account given by Joseph Raz.[37] There are differences as to what authority is, and differences as to how it is justified.

---

[34] Raz, 'Authority, Law and Morality', 303.

[35] Marmor, *Interpretation and Legal Theory*, 115.

[36] In Ch. 6, below, I will consider how far this particular difficulty can be met. I will argue that, with very slight modifications in Raz's schema, it is in fact possible to make a case that majoritarian outcomes are authoritative in his sense. (We may even show, paradoxically, that a piece of majoritarian legislation has a greater claim to Raz-ian authority than the intentions of any member of the majority.)

[37] See Raz, *The Authority of Law*, Chs. 1–2, and Raz, *Morality of Freedom*, Chs. 2–4. See especially ibid., 53 for what Raz calls *the normal justification thesis*: 'It claims that the normal way to establish that a person has authority over another person involves showing that the alleged subject is likely better to comply with reasons which apply to him (other than the alleged authoritative directives) if he accepts the directives as authoritatively binding and

The main demand that law makes on us as subjects is that we comply with it, and Raz's 'normal justification thesis' is oriented mainly to this demand. But constitutions, statutes and judicial decisions and opinions make additional demands on us as lawyers, jurists, politicians, and active, opinionated citizens. When something is enacted as law or as a source of law, I believe it makes on us a demand not to immediately disparage it, or think of ways of nullifying it or getting around it, or mobilizing the immune system of the *corpus juris* so as to resist its incorporation. This must be stated carefully, for systems like ours also make available generous structures like appeal, constitutional amendment, legislative reversal, judicial review, periodic elections, and so on; so, in a sense, no one is ever required to accept a legal or political defeat as final or irreversible. However, the demand that interests me operates in the logical space between defying or ignoring a statute or other legal decision and working responsibly for its repeal or reversal. It is a demand for a certain sort of recognition and, as I said, respect – that *this*, for the time being, is what the community has come up with and that it should not be ignored or disparaged simply because some of us propose, when we can, to repeal it.[38]

An example will help to illustrate what I have in mind. It concerns the administration of municipal housing policy in the United Kingdom.[39]

In 1972, the Conservative government in Britain passed a statute – the Housing (Finance) Act – requiring local authorities to raise public housing rents to market rates. When a socialist authority in Derbyshire (the borough of Clay Cross) refused to do this, the councillors' own assets were surcharged (in accordance with the relevant principles of local government finance) and several became bankrupt and thus disqualified from holding public office. In 1973, the opposition Labour party pledged not only to repeal the measure but to remove all penalties from, and indemnify against disqualification, the Clay Cross councillors 'who have courageously refused to implement the Housing (Finance) Act'. That pledge was widely condemned in the legal and political community as an attack on the rule of law, and when Labour was elected in 1974, the Minister

tries to follow them, rather than by trying to follow the reasons which apply to him directly.' (See also the discussion at the beginning of s. 4, above.)

[38] Clearly this is part of what is involved in Dworkin's argument about integrity in *Law's Empire*, 164–224, esp. the argument at 213: '[E]ach citizen respects the principles . . . instinct in the standing political arrangements of his particular community, . . . whether or not he thinks these the best principles from a utopian standpoint. . . . [Law as integrity] commands that no one be left out, that we are all in politics together for better or worse, that no one may be sacrificed, like wounded left on the battlefield, to the crusade for justice overall.' I explore the implications of this in Ch. 9.

[39] What follows is a summary of the account in Waldron, *The Law*, 8–18. In that discussion, I drew heavily upon Skinner and Langdon, *The Story of Clay Cross*, Austin Mitchell, 'Clay Cross', and Crosland, *Anthony Crosland*, as well as *Hansard* and contemporary newspaper accounts.

(Anthony Crosland) who had to sponsor the legislation indemnifying the councillors did so with great discomfort, describing it as 'this miserable promise', and saying 'I have not in my political life faced a problem as difficult as this.'

Those feelings of distaste and dishonour embody the sense of respect for law that I have in mind. Of course, it is true, as one supporter of the indemnification remarked, that 'the sovereignty of Parliament surely meant that Parliament could change its mind about any law'. It is true too that changing one's mind on a matter like this implies that one now thinks the penalties previously imposed were imposed inappropriately. But that is different from promising to expunge all traces of the statute from the polity, including the effects of its operation while currently in force. What Labour's opponents were maintaining, and what Crosland clearly felt, was that a piece of legislation should be treated, not just as an enactment of the current majority, but as something that stands for the time being in the name of the whole community. Once voted on in the legislature, it is entitled to whatever respect that communitarian status confers on it, without regard to – indeed bracketing away from – the substantive merits of its content.

At any rate, that gets at the sort of conception of authority I have in mind. It is, as I said, different from Raz's conception; certainly it is woollier and less well defined. The justification thesis has to be different too, for this conception of authority makes its demand *ex hypothesi* on someone who thinks he has good ground for believing that the legislature is mistaken. The problem, then, is how statutes and other sources of law can have authority and command respect among people who disagree about whether they satisfy Raz's *normal* justification thesis. In the sections that follow, we will explore the contribution that voting and majority-decision can make to the solution of that problem.

7. THE CIRCUMSTANCES OF POLITICS

An idea that I want to explore is that the dignity of legislation, the ground of its authority, and its claim to be respected by us, has to do with the sort of *achievement* it is. Our respect for legislation is in part the tribute we should pay to the achievement of concerted, co-operative, co-ordinated, or collective action in the circumstances of modern life.

In a variety of ways and for a variety of reasons, large numbers of us believe we should act, or organize things, together. There are lots of things that can only be achieved when we play our parts, in large numbers, in a common framework of action. Enterprises like protecting the environment, operating a health care system, securing the conditions for the operation of a market economy, or providing a basis for dispute resolution will founder unless people act in concert, following rules, participating in practices, and establishing institutions. Action-in-concert is not easy, particularly once people have a sense of themselves as individuals and of the ways in which acting with others might conflict with smaller scale projects of their own. In fact, when it actually takes place, action-in-concert is something of an achievement in human life.[40] Social choice theorists remind us that a common enterprise will often founder even when the potential participants agree about the project and share the same preference for its success. How much more of an achievement it is, then, when a large population act together in some common concern even though they disagree among themselves what exactly is to be done.

Consider the idea of 'the circumstances of politics', an idea adapted from John Rawls's discussion of 'the circumstances of justice'. The circumstances of justice are those aspects of the human condition, such as moderate scarcity and the limited altruism of individuals, which make justice as a virtue and a practice both possible and necessary.[41] We may say, along similar lines, that the felt need among the members of a certain group for a common framework or decision or course of action on some matter, even in the face of disagreement about what that framework, decision or action should be, are *the circumstances of politics*. The circumstances of politics deserve much greater attention than they have received in legal and political philosophy.[42] I believe they are essential for understanding many of the distinctively political virtues, such as civility, the toleration of dissent, the practice of loyal opposition, and – not least – the rule of law. Certainly they are indispensable for our understanding of procedural decision-rules, like majority-decision, and the concomitant ideas of authority, obligation, and respect.[43]

Like scarcity and limited altruism in the case of justice, the circumstances of politics come as a pair. Disagreement would not matter if there did not need to be a concerted course of action; and the need for a common course of action would not give rise to politics as we know it if there was not at least the potential for disagreement about what the concerted

[40] The emphasis on action-in-concert and the fragility of its achievement dominates Hannah Arendt's political philosophy. See Arendt, *The Human Condition*, 199 ff.

[41] Rawls, *A Theory of Justice*, 126–30.

[42] There is, however, an illuminating discussion of a similar idea (referred to as 'the conditions of politics') in Barber, *Strong Democracy*, 120–38. Barber describes the conditions of politics as 'conditions that impose *a necessity for public action, and thus for reasonable public choice, in the presence of conflict and in the absence of private or independent grounds for judgment'* (ibid.,120; emphasis in original). The last clause differs sharply from the account given here: I do not assume, as Barber does, that '[p]olitics concerns itself only with those realms where truth is not – or is not *yet* – known' (ibid., 129).

[43] I discuss the circumstances of politics in more detail in Ch. 9, below, relating the idea to Dworkin's notions of fairness and integrity in *Law's Empire*.

course of action should be. Both need some further discussion before we proceed.

8. CONFLICT AND COORDINATION

I want to begin with some comments about the game-theoretic structure of the difficulty of *acting together*.

We are accustomed to contrast two kinds of collective action problem – Prisoner's Dilemmas (PD) and pure Coordination Problems (CP). I shall assume that readers already have a good understanding of these problems. For simple two-person cases (covering choices by 'Row-Chooser' and 'Column-Chooser', each choosing between two options) they look like the representation in Figure 1.

PD

	co-op	defect
co-op	Q,Q	S,P
defect	P,S	R,R

CP

	do X	do Y
do X	P,P	Q,Q
do Y	Q,Q	P,P

Figure 1.

In each cell, Row-Chooser's pay-off is stated first, and Column-Chooser's second. The pay-offs are valued ordinally in each case and for each player as follows: $P > Q > R > S$.

Law can make various contributions to the solution of such problems – in the PD case by providing incentives (sanctions) to offset the tempting difference between P and Q, and in the CP case by marking either the doing of X or the doing of Y as salient for the parties.[44]

What I have called action-in-concert requires coordination. However, CP fails to capture the sort of coordination problem I have in mind in talking about the circumstances of politics. The form is more like a Partial Conflict coordination problem (PC) – see Figure 2. Each prefers either of the coordinative outcomes to non-coordination; but they differ in the particular coordinative outcome they prefer. (PC is sometimes known as 'The Battle of the Sexes': he prefers to go to a boxing match, she prefers to go to

---

[44] Though see Green, 'Law, Coordination and the Common Good', for an argument that law is unlikely to be able to contribute anything *distinctive* to the solution of a pure coordination problem.

PC

	do X	do Y
do X	P,Q	R,R
do Y	S,S	Q,P

Figure 2.

the ballet; but most of all they want to go out together rather than each to his or her favourite entertainment alone.) I believe that PC suggests a lot that is important about law in the circumstances of politics.[45]

Whether a PC gets solved depends on the circumstances of each case, including how much more each prefers his or her favourite outcome to the one less favoured, how likely each thinks it is that they will get their favourite outcome by holding out, etc. This is all reasonably well understood.[46] I do not want to claim that law *solves* PCs and that this is why we should respect it.[47] A legal system can make some contribution by associating sanctions with just one of the coordinative options and thus diminishing the difference between P and Q for one of the players. But before it can do that, the society must have decided which of the coordinative outcomes to select as the one to be bolstered by sanctions in this way. That itself is no mean achievement – and I want to say that it is by embodying that achievement that law commands our respect.

Joseph Raz has argued that pure CPs tell us very little about the point of legal authority. He is right about that. He also suggests that collective action problems in general cannot provide the basis of an adequate theory of legal authority, for there are many legal rules they do not explicate at all. 'Laws like the prohibition of rape and murder differ', he says, 'from laws which coordinate the efforts of large groups.'[48] Certainly it would be a mistake to try and force laws of all kinds into the same Procrustean bed. Nevertheless, it may help, to see what I am getting at, to focus on one of the examples Raz provides.

[45] None of this is original. I learned it from Hampton, *Hobbes and the Social Contract Tradition*, Ch. 6. Hampton shows how a PC game may be implicated in the solution of a PD. In Hobbes's theory, for example, we face a many-person version of PD in the state of nature; to solve it we must set up a sovereign; we may all accept that fact; but if more than one person wants to be sovereign, then we face a PC.

[46] See ibid., 155, for the formulae.

[47] Again, see Green, 'Law, Co-ordination, and the Common Good'. Note, however, that for reasons having to do with the shape of the particular theory he was attacking – Finnis, *Natural Law and Natural Rights* – Green did not dwell on PCs.

[48] Raz, *Ethics in the Public Domain*, 333.

Consider the law about rape. Raz is right to be horrified by any suggestion that a man's reason for refraining from rape has anything to do with
respect for law;[49] it should have to do with his respect for women. And
clearly it has nothing to do with collective action: rape is wrong even in
societies where it is a common practice. So an analysis of rape law in terms
of any sort of coordination problem looks unpromising. However, the
matter is more complicated when we consider aspects of the law of rape
which are complex and controversial: for example, statutory rape, marital
rape, homosexual rape, the bases (if any) on which consent is to be
inferred, mistakes as to consent, etc. Reasonable people differ on matters
like these. Yet each may have an interest – of the sort represented in a PC
– in sharing with others in society a common scheme of rape law that deals
unequivocally with these matters, a scheme which sets a specific age of
consent, which states whether mistakes have to be reasonable in order to
be exculpatory, and so on. Each may prefer that these matters be settled
even in a way that he opposes, if the alternative is no rape law at all (with
everyone who has a view enforcing it as best he can), or a law confined
only to those cases where it is uncontroversial in the community that a
wrong has been committed. No doubt this preference is partly due to the
fact that we cannot administer a law for the non-controversial cases unless
we settle some of the controversial issues. But that just reinforces my
point. As soon as we shift our focus from a simple prohibition such as
'Thou shalt not have sex with a woman without her consent' to the complex scheme of rules, procedures and presumptions in which such a prohibition is typically embedded, we see that many more issues addressed
by the law can be associated with the PC format – and thus with the circumstances of politics, as I understand them – than might at first appear.

9. DISAGREEMENT

As to the second circumstance of politics – disagreement – I mainly want
to rest with what I said in section 2: whatever else we wish away in our
elaboration of ideal models of civic republicanism and deliberative
democracy, we should not wish away the fact that we find ourselves living and acting alongside those with whom we do not share a view about
justice, rights or political morality.

Liberals do a good job of acknowledging this, so far as comprehensive
views of religion, ethics, and philosophy are concerned. Thus John Rawls
insists that 'a diversity of conflicting and irreconcilable comprehensive
doctrines' is 'not a mere historical condition that may soon pass away; it is

---

[49] Ibid., 327.

a permanent feature of the public culture of democracy'.[50] And he says it is therefore fortunate that we do not need to share a common view in society about religion, ethics, and philosophy. But liberals have done a less good job of acknowledging the inescapability of disagreement about the matters on which they think we *do* need to share a common view, even though such disagreement is the most prominent feature of the politics of modern democracies.[51]

Rawls and his followers may respond that their job is to explore the idea of 'a well-ordered society,' defined as a society whose members share a view about justice.[52] They think this an important idea to explore in part because they believe (quite rightly) that an issue of justice is an issue on which we need to act together on the basis of a common view. But the *need* for a common view does not make the fact of disagreement evaporate.[53] Instead it means that our common basis for action in matters of justice has to be forged in the heat of our disagreements, not predicated on the assumption of a cool consensus that exists only as an ideal.

These are not just abstract considerations. In the United States, in Western Europe, and in all other democracies, every single step that has been taken by legislatures towards making society safer, more civilized, and more just has been taken against a background of disagreement, but taken nevertheless in a way that managed somehow to retain the loyalty and compliance (albeit often grudging loyalty and compliance) of those who in good faith opposed the measures in question. The prohibition of child labour, the reform of the criminal process, the limitation of working hours, the dismantling of segregation, the institution of health and safety regulations in factories, the liberation of women – each of these achievements was secured in what I have called the circumstances of politics, rather than in anything remotely resembling the justice-consensus that Rawlsians regard as essential to a well-ordered society. What is more, each of these legislative achievements claims authority and respect as law *in* the circumstances of politics, including the circumstance of disagreement as to whether it is even a step in the right direction. Such legislation does not claim authority and respect simply as an intimation of what an ideal society would be like; if it did, those with a different vision or social ideal would simply turn away.

---

[50] Rawls, 'The Domain of the Political and Overlapping Consensus', 246.

[51] It is the most prominent feature not just of politics but of our own interactions with colleagues when we are debating the issues of rights and justice on which we are all supposed to be experts.

[52] Rawls, *Political Liberalism*, 35. Calling a society well-ordered, Rawls says, conveys among other things that 'it is a society in which everyone accepts, and knows that everyone else accepts, the very same principles of justice . . .'.

[53] I pursue this further in Ch. 7, below.

10. A MERE TECHNICALITY?

In the circumstances of politics, tossing a coin might be a way of settling on a common course of action. If the deadline for action was near enough and the need for concerted action sufficiently compelling, we might adopt any arbitrary method that made one course of action more salient. If the matter were particularly grave, we might even *admire* such methods, in a sort of Nietzschean or existentialist spirit: I remember the bracing feeling when a faculty meeting once prepared to toss a coin to decide which of two candidates to hire, after several hours of deadlock.

Is majority-decision to be respected in that spirit? Is it simply a technical device which enables us to choose one course of action – any course of action – in circumstances where we want to act together but are deadlocked about what to do?

Certainly any decision-procedure which addresses the circumstances of politics has to *look* technical. In section 4, we went over an argument by Joseph Raz to the effect that law can be authoritative (in his sense) only if recognizing something as law is *an alternative to* trying to figure out for oneself what is to be done about the matter that the law addresses; it can be authoritative therefore only if the method of recognizing something as law seems arbitrary in relation to the substantive merits. That applies also to decision in the circumstances of politics. Suppose my friends and I face a decision-problem of the kind labelled 'PC' in Figure 2 of section 8: we want to act together in regard to some matter M, but one of us thinks it is important to follow policy X while the others think it important to follow policy Y, and none of us has reason to think any of the others a better judge of the merits of M than himself. Suppose, too, that we all know M requires a common policy in which each of us will play an independent but necessary part; moreover the part that each of us would play in X is contrary to the part that each of us would play in Y (in the sense that anyone's playing the part assigned to him in the one policy would make it impossible for the other policy to succeed).

In these circumstances, the following will obviously *not* be a way of settling on a common policy: each does whatever he thinks it is important to do about M. We must find a way of choosing a single policy in which the three of us can participate *despite* our disagreement on the merits. And, since each is to act independently once this method of choice has been followed, each must have a way of identifying just one of the proposed policies as 'ours', i.e. as the one which 'we' are following. That ability must not involve the use of any criterion such as C: 'What it is important to do about M', for it is precisely disagreement about the application of C that gives rise to the decision-problem in the first place. The way in which any of us identifies a policy as 'ours' must therefore seem arbitrary in relation to C (though of course it will not be arbitrary in relation to the decision-problem). Majority-voting satisfies this requirement, for any member of the group may identify (say) Y as 'the policy favoured by the majority', whether or not he thinks that Y satisfies C.

Is that all we can say for it – that it is a successful technicality? Hannah Arendt seems to hold this opinion: she calls majority-decision 'a technical device', though she goes on immediately to say that it is 'inherent in the very process of decision-making' and that it is 'likely to be adopted almost automatically in all types of deliberative councils and assemblies'.[54] There is in fact considerable disagreement among political theorists as to whether majority-decision is natural or conventional.[55] Probably, the question is a silly one. Bernard Bosanquet refers to majority-decision as an *invention*:

> The very instrument of all political action was invented, so far as we can see, by the Greeks. The simple device by which an orderly vote is taken, and the minority acquiesce in the will of the majority as if it had been their own – an invention no less definite than that of the lever or the wheel – is found for the first time as an everyday method of decision in Greek political life.[56]

But the fact that the lever is an invention does not mean that it does not work on natural principles, or that we can vary it as we please (as we might vary a 'mere' convention) and still achieve the same effect. Something similar may be true of majority-decision: it may be a technical procedure which we have invented, but *also* a method that is morally respectable in a way that other technicalities and conventions might not be.

11. RESPECTING MILLIONS

A piece of legislation deserves respect because of the achievement it represents in the circumstances of politics: action-in-concert in the face of disagreement. That is what I tried to capture at the end of section 9. It may

---

[54] Arendt, *On Revolution*, 164. Notice also Arendt's contrast between 'majority-decision' and 'majority-rule': 'Only where the majority, after the decision has been taken, proceeds to liquidate politically, and in the extreme case, physically, the opposing minority, does the technical device of majority decision degenerate into majority rule' (*idem*).

[55] John Locke maintained it was natural: 'the act of the majority passes for the act of the whole, and of course determines, as having by the Law of Nature and Reason, the power of the whole' (Locke, *Two Treatises of Government*, II, para. 96, 332). The contrary view was held by Rousseau (*The Social Contract*, Bk. I, Ch. 5): 'The law of majority-voting is itself something established by convention', and has no authority among a people that have not unanimously selected it as their decision-procedure.

[56] Bosanquet, *The Philosophical Theory of the State*, 4–5.

also deserve our respect because it is a *respectful* achievement – because it is achieved in a way that is respectful of the persons whose action-in-concert it represents.

We often think of majority-decision as an impersonal principle – one that is purely aggregative and, like utilitarianism, fails to take individuals seriously.[57] But I want to stress the regards in which majority-decision respects the individuals whose votes it aggregates. It does so in two ways. First, it respects their differences of opinion about justice and the common good: it does not require anyone's sincerely held view to be played down or hushed up because of the fancied importance of consensus. Second, it embodies a principle of respect for each person in the processes by which we settle on a view to be adopted as *ours* even in the face of disagreement.

Both points need elaboration; but first some preliminaries. Although our topic is legislation, it will be easier to explain the points I want to make about respect in terms of majority-decision in a direct democracy, rather than majority-decision in a representative legislature. I assume that in the latter context a representative's claim to respect is in large measure a function of his constituents' claims to respect; ignoring him, or slighting or discounting his views, is a way of ignoring, slighting, or discounting *them*. So let us deal direct.

Talking about direct democracy brings us up against the problem of numbers, however. In an assembly of a few hundred members, each representative may feel that his vote is significant. But direct democracy can seem impersonal and alienating because it deals in millions of votes. A single citizen who has thought things through carefully may feel that his contribution is simply lost among the millions, swamped by the daunting statistics that will determine what the community's view is eventually taken to be. Even though he knows that nothing but individual votes like his – millions of them – determine the decision, he may be hard put to think of himself as making a contribution to that decision, for his vote seems lost in the crowd. And certainly it will appear to him that it makes no difference to the statistics whether he voted as he did because he had thought the issues through or because he tossed a coin. In that sense, he might think that majority-decision does not respect him as a thinking individual, for it does not proceed on what he regards as a human scale.[58]

It is important not to think of this as a problem about *voting*. It is a problem rather about the nature and scale of the issues in whose resolution voting is involved. When I said, in section 7, that there are certain things that can only be achieved if we act in concert I meant 'act in concert *in very large numbers*'. Two or three people gathered together cannot resolve on any

---

[57] Cf. Rawls, *Theory of Justice*, 27.
[58] Cf. Constant, 'The Liberty of the Ancients Compared with that of the Moderns', 314 and 316. See also the discussion in Ch. 11, s. 3, below.

course of action, involving them alone, that will solve environmental problems, for example, or provide for public hygiene in a large urban society. Nor, since we live in the very close company of hundreds of thousands of strangers (and acquaintances), can two or three people acting together solve the sort of problems that we associated in section 8 with the administration of a law of rape. Because we live side by side with millions, we must address our common problems on that sort of scale. If we believe that everyone affected by a problem has a right to a say in its solution, then there is nothing to do but set up a procedure for counting and somehow assessing millions of individual opinions. Our unease with this, and our inability to relate it to a straightforward sense of our own importance as individual agents ('What are *you* doing about the environment?'), has nothing to do with majoritarianism. It is a function of our persevering with rather primitive individual-on-individual notions of agency, responsibility, harm, etc. in moral philosophy in circumstances where such notions are evidently unhelpful and distracting.[59]

Our models sometimes simplify away from large numbers for expository purposes: for example, the game-theoretic matrices in section 8 assume (absurdly) that the circumstances of politics involve only two individuals. But in thinking about the respect owed to legislation it is important not to lose sight of the scale on which the problem is actually posed. One way to see that collective decision among large numbers of people is not incompatible with respect for persons is to imagine a problem which affects a very large number of people (say, millions), *each* of whom has thought long, hard, and conscientiously about it. Assume that the problem requires a common solution, but that there is disagreement among the persons affected as to what the solution should be. Clearly it would be wrong to say of any of these citizens that his view should be *excluded* from consideration, simply to reduce the 'impersonality' of the decision-procedure. And if it is wrong to say that of any citizen in particular, it is obviously wrong to say it of all-but-a-handful, which is what reducing the decision-procedure to a human scale – where each could trace the impact of his own opinion and his own vote – would involve. There is no alternative: if the problem affects millions, then a respectful decision procedure requires those millions to listen to one another and to settle on a common policy in a way that takes everyone's opinion into account.[60]

---

[59] See Parfit, *Reasons and Persons*, 67 ff. See also Hardin, *Morality Within the Limits of Reason*. See also Waldron, 'Virtue *en Masse*'.

[60] I emphasize again that this is distinct from the question of representation; representation does reduce deliberation and voting to a (politically) manageable scale; but it is, as I said earlier, supposed to do so as *a way* of respecting citizens in their millions, not as an alternative to that. (Note for reviewers: one of the glaring defects of this book is that it does not include an adequate discussion of representation.)

12. RESPECTING DISAGREEMENT

I said that majority-decision respects individuals in two ways. The first is by respecting the fact of their differences of opinion about justice and the common good. Majority-decision does not require anyone's view to be played down or hushed up because of the fancied importance of consensus. In commanding our support and respect as a decision-procedure, majority-decision requires each of us not to pretend that there is a consensus when there is none, merely because we think that there ought to be – whether because any consensus is better than none, or because the view that strikes *some* of us as right seems so self-evidently so that we cannot imagine how anyone would hold to the contrary.

The more dangerous temptation is not to pretend an opposing view does not exist, but to treat it as beneath notice in respectable deliberation by assuming that it is ignorant or prejudiced or self-interested or based on insufficient contemplation of moral reality. Such an attitude embodies the idea that since truth in matters of justice, right, or policy is singular and consensus is its natural embodiment, some *special* explanation – some factor of deliberative pathology, such as the lingering taint of self-interest – is required to explain disagreement, which explanation can then be cited as a reason for putting the deviant view to one side.

The kind of respect I have in mind involves rejecting this inference. It need not involve rejecting the premise about the singularity of truth;[61] that is, it need not involve anything like relativism. Respect has to do with how we treat each other's *beliefs* about justice in circumstances where none of them is self-certifying, not how we treat the truth about justice itself (which, after all, never appears in politics *in propria persona*, but only – if at all – in the form of somebody's controversial belief).[62] Nor is it just a point about fallibility, though of course anyone who holds a view about justice must think it possible he is mistaken and must not act in a way that shows he thinks that possibility can be ignored. It is rather that, whatever the state of my confidence about the correctness of my own view, I must

---

[61] Thus, as I observed in fn. 42 above, I do not agree with Benjamin Barber that the circumstances of politics presuppose issues on which there is no question of truth or right answers. I do not agree with his claim that there is a contrast between disagreements resolved through politics and disagreements that may in principle be 'resolved by reference to the unity of truth' (Barber, *Strong Democracy*, 129).

[62] I have elaborated this argument in Ch. 8. Although the idea of objective values is the idea of one view being right and the others wrong in a dispute about justice, it is an idea which has little utility in politics. As long as objective values fail to disclose themselves to us, in our consciences or from the skies, in ways that leave no room for further disagreement about their character, all we have on earth are *opinions* or *beliefs* about objective value. The friends of truth will insist stubbornly that there really is, still, a fact of the matter out there. Really. And maybe they are right. But it is surprising how little help this purely existential confidence is in dealing with our decision-problems in politics.

understand that politics exists, in Arendt's words, because 'not man but men inhabit the earth and form a world between them'[63] – not one person but people – that mine is not the only mind working on the problem in front of us, that there are a number of distinct intelligences, and that it is not unexpected, not unnatural, not irrational to think that reasonable people would differ.

Here I want to draw on another Rawlsian idea – what he called 'the burdens of judgment, . . . the many hazards involved in the correct (and conscientious) exercise of our powers of reason and judgment in the ordinary course of political life' which stand in the way of any expectation of agreement among reasonable persons.[64] Many of our most important judgements, Rawls says, are made about matters and under conditions 'where it is not to be expected that conscientious persons with full powers of reason, even after free discussion, will arrive at the same conclusion'.[65] On any plausible account, human life engages multiple values and it is natural that people will disagree about how to balance or prioritize them. Also, on any plausible account, people's respective positions, perspectives, and experiences in life will give them different bases from which to make these delicate judgements. These differences of experience and position, combined with the evident complexity of the issues being addressed, mean that reasonable people may disagree not only about what the world is like but also about the relevance and weight to be accorded the various insights that they have at their disposal. Together factors like these make disagreement in good faith not only possible but predictable:

Different conceptions of the world can reasonably be elaborated from different standpoints and diversity arises in part from our distinct perspectives. It is unrealistic . . . to suppose that all our differences are rooted solely in ignorance and perversity, or else in the rivalries for power, status, or economic gain.[66]

Rawls uses the burdens of judgement to explain comprehensive philosophical disagreements. But the same idea can be used to characterize our political deliberations, including our deliberations about rights and justice, as well as ethics, religion, etc. The circumstances under which people make judgements about issues like affirmative action, the legalization of abortion, the limits of free speech, the limits of the market, the proper extent of welfare provision, and the role of personal desert in economic justice are exactly those circumstances in which we would expect, given Rawls's account of the burdens of judgement, that reasonable people would differ. As in the case of more comprehensive disagreements, we do not need to invoke bad faith, ignorance, or self-interest as an explanation. The difficulty of the issues – and the multiplicity of intelligences and

---

[63] Arendt, *On Revolution*, 175.   [64] Rawls, *Political Liberalism*, 56.
[65] Ibid., 57.   [66] Ibid., 58.

diversity of perspectives brought to bear on them – are sufficient to explain why reasonable people disagree.

13. COUNTING EQUALLY

Because we respect the fact of disagreement, we face a decision-problem that an individual, confident in his own view, would not face acting on his own. The second point about respect has to do with how we deal with others in the way we address that decision-problem.

Once I notice that others disagree with me (even after deliberation) on a matter on which we desire to act in concert, we could (as I said at the beginning of section 10) choose a common policy by tossing a coin. Or the group might single out one person for leadership and announce, Hobbesian fashion, that following that person's view is going to be the only basis on which the group is able to do anything. Or we could take a vote and act together on the majority view. Though this is by no means an exhaustive list of possible decision-methods, the first two methods – random choice, on the one hand, Hobbesian leadership on the other – throw into relief distinct aspects of the way in which the third method – majority-decision – values and respects individuals.

In the first place, majority-decision differs from the coin-tossing method in giving positive decisional weight to the fact that a given individual member of the group holds a certain view. Tossing a coin may give some weight to that fact in setting out the options, for we would not use the coin-toss to choose among options that nobody favours. And in certain circumstances, coin-tossing will give an option decisive weight just because someone favours it – namely, the circumstance in which no one holds an opposing view. However, once a set of options (> 1) is established, the principle of majority-decision goes further and says that in the case of each individual, the fact that that individual favours option X is a reason for the group to pursue option X, even though there is disagreement. Because there *is* disagreement, it is not yet a conclusive reason; still, it counts in favour of the group's pursuing X.[67]

---

[67] Ackerman, *Social Justice in the Liberal State*, 283, describes this contrast in terms of tie-breaking: 'If, say, there are 99 people in the Assembly, then majority-rule gives me a decisive voice when the rest of you are split 49-49; and the same is true of your decision as well. When confronted with the prospect of a tied vote, the majoritarian does not appeal to some unresponsive decision-procedure, but instead recognizes each citizen's right to have his considered judgment determine the social outcome.' Ackerman calls this feature of majority decision 'minimal decisiveness', and says that a coin-toss among options favoured by various citizens does not accord each individual's view minimal decisiveness in this sense (ibid., 287).

The contrast with the Hobbesian method throws additional light on the way majority-decision respects individuals. The Hobbesian approach gives great weight to the fact that, out of all the citizens, one individual in particular – the wannabe sovereign – favours the option he does, while according little or no weight to the views of any of the others. The point is not that the Hobbesian approach ignores disagreement; it does not fail to respect individuals in the first sense. On the contrary, it is precisely *because* we recognize that we are stuck with disagreement that we move to the Hobbesian approach. The Hobbesian method therefore contrasts with any approach to political decision-making which assumes (along Rawlsian lines for example) that questions of constitutional design cannot be well-formulated among people who disagree about justice.

The Hobbesian method is to give decisive weight to just one of the competing views (it does not particularly matter which one), and little or no weight to any of the others. The method of majority-decision, by contrast, involves a commitment to give *equal* weight to each person's view in the process by which one view is selected as the group's. Indeed, it attempts to give each individual's view the greatest weight possible in this process compatible with an equal weight for the views of each of the others.[68] Not only may each person's view be minimally decisive, but the method accords maximum decisiveness to each, subject only to the constraint of equality. In this sense, majority-decision presents itself as a *fair* method of decision-making.

To be sure, the constraint of equality, which lies at the base of that claim to fairness, is a very demanding one, particularly when large numbers are involved. Large numbers may make it appear to individuals that each vote has minimal weight in the process, and that a vote not cast with the majority may be said to carry no weight at all (to be, as they say, 'a wasted vote'). But as we saw in section 11, the involvement of very large numbers of people is a consequence of the structure of the problems together with the entirely unexceptionable principle, 'What touches all should be decided by all.' If a social problem in its nature affects millions of people, then any attempt to give the illusion of great weight – or even considerable weight – to the vote of a single person (out of concern for his anxiety that his view not be lost in the crowd) could succeed only at the cost of diminishing even further the weight accorded to the views of others who are equally affected.

14. A PROOF?

I have said that according equal weight or equal potential decisiveness to individual votes is a way of respecting persons. In this sense, majority-

---

[68] For an argument that equal weight *implies* equality at the highest level possible, see Vlastos, 'Justice and Equality', 62–8.

decision is a respectful procedure – not just an admirable technical device for securing action-in-concert in the circumstances of politics. What Bosanquet called the Greek invention – the device by which an orderly vote is taken, and the minority acts on the view of the majority as though it had been their own – evinces a certain conception of respect, a certain conception of fairness.

What I am *not* saying, however, is that either fairness or equal respect for persons *requires* majority-decision.[69] John Stuart Mill's position in *Considerations on Representative Government* embodies the possibility that it does not. Mill maintained ferociously that

it is a personal injustice to withhold from anyone . . . the ordinary privilege of having his voice reckoned in the disposal of affairs in which he has the same interest as other people. If he is compelled to pay, if he may be compelled to fight, if he is required implicitly to obey, he should be legally entitled to . . . have his consent asked, and his opinion counted at its worth . . .[70]

But 'not at more than its worth', Mill added. Fairness does not require that the view of a wise and intelligent person have the same weight – the same potential for decisiveness – as the view of a person who is ignorant and unreasoning. Indeed it is arguable that fairness requires the opposite, at least if fairness means something like 'that to which no one can reasonably object'. As Mill puts it:

Every one has a right to feel insulted by being made a nobody, and stamped as of no account at all. No one but a fool . . . feels offended by the acknowledgment that there are others whose opinion, and even whose wish, is entitled to a greater amount of consideration than his.[71]

Thus a conception of equal respect which is responsive to proven or acknowledged differences in reason, wisdom, and experience may justify some sort of plural voting scheme, rather than the equal weight implicit in plain majority-decision.[72]

Whether it is possible in the circumstances of politics to *justify* (or agree upon) criteria of wisdom etc. for the purposes of these differentiations is another matter. If the mark of wisdom is having come up with just decisions in the past, and people disagree about what counts as a just decision, then it is not clear how we can determine who is wise and who is not without failing in respect for persons in the first of the senses set out above (the sense discussed in section 12).

[69] For the theorem (in social choice theory) that majority-decision alone satisfies elementary conditions of fairness and rationality, see May, 'A Set of Independent Necessary and Sufficient Conditions for Simple Majority Decision'. See also Sen, *Collective Choice and Social Welfare*, 71–3. There are useful discussions in Ackerman, *Social Justice in the Liberal State*, 277–93 and Beitz, *Political Equality*, 58–67.

[70] Mill, *Considerations on Representative Government*, Ch. VIII, 329.   [71] Ibid., 335.

[72] See also Rawls, *A Theory of Justice*, 232–4.

Something similar can be said about a point that Charles Beitz makes, that any inference from equal respect to majority-decision would have to 'reflect an implausibly narrow understanding of the more basic principle [i.e. equal respect], from which substantive concerns regarding the content of political outcomes . . . have been excluded'.[73] Beitz is surely right that the concept of equal respect for persons is normally used in a way that conveys not just the speaker's view about how political decisions are reached but also his view about the substantive impact on individuals of the outcome itself. Such a speaker will not be convinced, then, that equal respect entails majority-decision, for he will know that majority-decision can lead to outcomes which (as he believes – and maybe rightly) do not give individuals the substantive respect to which they are entitled.[74]

Once again, however, we can see that this broad notion of respect is unusable in society's name in the circumstances of politics. It is because we disagree about what counts as a substantively respectful outcome that we need a decision-procedure; in this context, folding substance back into procedure will necessarily privilege one controversial view about what respect entails and accordingly fail to respect the others. Thus in the circumstances of politics, all one *can* work with is the 'implausibly narrow understanding' of equal respect; and I suspect (though, again, I doubt that one can prove) that majority-decision is the only decision-procedure consistent with equal respect in this necessarily impoverished sense.[75]

15. THE REASONABLENESS OF LEGISLATION

We began by exploring a common source of discomfort about statutes – a feeling that legislation is unsatisfactory as a source of law, since it comes into being by processes that appear quite arbitrary – for example, a single swing vote among hundreds, which for all we know may have been cast for any reason or for none. That sort of provenance seems quite at odds with the elements of deliberation and reason that we treasure and value in the law. I hope I have shown that this sense of arbitrariness is unfounded. Every feature of the majority-decision method that seems arbitrary can be defended as *reasonable in the circumstances of politics*, and indeed as

---

[73] Beitz, *Political Equality*, 64.   [74] Cf. Dworkin, *A Matter of Principle*, 59–69.

[75] Beitz might respond by saying that if we *do* have to work with a narrow procedural notion of respect for persons, the only decision-method we can infer from it is the unanimity requirement embodied in something like Rawlsian contractarianism. (Cf. Beitz, *Political Equality*, 63.) But of course unanimity is precisely what is not available in the circumstances of politics, the only circumstances in which we actually need a decision-procedure. Anyway, as Beitz himself notes, the contractarian requirement of unanimity is usually seen these days as a substantive heuristic, not the basis of a procedural model – which is why it overlooks, as all substance-oriented approaches do, the fact of substantive disagreement.

expressive of perhaps the most robust conception of respect for persons that we are entitled to work with in those circumstances.

Majority-decision is sometimes described as mechanical and impersonal,[76] a 'crude statistical view of democracy'.[77] But what seems like its mechanical nature is the tribute it pays to the felt need for action-in-concert, even in the face of disagreement about the only things that would qualify it, in some critics' eyes, as non-mechanical. It is a mechanical procedure precisely because recourse to a substantive procedure would reproduce not resolve the decision-problem in front of us. What seems like the majoritarian obsession with statistics is – as we saw in section 11 – the tribute that politics pays to the reality that social problems and opportunities confront us in our millions, not in the twos and threes that moral philosophers are comfortable with. And what seems like its impersonality is a commitment to equality – a determination that when we, who need to settle on a single course of action, disagree about what to do, there is no reasonable[78] basis for *us* in designing our decision-procedures to accord greater weight to one side than to the other in the disagreement.

At the end of section 6, I said that our problem was to explain how statutes and other sources of law can have authority among people who disagree about the merits of their provisions. Readers may feel that this issue of authority has been left hanging. After all, noting that a decision-method is neither mechanical, nor impersonal nor statistical is not the same as showing that it has or should be accorded *authority*. And saying that it evinces respect for persons does not establish that either – especially since (as I said in section 14) it is not clear whether one can *prove* that majoritarianism is the only decision-method consistent with equal respect, let alone that it is required by equal respect. We still seem to be lacking the sense of constraint associated with authority.

I think this is appropriate; an account of majority decision cannot itself explain the authority of legislation (in this constraining sense). That explanation must come primarily from our sense of the moral urgency and importance of the problems that it is necessary for us to address – the things that (morally) *need* to be done and must be done by us, in our millions, together, if they are to be done at all. That is where the imperative

---

[76] See Selznick, 'Defining Democracy Up', 106.

[77] Dworkin, *A Bill of Rights for Britain*, 36.

[78] The idea of reasonableness that I am using is adapted from Rawls, *Political Liberalism*, 61: '[T]hose who insist, when fundamental political questions are at stake, on what they take as true but others do not, seem to others to simply insist on their own beliefs when they have the political power to do so. Of course, those who do insist on their beliefs also insist that their beliefs alone are true: they impose their beliefs because, they say, their beliefs are true and not because they are their beliefs. But this is a claim that all equally could make; it is also a claim that cannot be made good by anyone to citizens generally. So, when we make such claims others, who are themselves reasonable, must count us unreasonable.'

sense of constraint must come from; and obviously it will vary depending on a proper estimation of how important the problems actually are. But once this sense of constraint is established, then what I have said about the respectability of majority-decision comes into its own; for the problems we face pose themselves urgently for us *in the circumstances of politics*, and in particular in the circumstance of disagreement about what would be a just, a moral, or at any rate an appropriate solution. The appeal of majority-decision is that it not only solves the difficulty that this circumstance generates, but it does so in a respectful spirit, while its constraining authority consists in the fact that the problems it allows us to address in this way in these circumstances are problems that are on any account important and compelling. The two, then – constraint and respectfulness – combine to make a particular demand on each citizen (which is, I think, a demand characteristic of law and the rule of law) that he should not insist unreasonably on what appears to him to be the *right* solution to the urgent problems we face, if the result of such insistence is likely to be that the problems we face do not get any sort of solution at all.

Chapter Six

Legislators' Intentions and Unintentional Legislation

1. LEGISLATIVE INTENT

A bill has been debated and a statute has been enacted. How now is it to be interpreted? One initially appealing answer is that we should interpret the statute in the way the legislators intended, resolving any vagueness or ambiguity by finding out as much as we can about what the legislators had in mind. In this chapter, I shall discuss the latest attempt in analytic jurisprudence to revive the view that reference to legislators' intentions should play a role in the interpretation of statutes. I use 'revive' advisedly. It is true that reference to legislative intent is reasonably common among judges and lawyers in America,[1] and the appeal to 'original intent' is common too in the politics of American constitutional law.[2] Philosophically, however, the idea of appealing beyond the statutory text to independent evidence of what particular legislators are thought to have intended has been subject to such powerful criticisms, most notably by Ronald Dworkin,[3] that one is surprised to find it appearing again in anything other than a trivial form in respectable academic jurisprudence.[4]

Yet in a recent book, entitled *Interpretation and Legal Theory*, Andrei Marmor makes an argument for the intentionalist thesis which is not only respectable, but novel and almost persuasive.[5] Its originality consists in eschewing any argument based on democratic considerations. Marmor advances no version of the claim that judges ought to defer to legislators' intentions because legislators are elected and acountable and judges are

---

[1] It is less common in England, though for a recent change of approach see the decision of House of Lords in *Pepper* v. *Hart* 2 All ER [1993].

[2] See Meese, 'Interpreting the Constitution'.

[3] Dworkin, *Law's Empire*, 312–37.

[4] For a trivial version of intentionalism, see Stanley Fish, 'Play of Surfaces: Theory and Law', 300–1: 'Intentionalism properly understood involves no methodology, no prescriptive direction. . . . [T]here cannot be a distinction between interpreters who look to intention and interpreters who don't, only a distinction between the differing accounts of intention put forward by rival interpreters. . . . [E]veryone who is an interpreter is in the intention business, and there is no methodological cash value to declaring yourself (or even thinking yourself) to be an intentionalist because you couldn't be anything else.'

[5] Marmor, *Interpretation and Legal Theory*, esp. Ch. 8.

not.[6] His argument is based instead on a consideration of Joseph Raz's theory of the authority of law. The normal justification of X's having authority over Y, Raz says, is that Y is more likely to follow the reasons that apply objectively to his decisions if he follows the directives of X, than if he tries to work out the reasons himself.[7] If this is true of X's directives, Marmor reckons, it is likely to be true also of the intentions that lie behind those directives, even when such intentions are not fully disclosed in the directives themselves and have to be recovered by other means.

The application of this general argument to the case of legislation is obvious enough. A statute is conceived as the work of a lawmaker, X, and it is said to have authority just in case X has some sort of technical or moral expertise in the field that the statute addresses. X is the expert and so ordinary citizens will do better by deferring to his directives than by trusting their own judgement on the matter. Now, this expertise is disclosed in the first instance in the explicit words of the statute that X has written. It is, however, unlikely to be exhausted by that. If his text turns out to be vague or infelicitous, his subjects may have recourse to his expertise in other ways, by gathering clues as to the thoughts and purposes that were in his mind at the time the original statute was passed. The law's authority, after all, is a matter of X's authority, and that authority is defined dispositionally as the likelihood that others will do better by deferring to him. Thus, an argument for the authority of law based on the fact that the legislator is more enlightened than his audience may generate a case for appealing also to legislative intent as a further basis of enlightenment in determining what a citizen or official ought to do.

An argument of this kind depends, at least for its initial attraction, on a rather primitive picture of legislation. It gains its greatest plausibility by stressing the features that statutes have in common with simple commands. If we understand legislation along Hobbesian lines – 'where a man saith, *Doe this*, or *Doe not this*, without expecting other reason than the Will of him that sayes it'[8] – we may indeed be inclined to turn to the lawmaker's intentions as a basis for interpreting the statutes that he has passed. For if there is something about *his will* that makes his original command authoritative, it seems natural to have recourse to that will – as far as one can ascertain it – if one is in need of further guidance in putting the command into effect.

---

[6] Certainly, most appellate judges are not elected, i.e. most judges whose interpretations will be influential in the legal system. Moreover those judges who are elected are seldom regarded by voters (and hardly ever regard themselves) as popular *representatives* in the way that legislators are.

[7] See Raz, *The Morality of Freedom*, 53. See also Ch. 5, above, at fn. 37 and accompanying text.

[8] Hobbes, *Leviathan*, Ch. 25, 176.

I shall spare the reader any reiteration of the difficulties of this style of jurisprudence. The most important point is that Marmor does not take adequate account of the fact that modern statutes are not the products of single expert authors. They are produced by the deliberations of large multi-member assemblies whose claim to authority in Raz's sense (if indeed they can make any such claim at all) consists in their ability to integrate a diversity of purposes, interests, and aims among their members into the text of a single legislative product. The modern situation, in other words, is not that of a *person* having authority, but (at most) of a *group* having authority, and of its having that authority only by virtue of the way in which it combines the interests and knowledge of its members in the act of legislating. In this situation, it is unwise to make any inference from the authority of legislation to the authority of anything said or any purpose expressed by particular members of the legislature that does not amount in itself to a legislative act. That, in outline, is the argument I shall make.

Someone may ask: What if the conditions under which a statute is passed are such as to make single-author jurisprudence more appropriate? A particular law may have been conceived by just one legislator and his staff and passed 'on the nod', so to speak, by others in the chamber, in deference to his expertise in the area. In a case like this, surely it is not inappropriate to regard the particular legislator as the author, and to appeal to his intentions when we want to clarify what he has done.[9] But whether this line of argument works will depend on whether we can plausibly attribute *authority*, not just legislative efficacy, to the single legislator in question.

We have to remember that theories of legal authority (and any concomitant theories of interpretation) are usually purchased wholesale not retail. The question for jurisprudence is seldom about the authority or interpretation of this or that statute in particular, but about the relation between authority and interpretation generally. We must ask, then, whether there is anything true in general about the way in which statutes are produced that makes appeal to legislators' intentions a proper strategy of interpretation. How we answer that question will depend on what we take to be the most helpful general model of the legislative process, so far as theories of authority are concerned. My submission is going to be that, at that level, we will do better by eschewing any model that regards legislation as most commonly the intentional product of a single law-making author. We do better – as I have argued throughout this part of the book – by focusing on the structures and proceedings of legislative *assemblies*.

The argument that follows will proceed in three stages. After some preliminaries, I will address the general issue of the intentionality of statutes. I will argue in section 3 that, under the conditions of modern legislation, it

---

[9] I am grateful to Chaim Gans for this point.

is often implausible to describe legislative acts as intentional acts, even though they take place in an intentionally-organized context. In section 4, I will show how Raz's thesis about authority (or a plausible version of that thesis) might nevertheless apply to legislative acts, despite the fact that they are not conceived as intentional acts. Then, in section 5, I will show that the best arguments for the authority of statutes produced under these conditions are arguments which actually preclude any appeal to the intentions of particular legislators as a general interpretive strategy. I will end, in section 6, with some further general comments on the significance of the considerations about legislation on which I have been basing my arguments.

2. LEGISLATORS NOT FRAMERS

First, I want to deal with some preliminary matters. Like Marmor, I take the subject of this discussion to be statutory not constitutional interpretation.[10] The hardest case for an opponent of the intentionalist strategy – and thus the case that I have to address – is a statute passed recently, in a deliberative session of which there is an undisputed public record, by legislators familiar with the conditions of the society to which the statute is going to apply. If questions arise about the interpretation of a law enacted under these conditions, it is not implausible to suggest that they might be answered by looking to the public record of debates, committee deliberations, etc. to see what the legislators had in mind. Of course, such exercises are not always successful. Still, even if the judges get the legislators' intentions wrong, or even if the legislators are for some other reason dissatisfied with the judges' answer, the legislators can always enact another statute to impose the interpretation or purpose they prefer.[11]

None of this applies in constitutional adjudication. Despite its popularity among conservative politicians, the appeal to the intentions of the framers of the US Constitution is ludicrously implausible. Those who make the appeal disagree about who counts as a framer. Is it the drafters of the text, the members of the Philadelphia Convention, the ratifiers, or the people who elected the ratifiers? Not only that, but whoever the framers are taken to be, their actual intentions are largely a matter of conjecture and at least as controversial as any less historical form of 'interpretation'. We know 'practically nothing', for example, about what went on in state legislatures during the ratification debates.[12] Moreover, even if we knew the framers' intentions, it would be unwise to rely on them. The

---

[10] Marmor, *Interpretation and Legal Theory*, 172–3.   [11] Ibid., 173.
[12] Schwartz, *The Bill of Rights: A Documentary History*, Vol. II, 1171; I am obliged for this reference to Post, 'Theories of Constitutional Interpretation', 22.

framers lived two centuries ago and, despite their revolutionary virtue, they were utterly unacquainted with the conditions of modern politics and society in America. They lived in a loosely federated set of sparsely populated post-colonial white supremacist states, whose economies were based on the exploitation of African slaves in agriculture, and whose politics were confined to those who owned slaves, women, or property. For the purposes of the Raz/Marmor argument, these men would not even have understood, let alone have had a better grasp than us of, the conditions for the subsistence of a continental superpower as a free and constitutional republic, under conditions of ethnic diversity, democratic equality, and post-industrial crisis. There may be a case for regarding the text of the Constitution as a stable and indispensable framework to house the volatility and vicissitudes of modern politics.[13] But that stabilizing function has more in common with coordinative authority – which Marmor acknowledges can generate no justification for an appeal to original intent[14] – than with the authority of moral expertise on which deference to framers' intentions is more usually based.

I take it, then, that we are to discuss the role of legislative intent in the interpretation of ordinary statutes under modern conditions. I shall assume, in addition, that when we talk about legislation, we are envisaging the work of a Congress, a Parliament or a state assembly: that is, a body comprising a number of members (usually in the hundreds) of various political persuasions, elected as representatives by the people of the state to whom the legislation is going to apply. I shall assume, too, as I did in Chapter Four, that the legislators are a diverse body of people, drawn from different groups in a heterogeneous and multicultural society. I assume in other words that there is very little in the way of shared cultural and social understandings among them beyond the rather stiff and formal language that they address to one another in their legislative debates. I shall assume finally that the legislature possesses fastidiously defined procedures to determine how a piece of legislation is introduced, debated, and passed, what it comprises (that is, what its final authoritative text is), and when it takes effect. These procedures amount to the constitution of the legislature, and reference to them will form part of the rule of recognition for the legal system.

Though these assumptions are obvious enough in the modern world – and no doubt wearying to my readers at this stage! – they turn out to be crucial for my argument against appeals to legislators' intentions. Accordingly, I will spend some time examining their grounds in section 6.

---

[13] See Arendt, *On Revolution*, esp. Ch. 4.
[14] Marmor, *Interpretation and Legal Theory*, 179–80.

3. UNINTENTIONAL LEGISLATION

It is sometimes said, as though it were a truism, that anything we interpret must necessarily be conceived as a product of someone's intention.[15] The point is taken to be an elementary one about what counts as a linguistic artefact. Wave action on sand or the rustling of the wind might produce marks or noises that look or sound like texts. But one cannot treat them as texts – it is said – and one cannot set about discerning their meaning, unless one attributes their appearance to the intentions of some intelligent author. Stanley Fish puts the point this way:

> [I]n order to hear sense in arbitrarily produced sounds or marks we have to hear those sounds and marks within the assumption that they have been produced by some purposeful agent; that is, we have to hear them *as not arbitrarily produced*, even if to do so we must attribute purpose and intention to the waves or to the wind or to the great spirit that rolls through all things.[16]

The positing of intention comes first on this account; the positing of meanings second.[17]

In exactly the same way, many legal theorists think it obvious that a statute must be conceived as something which has been produced intentionally; and they infer from this that the only possible object of interpretation in the law is the meaning envisaged by those whose purposes constitute the intentionality of the provision under consideration.[18] Thus, imagine that a piece of paper duly certified in accordance with proper parliamentary procedure appears in front of a judge with marks on it that look like the following:

Vehicles in the Park Act 1993. (1) With the exception of bicycles and ambulances, no vehicle shall be permitted to enter any state or municipal park. (2) Any person who brings a vehicle into a state or municipal park shall be liable to a fine of not more than $100.

According to Stanley Fish and others who take the view that I am discussing in this section, if the judge views this as a statute and begins the laborious business of working out, for example, whether its provisions apply to the proverbial jeep on a plinth,[19] he must be treating the marks on the paper as the product of someone's intention.

---

[15] For the best-known recent argument to this effect, see Knapp and Michaels, 'Against Theory', 723.

[16] Fish, 'Play of Surfaces: Theory and Law', 299.

[17] Fish, *Doing What Comes Naturally*, 296.

[18] See, e.g., Knapp and Michaels, 'Intention, Identity and the Constitution', 187.

[19] The case is from Fuller, 'Positivism and Fidelity to Law', 633: 'What would Professor Hart say if some local patriots wanted to mount on a pedestal in the park a truck used in World War II, while other citizens, regarding the proposed memorial as an eyesore, support

Fish concedes that it is a further question whether we should search the legislative record in order to find intentionalist clues to the solution of the jeep-on-a-plinth problem. Acknowledging legislative intentionality, he says, is not the same as deferring to legislators' intentions, especially when the latter are not the intentions disclosed immediately in the text of the statute itself. We may end up answering our question about the jeep by reading the statute in a way that would have surprised its authors.[20] Still, the crucial point, according to Fish,

is that one cannot read *or* reread independently of intention, independently, that is, of the assumption that one is dealing with marks or sounds produced by an intentional being, a being situated in some enterprise in relation to which he has a purpose or a point of view.[21]

The fact that 'intention' and 'meaning' are heavily theory-laden terms does not, according to Fish, undermine the point that interpreting a text is always a matter of determining what the intentional being who produced it meant. It is always, he says, a matter of discovering the meaning of which the statutory text was intended to be the expression.[22]

Though this position may seem uncontroversial with regard to novels and poems, it is confused – and significantly confused – in regard to modern legislation. Legislation, I have assumed, is the product of a multi-member assembly, comprising a large number of persons of quite radically differing aims, interests, and backgrounds. Under these conditions, the specific provisions of a particular statute are often the result of compromise and line-item voting. It is perfectly possible, for example, that our imagined Vehicles in the Park Act, considered as a whole, does not reflect the purposes or intentions of any of the legislators who together enacted it. Let me spell out this possibility. With regard to section 1 of the Act, the legislators might have been divided on the exception for bicycles (which I shall call B), on the exception for ambulances (A), and on the inclusion of state parks as well as municipal parks (S). Suppose the legislators divided into three equal factions on these issues as in Figure 3.

Faction 1	Faction 2	Faction 3
B	B	~B
A	~A	A
~S	S	S

Figure 3.

their stand by the "no vehicle" rule? Does this truck, in perfect working order, fall within the core or the penumbra?' The case is discussed by Marmor, *Interpretation and Legal Theory*, 130.

[20] Hence the prescriptive triviality of Fish's intentionalism: see fn. 4, above.
[21] Fish, *Doing What Comes Naturally*, 99–100.   [22] Fish, 'Play of Surfaces', 302.

Successive majority voting on these various questions would produce our familiar statute – B & A & S – even though that combination corresponded to nobody's preference.

Someone may respond: surely, after the amendments are in, the legislators will vote on the bill as a whole, in its final form (B & A & S). Thus even if they initially disagree, the enacted statute will at least reflect the intentions of a majority at that last stage, taking into account their awareness of what was politically possible. But this is purely an artefact of our particular parliamentary procedures – that we have a 'third reading' debate and division, for example, after the amendment stage. One could imagine a legislature that proceeded quite differently. There might be a preliminary discussion during which all the issues likely to provoke a division were identified. General debate would ensue, at the conclusion of which members would feed their votes on the various issues into a machine which would produce the statute in its final form on the basis of the voting and promulgate it automatically to judges, officials, and the population at large. The possibility of such a machine was considered by Richard Wollheim in his famous article 'A Paradox in the Theory of Democracy':

I now want to . . . envisage Democracy in terms of a certain machine which operates according to [the following] method or rule. The machine – which we may for convenience call the democratic machine – operates in a discontinuous fashion. Into it are fed at fixed intervals the choices of the individual citizens. The machine then aggregates them according to the pre-established rule or method, and so comes up with what may be called a 'choice' of its own. Democratic rule is said to be achieved if throughout the period when the machine is not working, the most recent choice of the machine is acted upon.[23]

Now, theorists of public choice are familiar with various tangles of cyclicity that such a machine might get into. Let us assume, however – as Wollheim did – that these are not a problem for the cases we are considering.[24] The point of this thought-experiment (which is not the same as Wollheim's use of it)[25] is that it enables us to envisage a piece of legislation

---

[23] Wollheim, 'A Paradox in the Theory of Democracy', 75–6.

[24] Ibid., 75. I also want to evade a complaint that Ronald Dworkin might make, that the Wollheim machine is capable of yielding something like 'a checkerboard statute', that is, a statute that lacks internal coherence. (Dworkin, *Law's Empire*, 178–84.) Even if Dworkin is right in thinking that there is something objectionable about a statute so compromised that it does not reflect any coherent set of principles or policies, he can hardly deny that it is a text and that a judge might make a good faith effort to interpret it. Remember too that 'integrity', the value which Dworkin says is at stake here, is just one legal value among several, and must often be considered alongside justice and fairness. (See also the discussion in Ch. 9, below.) In any case, the Wollheim machine *need* not produce statutes that lack integrity. At most, a requirement of integrity would imply only that the machine's output *could* be interpreted as the product of someone's intention, not that it *must* be so interpreted.

[25] Briefly, Wollheim was interested in the question of why a person whose input into the machine was a firm and whole-hearted vote against policy A, should ever regard the

that cannot be conceived as, in Fish's words, something produced 'by an intentional being, . . . situated in some enterprise in relation to which he has a purpose or a point of view'.

Of course, this is just a model: in the real world, statutes are never produced exactly like that. But also, in the real world, statutes are never produced exactly as the product of one person's coherent intention. The interesting question is which picture is more helpful for our thinking about the intentionality of statutes under modern legislative conditions. Given the large part that is played by compromise, logrolling, and last-minute amendments in contemporary legislation, my money is on the machine.

Fish may make another response. He may say: even if it is the product of Wollheim's machine, still the text of our statute is quite unlike the cases mentioned earlier of marks made by waves in the sand or noises in the wind.

He is right. There are three important differences. (1) The machine does what it does on the basis of the legislators' inputs, and those inputs are fully intentional. (2) The machine is programmed to produce the particular signs (words) that it does (under particular input conditions) because those signs are taken to have certain meanings by those who program it. It is the programmers' intention, for example, that the English words 'with the exception of bicycles' be produced by the machine in the event that a majority of legislators press button 'B'. This is their expectation about how the machine's output – whatever it is – will be understood by those to whom it is sent: they will read it as a set of English sentences. And it is this expectation that the legislators share as they input their votes. (3) The whole system (the machine itself and the conventions surrounding its use) has been set up intentionally, pursuant to certain democratic procedural aspirations. The entire exercise, then, is an intentional one, and that is enough to distinguish it from waves in the sand.[26]

But none of that is sufficient to establish Fish's conclusion that the text must be taken to embody *a particular intention*, for example, an intention to

machine's output as giving him a reason to act in favour of A. We will discuss this aspect of his example in s. 5 of Ch. 11, below.

[26] Point 2 is sufficient to address the argument of Knapp and Michaels, 'Intention, Identity and the Constitution', 190–2, that the assignment of meaning to marks produced by chance involves an arbitrary choice among all actual and possible languages which might give semantic value to such marks. Knapp and Michaels say that 'the only plausible reason for restricting the text's meanings to the language in which the author wrote it is that one is interested in the author's intention; otherwise, the choice of this rule over an infinite number of others would be arbitrary'. (Ibid., 192.) This argument is invalid, at least as it applies to our legislative example. Those who set up the Wollheim machine have determined intentionally that the marks it produces are to be understood as English words and sentences. But it does not follow from this that the particular marks that emerge from the machine should be taken to express the particular intentions of any user of the English language.

ensure that vehicles other than bicycles and ambulances do not enter state
or municipal parks. For neither that intention nor anything like it figures
among the intentional elements 1–3 that we have just identified.
Accordingly, when the statute is read for the first time by an official or a
citizen (or for that matter by a legislator interested to know what he and
his colleagues 'decided'), Fish is not entitled to say that the aim of the reading must be to determine what somebody meant.

Max Radin once wrote that it is the job of a legislature to pass statutes
not form intentions.[27] A legislature is an artificial actor, and the passage of
a statute is its action: indeed we refer to statutes as *acts* of Congress or
Parliament or whatever. But though we use the language of agency in this
way, we must not be misled by an obsessive analogy with the actions of
natural persons into searching for a legislative equivalent for every event
or state associated with action in the psychology of individual agents. Few
would say, for example, that legislatures (as opposed to particular legislators) have motives as well as intentions associated with particular acts;
few would be willing to put the kind of weight on the motive/intention
distinction that we apply in the individual case.[28] So why insist on a cor-
relate for intention at all? Why not simply say that the act of a legislature
is an artificial resultant of the acts of individual legislators, structured and
related to one another through certain procedures, decision-functions and
perhaps machines? Why not say that while each of the latter actions – the
individual actions – is of course the product of an intention, the resultant
action – the act of the legislature itself – need not be?[29]

Part of the confusion tempting us to ascribe intentions to legislatures has
to do with the concept of meaning. It may be thought that the very fact that
legislation is a *speech*-act – the production of a meaningful utterance or text
– means that it cannot be regarded as non-intentional.[30] What is it after all
to say 'No vehicle shall be permitted to enter any state or municipal park'
but to utter a string of sounds with the intention to produce a certain effect

---

[27]   Radin, 'Statutory Interpretation', 863; I am indebted for this reference to Moore, 'A
Natural Law Theory of Interpretation', 355.

[28]   Cf. the discussion in Marmor, *Interpretation and Legal Theory*, 167.

[29]   Then what becomes of the inquiries into legislative intention that are occasionally
undertaken in constitutional law – for example, in querying whether a piece of legislation
was intended to unduly burden some religious practice? What becomes of the familiar distinction between (a) neutral and non-neutral impacts and (b) neutral and non-neutral intentions? There is not space here to go fully into this issue. However, it has always seemed to me
that the more useful distinction is between (a) consequential inquiry into neutrality of
impacts, and (b*) justificatory inquiry as to whether there are neutral *reasons* favouring the
legislation, whether or not those reasons surfaced in anyone's intentions at the time. If a court
can discover a good neutral reason for a given law, the fact that it happens to have been
enacted for a non-neutral purpose is surely not a justification for striking it down. By striking it down, we would be depriving ourselves of something useful purely in order to retali-
ate against the legislators' bad intentions.

[30]   I am obliged to Joseph Raz for this point.

or response in one's audience by virtue of their recognition of that very intention?[31] Even if one were to eschew the idea of a single utterer for cases like this and concentrate just on the meaning of the sentence, it remains the case that our most plausible accounts of sentence-meaning make that notion a function (albeit a complex one) of individual intention.

I do not think that considerations like these drive us towards any notion of legislative intentionality. I have noted already – item 2 above – that even a Wollheim machine would have to be programmed and operated on the basis of certain assumptions about the meanings of various signs and sounds. A legislator who votes for (or against) a provision like 'No vehicle shall be permitted to enter any state or municipal park' does so on the assumption that – to put it crudely – what the words mean to him is identical to what they will mean to those to whom they are addressed (in the event that the provision is passed). He can entertain that assumption only on condition that the words are meaningful elements in a language – that is, only on condition that there is a community in which it is well known that members of that community commonly use such words to produce a certain effect or response in their audience by virtue of the audience's recognition of that very intention.[32] That such assumptions pervade the legislative process shows how much law depends on language, on the shared conventions that constitute a language, and on the reciprocity of intentions that conventions comprise.[33] But though they indicate a place for referring to intentions – the intentions of language-users as such – in any comprehensive account of what is going on, they provide no warrant for the view that, simply because a particular piece of legislation has a linguistic meaning, it must embody a particular intention attributable to a language-user.

4. AUTHORITY

It is one thing to play with the possibility of unintentional legislation, along the lines of my thought-experiment involving the Wollheim machine. But what becomes of the authority of a legislature if its statutes are not conceived as intentional acts? How can a legal provision be regarded as authoritative if the legislature employs a Wollheim machine to generate its laws? To address this question, we have to look again at the notion of authority.

---

[31] See Grice, *Studies in the Way of Words*, 92.
[32] Ibid., 117–37. See also Ch. 4, s. 5, above.
[33] Legislation may also rely on certain quasi-linguistic conventions common to legislative draftsmen and the legal/judicial community. I am obliged to Joseph Raz for this point.

In what follows, I shall concentrate on the theory of authority presented by Joseph Raz,[34] for this is not only the leading conception, but the one on which Marmor's argument is based. It may not, however, fully capture the claim that legislation makes on our respect: I have tried to describe this further and deeper claim in Chapter Five.[35] So far as that deeper claim is concerned, there is no particular difficulty about legislation which is the product of a Wollheim machine. The difficulty lies solely with the Raz-ian conception of authority; so, for the sake of argument, this chapter focuses almost exclusively on Raz's conception.

The thesis about authority that Marmor invokes from Joseph Raz talks about 'the normal way to establish that *a person* has authority over another person'.[36] It is persons who have authority, on this account, not organizations or laws. In a subsequent chapter of the book, Raz asks whether anything changes when we move from a one-on-one situation to an issue involving the authority of the state. However, the change that seems to interest him there is the fact that 'political authorities govern groups of people' rather than particular individuals.[37] He does not appear to be interested in the ramifications for his thesis of the fact that political authorities like legislatures *are* groups of people. The closest Raz comes to considering the issue is in the following passage that Marmor cites from an article published earlier than *The Morality of Freedom*: '[A] directive can be authoritatively binding only if it is, or is at least presented as, someone's view of how its subjects ought to behave.'[38] Marmor glosses this as 'the idea that only an agent capable of communion with others can have authority over them'.[39] (He uses it to argue against Ronald Dworkin's view that the norms judges should take as authoritative are norms they themselves produce by a process of interpretive construction.)

The fallacy in Raz's thesis (or at least in Marmor's presentation of Raz's thesis) about the normal justification of authority lies in forging too tight a connection between *authority* and *authorship*. On the Raz/Marmor account, authority cannot be systemic: it must be attributable to an author. Their claim seems to be that the reasons of ordinary citizens can be affected in the way that authority affects reasons only if there is some identifiable person (natural or artificial) who *has* the authority in question. Thus Marmor assumes that a statute, S, can have authority only if the following is true about the person, X, who issued it: namely, that any person Y to whom the statute is addressed does better by following $X's$ view of the reasons that apply to $Y's$ conduct than by attempting to work out those

---

[34] See Raz, *The Morality of Freedom*, 21–195.   [35] See above, Ch. 5, especially s. 6.
[36] Raz, *The Morality of Freedom*, 53 (my emphasis).   [37] Ibid., 71.
[38] Raz, 'Authority, Law and Morality', 303, cited by Marmor, *Interpretation and Legal Theory*, 114.
[39] Marmor, *Interpretation and Legal Theory*, 115.

reasons for himself. For a statute to have authority, on this account, is for its author to have (or to have had) a view which is superior in some regard to any view likely to be formed by the person to whom the statute is addressed.[40]

I want to suggest, however, that the situation in which statutory authority (in Raz's sense) is traceable back to personal authority is a special case. In other cases, it is possible to talk about the authority of the statute *tout court* and develop a version of the normal justification thesis which refers only to the likelihood that person subject to it will do better by following its provisions. What I have in mind is something along the following lines (which I shall label 'thesis [J]' because I will want to refer to it later):

[J]: A statute (or any text) S has authority over a person Y only if person Y is likely better to comply with the reasons which apply to him by following the provisions of S, than if he tries to follow those reasons directly.

Now, [J] *may* be true on account of something about the views or the intentions of the person X who authored or voted for S. But that need not be the reason for its truth: S may satisfy [J] despite the fact that S has no author, or satisfy it in virtue of features that make no reference to any person's expertise.

Marmor of course does not consider [J] – for I have just invented it. However, in his discussion of Dworkin's arguments, he seems to suggest that whenever anything like [J] is true, we must either locate an individual X, whose view on the matter in question is taken to be superior to Y's, or we must *pretend* that there is some such individual. This insistence on producing or imagining a singular X is never defended (except by reference to Raz's formulations). I suspect, however, that it is due to an inability to

---

[40] Marmor defends this thesis in a response to an earlier version of this chapter. In Andrei Marmor, 'Authorities and Persons: A Reply to Jeremy Waldron', he argues that the connection between authority and personal authorship is indispensable for what Raz calls the 'content-independence' of the reasons that authoritative directions are supposed to yield. A text cannot have authority in its own right, Marmor argues, because one's only reason for deferring to it would be some belief about the verisimilitude or reliability of its contents, and that belief is not content-independent in the relevant sense.

But surely – I want to respond – a democrat may have a content-independent reason to defer to the output of the Wollheim machine. Marmor acknowledges this, but maintains that the democrat's *real* reason for doing so is deference to the views of the human designer of the machine. He asks, '[I]n what sense is the machine's output authoritative, over and beyond the authority of the agreed method which is bound to be (as Waldron readily concedes) the product of someone's authorship? The answer is simple: in no sense whatsoever.' (Ibid., 347.) But even if we accept that the machine must have had a human designer – call him 'Madison' – the fact is that we defer to the machine's output *because of the sort of machine it is* not because it was designed by Madison. If Madison had designed an autocratic machine, calculated invariably to designate *Madison's* input as the social choice, we would pay the machine's output no attention whatsoever. And this is not because we have content-dependent reasons for rejecting that sort of output, but because we have content-independent reasons for rejecting *that sort of machine.*

conceive of how Y could do better by following the provisions of S than by following his own reason, unless S was an expression of someone else's view (someone who was smarter or more knowledgeable than Y was). So let me explain how that might be possible.

First, a trivial example. I am very bad at keeping track of credit card transactions. I use my card, several times a week, but I do not keep the receipts or write down the amounts, so I am never sure how much has been charged to my account. Any attempt I made to work it out for myself would probably be inaccurate. Fortunately, Chase Manhattan Bank provides an '800' number for me to call. I punch in my credit card account number, and the last four digits of my Social Security number to verify my identity, and the disembodied 'voice' of a machine will say something like this:

Your current balance $_{is}$ FOUR hundred $_{and}$ *thirty* FIVE dollars $_{and}$ *sixty* cents. Your available credit $_{is}$ FIVE thousand FIVE hundred $_{and}$ *sixty* FOUR dollars $_{and}$ *forty* cents.

Now I am under no illusion that there is anyone at the bank who has worked all this out and is waiting to communicate it to me, any more than I think the 'voice' I hear is that of some individual at Chase headquarters, sitting patiently by the phone waiting for people like me to call. The deliverance I have just quoted is nothing but the product of a machine responding on the spot to my touch-tone input, to various inputs from retailers, and to its record of my credit limit. No one has worked out what my balance is: there are just the noises recorded above. Indeed the machine may not even be storing a record of my balance; apart from the sending of my monthly account, it may be computed only as a response to my telephone call. Still, the machine's output is authoritative for me in terms of thesis [J]: I do better by relying on this text for information about the outstanding balance on my credit card than I would by relying on my own forgetful computations.

I know of course that someone has intentionally programmed the machine to produce outputs (in response to certain inputs) such that people who treat its sounds as English sentences will have reason to rely on the information such sentences conventionally convey. That is like the conditions 1–3 for the Wollheim machine that I mentioned in the previous section. But I can concede all that without saying (or pretending) that anyone is intentionally conveying to me the message that my outstanding balance is $435.60. That my reliance on the machine's output makes reference to someone's intentions (in programming the machine) does not make the machine, for me, an intentional system.[41]

---

[41] The philosopher Daniel Dennett is famous, among other things, for the claim that it is sometimes appropriate to treat machines as intentional systems. See Dennett, 'Intentional

In the case of the bank's computer, there are good reasons for me to respect the machine's output more than I respect the results of my own computations: the bank has an interest in keeping accurate records and no interest, as far as I can tell, in concealing the true state of my account from me. But legislatures are not banks. What reasons might there be for respecting the deliverances of a Wollheim machine?

I will consider three lines of argument: (A) the utilitarian argument, that a Wollheim machine might aggregate individual preferences in the way required by the applicable social welfare function; (B) the Condorcet Jury Theorem, that the view determined by a Wollheim machine to be that of the majority has a probability of being correct that is greater than the probability that any one of the views being counted is correct; and (C) the Aristotelian claim (which we considered briefly in Chapter Four) that a multitude of persons, by a process of deliberative synthesis, may forge a better view than even the wisest of them could come up with on his own.

None of these arguments is watertight. But in common with Marmor and Raz, I do not want to make a watertight case for the authority of such legislation. The claim by Marmor that is under consideration is only that *if* (and *to the extent that*) there is reason to accord authority to a statute, there may also be reason to accord authority to the intentions of some or all of the members of the legislature which passed it, even when these intentions are not disclosed in the text of statute itself. My claim in section 5 will be that even this inference of Marmor's is invalid, at least to the extent that the authority of a statute (such as it is) is based on argument A, argument B, or argument C.

Before moving to that, let me sketch out the three lines of argument in a little more detail.

A. *The Utilitarian Argument.* Historically, the utilitarian case for democracy has been that a majoritarian decision-procedure at the level of public choice can sometimes model an aggregative social welfare function at the level of utilitarian morality. For both cases – that is, for both a majoritarian decision-procedure and a Benthamite social welfare function – the fact that a course of action promotes the satisfaction of some preference counts in its favour, and when it becomes apparent that not everyone's preferences can be satisfied, one adopts the course of action that satisfies as many of them as possible. Thus as democrats, we follow the will of the majority; and as utilitarians, we try to promote the greatest aggregate

Systems'. But my claim falls far short of that here (even assuming Dennett's argument is accepted). It seems to me that an output S of a machine may sometimes be authoritative for a person in terms of thesis [J] whether that machine is (to be treated as) an intentional system or not.

happiness. The two may amount to roughly the same thing if individual votes are a reliable guide to the conditions of individual happiness.[42]

Now of course there are all sorts of difficulties with this equation. It presupposes that individuals are voting their own happiness; it assumes they are reliable judges of that; and it avoids altogether the question of the intensity of their preferences. Moreover, for the case of a representative legislature (as opposed to a directly democratic one), a number of epicycles have to be added to ensure that votes cast by each legislator accurately represent the proportion between various preferences of his constituents. Still, even if these difficulties cannot be perfectly overcome, it is easy to imagine that a Wollheim machine, registering and aggregating a large number of individuals' expressed preferences, might produce an output whose utilitarian credentials were much better than any rough-and-ready computation that could be made by the individual citizen. If an individual knows that his own computations of social utility are even less accurate than the machine's, and perhaps biased also by wishful thinking in his own favour, it might be wiser for him to forego self-reliance and rely instead on the somewhat less fallible outputs of the machine as his guide to what the general happiness demands. In these circumstances, anyone who believes that the truth about what ought to be done is utilitarian will have reason to regard the outputs of the machine as authoritative in the sense of thesis [J].

B. *Condorcet's Jury Theorem*. Under the previous heading, we assumed that individual legislators were asking themselves different questions as they voted: each was asking 'What do I want?' (so that legislator W was asking 'What does W want?' and legislator X was asking 'What does X want?'). The same would be true if each legislator was asking himself, 'What are the preferences of my constituents?' We imagined that the Wollheim machine would take each person's preferences and aggregate them using a social welfare function to produce, for the first time in this process, a conclusion about the general good. Often, however, legislators take themselves to be asking the *same* question: 'What is best for everyone, or for society at large, or what is most just?' Often, *each* takes himself to be expressing a view about the *general* welfare. When this is the basis of individual legislators' votes, is there any reason to believe that a Wollheim machine will produce an authoritative output, in the sense of thesis [J]?

There is; and the argument is a matter of simple arithmetic. Suppose that some voters are addressing a single question with two answers, one correct and one incorrect (for example, they are jurors deciding whether someone did or did not commit a robbery). Assume that the probability of

---

[42] This paragraph and the one that follows are adapted from Waldron, 'Rights and Majorities: Rousseau Revisited'.

each voter choosing the correct answer is greater than 0.5, that is, that each is more likely to get it right by thinking about the matter and then voting his best judgement than if he simply tosses a coin. Then provided the votes are cast independently of one another, the probability that the answer chosen by a simple majority of them will be the correct answer is somewhat greater than 0.5, and it rises toward the limit of certainty as the size of the group of people voting increases.[43]

This theorem, due to the Marquis de Condorcet, has its limits.[44] The same reasoning yields the conclusion that if the average competence of the individual voters dips below 0.5, then majority competence tends towards zero as group size increases. In other words, the theorem provides a ground for the authority of the outcome if individual voters are, on average, more likely than not to be correct in the alternative they choose; but it provides reason for doubting the authority of the outcome if on average the voters are more likely than not to choose incorrectly. As we saw in Chapter Three, Condorcet himself believed that, historically, average individual competence tended to decline as group size (for example in a legislature) increased. But of course there is no reason to think that this truth (if it is a truth) of political sociology exactly cancels out the arithmetical effect we have been discussing.[45]

In any case, Condorcet's theorem indicates a reason for according authority to the output of a Wollheim machine in at least some circumstances. If a large number of legislators address themselves scrupulously to some objective issue and if they each have a better than even chance of being right, then the ordinary citizen would be wise to trust the decision

[43] Suppose there are three voters – V, W, and X – voting independently, each with a .6 chance of being right. When V casts his vote, there is a .6 chance he's right and a .4 chance he's wrong. When W casts his vote: there is a $.6 \times .6 = .36$ chance that a majority comprising at least W and V will be right; a $.6 \times .4 = .24$ chance that V will be right and W wrong; and a $.4 \times .6 = .24$ chance that V will be wrong and W right. Now X casts his vote. If V got it right and W wrong, there is a $.24 \times .6 = .144$ chance that a majority comprising only V and X will be right. And if V got it wrong and W right, there is the same chance (.144) that a majority comprising only W and X will be right. The overall probability that a majority will be right then is

$$0.36 \text{ (VWX or VW)} + 0.144 \text{ (VX)} + 0.144 \text{ (WX)} = 0.648$$

which is somewhat higher than the 0.6 individual competence we began with.

For a sense of the difference that an increase in group size can make, consider that if we add to the group two additional voters of the same individual competence (0.6), we get a competence of 0.68256 for the five members deciding by a majority. To get a group competence of higher than 0.9, we need only add an additional 36 members with individual competencies of 0.6. (See Grofman and Feld, 'Rousseau's General Will: A Condorcetian Perspective', 571.)

[44] Condorcet, 'Essay on the Application of Mathematics to the Theory of Decision-making', 33–70.

[45] For Condorcet's awareness of the limits of the Jury Theorem, see the discussion in Estlund et al., 'Democratic Theory and the Public Interest', 1317–40.

generated by a majoritarian machine out of their individual votes. Indeed, on Condorcet's reasoning, *each individual legislator* will do better by observing the authority of the machine-produced legislation than he would by trusting the reasoning that led to his own individual vote. This, as we shall see, is fatal to Marmor's case. But before we consider that, let us look at the third of our arguments for legislative authority.

C. *Aristotelian Synthesis.* Condorcet's result is maddeningly mechanical. Forget truth, objectivity, and justice: the same arithmetical reasoning tells us about the prospects that a majority of balls pulled at random out of an urn will be black, given that more than half of the balls in the urn are black. Moreover, Condorcet's result takes no account of discussion, deliberation, and persuasion – the very processes that are likely to produce a legislative record to which Marmor's intention-seeking judge can appeal.[46]

The third line of argument I want to consider concentrates a little less on the Wollheim machine and the arithmetical blindness of its operations, and a little more on the real-world prospects that a multi-member legislature might come up with some result that satisfies condition [J]. Like the previous argument (and unlike the utilitarian theory), this one also assumes that legislators are addressing themselves in good faith – as they deliberate and vote – to a single question with an objective answer.

The argument this time is due to Aristotle, and it is the one to which we referred in Chapter Four.[47] When Aristotle asks in Book III of the *Politics* whether political power should be in the hands of the many or in the hands of a few men (or even one man) of extraordinary wisdom and virtue, he entertains the possibility that there is more to be said for the multitude than might at first appear:

For the many, of whom each individual is not a good man, when they meet together may be better than the few good, if regarded not individually but collectively, just as a feast to which many contribute is better than a dinner provided out of a single purse. For each individual among the many has a share of excellence and practical wisdom, and when they meet together, just as they become in a manner one man, who has many feet, and hands, and senses, so too with regard to their character and thought. Hence the many are better judges than a single man of music and poetry; for some understand one part, and some another, and among them they understand the whole.[48]

---

[46] See Estlund et al., 'Democratic Theory and the Public Interest', for a consideration of the view that the applicability of Condorcet's theorem actually precludes deliberation among the citizens. That view is incorrect. It does not matter at all how the individual competencies have been achieved, whether by discussion or by innate talent. What matters for the Condorcet result is that the individual competencies be determined at the moment of voting, and that the votes be logically independent of one another.

[47] See also Waldron, 'The Wisdom of the Multitude', 563.

[48] Aristotle, *The Politics*, Bk. III, Ch. 11, 66 (1281b1–10).

What lies behind this is the idea that a number of individuals may bring a diversity of perspectives to bear on the complex issues under consideration, and that they are capable of pooling these perspectives to come up with better decisions than any one of them could make on his own.

Suppose, for example, that the Athenian *ecclesia* is considering whether to mount an invasion of Sicily. One man may know the geography of the Sicilian coastline; another may know the character of the island's inhabitants; a third may have experience of amphibious expeditions to other regions; a fourth may be acquainted with the current state of the Athenian fleet; a fifth may be a bitter veteran of past military catastrophes; a sixth may know what is to be gained from the expedition; and so on. No one person may have all this information and experience himself. The most rational way to make the decision, then, is to pool the knowledge of the various individuals.[49]

That is why Aristotle takes it as the mark of man's political nature that he has been endowed with the faculty of *speech*.[50] Each can communicate to another experiences and insights that complement or qualify those that the other already possesses, and when this happens in dense interaction throughout a community, it enables the group as a whole to attain a degree of wisdom and practical knowledge that surpasses even that of the most excellent individual member.

Now, there are two ways we can model what goes on in this pooling of knowledge and experience: (i) *individual synthesis* and (ii) *group synthesis*.

i. *Individual Synthesis.* Each legislator listens carefully to the views of each of the others, and forms them into a synthesis which is then reflected in his voting. If he possesses a modicum of rationality and comprehension, the view that he ends up holding should count as authoritative, at least in comparison to the views of any persons who have not been exposed to a diversity of perspectives in this way. In addition, the view of a majority of such legislators would have whatever authority stems from the fact that it appears to embody the most persuasive of the various syntheses achieved in this way.

ii. *Group Synthesis.* Alternatively, if the issue is a complex and subtle one, an authoritative synthesis may emerge at the level of group action without necessarily emerging at the level of individual understanding at all. This is the model of public deliberation – sometimes referred to as 'the market place of ideas' – presented by John Stuart Mill:

Truth, in the great practical concerns of life, is so much a question of the reconciling and combining of opposites that very few have minds sufficiently capacious

[49] This and the paragraphs that follow are adapted from Waldron, 'Religious Contributions to Political Deliberation'. See also Waldron, 'The Wisdom of the Multitude'.
[50] Aristotle, *Politics*, Bk. I, Ch. ii, 1253a.

and impartial to make the adjustment with an approach to correctness, and it has to be made by the rough process of a struggle between combatants fighting under hostile banners.[51]

Here the suggestion is that people simply fling their experiences and opinions into the public forum and, whether others understand them precisely or not, they will have their effect, and the truth will emerge by a sort of 'invisible hand' process, analogous to that by which Adam Smith thought efficiency would emerge from the operation of the market. The difference between this model and the individual synthesis model is that Mill does not presuppose that each person's contribution is being carefully taken on board by every other person and synthesized by him with his own view before he sends his modified opinion out to engage with the views of others in a similar way. According to Mill's model, quite incommensurable ideas may yet have a dialectical effect on one another, so that something better emerges in the discussion, even though the 'adjustment' between the various views has not been made by the deliberate synthetic activity of any 'single mind'.

If anything like this happens, then once again there is a reason to accord to the output of such a process the sort of authority intimated in thesis [J], even though there is no such reason for according authority to the particular views of any individual participant.

5. THE AUTHORITY OF THE GROUP

I hope it is clear now what my argument against Marmor's thesis is going to be. It is not simply that useful legislation can be conceived to emerge non-intentionally, through the impersonal or mechanical processes we have been discussing. I also want to argue that in the case of each of these processes, any reason we have for according Raz-ian authority to the resultant legislation is also a reason for discounting the authority of the views or intentions of particular legislators considered on their own.

There is an intriguing point about the rule of law here. The model of authority used by Raz and Marmor presupposes that there is one person, X, whose knowledge or situation is such that any ordinary citizen, Y, should trust the directives of X rather than his (Y's) own reasoning. But it is an important part of our normative concept of legal authority that legislators themselves should be bound by the laws they enact.[52] On the

---

[51] Mill, *On Liberty*, Ch. 2, 58.

[52] See Hayek, *The Constitution of Liberty*, 155: 'The chief safeguard is that the rules must apply to those who lay them down and those who apply them – that is, to the government as well as the governed . . .'. There is a similar point in Locke's discussion of the desirability of vesting legislative authority in a representative assembly. Locke argued that legislators

Raz/Marmor approach, it is impossible that a law could have *authority vis-à-vis* a legislator, for it makes no sense to say that X has better reason to trust the directives of X than he has to trust his own reasoning on the matter that X is addressing. By contrast, the three arguments I have presented have the attractive ability not only to satisfy thesis [J] concerning the normal justification of authority, but also to make it clear why laws should have authority over the legislators who vote for them.

Let me now go through the arguments in turn, to discuss their implications for the respect we should accord to the views, hopes, intentions, and other non-canonical opinions of the individual legislators.

A. *The Utilitarian Argument.* On this account, each individual legislator is voting either his own interest or the interests of his particular constituents. But the authority of the resultant legislation is based on its claim to represent the *general* interest. The reasons that led the legislator to vote as he did, then, are not the same reasons that there are for respecting the result: the result should be respected because it embodies a conclusion about *social* utility, whereas the former claims to be counted on the ground that it embodies individual or sectional utility. The ground of the law's authority, therefore, is not reflected in the views or purposes of any particular legislator.

Maybe in very simple cases we can say that the general interest just *is* the shared interest of a majority of voters. In a straightforward pork barrel case, for example, the issue may be whether to benefit the East-Coasters with a new highway or to benefit the West-Coasters with a new dam (when we cannot do both). If the preponderance of individual preferences favours the latter, it might be thought that we *can* take the selfish purposes of the West-Coast voters as our best guide to the implementation of the socially-favoured policy. The social decision is about who to benefit; once that has been decided, we might as well take the interests of the victors as our best guide to what the general utility requires.

But a case has to be staggeringly simple to have this feature. If the legislative choice is complex, if benefits and costs are indirect as well as immediate, or if the general interest dictates any form of compromise, then the pork-barrel authority of the individual voters in the majority (such as it is) simply evaporates.

---

ought to be bound by the rules they enact in much the same way that ordinary subjects are bound. After bitter experience people found that they 'could never be safe nor at rest, nor think themselves in Civil Society, till the Legislature was placed in collective Bodies of Men, call them Senate, Parliament, or what you please. By which means every single person became subject, equally with other the meanest Men, to those Laws, which he himself, as part of the Legislative had established.' See Locke, *Two Treatises of Government*, II, para. 94, 329–40. See also Austin, *The Province of Jurisprudence Determined*, VI, 212–21.

B. *Condorcet's Theorem.* Condorcet's theorem amounts precisely to the claim that one will do better by following the majority decision than by following the judgement of a given legislator. What is more, *ceteris paribus* the wiser the legislators are on average, the more reason there is to follow the majority decision than to follow the views of any legislator chosen at random.

Suppose, however, that one is not picking one's legislator out at random, but choosing a member of the majority. (This after all is Marmor's suggestion as to *which legislators* are the ones whose intentions we should defer to.[53]) Surely Marmor could argue that the fact that a given legislator, L, is a member of the successful majority, shows (by Condorcet's theorem) that one will do as well by following L's view as by following the view that emerged by majority voting.

This argument would be faulty, for two reasons. First, the Condorcet theorem concerns *ex ante* probabilities and turns on the multiplicity of ways in which a majority can be constructed. Once a result has been arrived at by majority voting, the fact that L was a member of *the particular majority* that supported the result confers no additional authority on his judgement beyond the individual competence with which he began.

Secondly, the only way to determine whether L is a member of the majority – for the purposes of this argument – is by looking at whether his view matches the precise terms of the decision that has been arrived at by voting. It is only with regard to that issue that individual and majority competencies have been established. To the extent that his view varies from this, nothing can be inferred as to its reliability. If it is even subtly different, then the numbers may differ – and the whole gist of the Condorcet result is that small differences may make a big difference, so to speak. This difficulty, moreover, cannot be evaded by insisting that we consult L's intentions only when they correspond exactly to the issue that was voted on. The whole point about appeals to legislative intent is that evidence about L's intentions can cast *extra* light on the interpretive difficulties that courts are facing only to the extent that L's intentions are somewhat different from those represented conventionally by the *ipsissima verba* of the statute.

Let me put this last point in a way that takes it slightly outside the mechanics of the Condorcet framework. All suggestions about consulting the intentions of legislators are suggestions about consulting views, purposes and ideas that are not directly disclosed in the text of the legislation

---

[53] There is an interesting and subtle discussion in Marmor, *Interpretation and Legal Theory*, 159–65. Though he recognizes certain difficulties, Marmor's view seems to be that a legislator's intention is worth consulting when the legislator in question is a member of the majority who voted for the statute, and when the intention in question is also held by most (all?) other members of that majority.

itself. (Else what would be the point?) But it is only the text that has been voted on, and it is only relative to that text that we can talk about a majority view. Relative to any other understanding, the identification of a view as being held by the majority is always tendentious, and it is unlikely that its identification as such will ever be less controversial than the issue on which its alleged authority is supposed to cast light.

C. *Aristotelian Synthesis.* Once again the immediate argument is obvious. Aristotle's doctrine of the wisdom of the multitude is precisely the view that a group decision is sometimes more to be trusted than the judgement of its most knowledgeable and distinguished member. The latter, then, should defer like a good citizen to the decision in which he participated; and if *he* should defer, then surely every member of the group should defer. The opinions and intentions, then, that he is subordinating to the text, can hardly be taken by us as a basis for supplementing it.

Substantively, the point here is that a particular legislator's intentions may reveal only a partial view of the synthesis embodied in the legislation. To interpret the legislation in the light of such intentions would be to distort an integrated whole by biasing it towards one of its parts.

Admittedly, this does not take account of the *ex post* situation. For after the deliberation and the pooling of knowledge and experience have taken place, it may be true that some (or perhaps even every one) of the legislators is better informed on the issue than he or anyone else would be coming to it cold, with the benefit only of his own unaided judgement. That is the implication of model (i), of *individual* synthesis, which we considered towards the end of section 4. It may be thought, moreover, that such individual syntheses have to emerge at *some* stage or other in the process, otherwise voting by individual members would not ever reveal the wisdom of the multitude. John Stuart Mill's model (ii) might be all very well as a description of the informal emergence of veridical beliefs in a culture. But it is one of our basic assumptions about a legislature that its decisions are taken by *explicit* processes of voting. There are no invisible hands here; there are nothing but real individual hands on the voting buttons.

All the same, an awareness of the second model helps us realize how narrowly circumscribed the first may be for the purposes of statutory interpretation. For if a judge appeals beyond the text of a statute to the intentions of particular legislators, he will be appealing to things said or done *during* the course of the bill's passage. At that stage, the decisive synthesis may not have emerged or crystallized in individual minds, and we may be dealing with what can only be described pro tem as 'the reconciling and combining of opposites . . . by the rough process of a struggle between combatants fighting under hostile banners'.[54] At that stage, to

---

[54] Mill, *On Liberty*, Ch. 2, 58.

take the inscriptions on any one banner as indicative of the ultimate synthesis underlying the statute may be most unreliable. If, on the other hand,
one waits for the final synthesis to emerge, one will be waiting in effect for
the text of the final statute. So even if model (i) is the correct image of
Aristotelian synthesis, it gives little comfort to anyone who wants to establish the authority of legislators' intentions expressed otherwise than in the
chapter and verse of the text that embodies what the legislature ultimately
decides.

6. LEGISLATURES

I want to conclude with some remarks about the assumptions I have been
making about the character of modern legislation. I assumed – as I have
assumed throughout the book – that any legislature worth discussing is a
large multi-member assembly, comprising hundreds of persons with
diverse views, affiliations, and allegiances. I assumed too that such a body
would need formally specified procedures in order to determine what
counted as its decisions. And I have assumed implicitly that any bills it
considered and any statutes it enacted would be complex in their contents
and accordingly complex in the process of their passage. These assumptions tend to undermine any talk about 'the intentions of the author' of a
statute. To the extent that there is one author, it is the legislature considered as a body and as distinct from the individual members (or any subset
of the individual members) that it comprises. So far as that 'author' is concerned, all we have to go on are its formally specified actions; there is no
question of our being able to discern or attribute to it any thoughts, intentions, motives, or beliefs beyond that. I argued in section 3 that we would
do best to abandon all talk of such intentionality when we are considering
such bodies. A slightly more conciliatory way of putting the same point is
that we abandon all talk of legislative intentions apart from the intentionality that is part and parcel of the linguistic meaning (i.e. the conventional
or, in Gricean terms, 'sentence-meaning')[55] of the legislative text itself.
Beyond the meanings embodied conventionally in the text of the statute,
there is no state or condition corresponding to 'the intention of the legislature' to which anything else – such as what particular individuals or
groups of legislators said, wrote, or did – could possibly provide a clue.

The point, in other words, is this. There simply is no fact of the matter
concerning a legislature's intentions apart from the formal specification of
the act it has performed. Certainly, the specification yielded by the decision-procedure (that is, by the legislature's constitution) will be of an

---

[55] Grice, *Studies in the Way of Words*, 86 ff.

action under a certain intentional description, for legislation is, as I said earlier, a speech-act. The intentional description will be that such-and-such words were used with their conventional English meaning. That, however, is *all there is to say* about the institution's intentions. In the case of a natural person, we can go beyond that. We can always ask, 'Well what did you have in mind, what were you thinking of, when you did (or said) X?' if the meaning of X is unclear. The person's answer, though not necessarily definitive of the contents of his intention at the time, at least provides us with a clue; for there is *some* link in the case of a natural person, though certainly not a direct link, between intention and occurrent thought. In the case of a legislature or a corporation, there is no such clue, for there is nothing amounting to *the institution's occurrent thoughts.*

What are we to say, then, about the particular thoughts and hopes of individual legislators? Do they bear no relation at all to the legislature's action or intentionality? The answer is complicated. The intentional speech-acts of the legislature are constitutional functions of the intentional voting-acts of the individual members; but what matters here is simply the intentionality of 'yea' or 'nay' in relation to a given text, not any hopes, aspirations or understandings that may have accompanied the vote. A legislature is impotent – incapable of action – unless there is a rule for aggregating or combining the votes of its members: the principle of majority-decision, for example. But it does not need, in addition, any rule for combining their thoughts, hopes and understandings into something that would count as the thoughts or purposes of the institution.[56] Its intentionality – such as it is – is quite secure beyond that. Once again, the same point can also be stated in a more conciliatory form. Of course individual legislators have thoughts and intentions and of course those can be loosely associated with the human authorship of the statute. The point is that there is no way of going beyond that sociological platitude to settle any interpretive dispute. People only appeal to legislators' intentions when there is a disagreement, for example, in a court, about what purpose (or whatever) to attribute to the statute. If the two competing views (or any pair like them) are represented among the non-canonical intentions of the legislators, then there is no way any *one* such view can be singled out as authoritative for the purpose of settling the dispute.

The defender of legislative intent may make one last reply.[57] Surely – he will say – it matters whether the view we have in mind corresponds to the intentions of the majority or the minority in the legislature. Surely the majority view is – by reason of the rules that allow it to prevail – the more canonical.

---

[56] Cf. the largely ironic attempt to develop formulae for 'intentional majorities' in Brest, 'The Misconceived Quest for the Original Understanding', 213. See also fn. 53 above.

[57] This is not a reply that Marmor would make: see Marmor, 'Authorities and Persons'.

I think this is based on a deep misapprehension about the political authority of a legislature and about the principle of majority-decision. A statute passed in Parliament is an *Act of Parliament*, not an act of the majority party. Certainly, it claims whatever authority it has in the community on the basis of that non-partisan characterization (and I am thinking now of the deeper sense of authority explicated, above, in section 6 of Chapter Five). If we think, for example, that ordinary citizens supporting a minority party are bound to respect legislation sponsored by the majority, it is because they owe that respect to *the legislature*, and to the procedures and institutional forms that constitute it, not because they owe it to the majority as such.[58] Even if the legislative and elective procedures are majoritarian, the citizen's allegiance is to the principle of majority-decision not to the (members of the) majority.

Partly this is a matter of the complexity of modern legislation, of the multiplicity of views and considerations that must be brought to bear in debates and committee stages, and of the contribution that may be made by members of minority parties to the content of a bill through rhetoric, deal-making or amendment. Our discussion of Aristotelian synthesis here and in Chapter Four captures, I think, how important this can be, and how it undermines any simple appeal to the views of a few privileged members as providing us with a canonical legislative intention.

But above all it is a recognition – once again – that the elementary circumstance of modern politics is *plurality*[59] and that the form of legislation, as of all collective decision-making, is *e pluribus unum*. The authority of a law is its emergence, under specified procedures, as a *'unum'* out of a plurality of ideas, concerns, and proposals, in circumstances where we recognize a need for one decision made together, not many decisions made by each of us alone. The *'unum'* does not abolish the plurality, nor is it insensitive to it. It is one *decision* we need, not necessarily one personality, and so it is not merely as a matter of logic that we should refrain from attributing mental states to the legislature. By the same token, however, there is no justification for privileging *the mental states of any faction* in the legislature as canonical with regard to the decision that has been made by the whole. The decision is made in the name, and for the sake, of the entire community, and one hopes it has been made in a way that encourages

---

[58] Cf. Hobbes, *Leviathan*, 121: 'A Common-wealth is said to be instituted, when a Multitude of men do Agree, and Covenant, every one with every one, that to whatsoever Man, or Assembly of Men, shall be given by the major part, the Right to Present the Person of them all (that is to say, to be their Representative;) every one, as well he that Voted for it, as he that Voted against it, shall Authorise all the Actions and Judgements, of that Man, or Assembly of men, in the same manner, as if they were his own, to the end, to live peaceably among themselves, and be protected against other men.'

[59] Cf. Arendt, *The Human Condition*, 234: 'No man can be sovereign because not one man, but men, inhabit the earth . . .'.

rather than precludes a plurality of contributions from a variety of directions. What the decision is – what *we* have done – is the text of the statute
as determined by the institution's procedures.[60] Those procedures make
us *one* in action, and their identification of something as the text of a statute
makes us *one* as the authors of a deed. Before that, however, and beyond
that, we are many, and no further status as a part of the *unum* can be attributed to anything else that any of us says or thinks.

The other side of this coin is that we should not underestimate the difficulties in the way of a body of legislators understanding one another as
they proceed through the stages of law-making. I said in section 2 (it is
something I also elaborated in Chapter Four) that we must assume we are
not dealing with persons who are transparent to one another, or who share
a comprehensive body of common understandings. Legislators will come
to the chamber from different communities, with different ideologies, and
different perspectives on what counts as a good reason or a valid consideration in political argument. The only thing they have in common, in their
diversity and in the welter of rhetoric and mutual misunderstanding that
counts for modern political debate, is the given text of the measure currently under consideration. That is constituted by the conventions of the
shared official language as the only landmark, the only point of reference
or co-ordination, in a sea of possible misunderstanding – and even then it
is fragile enough and always liable to fly apart on account of the fragility
of shared meanings. The point is that the text of the statute, carefully
drafted, proposed and amended in accordance with the most formalistic
procedures, has a canonical status in legislation that is different in kind
from any common view or shared sense of purpose that one might discern
in the committee rooms or in the parliamentary corridors. The latter are
always tendentious, always likely to be the exclusive province of a few
like-minded legislators whose cozy understandings tend to defeat the
purpose of a solemn gathering of *all* the nation's representatives. By
appealing to such views, the courts take the side of what was 'implicit' or
'understood', and that may be harmless enough in a small homogeneous
legislature. But it strikes me that, in a multicultural society, legislators are
entitled to insist on the authoritativeness of the text and nothing but the
text as the only thing that one can be sure has been at the forefront of each
member's legislative endeavours.

One final point. I hinted at the beginning of this paper that some
American judges make a practice of appealing to certain statements on the
legislative record (a formal committee report, for example, or the unchal-
lenged statement of a bill's manager) which do not traditionally count as
part of text of the statute they are considering. It seems to me that Ronald

[60] See above Ch. 4.

Dworkin has this exactly right when he says in effect that the judges are developing a practice of recognizing such statements as *acts of the legislature* and that legislators are responding to that recognition by producing statements that are intended to be taken in that way.[61] Nothing I have said is incompatible with these practices: they represent in effect a gradual modification of the legal system's rule of recognition[62] from the judges' side, and, as far as the legislature is concerned, they represent a gradual modification of its constitutive procedures.

To the extent that these practices are well-established, they may require us to modify our view (perhaps quite subtly) about what counts as *the text* of our statute.[63] But they do not require us to deny that our best guide to what counts as that text are the reasons (related to the *e pluribus unum* considerations I mentioned a moment ago) for identifying certain things and not others as *acts* of the legislators in their *collective* capacity. Most importantly for the purposes of this chapter, such practices lend no weight at all to Marmor's argument that the intentions of a legislator might have authority over and above their status as disclosed in whatever turns out to count in fact as the authoritative text of the legislation itself.

What I hope to have shown, then, is that the force of Marmor's argument is narrowly confined to those very rare cases where legislation is produced by an individual author whose knowledge and expertise provide the same reason for respecting his intentions as for respecting the text he has produced. More positively, what I hope will follow from this is a greater recognition in jurisprudence of the conditions relating to plurality that are the very stuff and circumstance of our politics.

[61] Dworkin, *Law's Empire*, 342 ff.
[62] But I doubt that Dworkin would accept *this* part of my characterization. For his views on Hart's 'rule of recognition', see *Law's Empire*, 34–5.
[63] However, see Scalia, *A Matter of Interpretation*, 29–37 for a powerful and scathing critique of these practices.

II. Disagreement in Principle

Chapter Seven

Rawls's *Political Liberalism*

Disagreements come in all shapes and sizes. In this book I am concerned with disagreements about matters like social policy, social justice, and individual rights. In Part I, we considered the use of legislative assemblies as ways of arriving at decisions that can stand in the name of a whole society, even when the members of the society disagree about what the decisions should be. In Part III we will consider the view that a special method of decision-making must be reserved for disagreements about rights. Before turning to that issue, however, I want to consider some more abstract questions about the nature of principled disagreements and their relation to our understanding of truth, politics, law, and civic obligation.

What is the relation between disagreements of political principle and what we might call comprehensive philosophical disagreements about the good in a pluralistic society? I want to ask that question with particular reference to the recent work of John Rawls. Thus I use the phrase 'comprehensive philosophical disagreements about the good' as Rawls used it, to mean differences between various well-worked-out views about ultimate value or various conceptions of the nature and meaning of life. It includes, most prominently, religious disagreements; but it also includes disagreements among various secular conceptions of the good, such as hedonism, aestheticism, intellectualism, and various ethics of self-development and self-fulfilment. What is the relation between differences of these kinds and the disagreements we have in politics (and in political philosophy) concerning the fundamental principles of justice and right?

Here are a couple of models, a couple of ways of thinking about the relation between disagreements of the two kinds:

(1) In the first model, each conception of the good is associated with or generates a particular vision of the just society. Catholics, for example, have a particular conception of the good, and for many that conception issues in a particular vision of law and justice, expounded (say) in the jurisprudence of Thomas Aquinas. Muslims proclaim a comprehensive religious vision, and this generates for them a particular vision of the well-ordered society, a conception of law and justice which they refer to as *Sharia*. Also, on this model, someone who holds a secular view of human needs may develop a conception of justice which corresponds to that view;

his convictions about justice may be expected to differ somewhat from convictions of justice held by people who base them on different visions of human fulfilment. Disagreement about justice, on this first model, then, is just another aspect of disagreement about the good. It is what disagreement about the good amounts to in the social and political sphere.

(2) In the second model, particular theories of justice are not seen as tied to or generated by particular conceptions of the good. Instead, they stand apart from competing religious and philosophical conceptions. They present themselves as solutions to the various problems which disagreement about the good generates in society. Conceptions of justice, on this second model, are viewed as rival attempts to specify a quite separate set of principles for the basic structure of a society whose members disagree about the good. The rivalry between competing conceptions of justice is seen as independent of (and cutting across) the rivalry between competing conceptions of the good. Thus among Catholics there are socialists and libertarians, who, although they agree about ultimate values, disagree fundamentally about the principles that should govern the economic structure of a modern plural society. In the debate about justice, a Catholic socialist may have more in common with someone who is a Marxist-Leninist and thus an atheist, than he has with a fellow Catholic who is politically conservative. The disagreement between socialist Catholics and politically conservative Catholics – or between socialists and political conservatives generally – is motivated quite separately, on the second model, from disagreements about the good.

Which (if any) of these models is implied or assumed in the arguments of John Rawls's book *Political Liberalism*? The answer seems obvious: the second model is the one that corresponds to Rawls's view of the matter.

That answer *seems* obvious, in part because Rawls explicitly rejects the first model as a way of characterizing his own theory, justice as fairness (JAF). JAF is not the upshot of any particular conception of the good; it is presented as a 'free-standing' conception (12),[1] intended to represent the terms of an 'overlapping consensus' among the many ethical and religious conceptions that compete for adherents in society. And Rawls presents this not only as a claim about JAF; he maintains that *any* view of the kind he is defending must reject the first model as a way of specifying the agenda for discussions of justice:

[T]he problem of political liberalism is: How is it possible that there may exist over time a stable and just society of free and equal citizens profoundly divided by reasonable though incompatible religious, philosophical, and moral doctrines? This is a problem of political justice, not a problem about the highest good.

[1] In this chapter, numbers in parentheses in the text are page references to Rawls, *Political Liberalism*.

Thus Rawls's approach to justice seems to fit the second model inasmuch as it defines a task or an agenda in whose performance people may be at odds in a way that (as I said) cuts cross the disagreements which they have about the good.

2. CAN THERE BE REASONABLE DISAGREEMENT ABOUT JUSTICE?

On the other hand, fitting Rawls's account into the second model presupposes that he actually contemplates disagreements about justice in a well-ordered society. In fact, it is not at all clear that he does. I mean that last statement to be as tentative as it sounds. Rawls of course does not deny that people disagree about what justice requires. But he does not say much about these disagreements in his own discussion. Compared with what he says about ethical, religious, and philosophical disagreements, Rawls's treatment of disagreements about justice is really quite insignificant.

To see this, imagine the following way in which the second of our models could be defended. One might offer an *explanation* of people's disagreements about justice that differed from the explanation one offered of their disagreements about the good. The dissonance between these explanations would then yield a prediction that the two types of disagreement could be expected to cut across one another.

Now, as saw in Chapter Five, Rawls devotes a lot of attention to the aetiology of disagreement in society.[2] He asks, 'Why does not our conscientious attempt to reasʊɴ ... 'th one another lead to reasonable agreement? It seems to do so in natural science, at least in the long run' (55). Rawls uses the phrase 'the burdens of judgement' as a way of articulating his answer to this question. The burdens of judgement are 'the many hazards involved in the correct (and conscientious) exercise of our powers of reason and judgment in the ordinary course of political life' (56). Human life engages multiple values and it is natural that people will disagree about how to balance or prioritize them. What's more their different positions, perspectives, and experiences in life will give them different bases from which to make these delicate judgements. Together factors like these make disagreement in good faith not only possible but predictable:

Different conceptions of the world can reasonably be elaborated from different standpoints and diversity arises in part from our distinct perspectives. It is unrealistic ... to suppose that all our differences are rooted solely in ignorance and perversity, or else in the rivalries for power, status, or economic gain. [58]

Thus, Rawls concludes, 'many of our most important judgments are made under conditions where it is not to be expected that conscientious persons

---

[2] See above, Ch. 5, ss. 9 and 12.

with full powers of reason, even after free discussion, will arrive at the same conclusion' (58).

This account, as it stands, could characterize political as well as ethical and religious disagreements; it could characterize differences about justice as well as differences about the good. However, Rawls quickly orients the burdens-of-judgement argument purely in the direction of disagreements about the good. 'The evident consequence of the burdens of judgment,' he says, 'is that reasonable persons do not all affirm the same comprehensive doctrine' (60). A well-ordered society cannot be expected to be a society of religious or philosophical consensus. Nowhere, as far as I can tell, does he infer the equally evident conclusion that reasonable persons cannot be expected to agree about the proper balance to be assigned in social life to their respective comprehensive conceptions. Nowhere does he infer that for the same reasons, in a well-ordered society, reasonable people might be expected to disagree fundamentally about the basic terms and principles of their association.[3]

One of the things Rawls takes from the burdens-of-judgement argument is that 'a public and shared basis of justification that applies to comprehensive doctrines is lacking in the public culture of a democratic society' (61). This provides positive evidence for attributing to Rawls the belief that issues of justice are *not* subject to the burdens of judgement. The argument to that effect goes as follows.

According to Rawls, issues of justice are to be dealt with on the basis of public reason: 'As far as possible, the knowledge and ways of reasoning that ground our affirming the principles of justice . . . are to rest on the plain truths now widely accepted, or available, to citizens generally' (225). To apply the burdens-of-judgement idea in this area would suggest that some of the reasons which people appeal to in articulating their views about justice are not, and cannot be, widely shared in this sense. Thus, if he is to sustain the idea of public reason as a basis for argument about justice, Rawls must deny that the burdens of judgement affect such argumentation. If the burdens of judgement preclude the use of public reason in a given area, it would seem to follow that the burdens of judgement do not apply in areas where the idea of public reason is appropriate.[4]

---

[3] An arguable exception is a passage towards the end of Ch. IV of *Political Liberalism* ('The Idea of an Overlapping Consensus') in which Rawls hazards the suggestion that 'different social and economic interests may be assumed to support different liberal conceptions' and to 'give rise to ideals and principles markedly different from those of justice as fairness' (ibid., 167). He does not, however, dwell on this possibility.

[4] That is, Rawls seems to be committed to saying:

For all areas of dispute x, the existence of the burdens of judgement in x → the lack of public reason in x

from which it would follow:

For all areas of dispute x, the existence of public reason in x → the absence of the burdens of judgement in x.

This leaves us with the rather uncongenial conclusion that there is no such thing as reasonable disagreement in politics. The burdens of judgement explain how reasonable disagreement is possible. But the ideal of public reason seems to presuppose that that explanation does not apply to the public issues of justice and right that are under discussion in politics.

3. PUBLIC REASON

I am reluctant to attribute this conclusion to Rawls. Surely, there would be no need for public reason if there were *not* disagreement about justice. If they did not disagree about justice, what would people have to reason or argue (or vote) about in a democratic society? If, however, there *is* disagreement about justice, and people make proper use of public reason to articulate and resolve it, it would seem churlish to deny that such disagreement was – initially, at any rate – reasonable.

As far as I can tell, Rawls says that the idea of public reason is incompatible at most with the existence of reasonable disagreement about *the fundamentals* of justice. It is not incompatible with reasonable disagreement about the way the details are worked out:

Accepting the idea of public reason and its principle of legitimacy emphatically does not mean . . . accepting a particular liberal conception of justice down to the last details of the principles defining its content. We may differ about these principles and still agree in accepting a conception's more general features. [226]

But while he denies that the specific content of JAF is definitive of public reason, Rawls is unabashed about offering the general principles of JAF – 'the values expressed by the principles and guidelines that would be agreed on in the original position' (227) – as a criterion of whether political argument is being conducted in accordance with the idea of public reason or not.

We should pause to consider how remarkable this view is. In the world we know, people definitely disagree – and disagree radically – about justice. Moreover their disagreement is not just about details but about fundamentals. There are places where Rawls acknowledges this diversity. He says near the beginning of *Political Liberalism* that '[w]e turn to political philosophy when our shared political understandings . . . break down' (44). However, in the other passages we have been discussing, his view seems to be that these differences are to be aired and debated only within the medium of 'principles and guidelines . . . agreed on in the original position' (227). Can he really mean that? Important though Rawls's conception has been, we all know that there is barely a handful of academic political philosophers who accept the original position idea as Rawls expounds it or his view of the principles and guidelines that would be accepted therein. It seems odd to select this extraordinarily controversial conception as the basis of one's view of public reason, that is, as the basis of one's normative view about the terms in which citizens may properly conduct and attempt to resolve their disagreements with one another about justice. More abstractly, it is surely a mistake to identify the norms framing the public debate about justice with values and principles which are constitutive (even if only *broadly* constitutive, let alone constitutive in detail) of a particular position in that debate.

In the passage we have been discussing, Rawls acknowledges the controversial nature of his suggestion about the content of the criterion which determines whether people are arguing in accordance with the ideal of public reason or not:

Many will prefer another criterion. . . . It is inevitable and often desirable that citizens have different views as to the most appropriate political conception; for the public political culture is bound to contain different fundamental ideas that can be developed in different ways. [227]

Quite so. Why, then, in the face of such controversy select one of the participants as the criterion to set the terms in which the controversy will subsequently be conducted?

Rawls's answer is: 'An orderly contest between [different fundamental political ideas] over time is a reliable way to find out which one, if any, is most reasonable' (227). As I understand it, the idea is as follows. *Ex ante*, there may be many apparently reasonable approaches to justice, Rawls's approach among them. A process of argument must therefore take place in political philosophy to sort out which one, if any, is acceptable as a fundamental conception for a well-ordered society. Part of what we are trying to sort out in that argument is which one of the competing approaches to justice would be acceptable as a consensual basis for public reason. If we come up with an answer, then we can say *ex post* that the other views are unreasonable, because they have failed as candidates for criterion of public reason. *Ex ante*, we *can* talk about reasonable disagreement concerning political fundamentals; but having settled on a view about fundamentals we are no longer in a position to talk in that way. *Ex post*, the only reasonable disagreements that remain are disagreements about the working out of the details of the conception that the first phase of argument has yielded.

I think this is Rawls's position. But I hope it is not. For it seems to be open to a serious objection.

4. RAWLS ON CONSTITUTIONAL DESIGN

Before I outline that objection,[5] let me back up a little. The view I have just been unravelling is not very different from the line Rawls took in Chapter Four of *A Theory of Justice*. There he noted – quite properly – that 'the question whether legislation is just or unjust, especially in connection with economic and social policies, is commonly subject to reasonable differences of opinion'.[6] The existence of such disagreement necessitates constitutional procedures (such as voting) which enable decisions to be made even when the members of the society are divided as to what the decisions should be. Now of course people disagree also about these procedural arrangements. Thus, Rawls says, the public-minded citizen addressing the justice of his society's structure faces questions of two kinds:

> First of all, he must judge the justice of legislation and social policies. But he also knows that his opinions will not always coincide with those of others, since men's judgments and beliefs are likely to differ especially when their interests are engaged. Therefore secondly, a citizen must decide which constitutional arrangements are just for reconciling conflicting opinions of justice. We may think of the political process as a machine which makes social decisions when the views of representatives and their constituents are fed into it. A citizen will regard some ways of designing this machine as more just than others. So a complete conception of justice is not only able to assess laws and policies but it can also rank procedures for selecting which political opinion is to be enacted into law.[7]

How and on what basis are proposals about political procedure to be evaluated? Rawls's answer in *A Theory of Justice* is that people 'are to choose the most effective just constitution, the constitution that . . . is best calculated to lead to just and effective legislation'.[8] Of course, we cannot guarantee that the results of any procedure will be just: 'Clearly any feasible political procedure may yield an unjust outcome.'[9] At best, the situation is one of imperfect procedural justice. The task is to find a constitution that will maximize the prospect that legislative decisions will be good ones.

Actually, the fact that we have no way of designing a political system guaranteed to yield the right results is not the only reason the situation is one of imperfect procedural justice. The matter is not just technical feasibility. Rawls thinks there are also *moral* reasons – indeed, reasons of justice – which require us to put up with a political system less likely to

---

[5] Which I do in s. 5, below.   [6] Rawls, *A Theory of Justice*, 198–9.
[7] Ibid., 196.
[8] Ibid., 197. (The ellipsis indicates the presence of an additional criterion of constitutional choice: the chosen constitution must not only be effective in yielding just choices, but it must also in itself do justice to those procedural rights – such as equal political participation – embodied in the first of the two substantive principles of JAF.)
[9] Ibid., 198.

yield substantively right answers about justice than one might design in the absence of such reasons. On Rawls's view, justice itself constrains the political procedures that are acceptable. He regards political power as a primary good regulated by the first principle of JAF, and he believes that the first principle generates 'a principle of (equal) participation', so far as the political constitution is concerned. It requires that *all* (adult, sane) individuals have the right to participate, either directly or through elected and accountable representatives, in making laws and other decisions about the structuring of their society.[10]

Moreover, on Rawls's scheme of things, political participation is not just one basic liberty among others. He rightly insists that there is an intimate connection between the principle of participation and the contractarian spirit of the original position hypothesis:

Justice as fairness begins with the idea that where common principles are necessary and to everyone's advantage, they are to be worked out from the viewpoint of a suitably defined initial situation of equality in which each person is fairly represented. The principle of participation transfers this notion from the original position to the constitution as the highest-order system of social rules for making rules. If the state is to exercise a final and coercive authority over a certain territory, and if it is in this way to affect permanently men's prospects in life, then the constitutional process should preserve the equal representation of the original position to the degree that this is practicable.[11]

The right to participate is in a sense 'the right of rights'[12] in Rawls's theory, for it is the direct descendant, in political practice, of the principle of popular sovereignty underlying the whole contractarian approach in political philosophy.[13]

---

[10]   Rawls, *A Theory of Justice*, 221 ff.

[11]   Ibid., 221–2. I am grateful to Frank Michelman for discussion on this point.

[12]   The phrase is William Cobbett's, from *Advice to Young Men and Women, Advice to a Citizen* (1829), quoted in Macfarlane, *The Theory and Practice of Human Rights*, 142. For further discussion of this idea, see Ch. 11 below.

[13]   Participation, then, is in some sense *special* in a contractarian theory. Rawls does not however infer from this that political participation is to be accorded greater weight than other basic liberties covered by the First Principle. On the contrary, he toys with the idea – suggested in different ways by Benjamin Constant and Isaiah Berlin – that in modern liberalism, political liberties should be accorded less importance, and that greater weight should be attached to other basic liberties and the protections they provide against oppression and interference. (See Constant, 'The Liberty of the Ancients Compared with that of the Moderns', esp. 316–17 and Berlin, *Four Essays on Liberty*, 129–31, cited by Rawls, *A Theory of Justice*, 229–30.) In *Political Liberalism*, Rawls indicates greater sympathy for the Constant/Berlin position that political liberties are properly ranked low among the other basic liberties and that their value is mainly instrumental. (See Rawls, *Political Liberalism*, 299.) In the earlier work, he is more agnostic: 'Different opinions about the value of the liberties will, of course, affect how different persons think the full scheme of freedom should be arranged. Those who place a higher worth on the freedom of participation will be prepared to take greater risks with the freedom of the person, say, in order to give political liberty a larger place' (Rawls, *A Theory of Justice*, 230).

But although Rawls thinks there are moral grounds for a procedural element in our design of political institutions, my point is that his conception is definitely not mere procedural justice. We are to choose or frame a constitution in a way that respects the claims of participation certainly, but we are to frame it also with an eye to the substantive justice of the outcomes that a given system is likely to yield. Of the various participatory schemes that are available, we are to choose the one most likely to yield substantively just conclusions.

How, though, can citizens agree on issues of constitutional choice if they disagree about the telos of such choice? A libertarian will seek participatory procedures that maximize the prospect of legislation that is just by his own free market standards, while a social democrat will seek participatory procedures that maximize the prospects for legislation embodying collective and egalitarian concern. This indicates to Rawls that disagreements about justice must be dealt with first, before issues of constitutional design are even addressed. Thus what he says about constitutional choice (that is, about the choice of legislative process) is predicated on the assumption that we *already* know and *already* agree about the basic principles of justice:

In framing a just constitution I assume that the two principles of justice already chosen define an independent standard of the desired outcome. If there is no such standard, the problem of constitutional design is not well posed, for this decision is made by running through the feasible just constitutions (given, say, by enumeration on the basis of social theory) looking for the one that in the existing circumstances will most probably result in effective and just social arrangements.[14]

Rawls concedes that people do have 'reasonable differences of opinion' about whether legislation is just; but he characterizes those as disagreements about how to apply Rawlsian principles in a complex world, not disagreements about which principles to apply.

Thus the approach in *A Theory of Justice* is almost exactly the same as *Political Liberalism*, where Rawls suggests that political differences are to be played out in a medium of public reason which not only accommodates, but is defined in terms of, 'principles and guidelines that would be agreed to in the original position' (227). Both books assume that there will come a point at which reasonable politics can presuppose that participants are agreed, at least at a general level, about which principles of justice they are to apply.

5. TO THE REAL WORLD

Suppose, for a moment, that we buy this. Obviously, it would be a mistake to infer anything from it for the problems about politics, procedure and

---

[14] Rawls, *A Theory of Justice*, 198.

constitutional choice that *we* face – we, in the real world, where people do not at all agree about the fundamentals of justice. To think – as *we* have to – about the politics of a society whose members differ radically and in principle about what justice requires is – in Rawls's terms – to move from ideal (or strict compliance) theory to non-ideal (partial compliance) theory. Both of his books are about 'a well-ordered society' – 'a society in which everyone accepts, and knows that everyone else accepts, the very same principles of justice' (35). It follows that the application of his arguments to a society like ours, in which people neither accept, nor think of themselves as accepting, the same principles of justice is quite problematic. Ours is a society whose politics are dedicated quite explicitly to grappling with fundamental *dis*agreements about justice. For this reason, it is not a well-ordered society in Rawls's sense.[15]

I wonder whether, on reflection, Rawls is happy with the width of this gap between the politics of a well-ordered society and the politics of a society like ours. There are two signs that he is not.

First, he himself seems quite willing to draw conclusions about American constitutional law from his arguments about public reason etc. Though any such inference should be regarded as quite reckless, given the divergence between the politics of a well-ordered society and the politics which the US Supreme Court actually has to address, Rawls seems unabashed about drawing them.

Secondly, Rawls is in general much less comfortable in his later work with the characterization of a well-ordered society which he gave in *A Theory of Justice*. He now denies what he then maintained – that in a well-ordered society people affirm the same conception of justice on the same moral and philosophical grounds. The point of *Political Liberalism* is to argue that in a well-ordered society people can (and probably must) affirm the same conception of justice on different moral and political grounds. I wonder whether Rawls might be willing to yield a further concession. Maybe what is definitive of political philosophy – the philosophy of *politics*, after all – is that it asks how a society can be well-ordered in its procedures for debate and decision-making when its citizens disagree, not only about the good, but also about justice. The first concession, Rawls says, was motivated by the need to come to terms with the pluralistic circumstances of '[a] modern democratic society' (xvi). But 'pluralism of comprehensive religious, philosophical, and moral doctrines' (xvi) is not the only pluralism with which we have to deal in a modern democratic society. We also have to deal with justice-pluralism and disagreement

---

[15] Justice Holmes is famous for his observation in *Lochner* v. *New York* (1905) 198 US 45, that '[t]he Fourteenth Amendment does not enact Mr. Herbert Spencer's *Social Statics*'. More important, however, is the generalization he drew from that – viz. that the constitution 'is made for people of fundamentally differing views'. (Ibid., 75–6).

about rights. Maybe political philosophy should be required to come to terms with that circumstance also.

6. THEORY AND POLITICS

Against all this and in defence of *Political Liberalism*, it may be argued that Rawls cannot simply confront disagreements about justice as a spectator – carefully noting the diversity of views, the extent of disagreement, etc. For he *is* a theorist of justice. He engages in these disagreements *as a partici-pant*, and as an uncompromising opponent of conceptions other than his own. He surely cannot be required to make room, in his own normative conception of a well-ordered society, for views about justice that are incompatible with his, views which from his point of view have simply got things wrong. If JAF is offered as a theory of justice, its principles must do *all the work there is to be done by principles of justice*. As a conception of just-ice, JAF is not required to be fair to or accommodate its rivals. If a well-ordered society is a just society – and if Rawls is right about justice – then a well-ordered society *will* be one in which the principles he defends, and not any others, hold sway. After all, nothing is more important than just-ice in the basic structuring of society. To form the belief that *justice* requires X rather than Y, is to form the belief that nothing less than X will do and that a compromise or accommodation with Y or anything else would be pernicious. Of course a given belief about what justice requires may be mistaken. But what one would be mistaken about, is what categorically and uncompromisingly ought to be done, so far as the basic structure of society is concerned.

That is what one might say in defence of Rawls's approach – an approach which characterizes a well-ordered society purely in terms of the principles of justice he thinks correct, without reference to the compe-tition between them and what he regards as their fundamentally mistaken rivals. He is simply claiming truth for his theory and the falsity of any theory that contradicts it.[16]

I have no objection to this as a way of thinking about justice. But I have misgivings about it as a way of thinking about politics, certainly as a way of thinking about the politics of justice. What is normally understood by politics is that it is an arena in which the members of some group debate and find ways of reaching decisions on various issues in spite of the fact that they disagree about the values and principles that the merits of those issues engage. (As I said in Chapter Five, the existence of such disagree-ment and the felt need for a common decision notwithstanding the

---

[16] See also the discussion in s. 8 of Ch. 9, below.

disagreement are the elementary 'circumstances of politics' – in the same way that moderate scarcity, reasonable pluralism and limited altruism are among what Rawls calls 'the circumstances of justice'.[17]) The empirical science of politics is the study of the ways in which this deliberation and decision-making actually take place. Normative reflection on politics amounts to reflection on the values and principles that are implicated in these processes of deliberation and decision-making. To imagine that deliberative politics (or any form of peaceful politics) is possible is to imagine that people can agree on some of these procedural points even though they disagree on the merits of the issues that the procedures are, so to speak, designed to house. It is to imagine, in other words, that the procedural issues and the substantive issues are in some sense separable.

Now I can certainly think about politics without ceasing to be the partisan of a particular conception of justice competing uncompromisingly with its rivals in the political arena. But I cannot do so if my thinking about political and constitutional procedure is conducted entirely in the shadow of my substantive convictions. For me to think about politics, there must be limits on the 'logical space' that my substantive views occupy. To think about politics, I must be willing at least part of the time to view even my own uncompromising convictions about justice as just one set of convictions among others. I must be willing to address, in a relatively impartial way, the question of what is to be done about the fact that people like me disagree with others in the society about justice. That concession can be a demanding one. It is not just a matter of organizing neutral rules for a debating club. Political debate must issue in decision. To engage in politics is to subscribe to procedural principles (majority-decision is an example) that might yield outcomes at odds with my own substantive convictions, outcomes that my own substantive convictions condemn.

But how – it might be asked – can one contemplate this *on a matter of justice*? If justice is the *first* virtue of social institutions, how can there be any political virtue or principle that requires one to support injustice simply on the ground that (for example) the other side won a vote in a parliament, congress or court? If justice is the first virtue of social institutions, then surely nothing – including political procedures, including voting – is more important.

This response – which I have heard from others but which I am not attributing to Rawls – rests on an impoverished conception of the dimensions of political importance. To say that view Y, which we think unjust, should prevail because it has greater political support, is not to rank political or procedural considerations ahead of justice on some single dimension of moral importance. It is to come at the issue from a different

---

[17] See Rawls, *Political Liberalism*, 66. See also Rawls, *A Theory of Justice*, 126–30. See also Barber's account of 'the conditions of politics' in *Strong Democracy*, 120–38.

direction. When we say that a view which we think incorrect should prevail on political grounds, we approach it not in terms of intrinsic importance or priority, but in light of the basic circumstance of politics – that even on the matters we think *most* important, a common decision may be necessary despite the existence of disagreement about what that decision should be. The problem defined by that circumstance is the problem of selecting a substantive principle of justice to act on (together) when we disagree about which principles are true or reasonable and which not. To say that in such a case *justice* is being subordinated to procedural values in political decision-making would be to beg the question of which of the positions competing for political support is to be counted as just.[18]

7. OVERLAPPING CONSENSUS

I began this chapter by looking at the relation between disagreements about justice and disagreements about the good. Two models were suggested: on the first, disagreements about justice are the upshot of disagreements about the good; on the second model, the two sorts of disagreements are independent of one another. We have seen that Rawls is probably not, after all, committed to the second model, at least not as a model of a well-ordered society. For on his account, a well-ordered society may exhibit disagreements about the good but it will not exhibit disagreements about the fundamentals of justice.

What about the kind of society with which we are familiar, in which *both* types of disagreement are present. Which of our two initial models is more accurate with regard to a less-than-well-ordered society like our own? Here, I do not think Rawls would want to rule out the first model, or at least some version of it. If a religious or philosophical tradition has nurtured a rich and resourceful conception of the good, it would be odd to expect its priests, ideologues, or philosophers not to have developed that conception also in a social or political direction. Social and political concerns are, after all, among the most pressing concerns we have: it would be odd if a tradition had views about what made life worth living but no views at all about the basis on which we ought to live our lives together. This seems indicated, too, by Rawls's use of the term 'comprehensive' to describe views about religion and value that compete in society. 'Comprehensive' seems to imply an ambition on the part of such conceptions to answer all the big questions, from which questions about justice can hardly be excluded. It is significant that one of Rawls's most prominent examples of a theory of the good is utilitarianism (13); and utilitarianism certainly implies (some would say, it just *is*) a view about justice.

[18] See Ch. 9, s. 4, for an elaboration of this argument. See also Ch. 11, s. 5.

But if the first model explains even a part of people's disagreements about justice, then there is an interesting consequence for Rawls's account of the transition (so to speak) from a less-than-well-ordered society, in which people disagree about the fundamentals of justice, to a well-ordered society in which one particular conception of justice – say, JAF – is enshrined as a framework for public reason. The consequence has to do with Rawls's distinction in *Political Liberalism* between an overlapping consensus and a *modus vivendi*. Both overlapping consensus and *modus vivendi* are models of the many-to-one relation between conceptions of the good and a single favoured conception of justice. Though Rawls is adamant that they are 'quite different' from one another (147), he conjectures that 'an initial acquiescence in a liberal conception of justice as a mere modus vivendi could change over time . . . into an overlapping consensus' (168).

One way of understanding that change is as follows. So long as each conception of the good generates its own conception of justice – that is, so long as each conception of the good is truly 'comprehensive' in the way I described in the second paragraph of this section – it is impossible for competing conceptions of the good to be related to a single conception of justice (such as JAF) in the strong moral relation that Rawls refers to as 'overlapping consensus'. Why? Because each conception of the good generates a direct competitor to the conception of justice which is putatively the recipient of allegiance in overlapping consensus.

Thus, among a range of rival conceptions of the good, $G_1, G_2, \ldots G_n$, we are likely to find that $G_1 \to J_1$, $G_2 \to J_2$, and so on (where $J_1, J_2, \ldots J_n$ are rival conceptions of justice). Each of these pairs – G_1/J_1, G_2/J_2, etc. – defines a *comprehensive* philosophical conception $C_1, C_2, \ldots C_n$. Now suppose there is a liberal conception of justice, JAF, which could in principle represent a genuine overlapping consensus as between G_1, G_2, etc. From the point of view of J_1, J_2, etc., allegiance to JAF will be, at best, a mere *modus vivendi*. For J_1 and J_2 contradict JAF: they are rivals to JAF as they are to each other. They cannot offer JAF the sincere moral support that an overlapping consensus presupposes without compromising their own claims about justice. Moreover, inasmuch as J_1 is an integral part of C_1, J_2 an integral part of C_2, etc., the comprehensive conceptions $C_1, C_2, \ldots C_n$ will not be able to support JAF in overlapping consensus either.

However, if JAF can secure itself for a period of time as a *modus vivendi* among $C_1, C_2, \ldots C_n$, it may cause each of the justice-components of those comprehensive conceptions to gradually lose ground, even within its generating conception. J_1, for example, may gradually come to seem redundant even to the followers of C_1 as its work *qua* conception of justice is done – albeit as a *modus vivendi* – by the liberal conception of justice JAF. This opens up the possibility that over time, C_1 will decompose into its constituent parts – G_1 and J_1 – with J_1 being quietly dropped, and the conception of the good, G_1, being left to forge a genuine moral allegiance to JAF. And similarly, for many of the other comprehensive conceptions.

If this process captures anything along the lines of what Rawls has in mind, it might also provide an additional basis for characterizing certain comprehensive conceptions of the good as unreasonable, from the point of view of JAF. 'Unreasonable' has two meanings in *Political Liberalism*. On the one hand, as we have seen, it refers to a conception whose divergence from other conceptions is not intelligible in light of the burdens of judgement. On the other hand, it refers to a conception which makes claims for itself and its adherents without regard to a fair balance between its claims and those made in behalf of other conceptions. I have argued elsewhere that these definitions of 'unreasonable' can come apart.[19] Here, though, I want to suggest that one way of defining 'unreasonable,' in the second sense, is that it applies to any comprehensive conception, C_i, that has lived with other conceptions in *modus vivendi* for some time *without* being willing to abandon (or allow to wither away) its own tendentious theory of justice, J_i.

8. POLITICS AND DISSENSUS

What I have just set out are some ideas on how we might think about the relation between disagreements about the good and disagreements about justice towards the end of the era or phase in which disagreement about justice remains a reasonable possibility.

However, these speculations about the withering away of reasonable disagreement about justice in a well-ordered society should not blind us to the fact that full-blooded disagreement about justice remains the most striking condition of our own politics. In these circumstances, we should be very careful about inferring anything for our politics – including our constitutional jurisprudence – from the purely theoretical possibility of a well-ordered society as John Rawls understands it. Because it may encourage or license such inferences, the argument in *Political Liberalism* needs to be hedged around with serious reservations and qualifications. Students of political philosophy need to be made aware of how much distance there is between the sort of theorizing about justice that goes on in works like *Political Liberalism* and the sort of theorizing that would be necessary if we were really to try making sense of the place that politics, process, and constitution have in a society like our own.

[19] See Waldron, 'Justice Revisited'.

Chapter Eight

The Irrelevance of Moral Objectivity

1. OBJECTIVITY AND REALISM

We disagree on matters of principle, but of course that does not mean there are no right answers. Of the various views about justice and rights that compete in our society, surely some are more acceptable than others. Surely indeed some of them are true and others false. That at any rate is a philosophical possibility. And – some will say – it is a possibility that should not be without consequence for politics.

I think this last claim is mistaken, and that is why I have called this chapter 'The *Irrelevance* of Moral Objectivity'. I hope no one will infer from that title that I am disparaging objectivity in the sense of fairness, impartiality, or even-handedness. The sense of 'objectivity' I mean is the sense invoked when people claim that some moral judgements are objectively true, while others are objectively false. Those who make this claim about objective truth and falsity are called moral realists – or at least, that is what they are called by philosophers. Most non-philosophers find this term bewildering: I imagine 'moral realist' has Machiavellian resonances in the minds of many people. Those who teach moral philosophy to law students often have to spend time explaining that moral realism has very little in common with *legal* realism, and indeed that it contradicts it in several respects. The legal version is much closer to what realism means to the ordinary person – namely, the ordinary sense in which 'Let's be realistic' means 'Let's be cynical.' At any rate, 'moral realism' is what philosophers call the thesis that there are such things as objective moral truth and objective moral falsity; and 'anti-realism' is the term for the philosophical denial of that thesis. Since moral realism looks as though it might have important ramifications for the way we think about political disagreement, it is worth taking some time to explore its implications for law, legality, and adjudication.

There are all sorts of ways of formulating the realist position, but for convenience the realist's belief in moral objectivity can be stated technically as follows:

There are facts which make some moral judgements (that is, some statements of value or principle) true and others false, facts which are independent of anyone's beliefs or feelings about the matters in question.[1]

---

[1] Some realists insist that the facts referred to in this formulation must be 'external' or 'mind-independent'; but this is too strong, since many realists do not want to deny that there

Anti-realists deny this. They deny that there are moral facts which determine the truth or falsity of the judgements people make. They say: *there are only moral judgements and the people who make them.* Some of the judgements that are made we like, and some we do not like. Some we repudiate and some we cherish. Some we ignore, and some we ride out to kill for. But there are no objective matters of fact which justify these attitudes or which make any of the judgements correct or any of them incorrect.

Anti-realists differ in what they then go on to say about the idea of moral truth. For some, talk of the truth or falsity of a moral judgement is as sensible as talk of the truth or falsity of an exclamation like 'Long live liberty!' or 'Down with President Clinton!' For others, the predicates 'true' and 'false' are not meaningless so much as redundant. To say, 'It is true that abortion is wrong' is just a particularly emphatic or ponderous way of aligning oneself with the claim 'Abortion is wrong'. It adds nothing of substance to a simple repetition of that judgement. Either way – whether we reject the idea of truth for moral judgements or read it disquotationally – the idea of an objective matter of fact which makes a moral judgement true or false and which a moral judgement purports to represent or to which it purports to correspond, is rejected.

2. LEGAL POSITIVISM AND MORAL JUDGEMENT

What does anti-realism imply so far as the philosophy of law is concerned? One answer that many have found tempting is that anti-realism helps to bolster the claims of legal positivism. Positivism denies any necessary connection between law and morality, and this denial might be thought to be motivated by a desire to insulate the objectivity of law (such as it is) from the lack of objectivity that anti-realists associate with moral judgements about justice, rightness, and value.

Some legal positivists view the connection in this way.[2] Most, however, think that matters are not so simple. This may be because they think there are conceptual or philosophical reasons for keeping law and morality separate which have nothing to do with the issue of moral realism versus anti-realism. Or it may be because they think that there are actually moral reasons for maintaining the separation between law and morality, in which case they can hardly be in the business of disparaging morality. Both options are worth exploring.

would be no moral facts if conscious agents like ourselves did not exist, nor do they need to deny that reference to beliefs or feelings is sometimes included in the truth-conditions of moral propositions. The formulation I have used in the text is suggested in Walker, *The Coherence Theory of Truth*, 3.

[2] Hans Kelsen is an example. See Kelsen, *The Pure Theory of Law*, 59–69.

Legal positivism may be understood as a view about what legal deci-sion-making involves, or it may be understood as a view about what legal decision-making *ought* to involve: I shall call the former 'descriptive posi-tivism' and the latter 'normative positivism'. Common to each of these is the positivist conception of law. According to that conception, law is to be understood in terms of rules or standards whose status as *legal* rules or standards derives from their origination in some human source, sociolo-gically defined. Thus statements about what the law is – whether these are statements made in the course of describing a legal system, offering legal advice, or disposing of particular cases – may be made without exercising moral or other evaluative judgement. The judgement is simply one of social fact. That is not true, of course, of statements made in the course of law-*making*, for legislation always involves the exercise of moral or politi-cal judgement. But statements about legislative procedure and statements about which events in the legislature qualify as the enactment of a statute do fit the description we have given. And once a legal rule has been enacted by the legislature, no further exercise of moral judgement is required for its identification, interpretation or application. That, in gen-eral, is the positivist conception of law.

Descriptive positivism maintains that this is what law *is* – law as such (perhaps by definition), or law in (say) the United States or in England. In regard to those particular legal systems, descriptive positivism is almost certainly false. This is partly because many of the rules and standards iden-tified by the best available tests of positive law actually require those who administer them to exercise moral judgement. And it is partly because there are inevitably such gaps in positive law and such indeterminacy in the meanings of the legal rules as to make their administration in fact impossible without the exercise of moral judgement. I shall not waste time defending these claims; everyone is familiar with the evidence. Some jurists try to evade these points by definitional manoeuvre: they say that the existence of a legal rule which requires the exercise of moral judgement is incompatible only with 'positive' positivism, not with 'negative' posi-tivism (or it may be the other way around);[3] and they say that the existence of gaps and indeterminate meanings in a given set of positive rules indi-cates only that we may run out of law in some systems and have to switch to political decision-making, not that legal decision-making itself takes on a moral or political character. As far as I can tell, the motive behind such moves is to secure a victory in the descriptive debate for a position *called* 'legal positivism', no matter what that position turns out to be.

As a descriptive or a definitional thesis, legal positivism is meta-ethically neutral. It takes no position on the nature of moral judgement. It

---

[3] See Coleman, 'Negative and Positive Positivism'.

is compatible with moral realism and with moral anti-realism. All it says is that legal decision-making is one thing, moral judgement another. *Normative* positivism is a different matter. This is the thesis that the law *ought* to be such that legal decisions can be made without the exercise of moral judgement. Or, if we do not want to state it in the language of obligation: it is the thesis that it would be *a good thing* for the law to be as the descriptive positivist thinks it is. Normative positivism is itself a moral claim: indeed it is a moral claim about the making of moral claims in the particular area of social life we call *law*. It identifies the contamination of legal decision by moral judgement as a moral disadvantage; it says that we lose something of value thereby. It is by far the most interesting form of legal positivism (and indeed it is hard to imagine how a positivist definition of the concept of law could be sustained, without eventually having resort to some such normative thesis). Gerald Postema has argued convincingly that normative positivism was the legal philosophy of Thomas Hobbes, David Hume, and Jeremy Bentham.[4]

The striking thing about normative positivism is the way it views putative cases of moral decision-making in law. For the descriptive positivist, such cases are threats or counter-examples: they have to be reclassified or explained away if the descriptive thesis is to be maintained. His normative counterpart, however, views them in a different light. They are unsatisfactory aspects of the law to be condemned and minimized. The legal system should be reformed so that moral decision-making, by judges or officials, is eliminated as far as possible.

Why? The reasons in Hobbes's, Hume's, and Bentham's jurisprudence had to do with the desirability of certainty, security of expectation, and knowledge of what legally empowered officials were likely to require. If the decisions of an official turned on the exercise of his moral judgement, there would be no telling what he might come up with. From the point of view of the citizen trying to organize his life, the official's decisions would be *arbitrary*.

I want to spend some time on this notion of arbitrariness. I think it is very important for normative positivism, but I think also that many of those who perceive its importance are under a misapprehension about its connection to the issues of moral realism and anti-realism with which we began.

In modern jurisprudence, the word 'arbitrary' has at least three connotations, all of them bad. (1) Sometimes it means 'unpredictable', and that,

---

[4] Postema, *Bentham and the Common Law Tradition*. Jules Coleman has objected that normative positivism infuses morality into the concept of law, and thus commits 'the very mistake positivism is so intent on drawing attention to and rectifying' (Coleman, 'Negative and Positive Positivism', 11). Gerald Postema exposes the confusion of this objection clearly: see Postema, *Bentham and the Common Law Tradition*, 328–36.

as I said, was the charge that particularly worried Jeremy Bentham and other thinkers in the mainstream of British positivism. (2) Sometimes it means 'unreasoned', as when a decision is made on the basis of whim or reflex prejudice rather than on the basis of argument. Now these are not the same. A judicial decision can be unreasoned without being unpredictable: we may know in advance, for example, that a judge is a 'knee-jerk' conservative on some range of issues and be able to predict his response accordingly. On the other hand, a legal decision can be unpredictable without being unreasoned. We may know that the judge is going to reason morally (by his own lights) but not know what his moral framework will be. Or even if we do know that he is, say, a utilitarian, we may be unable to predict his decision because we do not know enough about his reasoning powers or about the information available to him. (3) A third sense of 'arbitrariness' is particularly important with regard to American constitutional law. Some feel that even if judges are making moral decisions as reasonably and as predictably as they can, still their decisions lack *political legitimacy*. It is for the people or the legislators they have elected to make that sort of decision; it is not for the judges to take the determination of social principle and social value into their own hands. In this democratic sense, 'arbitrary' means something like 'without authority or legitimacy'.

For reasons like these, normative positivists oppose and seek to minimize the amount of moral decision-making exercised by judges and other (unelected) officials in the legal system. Moral judgement by officials, they say, adds an arbitrary dimension to the areas of social life which it affects, whereas it is the mission of law to diminish arbitrariness.

Those who disagree with them on this issue sometimes refer to themselves as proponents of the idea of *natural law*. In modern Anglo-American jurisprudence, the term 'natural law' is used most often for opposition to descriptive or definitional positivism. Natural lawyers deny that law consists only of positive rules; they say that the whole concept of law and the application of particular laws inevitably implicate moral principles and moral values. But if they add, '. . . and a good thing too', they become opponents not only of descriptive, but of normative positivism. These natural lawyers deny that there is anything arbitrary or undesirable about judges making moral decisions; indeed they welcome the introduction of values and principles into public life. They think of it as one of law's affirmative contributions.

Many, but not all of those who oppose normative positivism, are also moral realists. One arguable exception is Ronald Dworkin. Dworkin emphatically denies that there is anything wrong or arbitrary about judges incorporating moral and political views into their judgments. He thinks it is unavoidable, and he believes it is an integral part of what good adjudication requires.[5] He insists that such judgments be reasoned, and he repudiates both the democrat's charge of illegitimacy and the Benthamite worry about unpredictability. However, he has said more than once that he is not a moral realist in the sense defined at the beginning of this chapter, or at least that he does not think the debate about moral realism worth participating in.[6] Other opponents of normative positivism, however, *are* moral realists, and indeed the term 'natural law' is sometimes reserved for the position that conjoins moral realism with opposition to positivism in one or other of its forms.[7] That is an understandable usage, since outside analytic jurisprudence, 'natural law' is often used to refer simply to the facts which, according to a moral realist, make judgements of value true or false.

Dworkin apart, is there anything natural or understandable about the connection between moral realism, on the one hand, and opposition to normative positivism, on the other? Is there reason to expect a normative positivist to be an anti-realist? Conversely, should we expect someone who believes in moral objectivity to think that moral decision-making by judges and other legal officials is a good thing? I am going to argue for a negative answer to these questions.

The attractions of an affirmative answer are fairly obvious. According to the realists, those who are sceptical about moral objectivity present moral judgements as simply the arbitrary expression of emotion. Cut loose from any independent criterion of truth or objectivity, judgements about right and wrong become purely matters of private opinion, as whimsical and contingent as the feelings of those who make them. Your judgement is as good as mine, because there is no true or false of the matter. Now these sound exactly like the accusations that lead jurists in the direction of normative positivism. If an individual's moral judgement is just the idiosyncratic expression of his attitude, then it is unpredictable, unreasoned, and lacks authority; in a word, it is *arbitrary*. Those who want to eliminate arbitrariness from law, therefore, would seem to have good reason to be normative positivists if anti-realism is true. On the other hand, if anti-realism is false, then moral judgements regain the status of truth claims, and they acquire all the authority, reasonableness, and predictability that that entails. With this status, they can be allowed back into the law. So, the common view concludes, moral realists are likely to feel much more comfortable than anti-realists in allowing judges to make moral decisions.

That is the view I want to attack. That is the difference moral realism is supposed to make in jurisprudence which I shall argue it should not make. In the three sections that follow, I shall make some general points about

[5] Dworkin, *Law's Empire*, 256.
[6] Ibid., 82–3. For a different emphasis, see Dworkin, 'Objectivity and Truth'.
[7] See Moore, 'Moral Reality'.

realism and anti-realism in moral philosophy, before resuming my argument, in section 6, to the effect that moral decision-making in law is likely
to be as arbitrary (in all three of the senses I mentioned) for a moral realist
as it is for any opponent of moral objectivity.

3. QUASI-REALISM AND THE NO-DIFFERENCE THESIS

Some philosophers argue that the issue of moral objectivity is irrelevant
generally, not merely with regard to the law. Ronald Dworkin toys with
this view in his response to those he calls external sceptics. 'We use the language of objectivity,' he says in *Law's Empire*, 'not to give our ordinary
moral . . . claims a bizarre metaphysical base but to *repeat* them, perhaps in
a more precise way, to emphasize or qualify their content.'[8] Maybe we use
it to indicate our seriousness, or our belief that the claim we are making
has ramification for the lives of everyone, not just our own. But, he goes
on:

[T]here is no important difference in philosophical category or standing between
the statement that slavery is wrong and the statement that there is a right answer
to the question of slavery, namely that it is wrong. I cannot intelligibly hold the
first opinion as a moral opinion without also holding the second. Since external
skepticism offers no reason to retract or modify the former, it offers no reason to
retract or modify the latter either. They are both statements within rather than
about the enterprise of morality . . . I hasten to add that recognizing the crucial
point I have been making – that the 'objective' beliefs most of us have are moral,
not metaphysical, beliefs, that they only repeat and qualify other moral beliefs – in
no way weakens those beliefs or makes them claim something less or even different from what they might be thought to claim. For we can assign them no sense,
faithful to the role they actually play in our lives, that makes them not moral
claims. If anything is made less important by that point, it is external skepticism,
not our convictions.[9]

Notice that this is distinct from the disquotational conception of truth
referred to earlier.[10] Someone might hold a disquotational theory about
'true' in moral contexts, but still think that the question of moral objectivity was a robust and important philosophical issue. Dworkin, however,
seems to be suggesting in this passage that it is a non-issue (though elsewhere on the pages from which I have quoted he indicates that it might be
an interesting debating topic 'for a calm philosophical moment, away
from the moral or interpretive wars').[11]

---

[8] Dworkin, *Law's Empire*, 81.   [9] Ibid., 82–3.
[10] See the last paragraph of s. 1 above.
[11] Dworkin, *Law's Empire*, 82. See also ibid., 80: 'There is an ancient and flourishing philosophical debate about whether external skepticism, particularly external skepticism directed

The view that there is no significant difference at all between realism and anti-realism (about morality, or anything) seems difficult to sustain without a general attack on metaphysics and on the whole business of discussing the meanings of words and the sorts of things they refer to. Realists claim that there are real properties corresponding to the predicates 'good' and 'right', and that no one understands the meaning of these terms unless they grasp that. Anti-realists say that the use of evaluative predicates can be understood without invoking any ideas along those lines at all. If that does not count as a philosophical disagreement, nothing does.

A more modest version of the no-difference position is Simon Blackburn's thesis of 'quasi-realism'.[12] Though Blackburn insists that there is a live philosophical issue between realists and their opponents, he denies that anti-realism does any violence to the way we ordinarily think about ethics and morality. Quasi-realism, he says, is the enterprise of 'trying to earn our right to talk of moral truth, while recognizing fully the subjective sources of our judgements, inside our own attitudes, needs, desires, and natures'.[13] In carrying through this programme, Blackburn has contributed considerably to the debate about moral objectivity by answering some of the cruder criticisms and disarming some of the sillier caricatures of emotivist and other anti-realist positions. However, I think it is a mistake to promise that one can produce an anti-realist counterpart for *everything* ordinary moralists want to say. Even if ordinary moral discourse is not systematically infected with a false metaphysics, it has been so influenced in the minds of many of its practitioners by a belief in moral objectivity, particularly the objectivity of Divine Command, that it is unlikely to have remained entirely free of metaphysical distortion. It may be wiser, I think, for the anti-realist to remain agnostic on the question of whether ordinary ways of talking about morality make sense. (One disadvantage of Blackburn's term 'quasi-realism' is that it indicates a willingness to let the realists dictate the terms of the discussion, with the anti-realist struggling along, showing that he too can keep up with the realist idioms.[14])

A couple of other considerations reinforce this. First, it is simply no longer true that ordinary moral discourse is characterized unambiguously by realist-sounding talk of truth and falsity, logic and argument, reasonable and unreasonable positions. Some is and some is not. For every stern

---

to morality, is a significant theory and, if it is, whether it is right.' In Dworkin, 'Objectivity and Truth', however, the argument seems to be that moral scepticism cannot be coherently stated.

[12] The most general statement of quasi-realism is found in Blackburn, *Spreading the Word*. Its application to ethics is indicated clearly in his essays, 'Rule-Following and Moral Realism', esp. 174 ff., and 'Errors and the Phenomenology of Value'.

[13] Blackburn, *Spreading the Word*, 197.

[14] I am grateful to Bob Hargrave for this point.

preacher who talks about the reality of obligation, there is a gum-chewing sophomore who says that all morality is just a matter of opinion. The ordinary talk one hears is infested as much with relativist idioms as with truth-claims. Moral realists often *claim* that their meta-ethic gives a better account of what people ordinarily think about morality. But that is because they are not listening to what actually gets said in our culture, or they are filtering or discounting some of it already on the basis of the very theory they take themselves to be supporting with this evidence. Their theory may offer a better account of their own moralizing and that of their chums. But ordinary moral discourse, as I hear it, is a meta-ethical Babel. It is the job of a moral philosopher to try and sort that out, not to promise in advance to accommodate as much of it as he can.

Second, we should remember that 'realism' and 'anti-realism' are terms that pick out *types* of meta-ethical view, not particular theories. There are several different anti-realist theories (Humean projectivism, emotivism, prescriptivism, conventionalism, existentialism, etc.). Though a given anti-realist might feel some common cause with all such views ('It's us against the realists'), in fact he will reject all but one of them. Similarly, there are many different versions of moral realism (ranging from naturalism through moral rationalism to some version of God-and-hellfire); and, again, one presumes that a given realist will reject all but one of these. Many modern realists do not want to associate themselves, for example, with any view that defines 'right' and 'wrong' in terms of the will of God. But it seems likely that if any version of moral realism has shaped the way we talk about morals in ordinary discourse, it is this one. Since most of their philosophical opponents reject that, it seems crazy for anti-realists to promise that their theories can cope with and explain the legacy of Divine Command conceptions in our moral feelings and our moral vocabulary.

4. THE PANIC ABOUT EMOTIVISM

Still, it is worth reiterating the points Blackburn and others have made in answer to some common criticisms of anti-realism, particularly emotivist and projectivist versions of anti-realism. Their points may not fulfil the quasi-realist promise that emotivism can accommodate all realist idioms in ordinary discourse. But they are a useful antidote to the panic realists pretend to feel about the consequences of adopting an emotivist approach. Since emotivism remains the most interesting sceptical view, it is worth dealing with that panic before we look at the implications that moral realism and anti-realism have for law.

Emotivism is the theory that moral terms are used to express and evoke emotions, rather than primarily to convey information. Emotivists are

often accused by their opponents of not taking morals seriously, of making morality merely a matter of whim, of suggesting that our moral judgements are as capricious and arbitrary as our feelings about the people,
situations, and actions being judged. The implication is that realists are
able to take their moral commitments more seriously than emotivists can
because they (the realists) regard moral commitments as a perceptive
response to some matter of objective fact rather than a product of contingent feeling. But the idea of taking one's moral judgement seriously needs
a little scrutiny. Taking one's judgements seriously might mean (a) being
ready to act on them, being moved by them, having them play an important role in practical life and action, and actually doing what one judges to
be right (even when tempted not to). Or it might mean (b) being unwilling
to budge in debate and argument from the moral claims one makes, sticking with one's judgements, refusing to countenance the possibility of
changing one's view, and so on.

I take it that what the realists have in mind when they talk about being
serious about one's moral judgements is something like (b) as opposed to
(a). If a moral judgement is an accurate report of a matter of fact, then one
who regards himself as a reliable observer should stick with his report –
sternly, strictly, sonorously, or whatever – and refuse to be tempted to
adopt a more seductive-sounding but factually less accurate position. But
actually, nobody is particularly interested in this form of moral steadfastness, or at least in this form taken alone. What attracts us to the idea of
taking morals seriously is not someone sticking to a particular *view* (a
moral description, a moral characterization) in the face of temptation away
from it. What attracts us is someone being prepared to *act* on a moral judgement. We are attracted by a person's being practically and not just theoretically steadfast. The moral person we admire has the ability to be *moved* by
the good, not just the ability to accurately detect and report its presence.

Now, it is a well-known feature of moral judgements that their sincere
adoption indicates a commitment to action. Emotivists have a ready explanation of this: since moral judgements are expressions of emotion, and
since (by definition) emotions move us (albeit in complicated ways), then
obviously one who makes a moral judgement that x is good is moved to
act in favour of x, since that disposition is precisely what his judgement
evinces. Realists, on the other hand, have a notoriously difficult time with
this feature of moral language. Since moral properties are just factual
properties on their account, it is hard to see why their recognition should
indicate any willingness to act in any particular way. This difficulty is
often used as the basis of an independent argument against realism – one
aspect of J. L. Mackie's so-called 'argument from queerness'.[15] I do not

---

[15] Mackie, *Ethics: Inventing Right and Wrong*, 40.

want to use it, in this chapter, as a line of argument in its own right, for I believe the realist has an answer. He simply denies the assumption that knowledge of the good is necessarily motivating.[16] Still it is worth seeing how it affects the present issue – of whether realists take their moral views more seriously than emotivists do.

We have seen that the realist can be embarrassed by having his vaunted moral seriousness characterized in terms of (b) rather than (a), above. Now the more he tries to escape from this embarrassment, the more he runs into the difficulty posed by the argument from queerness. To move from (b) to (a), it has to be the case that accurate perception of moral facts disposes one to act morally. But for that to be the case, moral facts *do* have to be presented as something queer – and not 'queer' in the sense of unusual or odd (like giraffes or neutrinos), but 'queer' in the sense that it looks as though the metaphysical account of them has been cobbled together in an *ad hoc* way purely to meet this difficulty. It looks, then, as though we should turn to emotivism if we want a meta-ethic that shows how people take their morals seriously – at least in a sense of 'seriously' that is of some practical interest.

Underlying the attack on emotivism, there is an insinuation by the realist that people's emotions are flighty and contingent – too much under their control and too subject to self-serving manipulation to be an appropriate foundation for morality.[17] But even the realist has to concede that *something* in our moral practice is as fickle and manipulable as emotion. If it is not our moral judgements, then it is our motivation to act on those judgements. Since in the end it is how people act that really concerns us, the realist cannot claim any advantage.

There are also things to be said about the implied account of emotions in this discussion. Realists seem to crave a foundation for our moral commitments in something more stable than what Thomas Nagel has referred to as 'fortuitous or escapable inclinations'.[18] But in fact that is not a sensible way to characterize many deep emotions, which are strong, steady, and remarkably resistant both to deliberate change and to the vicissitudes of circumstance. Think, for example, of parental love and concern. Why should the feelings that find expression in moral judgement not be more like that, than like a whimsical taste for cookies, a whoop for a football

---

[16] See, e.g., Moore, 'Moral Reality', 1122–3. See also Brink, *Moral Realism and the Foundations of Ethics*, 37–50. Brink calls this position 'externalism' – i.e. that the link between moral judgement and action depends on some independent motivation, external to the moral judgement. For an 'internalist' response by the realist, see Platts, 'Moral Reality', 295: 'Why should it not just be a brute fact about moral facts that . . . their clear perception does provide sufficient grounding for action?'

[17] See the interesting discussion in Lovibond, *Realism and the Imagination*, 1–9.

[18] Nagel, *The Possibility of Altruism*, 6. I owe this reference to Lovibond, *Realism and Imagination*, 4.

team, or an afternoon's inclination to take a nap? Realists become awfully prone to caricature when they hear the term 'emotion' in a meta-ethical theory. They say things about human feelings – their alleged crudity, simplicity, fickleness, and inarticulacy ('boo!' and 'hooray!') – in order to lampoon the opposing position which (one hopes) they would never dream of saying in any other context where feelings were being discussed. Does anybody think that one's emotional attachment to one's child is best captured by 'Hooray for Sam!'? Does anyone use these crude terms to characterize the way in which they are moved by *King Lear*? If not, why should anyone think that a characterization as crude as that must be the emotivists' best candidate for what is expressed in a moral commitment?

We should remember also what is being compared with what. The realist is tempted to say that we are comparing the fickleness of an individual's feelings, on the one hand, with the solidity of hard moral fact, on the other. But that is a mistake. What is being compared with the alleged fickleness of emotion is not the solidity of moral facts themselves, assuming there are such things, but the solidity or fickleness (whichever it is) of people's *beliefs* about moral facts. Even if there are such objective facts, there is no privileged, easy, or uncontroversial access to them; there is certainly no mode of belief which is straightforwardly and indubitably reflective of the facts' solidity. We know that there are psychological phenomena like self-deception, wilful blindness, deceit, capricious and unpredictable misapprehension, and illusion with regard to other matters of fact. People can mislead themselves and others, and change their minds deliberately or arbitrarily back and forth as easily when they are surveying the world of real and tangible objects, as when they are taking on or sustaining an emotional commitment. The realist is not entitled to assume that our beliefs about moral facts are any steadier in regard to these vicissitudes than our factual beliefs generally. But once that is conceded, the contrast with the fickleness and unreliability of 'mere' emotions evaporates.

Perhaps, in the end, what worries the realist is the contingency of judgement and feeling on the emotivist account. Not contingency in the sense of fickleness; we have already dealt with that caricature. But contingency in the sense that emotivism makes moral judgements depend on the wrong sort of thing. The emotivist seems to think that every person must be prepared to say the following about his own moral sensibility:

I only make the moral judgements I do (at whatever level) because of how I feel. If I felt differently I would make different moral judgements.

But that characterization can be misleading, for the 'because' and the counterfactual that go with it are ambiguous. If the 'because' is supposed to connote simple causality (i.e. 'Among the causal antecedents of some moral judgement I make are some feelings of mine'), then the emotivist is indeed committed to it. That is what it is for a judgement to express a feeling. (The realist can accept that as well, since on his account the emotive genesis of a judgement need not detract from its status as a descriptive bearer of truth-value.) But the 'because' of causality is not the 'because' of justification or reason-giving. The emotivist is emphatically not committed to saying that his own feelings *justify* the judgements that he makes. When I condemn an action, I usually do so in virtue of some feature F that it has (F may be the action's cruelty, for example, or its hurtfulness), and I may express that relation in the counterfactual: 'If the act had not been F, it would not have been wrong.' Critics sometimes accuse the emotivist of thinking that the feature of arousing a negative emotion in the speaker is the paradigm value for F. But, as Simon Blackburn argues, emotivists are not committed to that at all:

The counterfactual 'If we had different attitudes it would not be wrong to kick dogs' expresses the moral view that the feature which makes it wrong to kick dogs is our reaction. But this is an absurd moral view, and not one to which [an emotivist] has the least inclination. Like anyone else he thinks that what makes it wrong to kick dogs is that it causes them pain. To put it another way: he approves of a moral disposition which given this belief [about the dogs' pain] as an input, yields the reaction of disapproval as an output; he does not approve of one which needs belief about our attitudes as an input in order to yield the same output, and this is all that gets expression in the counterfactual.[19]

5. MORAL DISAGREEMENT

The impulse to anti-realism in ethics has many sources. For some philosophers, it is simply that emotivism or prescriptivism provide what appear to be the best accounts available of what is going on when moral judgements are made and thought about and followed. These philosophers do not come into meta-ethics with any particular sceptical axe to grind. They just start from the position (which everyone acknowledges) that moral judgement has *something* to do with attitude, feeling, and the determination and guidance of action, and they build up their account from that. Having developed their analysis, they then discover that there is no room for any realist notion of moral truth and moral objectivity, and they put those ideas quietly aside.[20]

Others are led to anti-realism more directly, from their reflections on the intractability of moral disagreement. There seems to be disagreement or

[19] Blackburn, 'Rule-Following and Moral Realism', 179.
[20] I suspect this is how R. M. Hare was led to an anti-realist position: see Hare, *The Language of Morals*. See also the discussion in Hare, *Moral Thinking*, 65–86.

opposition about almost everything in ethics – about values, principles, virtues, desert, God, the nature of the good life, our obligations to one another, the appropriate way to deal with conflict, politics, democracy, rights, the respect due to humanity in all its forms, our relations to the animals, and on and on – and there is no consensus at all about how such disagreements may be resolved. Of course the existence of disagreement does not imply the truth of anti-realism. But it is not entirely crazy to explore the anti-realist option in the face of disagreements as apparently intractable as these.

It may be worth expanding on this last point. J. L. Mackie thought that the differences that exist in people's moral, ethical, and political views were the basis of one of two main arguments supporting moral scepticism: 'Radical differences between first order moral judgements make it difficult to treat those judgements as apprehensions of objective truths.'[21] Certainly they make it impossible to treat *all* the different views as apprehensions of objective truths, but I take Mackie's point to be that they make it difficult to treat *any* moral views in that way. Given what morality is and what it is for (given the sort of fact it must be, if it is a matter of fact), how could there be objective truth and falsity certified by the way the world is, and yet so much disagreement?

Realists' reactions to this argument differ. Nicholas Sturgeon writes that it is 'one argument for moral skepticism that I respect even though I remain unconvinced',[22] while Michael Moore insists that it is

subject to the crushing rejoinder that the mere fact of disagreement among the judgments of people hardly shows there is no fact of the matter to be agreed upon. People within a culture, and people in different cultures, may disagree about all sorts of things, such as whether the winds are influenced by the earth's rotation, or whether the moon is made of rock. The simple fact of disagreement for certain sorts of belief cannot itself show that there is no fact of the matter being argued about. To think otherwise is to confuse intersubjective agreement with objectivity.[23]

Moore is right about the logical gap between disagreement and there being no objective fact of the matter. But he talks as though *this is all that needs to be said* about moral disagreement in order to avoid embarrassment for the realist. And it is not: moral disagreement remains a continuing difficulty for realism, even if it does not entail its falsity, so long as the realist fails to establish connections between the idea of objective truth and the existence of procedures for resolving disagreement.

If we disagree about whether the moon is made of cheese, both of us will say that the matter could be settled if someone actually went there and

---

[21] Mackie, *Ethics: Inventing Right and Wrong*, 36. The second argument is 'the argument from queerness', which I mentioned in the previous section.
[22] Sturgeon, 'Moral Explanations', 229.   [23] Moore, 'Moral Reality', 1089–90.

tasted it. If we disagree (to use Moore's less trivial example) about the impact on wind of the earth's rotation, we look to meteorology and physics for complicated ways of sorting this out. Now moral realists have pointed out, quite properly, that scientific method is enormously complicated and subtle: the simple positivist image of indubitable observation-statements that either refute or confirm a disputed hypothesis is naive and uninteresting, and it does not count at all against moral realism that there is nothing similar available in ethics. Still, our conception of reality in science is associated with the whole complex apparatus of method, heuristic, observation, and experimentation. We know how to proceed in the face of disagreement. There is nothing equivalent in morals, nothing that even begins to connect the idea of there being a fact of the matter with the idea of there being some way to proceed when people disagree.

The point has to be stated carefully. I am not saying that there is no procedure or methodology in ethics that commands universal assent; there is no such procedure in science either. Astronomers say one thing, astrologers another.[24] But at least in mainstream science, there is a broad conception of method acknowledged by a large group of practitioners, all of whom regard that acknowledgement as something independent of the scientific disagreements they have with one another. No doubt the conception is loosely defined and controversial in places. No doubt also, the group excludes some of those who purport to practice science. Still it is understood by its members, at any rate, and by a substantial consensus in the culture at large, to include the protagonists in a large number of important disagreements. In other words, a single (albeit loosely defined) conception of method for settling disagreements is shared by a significant group of people who regard themselves as engaged in serious disagreement with one another. And what is more, disagreements do get settled by this method, and when they do not, we can often refer to the terms of the method to explain why.

Among moralists, there is nothing remotely comparable. Instead each view comes along trailing its own theory of what counts as a justification: utilitarians have one view, Kantians another, Christian fundamentalists yet another, and so on. Aristotelians, Nietzscheans, Marxists, traditional conservatives like Burke, liberals like Rawls, feminists like Gilligan – all acknowledge that the disagreements between them are important (if any are). Yet unlike their counterparts in the scientific community, they share virtually nothing in the way of an epistemology or a method with which these disagreements might in principle be approached. If two utilitarians disagree about social policy, they can refer that disagreement to the complex apparatus of modern consequentialism: different levels of moral

---

[24] See Gewirth, 'Positive Ethics and Normative Science', 311.

thought, different models of inter-personal comparability, strategic and game-theoretical models, sophisticated points about moral mathematics, and so on. But all this counts for nothing if the moral disagreement is between a utilitarian and a deontologist, or between Bentham and Nietzsche. Perhaps a utilitarian who is also a moral realist will maintain that the basic propositions of his theory are true and those of his deontological opponent false. He will claim that the development of utilitarian ethics beginning in the late eighteenth century is progress towards the truth, and that it represents an improvement in our moral sensibility. He will say, too that the Nietzschean is making some sort of appalling mistake. *But there is nothing he can say to support these claims* – indeed, nothing he can say about how a statement of this kind could be found to be true, how people might be mistakenly convinced that it was false, and so on.

Modern moral realists are quite disingenuous about this. Mark Platts writes that (on the realist view he espouses) 'moral judgments are viewed as factually cognitive, as presenting claims about the world which can be assessed (like any other factual belief) as true or false, and whose truth or falsity are as much possible objects of human knowledge as any other factual claims about the world'.[25] But how exactly are we to assess the truth or falsity of a moral judgement? What does the assessment involve? What procedures? What methodology? We are never told. For a proposition to be a possible object of knowledge, it is not sufficient for it to be capable of being true and being believed to be true: there must also be some gesture in the direction of justification for the true belief in question, and in particular a non-trivial sense of justification that would have some connection and sensitivity to the distinction between the genesis of true belief and the genesis of false belief.

Platts says that '[w]e detect moral aspects of the world in the same way we detect (nearly all) other aspects: by looking and seeing'.[26] But in non-moral cases, where two people disagree about something (say, the colour or size of an object) and each of them claims to have based her belief on visual detection, we can supplement the simple epistemology of looking-and-seeing with a whole apparatus on which we agree and which explains mistake, illusion, and perspective – a whole paraphernalia which connects the epistemology to complicated procedures for distinguishing truth from falsity, accuracy from error, and which is rooted eventually in a physiological account of perception.[27] There is nothing comparable in ethics.

---

[25] Platts, 'Moral Reality', 282.   [26] Ibid., 285.
[27] Partly what this means is that we can give an account of the subjectivity of perception that is 'objective' in the sense discussed by Nagel in *The View from Nowhere*, 5.

Platts also writes: 'By a process of careful attention to the world, we can improve our moral beliefs about the world, make them more approximately true.'[28] He adds that this process of improvement has no end point, nothing that counts as final certainty. But he fails to say anything about what 'care' is or involves in this context. Again, in straightforward cases of looking-and-seeing, an account can be given: 'Look at an object from several angles before you pronounce on its shape, because angle of vision affects shape perception'. We give an account of what it is to be careful which has an agreed and independent basis in our theory of perception. Nothing similar is agreed on in ethics, and nothing along these lines is offered by Platts.

By their own lights, moral realists ought to be very concerned that they have nothing to offer in the way of a method for approaching moral disputes. Consider what Michael Moore has written about what he thinks of as the sad predicament of the moral sceptic:

A skeptic will regard his own values with embarrassment, for they hold out a promise on which he thinks he cannot deliver. His value judgments, that is, purport to be descriptive in form. For example, he may say such things as 'Killing is wrong,' a statement that seems capable of being true or false. Moreover, others expect that when he says these things, he has reasons with which he can demonstrate the truth of such propositions, reasons that others will find persuasive. Yet his skepticism tells him that none of this is true. He is merely playing a peculiar form of language game when he makes his value judgments. Accordingly, when he wishes to engage in honest debate and not merely to issue propaganda, he will qualify his value judgments with 'I think,' or 'of course, it's only my opinion.' He will try to cancel the promissory note as he issues it, because he believes he cannot otherwise pay it.[29]

As a matter of fact, many anti-realists deny that their (or anyone else's) moral judgements hold out such a promise. 'Error Theorists' (such as Mackie) believe they do, but non-cognitivists (such as R. M. Hare) do not.[30] Be that as it may, moral *realists* certainly believe this about *their own* judgements. But since they are quite unable to demonstrate the truth of their judgements or show how they correspond to moral reality, *they* should be the ones in all honesty to qualify their claims with 'Of course, it's only my opinion'. For though they insist that there is some fact of the matter, they offer nothing which would help distinguish a mere arbitrary opinion from a well-grounded belief.

6. MORAL JUDGEMENT AND ADJUDICATION

Let us turn back finally to the law, and to the desirability of moral decision-making by judges and other officials in legal contexts.

---

[28] Platts, 'Moral Reality', 285.   [29] Moore, 'Moral Reality', 1063.
[30] Compare Mackie, *Ethics: Inventing Right and Wrong*, 35 with Hare, *Moral Thinking*, 80.

We know there is moral disagreement in society and that even those who believe that there are right answers in these controversies are unable to agree about how we might arrive at them. In the face of all this disagreement, how should a judge or other official behave? How should he respond to the fact that many of the people whose lives are affected by his decisions, and many of the other officials in whose company he must make his decisions, hold views on issues of social and political morality that are radically at odds with his own?

In particular, given everything that has been said so far, what difference would the truth of moral realism make to his dilemma? The main misgiving, we recall, is about the *arbitrariness* of moral decision-making by judges: arbitrariness in the sense of unpredictability, irrationality, and democratic illegitimacy. This is what normative positivists fear about judicial moralizing. Are their fears likely to be allayed at all by a belief in moral objectivity? Is it an apprehension that arises only on account of the emotivist theory of ethics?

Michael Moore, for one, seems to believe that the answer to these last two questions is 'Yes.' Judges have to believe in objectivity, he claims, in order to dispel the suggestion of arbitrariness in their moral judgements. They cannot afford to be sceptics:

> Judges are subject to [the] debilitating psychological consequences of skepticism no less than the rest of us. The institutional role may even intensify these effects, for judges must not only make value judgments, but also impose them upon other people. If one's daily task is to impose values on others, to think that these are only one's own personal values doubtlessly makes the job hard to perform at all. To foist personal values onto hapless litigants is not for many temperaments a satisfying role.[31]

In the light of what we have said, this now seems completely wrongheaded. Even if scepticism is rejected, even if there *are* moral facts which make true judgements true and false judgements false, still the best a judge can do is to impose his *opinion* about such facts on the 'hapless litigants' who come before him. They will have beliefs and opinions of their own about the matter, and even if they too become card-carrying moral realists, they will continue to ask why the judge's view of the moral facts should prevail over theirs. The truth of moral realism (if it is true) does not validate any particular person's or any particular judge's moral beliefs. At best, it alters our understanding of the character of a moral disagreement without moving us any closer to an understanding of who is right and who is wrong.

We saw earlier that Moore thought an anti-realist, if he is honest, ought always to qualify his value judgements with 'I think', or 'Of course, it's

---

[31] Moore, 'Moral Reality', 1064.

only my opinion' and he seems to hold that this will embarrass the judge because, in the same breath, the judge will be imposing the views he is qualifying in this way upon people who disagree with him. In fact, it is quite unclear why Moore thinks this retiring posture is either appropriate for or distinctive of the anti-realist position. For one thing, if an anti-realist is going to be coy about his value-judgements in a way that is meta-ethically transparent, he ought to be saying, not 'I think', but 'I feel'. He ought to characterize his judgement not as a personal opinion ('Opinion about what?') but as some sort of complicated affect. Talk of opinion is appropriate when there is some *matter of fact* about which people disagree. It is not appropriate in cases of contrary emotions.

But then the next point is obvious. Since, on any account, there *is* moral disagreement, and since we do not agree even in principle on any way of settling such disagreements, a judge who is assigned the task of making moral judgements ought to be saying 'I think' and 'Of course, it's only my opinion', *even if realism is true*. If he pays any attention to the fact that he is not the only person in society with an opinion on the (allegedly factual moral) issue he is addressing, he will certainly be conscious of some arbitrariness in his own opinions prevailing over others', whether he is a realist or not.

Consider now the three aspects of arbitrariness we listed in section 2 of this chapter: worries about the unpredictability, the irrationality, and the democratic illegitimacy of judicial moralism.

(1) *Unpredictability.* Does moral realism make any difference to the predictability of those judicial decisions that involve a moral element? If some version of emotivism is true, there will surely be a modicum of empirical predictability. We know, for example, that Chief Justice Rehnquist is a conservative and Justice Stevens is something of a liberal, and political scientists use observations like these as a basis for fairly reliable predictions about the attitudes they will express and the positions they will take, without assuming anything in the way of moral objectivity. What would moral objectivity add to this?

Without an epistemology, the answer I think is 'nothing'. The only basis for predicting what a judge's beliefs will be about the moral facts today is the record of his beliefs about them in the past, and as we have seen, something similar to this form of predictability is already available even if realism is false. Maybe if realists came up with a psychology of moral perception, predictability could be improved. We know that in the presence of a red patch, most observers who are not blind will detect redness (and we can explain why), and we know that if an elephant wanders into the courtroom, the judge along with everyone else is likely to report 'There goes an elephant.' If responses to the presence of moral value were as predictable as this, then maybe realism would have something to offer in the way of dispelling arbitrariness. But no modern realist wants to associate himself with such an epistemology. Very few regard perceptions of value as on a par with colour discriminations or the discrimination of large visible objects. And any who did would find himself having to denigrate his moral (as opposed to his meta-ethical) opponents as colour-blind, on such a wide front as to deprive the analogy with sense-perception of any usefulness at all in dealing with interpersonal disputes.[32]

(2) *Irrationality*. It might seem as though the worry about irrationality is the one where realism clearly has the advantage over moral anti-realism. After all, realists say that moral judgements are reasoned reports of the presence of moral properties, while anti-realists explicitly deny this.

But the worry about the irrationality of judicial moralizing is not about what judges say, but about what they do. It is a concern about whether they are prepared to argue or assemble reasons for their views, or whether they simply announce them flatly, saying that though they cannot argue about virtue or vice, they know it when they see it. And here it seems that anti-realist and realist accounts of moral judgement are simply on a par. Some realists do take the flat 'I know it when I see it' approach to the detection of moral value. They will *say* it is a perception (and in principle correctable etc.), but that has no impact on the way they argue. The counterpart of this position is the emotivist who *simply* expresses or gives vent to what he takes to be his attitude on some issue. He too may draw attention to the mutability of his disposition, and he may even express a favourable attitude towards that. But again, it need not affect how he argues. Often – and I suppose this is some evidence for quasi-realism – it will be impossible to distinguish such a realist judge from such an anti-realist judge on the bench.

On the other hand, an emotivist may articulate his moral judgement on a particular issue in terms of the ramification of some more general attitude that he has. He may indicate for example that he cares about human starvation in all its forms, and so in this particular case he is going to act to protect some plaintiff from the possibility of starvation. In this case, he has something that looks quite like what a realist would call *a reason* to offer in support of his verdict. The verdict is not simply *there* starkly staring at us, as an arbitrary moral reflex. Once again, if the question about arbitrariness is, 'Is the moral judgement simply posited, or does it derive from more general considerations?', then such an emotivist is no worse off than the realist in terms of the way he regards his moral dispositions.

---

[32] This, by the way, is the appropriate way to deal with McDowell's analogy between moral predicates and the terms for secondary qualities: see McDowell, 'Values and Secondary Qualities', 110.

(3) *Democratic Illegitimacy.* Particularly in American constitutional adjudication, a judge sometimes has to assert his view of what is right over the view taken by a legislature or electorate. In Part III of this book, I shall argue that there are – to say the least – considerable difficulties in explaining the democratic legitimacy of this. But I do not want to take advantage of *bad* arguments against judicial review – at least to the extent I can help it!

The theory that moral and political views are merely matters of attitude is often associated – I think quite wrongly – with an uneasiness about permitting judges to strike down legislation in spite of its democratic credentials. Those who have been persuaded of some anti-realist view such as emotivism often present the institution of judicial review as though it allowed the simple preferences of nine judges to prevail over the preferences of the mass of voting citizens or their elected representatives. If it is simply preferences versus preferences, or attitudes versus attitudes – if there is nothing objective about any of them – then surely the only thing to do (the argument goes) is to let the numbers count. Emotivism, therefore, is often taken as a reason for supporting majority rule and opposing judicial review.

As I shall argue in Chapters Ten through Thirteen, there *are* good reasons for opposing the judicial review of legislation, but they are not these. To see this, consider again how little difference the recasting of the judges', legislators', and voters' moral views in *realist* terms would make. If moral realism is true then what the judge is imposing on his fellow citizens is not something which is merely a subjective preference of his, but something which is a belief of his about the moral facts. That looks reassuring until we remember that what his view is opposed to is, equally, not the subjective preferences of legislators and voters, but *their* beliefs about the moral facts. As before, in the absence of any account of how one could tell which of two conflicting beliefs about the moral facts is more accurate, the imposition of one person's or a few people's beliefs over those of the population at large still seems arbitrary and undemocratic.

The issue comes down to comparing like with like. If moral realism is true, then judges' beliefs clash with legislators' beliefs in moral matters. If realism is false, judges' attitudes clash with legislators' attitudes. What we must not allow the realist defender of constitutional review to say is that it is a case of judges' beliefs clashing with legislators' attitudes. The defender of judicial review is not allowed to confine the benefits of his meta-ethics to those whom he favours as decision-makers.

The sense one often gets from discussions that attempt to legitimize constitutional review is that the judge is an elevated moral deliberator holding views of principle while the demos and its representatives are stuck at the level of articulating their sordid interests and their shabby prejudices.

There may be points to be made about the extent to which the political decisions of different agents are governed by their own narrow self-interest; maybe judges work in an institutional setting that leaves them less concerned with self-interest in their decision-making than directly elected politicians have to be.[33] But even if this is so, it has nothing to do with realism or anti-realism about morality. If the institutional setting is such as to taint a legislator's moral position with narrow self-interest, then the very same constraints are likely to influence the *beliefs* that he holds about (moral and other) matters of fact. Once again, we must remember that attitudes are not the only things that can be affected by interest. We are familiar with wilful blindness and self-deception in uncontroversially factual areas, and there is no reason to expect that this will be diminished (indeed, depending how you approach the connection between moral judgement and motivation, there is every reason to expect it to be enhanced) in the arena of moral fact. Defenders of judicial review may argue that judges have greater expertise in moral matters than ordinary citizens, so that their beliefs and their reasoning are more likely to be reliable. But we have already noticed that moral realists can produce no epistemology to match their ontological commitments. Without an epistemology – and an epistemology which is to some extent less controversial (or at any rate differently controversial) than the knowledge claims it covers – there cannot be a theory of expertise. Thus the epistemic inadequacy of moral realism is far-reaching: in practical matters, it deprives realists of almost everything that they might want to say or argue for in the name of objectivity.

I am arguing that the moral realist is no better off than the emotivist in supporting the legitimacy of judicial review. The converse holds also: the emotivist is no worse off than the realist in this regard. The case for judicial review must be won or lost on the moral and political merits of the matter, on the basis of moral arguments about fairness, justice, and democracy. And that is likely to be an area where there is no less disagreement (again, disagreement that can be analysed in either of these ways) than on the merits of the substantive decision itself.

To sum up, then. If moral realism is false, then what clash in the courtroom and in the political forum are people's differing attitudes and feelings, and there will seem to be something arbitrary about any one of them prevailing over any of the others, when none can be certified, so to speak, on any credentials other than the fact that some people find it congenial. If realism is true, then what clash in the courtroom and in the political forum are people's differing beliefs (hunches, hypotheses, speculations,

<hr />

[33] Again, I doubt this. To the extent that it is true in America, I suspect it is a matter of self-fulfilling prophecy with regard to legislatures. ('Let's not worry about the issues of principle. Let's leave those for the courts to decide.')

prejudices) about moral matters of fact. But that these are beliefs *about matters of fact* does not detract in any way from what will still seem to be a certain arbitrariness in one of them prevailing over any of the others. Since most moral realists abjure the sort of foundationalist epistemology that might make some such beliefs self-certifying and since they are unable to secure support for any other epistemology that might serve as a basis for a theory of error or a theory of expertise, all we have is a set of different persons with their conflicting beliefs. Exactly as in the case of attitudes, none of these can be certified as superior or naturally prevalent on any credentials other than the fact that some people find them congenial. Either we have the arbitrariness of taking one attitude over others equally eligible, or we have the arbitrariness of taking one belief over others equally eligible. But arbitrariness is there, on either meta-ethical account.

7. CONCLUSION

Why did natural lawyers ever imagine the contrary? I can only think that they were seduced by the idea that facts themselves might operate as constraints on the arbitrariness of judicial decision. Liberals and conservatives alike are concerned that judges should not think of themselves as free agents when they make their decisions, at liberty to determine the fate of the litigants and their fellow citizens, just as they please. They should think of themselves as constrained rather than unconstrained decision-makers. But if a judge's decision contains an essential moral element, and if moral realism is false, then the sense of constraint disappears. Outcomes are determined by the judge's subjective preference, and to the extent that his attitudes are under his control, he can make any decision he likes. (Which naturally invites the question of why he, rather than anyone else, should be the one who is allowed to do what he likes in this area.) If, on the other hand, moral realism is true, then there is a right answer to whatever questions of principle the judge puts to himself. We are apt to think of this as some sort of comfort: the right answer is there, so the judge is constrained after all.

But the existence of a right answer, if there is one, is so far a mere matter of ontology. There is some fact of the matter that makes one answer the judge might give true and another answer that he might offer false. But making true and making false are not things that facts do to judges. The facts do not reach out like little gods and grab the decision-maker, preventing him from deciding capriciously or dictating themselves to him in any unavoidable way. Making true and making false are semantic relations, and for all that any realist has told us they have nothing whatever to do with the social, psychological, political, or institutional determinants of judicial decision- making. Moral facts do not constrain us in the sense of constraint that interests us in politics. That there is a right answer 'out there' certainly means that a judge is not making a fool of himself when he goes out ponderously in search of it. But its mere existence does not drive the judge to pursue it, let alone determine that he will reach it. Different judges will reach different results even when they all take themselves to be pursuing the right answer, and nothing about the ontology of right answers gives any of them a reason for thinking his own view is any more correct than any other.

In the end it is moral disagreement, not moral subjectivity, that gives rise to our worries about judicial moralizing. And since realists have almost nothing of interest to say about the resolution of moral disagreement, they have nothing to offer to allay those concerns.

Chapter Nine
The Circumstances of Integrity

Because people disagree about justice, societies need what Ronald Dworkin calls principles of fairness (164–5).[1] Even if political authority is not prized in its own right as a distributable good, there have to be fair methods for making decisions when people disagree about what those decisions should be. Majority-decision is a fine example of a principle of fairness: as we saw in Chapter Five, it provides a basis on which a divided group can commit itself to a single course of action, a basis which takes the views of each member into account, and gives as much weight as possible to each on the condition that it gives no greater weight to any one of them than it gives to any of the others. Elective dictatorship is a fairness principle of a different kind: instead of prescribing a procedure for settling decisions in particular cases, it prescribes a procedure for settling on an individual who will be empowered, for a certain period, to make decisions on the basis of his own judgement in the name of the whole society. And of course there are also the much more complicated fairness principles embodied in the institutions of representative democracy.

We need principles of fairness because, as I said, people disagree about justice. Attractive principles of fairness are unlikely to confer decisional authority on the partisans of just one of the competing views about justice. Over time in a democratic society, political power can be expected to alternate back and forth between the major competitors (between conservatives and social democrats, for example). And even in a given period, constitutional arrangements will often ensure that no one party or faction monopolizes all the bases of current decision-making.

A past political decision has current force in a society if it has established a standing institution, rule, policy, or principle that continues to govern some aspect of social life. What I have just said about principles of fairness raises the possibility that some of the political decisions currently in force will be based on views about justice that are at odds with those underlying some of the other political decisions currently in force. When conservative parties replace social democratic parties in power, they seldom

---

[1] In this chapter, numbers in parentheses in the text are page references to Dworkin, *Law's Empire*.

attempt to wipe the slate clean.[2] Many decisions and practices inspired by social democratic values will remain in effect, coexisting uneasily with the fresh decisions of the new regime. Moreover, though the leadership of the society may be conservative, there will still be judges and officials who hold power on a basis that is independent of that leadership and who may continue to refer to social democratic ideals in their decision-making. Checks and balances, the separation of powers, and a history of political competition are thus likely to yield a patchwork of standards and institutions which no political party and no conception of justice can acknowledge as peculiarly its own.

2. THE CIRCUMSTANCES OF INTEGRITY

John Rawls has described moderate scarcity and limited altruism as *the circumstances of justice*: they are among the conditions, he says, that explain both the need for and the possibility of principles governing the distribution of primary goods.[3] Similarly, the fact of political disagreement together with the strongly felt need for social decision on certain matters are 'the circumstances of fairness,' or, as I called them in Chapter Five, 'the circumstances of politics'.[4] They define a role for procedural principles which determine whose (or which party's) decisions are to be accorded political authority. In much the same way, the possibility of a political patchwork may be regarded as 'the circumstance' of something that Ronald Dworkin posits as a third ideal: *integrity* (166).

Integrity, in Dworkin's theory, is a response to the fact that the various political decisions currently in force in a given society, coming as they do from different sources, are not guaranteed to cohere with one another. The task of integrity is to deal with what happens when principles of political fairness legitimate the making and enforcement of decisions in one and the same political system by partisans of competing views about justice. The point of specifying 'the circumstances of integrity' is to give us a general idea of integrity's 'problematic' (in the jargon sense of that term). It defines the array of difficulties and concerns that make our talk of integrity seem sensible. It is the answer a jurist would give to someone who kept saying 'What's your problem?' when he heard a jurist going on and on about integrity.

The circumstances of integrity are therefore not the same as Dworkin's particular theory of integrity. They are more like the presuppositions of

[2] Cf. Raz, 'The Relevance of Coherence', 307–8.
[3] For the idea of 'circumstances of justice', see Rawls, *A Theory of Justice*, 126–30.
[4] Above, Ch. 5, ss. 7–9. See also Benjamin Barber's account of 'the conditions of politics' in Barber, *Strong Democracy*, 120–38.

Dworkin's theory. The theory is Dworkin's prescription for dealing with the possibility of a political patchwork – a prescription based on his particular sense of the values and ideals at stake in this problematic. Dworkin believes that there is a distinct political virtue in maintaining and promoting coherence in our existing principles and institutions.[5] Any official (a legislator or a judge, for example) will be aware that people with views like his are not the only ones contributing to the shape and character of existing arrangements. Nevertheless, Dworkin says, each official should try to present the overall package of society's laws as though it conveyed a single view about justice that made sense in its own right. Thus a legislative principle of integrity 'asks law-makers to try to make the total set of laws morally coherent', and an adjudicative principle 'instructs that the law be seen as coherent in that way' by judges when drawing on it as a basis for current determinations (176). Though in fact as political participants we speak in different voices on matters of justice, Dworkin's ideal of integrity commands us to speak in the name of the community in just one voice. 'Integrity becomes a political ideal', Dworkin says, 'when we insist that the state act on a single, coherent set of principles even when its citizens are divided about what the right principles of justice and fairness really are' (166).

I said this is Dworkin's particular view of how and why we should respond to the possibility of disparate decisions. Other responses are imaginable. Some may deny that incoherence among current standards presents a problem. They may be indifferent to that possibility, figuring it is simply inevitable in the conditions of modern politics. They may think it more honest (more expressive of *real* integrity) for a community to present itself as torn among competing views of what members owe to one another, just as individuals – on any sensible account of personal ethics – are torn and conflicted about the principles that inform their daily lives. Or they may actually celebrate the incoherence: they may think, for example, that the prospects for freedom are promoted when the individual no longer has to deal with a monolithic state that speaks with just one voice.[6] Even those who are concerned at the prospect of incoherence may not agree with Dworkin's prescription. They may turn their concern back to the principles of fairness that generate the incoherence. They may argue for a more unified state apparatus – eliminating checks and balances, for example, and limiting the diversity of sources of decision in society. Or they may propose a change in the political culture that currently requires a new regime to show the same respect for the standing decisions of its

[5] I am not convinced by what I take to be the mischievous suggestion of Raz, 'The Relevance of Coherence', 317, that Dworkin does not believe in coherence at all as a political ideal for judges.

[6] Cf. Friedman, *Capitalism and Freedom*, Ch. 1.

predecessors (until they are formally amended) as it shows for its own.[7] Finally, those who agree both with Dworkin's diagnosis and with his prescription may yet disagree with him about the values underlying integrity. Though his main argument for integrity is based on the conditions of political legitimacy (190–216), Dworkin acknowledges that other arguments for it are possible (188–90). He would concede, presumably, that each argument will generate a slightly different conception of integrity (a slightly different view, for example, about what 'coherence' requires).

I mention these alternatives not to discredit Dworkin's own particular conception, but to reinforce our sense of articulation in this area of political argument. The central chapters of *Law's Empire* do not simply present a theory – law as integrity – in a 'take-it-or-leave-it' fashion. They highlight an important feature of political life in a pluralistic society: not only do we disagree about justice, but fair procedural principles allow disparate views about justice to hold force in society at a given time. The chapters outline grounds for concern about the incoherence that may result from this. They propose a particular heuristic for dealing with that possibility: namely, that in using past decisions as a ground for present ones, we should do so in a way that constructs the past as a coherent body of principle. The adoption of that heuristic is then identified, boldly, with the very foundations of law, legality, and legal rights; for on Dworkin's account its adoption is motivated by consideration of the conditions under which alone law can have a legitimate claim on the allegiance and obedience of those it governs.

The whole package as presented in *Law's Empire* is tremendously ambitious. But the individual parts are also worth considering on their own. Each is important, and none of them has been identified so clearly before. That is why I talk of 'the circumstances of integrity', not just of 'Law as Integrity: The Theory'. For even if we do not buy Dworkin's solution and the jurisprudence he constructs on the basis of that solution, still his isolation of a potential issue along these lines is already a substantial contribution to legal and political philosophy.

3. POINT AND PRACTICABILITY

Dworkin does not use the phrase 'the circumstances of integrity', nor does he draw the analogy with Rawls's talk of 'the circumstances of justice' in the way I have proposed. Nevertheless his discussion of integrity is strongly suggestive of such an analogy.

---

[7] See the discussion of an example concerning municipal housing policy in the UK in s. 6 of Ch. 5, above.

When Rawls – and, before him, David Hume – described moderate scarcity and limited altruism as 'the circumstances of justice,' they meant to contrast the real world, in which justice is both necessary and practicable, with two imaginable ways in which the world could be. On the one hand, the world could be such as to render justice redundant or superfluous:

> [I]f every man had a tender regard for another, or if nature supplied abundantly all our wants and desires, . . . the jealousy of interest, which justice supposes, could no longer have place. . . . Encrease to a sufficient degree the benevolence of men, or the bounty of nature, and you render justice useless, by supplying its place with much nobler virtues, and more valuable blessings.[8]

The circumstances of justice are thus what distinguish the real world from this imagined utopia or 'Golden Age'. Alternatively, the world could be so awful as to make unbearable the normative burdens that justice requires:

> Suppose a society to fall into such want of all common necessaries, that the utmost frugality and industry cannot preserve the greater number from perishing, and the whole from extreme misery; it will readily, I believe, be admitted, that the strict laws of justice are suspended, in such a pressing emergence, and give place to the stronger motives of necessity and self-preservation.[9]

The circumstances of justice thus include the conditions which make it plausible to assume that the demands of justice could be heeded and its prescriptions carried out by beings like us.[10]

Analogously, to talk of the circumstances of integrity, we must identify features of the real world which distinguish it, on the one hand, from a utopia in which integrity would be redundant, and, on the other hand, from a nightmare world in which integrity would be impracticable. And in fact Dworkin's conception of integrity is structured by exactly these distinctions.

The first contrast – between the real world and a utopia in which integrity would be redundant – is the most obvious. 'Integrity', Dworkin says, 'would not be needed as a distinct political virtue in a utopian state. Coherence would be guaranteed because officials would always do what was perfectly just and fair' (176). There would be no need in this utopia for a separate requirement that the community speak with one voice, for it would necessarily speak with one voice in speaking nothing but the truth about justice. The world *we* know, however is not like that. 'I am defending an interpretation of our own political culture,' Dworkin writes, 'not an abstract and timeless political morality' (216).

---

[8] Hume, *A Treatise of Human Nature*, Bk. III, Part II, s. ii, 494–5.

[9] Hume, *An Enquiry Concerning the Principles of Morals*, S. III, Part I, 186.

[10] See also the discusssion of 'limited strength of will' in Hart's account of 'the miniumum content of natural law' in *The Concept of Law*, 197.

The contrast here is not between the perfect justice of utopia and the moral imperfection of the real world. If just one imperfect view held sway in society (and we all believed it) there would be no role for integrity either; integrity is a response to variety and dissonance, not imperfection as such.[11] That integrity would not be a distinct concern in a society all of whose members agreed on one view about justice (even a false view) seems to assume that any one view about justice will be coherent in itself. That may be questioned: surely the phrase 'an incoherent theory of justice' is not an oxymoron. But we need not be troubled by this. *Coherence* is a concept of which there are many conceptions. Although there may be tests of coherence which some theories of justice fail, Dworkin has no independent reason for being interested in the conceptions of coherence which those tests presuppose. His prescriptive claim is that society as a whole should exhibit a concern for justice that is *as coherent as any individual theory of justice might be*. To get at the relevant notion of coherence, we must ask: 'In what way must a set of propositions about justice cohere in order to be regarded as a single *theory* or *view* about justice?' That will provide the test for coherence which we are then to apply to the principles underlying social arrangements as a whole, according to Dworkin.[12]

A single view, then, would *eo ipso* guarantee coherence in the relevant sense. Incoherence is a prospect – and thus integrity can be a distinct and important principle – only because multiple views about justice are in play. What Dworkin calls the 'background assumptions' of his interest in integrity are that 'different people hold different views about moral issues that they all treat as of great importance', and that, despite these

[11] I am assuming that a conception of justice could be both coherent and false. Some philosophers have held coherence theories of truth, according to which truth in some domain is simply identified with membership of a coherent set of propositions in that domain. (See Walker, *The Coherence Theory of Truth*.) It is tempting to say that Dworkin's jurisprudence is a coherence theory of truth in the domain of legal propositions. That temptation should be resisted. Apart from anything else, the coherence demanded by integrity is just one dimension of legal truth (or soundness or assertibility) in Dworkin's theory. I do not believe, either, that he holds a coherence theory of truth about justice. Like almost everyone else, he thinks coherence is necessary for truth in this area – hence the point about utopia. But there is no evidence of his subscribing to the view that incoherence is an inevitable companion of falsehood.

[12] It is possible to make the test even tighter than this. Instead of asking how coherent a set of propositions must be in order to be regarded as a single view about justice, we might focus our attention simply on the issue of disagreement and conflict. Is the set of propositions capable of generating disparate prescriptions as to what is to be done – i.e. prescriptions that directly contradict one another at the 'all-things-considered' level? If so, it does give rise to the problems that spur our interest in integrity. On the other hand, if a theory *looks* incoherent by some formal standard but does not generate, or is not capable of generating, such stark prescriptive conflicts in the real world, then its putative incoherence is not what we are interested in. Its putative incoherence would be more a matter of philosophical aesthetics than of the legitimacy-related issues invoked in Dworkin's discussion of integrity. (I am grateful to Stephen Perry for this point.)

differences, political fairness demands that 'each person or group in the community should have a roughly equal share of control over the decisions made by parliament or Congress or the state legislature' (178).

The other contrast – between the real world in which the demands of integrity can be met and a dystopic world in which that is impossible – is also implicit in Dworkin's conception, though his account of the conditions that distinguish the real world from this dystopia is somewhat less developed. The dystopic possibility is posed by what Dworkin calls 'internal skepticism' (78). Internal sceptics allege that the institutions and standards current in modern pluralist societies are too chaotic in their provenance and too inconsistent in their ideology to admit of the sort of 'tidying up' or constructive imposition of coherence that integrity recommends. The best known contemporary version of this, according to Dworkin, is the Critical Legal Studies (CLS) movement. CLS scholars argue that there are at least 'two deeply antagonistic ideologies at war within the law', and that 'our legal culture, far from having any shape amenable to a uniform and coherent justification of principle, can only be grasped through the infertile metric of contradiction' (272).

Dworkin claims to take this possibility seriously. It is useful, he says, to remind the liberal jurist that 'nothing in the way his law was produced guarantees his success in finding a coherent conception of it' (273). Unfortunately, however, Dworkin says very little about the real-world conditions that moral pluralism and political competition must satisfy in order to avoid this possibility.

The main argument in *Law's Empire* against CLS scepticism is that it neglects the distinction between *competing* principles (such as autonomy and mutual concern) which may figure in a single view about justice, and *contradictory* principles (such as equality and inequality) which cannot possibly be combined in one coherent conception (269–75). This might suggest the following as one of the circumstances of integrity. If integrity is to be practicable, the rival views about justice that have secured footholds in society's current standards must not directly contradict one another; suitably weighted, they must be capable of being held – albeit in tension – in some single complex view.[13]

Such a condition, however, would be far too strong. For one thing, it comes perilously close to denying the basis of the *other* circumstance of integrity – the circumstance that distinguishes our world from a morally homogeneous one. That assumption, remember, is that people really do

---

[13] Earlier in *Law's Empire*, Dworkin says that integrity is violated 'whenever a community enacts and enforces different laws each of which is coherent in itself, but which cannot be defended together as expressing a coherent ranking of different principles of justice . . .' (184). It is not clear, however, whether he means to suggest that the constructive task of the judge is rendered impossible once integrity has been violated in this way.

disagree about justice, and that views genuinely (not just apparently) at odds with one another may both be represented among the standards currently in force. For another thing, it ignores the fact that each of the rival views about justice in society is already a view about how competing principles such as autonomy and mutual concern should be ranked, related, and weighed within a single conception. It is not a case of one statute having been passed by an autonomy faction and another statute having been enacted by the party of mutual concern, and of its never having occurred to anyone except the judge (now faced with the two statutes together) that a suitably complex position could accommodate both principles. Social democrats and conservatives directly contradict one another in their assignment of weight to principles like these and in their account of the principles' relations to one another, and it remains to be seen how coherent sense can be made, by the constructive jurist, of these apparently contradictory weightings.

4. INTEGRITY VERSUS JUSTICE?

An advantage of describing disagreement about justice as one of the circumstances of integrity is that it gives us a clearer view of what is going when the two values – justice and integrity – appear to conflict.

Dworkin's view is that the two values often do conflict (188) and that when they do, 'justice must sometimes be sacrificed to integrity' (178). Such conflicts among ideals, he says, are common in politics. Even if we rejected the idea of integrity, we would still have to deal with conflicts between justice and political fairness (177).

I am not sure that 'conflict' is the right word to describe what happens when a person finds himself commanded by principles of fairness or integrity to do what his own convictions about justice oppose. We usually talk about a conflict between principles A and B (in some situation X) when the two principles are held by a single agent, and it is clear what A requires of that agent in X and clear what B requires of that agent in X and those requirements are incompatible.[14] That is seldom the situation as between justice and fairness or as between justice and integrity. We may know and agree what fairness or integrity require in a given situation, but the condition of our talking about fairness or integrity is the existence of disagreement about what justice requires. Principles of political fairness, for example, are principles used to guide social decision-making in circumstances where some members of the society think that justice requires one thing and some members of society think justice requires another.

---

[14] Thus conflict is not the same as disagreement.

When fair political procedures indicate that one of these factions is to pre-vail at the level of social decision, the result will seem to the members of that faction to be congruent with justice, even as it seems to members of the other faction to be at odds with justice. This disparity – as to whether there is a conflict with justice or not – should alert us to the possibility that there is something of a 'category-mistake' in treating justice and fairness as co-ordinate principles, competing on the same level.

It is significant that Dworkin's view of the potential for conflict between justice and fairness turns on his characterization of them as values which 'are to some degree independent of one another' (177). The clearest cases of moral conflict do involve such independence. For example: we are inter-ested in aesthetic value, but we are also interested in the relief of poverty; thus a political proposal to fund a new museum engages independent and conflicting values, as we imagine other things – such as a new welfare scheme – that could be achieved using the same resources. Justice and fair-ness, however, are *not* independent in this way. Instead, one is functionally related to the other. It is the task of political fairness to address the situation that arises when people in a society cannot agree about justice, and thus can-not act univocally *as a society* on the basis of an appeal to justice alone. The invocation of fairness is not the introduction of any new and independent value to alter the odds in that stand-off. It is rather the elaboration of respectful procedures for settling on social action *despite* the stand-off.

Another way of understanding the relation between justice and fairness uses Joseph Raz's notion of second-order reasons for action.[15] A second-order reason is a reason to act or to refrain from acting on a first-order reason. Now one's views about justice are usually conclusions about the first-order reasons (i.e. the substantive merits) for society's distributing rights and resources in certain ways. Once one becomes aware that those views are not shared by everyone in society, one acquires a second-order reason not to act peremptorily – at least not in the name of the whole soci-ety – on the basis of one's own estimate of those first-order reasons. Justice – certainly *social* justice – is something we must secure together; no one can do it on his own. Our acting together as a society is going to require us to take a view about what is to be done (about justice) in the light of our dis-agreement concerning the first-order reasons that apply to the matter in issue. If we decide to settle the issue by majority-voting, we are deciding to act in the light of reasons that are second-order in relation to the reasons that people properly act on in forming their substantive views (and in deciding how to vote).

An example may help here. Suppose someone urges the abolition of welfare assistance for unemployed single men. There are all sorts of

---

[15] See Raz, *Practical Reason and Norms*, 39.

reasons for and against this proposal. Since we are likely to disagree about what those reasons are and how they should be balanced, we must as a society have recourse to fair principles of political decision to determine the matter one way or the other. So we take a vote, and we find that abolition has the support of most members of the group. Now that political fact is not itself a reason for being in favour of abolition. If the majority-decision were to be reliably predicted *before* the vote, it would be quite inappropriate for that prediction to tilt the balance of reasons for a voter who was genuinely undecided on the merits.[16] The prospect of majority support adds nothing to the reasons in favour of abolition (reasons such as providing incentives for work, reducing public expenditure, freeing up resources for museums, etc.), nor does it compete directly with the reasons there might be for continuing the welfare provision (reasons like avoiding homelessness, diminishing incentives for crime, satisfying needs, etc.). Majority support offers a different kind of reason, operating at a different level: it is a reason *for society and for those who act in society's name* to settle on abolition as a social decision given that a social decision is needed and that people disagree about the first-order reasons in the matter. The difference of level, then, makes it misleading to talk about a conflict between justice and fairness.[17]

Talk of such conflict is not just theoretically misconceived; it can be politically confusing as well. If we talk about a conflict between justice and fairness, we seem to imply that sometimes fairness might weigh more heavily, and sometimes justice might weigh more heavily. But the problem is not about weighing and balancing; the problem is that we disagree about what justice requires, and thus we disagree about what goes into one side of the balance. If we *were* to decide, in a given case, that justice mattered more than fairness, what should we do? In the example above, should we abolish the welfare provision or maintain it? Which view of justice should we act on, having decided that justice matters more than

[16] The possibility of strategic voting does not affect this. The strategic voter does not alter his reasoning about the first-order issue once he discovers how others are likely to vote. He simply alters his voting behaviour. Indeed if he is going to engage in strategic voting, it is all the more important for his substantive reasoning to remain intact, so that he can hold on to a healthy sense of his overall priorities.

[17] This analysis is along the lines of the suggestions made at the end of Wollheim's fine essay, 'A Paradox in the Theory of Democracy', 71. The paradox of democracy is as follows: a person who voted for policy A, believing that policy A (and not policy B) is the one that should be implemented, is required by democratic principles to believe that policy B is the one that should be implemented in the event of B's attracting majority support. Wollheim's solution is to distinguish between 'direct' principles like 'Provision should be made for desperate need' and 'oblique' principles like majority-decision. But the basis of the distinction is never satisfactorily explained, and Wollheim offers only a sketch of the argument that is necessary to show that 'A should be done' and 'A should not be done' are not incompatible when the former follows from a direct principle and the latter from an oblique principle.

fairness? Should we each act on our own view of justice? But these problems only arise in the context of *social* decision.

Reminding ourselves that disagreement about justice is the circumstance of fairness has an additional consequence. It cautions us against adopting principles of fairness whose operation turns on considerations of justice. Such principles do not help us to settle on social decisions in the face of disagreement. Quite the contrary: they threaten to reproduce the very conflict about justice with which we began. An example of such a principle is the following, which I shall call Modified Majoritarianism: *'Let the majority prevail except in cases where the majority decision threatens individual rights.'* If people disagree (as we know they do) about what rights we have or about what threatens them, this principle will be hopeless. Suppose, in the example given above, that many members of the minority believe single unemployed men have a moral right to welfare assistance, and that the majority who favour abolition deny this. Then *both* sides will claim a victory under the principle of Modified Majoritarianism, and they will be no further ahead in their decision-making. They will need to set up *another* principle of fair political procedure (say, *Pure* Majoritarianism) if they are to make a social decision.

I have concentrated for a few pages on criticizing the common view that there can be conflicts and trade-offs between justice and political fairness. It is a while since anything was said about integrity. However, I believe the same considerations apply there also. The circumstances of integrity (like those of fairness) include the existence of disagreements about what is just and unjust. Therefore any putative trade-off between justice and integrity begs the question of which contestant view about justice is being privileged in our account of such a trade-off. It seems better to say, not that justice and integrity conflict, but that integrity like fairness is a political value that approaches issues of justice from an oblique angle – an angle defined functionally by the need to deal with the fact that various decisions to which our community has already committed itself have been made on the basis of disparate and conflicting conceptions of justice.

Thus Dworkin's talk of competition between justice and integrity is misleading. Integrity is not a value which *competes* with justice. It is rather a value whose job it is to come into play when the place properly assigned to justice in the life of a community – the role of determining a proper distribution of rights and duties, burdens and benefits, etc. – turns out to have been filled by disparate and competing conceptions of justice itself.

5. A PARTICIPANT'S POINT OF VIEW

The analysis just given may seem unsatisfactory. Surely Dworkin is right when he says that integrity (or fairness or both) may sometimes command a result which justice condemns. We can think about that possibility in the following way.

Though people disagree about justice, each person may hold a firm view. So it is possible to say, *at least from the point of view of a particular person*, that justice as he sees it is being sacrificed to integrity (or to fairness). Moreover, though people disagree about justice, some claims about what justice requires are true and others false. So, we might say, it is objectively either true or false in a given situation that integrity (or fairness) is at odds with what justice actually requires. We saw in the last chapter how careful we must be with the latter formulation. No matter how often or emphatically we deploy words like 'objective', a claim about what justice *objectively* requires never appears in politics except as someone's view – someone's view which of course, in the sort of situation we are considering, is directly contradicted by the view of someone else. Although there may *be* an objective truth about justice, such truth never manifests itself to us in any self-certifying manner; it inevitably comes among us as one contestant opinion among others.[18]

Let us concentrate, then, on some particular person who passionately holds a particular view about justice and is utterly convinced of its truth – notwithstanding the fact that he knows others in society, equally sincere and equally passionate, disagree with him. On the occasions when he is outnumbered, it will seem *to him* that justice is being sacrificed to democratic principles of political fairness. And he may be right. Similarly, in a situation in which society has already committed itself to principles of justice that he regards as misguided, the demand of integrity that the law remain coherent may seem *to him* to further compromise what justice truly requires. And he may be right about that also.

The point of view from which these judgements are made – that is, the point of view from which it appears that there really are conflicts and trade-offs among justice, fairness and integrity – is the point of view of just one contestant, in a society whose politics are defined by controversy. For a politically literate contestant, each of these judgements is matched by an awareness that there are, among his fellow citizens, people who believe (as he thinks, wrongly) that justice is *not* conflicting with fairness or integrity in these cases, people who disagree with him about what is just and unjust. It is matched, too, with an awareness of the point I emphasized in the last section: that it is only because we disagree about justice in this way, that there is any need for principles of fairness or integrity at all.

It seems, then, that a belief in the existence of conflicts and trade-offs between justice and integrity is a matter of purely personal politics, a tendentious belief that must be transcended when one takes up the

---

[18] See the discussion in Ch. 8, above.

perspective of society as a whole (the perspective we take as jurists or political philosophers). From that perspective, we must not say 'Society faces a trade-off between justice and integrity', though we may say that what society does in the name of integrity will inevitably (and more or less *ex hypothesi*) conflict with what *some* individuals believe about justice (and thus that it will, according to those individuals, conflict with what justice actually requires).

6. SCEPTICISM AND HESITATION

Throughout *Law's Empire*, Dworkin is at pains to insist that although disagreement about justice is one of the circumstances of integrity, it should not affect or undermine the confidence with which we advance particular claims about justice. For example, he dismisses as 'singularly inept' the following objection to his constitutional jurisprudence:

Someone will think one interpretation of the due process or equal protection clause better than another only because he thinks one theory of justice or equality better than another. But theories of justice and equality are only subjective; there is no right answer to which is best, only different answers. [373][19]

Dworkin says this objection is based on what he calls 'external skepticism' (78) – a general philosophical suspicion of the credentials of all justice-claims, indeed of moral claims in general. He insists that even if external scepticism raises important issues in metaphysics and the philosophy of language, it is wrong to infer anything from it so far as the validity of our practice of making moral judgements or judgements about justice is concerned (78–83). A lack of moral consensus, a recognition that different folks give different answers to questions about justice, even an imputation of 'subjectivity' – none of this should be used to dissuade us from participating in the very disagreements that are supposed to give rise to the sceptical difficulty. After all, as we saw in Chapter Eight, even if the sceptics are right and judgements of justice are nothing but expressions of subjective attitudes, that is no reason to be coy about expressing one's attitudes.

But is there any special problem about advancing tendentious claims about justice in the *political* realm? From one point of view, obviously not. If no one advanced controversial claims about justice, there would be nothing for fairness and integrity to address. One cannot therefore argue backwards from the circumstances of integrity and fairness to the inappropriateness of people advancing particular views *qua* citizens, *qua* voters, *qua* political partisans.

[19] Dworkin attributes this objection (Dworkin, *Law's Empire*, 451 n. 12) to Bork, 'Neutral Principles and Some First Amendment Problems', 10.

Still, there may be a little more to think about here. I mentioned earlier that a just social structure is something we must secure together; no one can do it on his own. Yet often we proceed in political philosophy as though the proper mode of thinking about justice were the careful formulation of a view or theory *by each individual* – a view or theory which ideally will amount to a comprehensive social vision. Of course we hope that each will be open to suggestions and criticisms from other individual view-formers. But the telos of thought-about-justice is a view formed finally in the mind of one agent, and then acted on conscientiously by that agent, no matter what others think or say. And if someone reminds us that justice is a social task, we simply respond with the hope that the unity of truth will secure a convergence of individuals' thinking. Whether or not that is a plausible assumption is another matter. But, at any rate, reflection on the fact that each is deliberating about something *social* does not intimate for us – as perhaps it should – any philosophical difficulty with the possibility that one person is right and everyone else around him wrong, so far as justice is concerned.

We proceed, I said, as though the crucial thing in political philosophy were for each of us to give his whole-hearted support to the theory that he thinks gets justice right. Certainly that sort of Thoreau-like steadfastness makes sense if we suppose that the fundamental question about justice is always in the end a question for the individual agent, 'What am I to do?'[20] It is striking, however, that today when a philosopher forms a view about justice and talks about 'What I would do' (about immigration, for example, or school prayer, or welfare provision), he usually means not what he would do as an individual agent, but what he would do in the unlikely event that he were in charge of the whole society and his conscience could mobilize us all. And we say the same about political philosophers: what Plato would do about gender equality; what Hobbes would do about religion; what Mill would do about prostitution; etc. Is this a valuable way of proceeding in political theory? I am not sure.[21] Perhaps we should hesitate before substituting the individual thinker for the society in these academic manifestos – the 'I' for the 'we' who in the end constitute the only possible agent of social change. When we do this, are we in fact despairing of collective action, and imagining instead that each of us can make a difference – and this time the *right* difference – on his own? Do we think of ourselves or of the philosophers we read as prophets or lawgivers? Or do we accept

---

[20] See Thoreau, 'Civil Disobedience', esp. 644: 'If the injustice has a spring, or a pulley, or a rope, or a crank, exclusively for itself, then perhaps you may consider whether the remedy will not be worse than the evil; but if it is of such a nature that it requires you to be the agent of injustice to another, then , I say, break the law. . . . What I have to do is to see, at any rate, that I do not lend myself to the wrong which I condemn.'

[21] See Waldron, 'What Plato Would Allow'.

that they are citizens, each of them one citizen among millions? Perhaps we should pause and reflect, for example, on the tension between the pronouns in William Blake's lines (from the poem *Milton*):[22]

> *I* will not cease from Mental Fight,
> Nor shall *my* Sword sleep in *my* hand,
> Till *we* have built Jerusalem,
> In England's Green & Pleasant Land.

The first two lines of the stanza are the rhetoric of John Brown, the last two are the rhetoric of legislative reconstruction; and what is troubling me in these paragraphs is some sense of mismatch between the thinking and conscience that animates the former and the sense of collective enterprise that finds expression in the latter.

I am not sure how far to pursue these worries,[23] but I am convinced we need to hold on philosophically to the sense of unease and hesitation here.

7. OFFICIALS

Perhaps there is nothing inappropriate about people advancing particular views of justice *qua* citizens, *qua* voters, *qua* political partisans. For mostly when we do this, we are offering it as a contribution to a process of social decision: we understand that we are not dictators, and that each of us is not the only candidate for *conscience of the society*. When it comes to officials, however – legislators, executive officers, and judges, those empowered to act in the name of the whole society – we must be a little more careful. To act in the name of a society in the circumstances of fairness is to act in a situation where no view about justice (including one's own view) is uncontested. In those circumstances, it is incumbent on the official to proceed in a way that shows some respect for the others who will be bound by his decision but who may not necessarily agree with its grounds.

There is a famous line from Thomas Hobbes's exchange with Bishop Bramhall: 'Because neither mine nor the Bishop's reason is right reason fit to be a rule of our moral actions, we have therefore set up over ourselves a sovereign governor.'[24] Hobbes's claim here is not that a particular person's reason is the wrong sort of thing to govern collective action: after all, the sovereign may be just a natural person too.[25] Rather, the claim is that,

---

[22] Emphasis added.

[23] I am grateful to Bob Hargrave, Sidney Morgenbesser, and Thomas Pogge for conversations along these lines. More are clearly needed.

[24] Quoted in Postema, *Bentham and the Common Law Tradition*, 54.

[25] Cf. Postema, *Bentham and the Common Law Tradition*, 55: 'The sovereign has no special claim to wisdom, insight, or truth . . . The [social contract] simply erects the sovereign's garden-variety natural reason as the standard of right reason . . .'.

as things stand, a particular person's view (even a bishop's or a philosopher's view) is just one view, denied and disputed by others, in a contest of substance that constitutes the problem of politics. The problem can only begin to be solved when there is a way of identifying one of the contestant views as *'ours'* – that is, as 'right reason' *for us* – as a view on which *we* will act and co-ordinate even though many of us disagree about its merits. When the matter is stated like that, it is clear that no one can believe his view of justice is *right reason* (and hence appropriately *ours*) merely because he is convinced (even if rightly) that his view is really correct.[26]

Still, it is not always inappropriate for an official acting in a public capacity to act on the basis of his own tendentious views about justice. The clearest case is when the society embraces principles of fairness that empower him to do precisely that. Elective dictatorship, as I said at the beginning, is a possible solution to the problem of social action in circumstances of disagreement, and under certain conditions it is a fair and attractive solution. Indeed, every democratic system embodies to some degree the principle that certain officials are empowered to take decisions in the name of the whole society on the basis of their own views about justice. This is how most political systems actually solve the problem of settling on social choices in the face of justice-disagreements: we designate one of the contestant views as the one to govern us for the time being.

Apart from such specific fairness-based designations, there is also a sense throughout *Law's Empire* that making judgements about justice in one's own voice – even though one is aware that such judgements are controversial and contested – is the default mode of all political action.[27] Neither integrity nor fairness make sense, Dworkin says, except among people who are committed to justice (263) – that is, except among people who are in the business of making and implementing judgements about what justice requires. Assuming that the demands of integrity, for example, sometimes leave judges with a choice between two coherent schemes of principle, each fitting most of the precedents and the existing law, Dworkin thinks it is *obvious* that the judge must choose between them on grounds of justice:

[H]e must choose between eligible interpretations by asking which shows the community's structure of institutions and decisions – its public standards as a whole –

[26] See also the Hobbesian motto to this book: 'And when men that think themselves wiser than all others, clamor and demand right Reason for judge; yet seek no more, but that things should be determined, by no other mens reason but their own, it is as intolerable in the society of men, as it is in play after trump is turned, to use for trump on every occasion, that suite whereof they have most in their hand.' (Hobbes, *Leviathan*, Ch. 5, 33.)

[27] This sense is clearest at the end of the book, where Dworkin speaks of the special prominence of justice in the constellation of political virtues: Dworkin, *Law's Empire*, 406.

in a better light from the standpoint of political morality. His own moral and political convictions are now directly engaged. [256]

The judge's awareness of dissensus in the community should not make him coy about engaging his own convictions. For if proper tribute has *already* been paid to the need for coherence and to whatever fairness-principles govern his official position, there is nothing else for the judge to do but make a judgment as to justice on the merits. The whole business of governance is *about* taking a view about justice and implementing it. If dissensus of views and diversity of current standards are, respectively, the circumstances of fairness and integrity, then the practice of forming and applying a view about justice is the primal or elementary circumstance of those circumstances.

8. THE CLAIMS OF INTEGRITY

So officials as well as citizens may make judgements of justice in their own voice, notwithstanding their awareness that others in society do not share their views. Still, there is a difference.

If I am a theorist setting out and elaborating a particular conception of justice, or if I am an individual voter or partisan propounding that conception in public debate, I can be expected to present it in a way that is not only tendentious but uncompromising. 'Here is what justice really requires', I will say. 'The theories held by other citizens, the theories that rival mine in public debate, are simply mistaken.' I may be wrong about that of course: my view might be false, and theirs closer to the truth. But subject to familiar requirements of sincerity, fallibilism, and openness to criticism, that is what the partisan of each view can be expected to say.

In this context, the suggestion that each theory ought to accommodate or seek some compromise with its rivals will seem quite inappropriate. How can there be a compromise about justice? If I give an inch to my rivals, I will be suggesting that we as society do less than what justice actually demands. The matter is not trivial. To form the belief that *justice* requires X rather than Y, is to form the belief that nothing less than X will do and that a compromise or accommodation with Y or anything else would be pernicious. Of course, as I have said, a given belief about what justice requires may be mistaken. But what one would be mistaken about, is what categorically and uncompromisingly ought to be done, so far as the basic structure of society is concerned.

This point, about 'no compromise, no accommodation', cannot be better explained than by Ronald Dworkin himself, in an account he gave (several years before the publication of *Law's Empire*) of why a decent utilitarian calculus should exclude 'external' preferences held by people as the upshot of political convictions that are incompatible with the grounds of utilitarianism itself. Dworkin wrote:

Utilitarianism must claim (as . . . any political theory must claim) truth for itself, and therefore must claim the falsity of any theory that contradicts it. It must itself occupy, that is, all the logical space that its content requires. . . . Suppose the community contains a Nazi, for example, whose set of preferences includes the preference that Aryans have more and Jews less of their preferences fulfilled just because of who they are. A neutral utilitarian cannot say that there is no reason in political morality for rejecting or dishonouring that preference, for not dismissing it as simply wrong, for not striving to fulfil it with all the dedication that officials devote to fulfilling any other sort of preference. For utilitarianism itself supplies such reason: its most fundamental tenet is that people's preferences should be weighed on an equal basis in the same scales, that the Nazi theory of justice is profoundly wrong, and that officials should oppose the Nazi theory and strive to defeat rather than fulfil it. A neutral utilitarian is in fact barred, for reasons of consistency, from taking the same politically neutral attitude to the Nazi's political preference that he takes to other sorts of preferences.[28]

At the level of expounding and defending utilitarianism as a theory of justice, this seems exactly right. As Dworkin puts it, one cannot commit oneself to defeating the theory that some people's preferences should count for more, and at the same time count that theory, as held by its proponent, as one preference among others, to be accorded equal weight and counted in a social calculus, to determine what justice actually requires.[29]

What appears, however, as principled opposition to compromise at the level of partisanship, may seem blinkered, self-centered, and obtuse when one is acting in the name of the whole society. At the level of partisanship, a theory of justice must 'claim truth for itself' and occupy 'all the logical space that its content requires'.[30] But at the level of social decision, the game is not one 'in which each person tries to plant the flag of his convictions over as large a domain of power or rules as possible' (211). Exercises of social power must claim legitimacy in relation to the community as a whole; they must claim also the allegiance and obligation of every member of the community.[31] They will be hard put to do this if their legitimacy is based solely upon conceptions of justice which some members of society reject. Thus, given the circumstances of fairness and integrity, the appropriate sense of community – appropriate for making power and coercion legitimate and for evoking allegiance and a sense of obligation from all citizens – must go beyond particular views about justice, no matter how sincerely and passionately those are held. It is Dworkin's view that community, in this sense,'commands that no one be left out, that we

---

[28] Dworkin, 'Rights as Trumps', 155–6.   [29] Ibid., 157.   [30] Ibid., 155.
[31] See also Copp, 'Could Political Truth Be a Hazard for Democracy?'

are all in politics together for better or worse, that no one may be sacrificed, like wounded left on the battlefield, to the crusade for justice overall' (213).

The passage is an important one. Read superficially, the prescription sounds anodyne. Of course, in a true community, no one should be left out, sacrificed, or abandoned. A community takes care of its casualties. But *casualties in the crusade for justice?*

It is clear, in context, that Dworkin does not mean by 'casualties' those who have given their lives or sacrificed their interests so that the society may be more just. He means those whose views we believe wrong or defective on matters of justice – those who have attempted to uphold what we (who might leave them behind on the battlefield) regard as unjust principles or inequitable arrangements. And when he talks about our sacrificing them or leaving them behind on the battlefield, Dworkin does not mean to refer to the possibility that we might suppress or liquidate those who disagree with us about justice. He means to refer to – and condemn – the possibility that, after the victory we have won for our principles (as we think, the true principles of justice), we might seek to prevent the unjust principles our opponents have sponsored from playing any part in or continuing to influence social arrangements. This is the possibility which, he suggests, a principled model of community prohibits.

Read in this way and fleshed out with obvious examples, Dworkin's suggestion can easily seem shocking. The Civil War is over, the forces of slavery and racism have surrendered, and now reconstruction of the nation – at last, thank God, on true principles of justice – can begin. Not so fast, says integrity. The views about justice held by those we defeated must not simply be abandoned on the battlefield at Antietam or Gettysburg. If the defeated views are embodied in standards or institutions already in force in society, then any decisions we make – even in the flush of our moral triumph – are constrained by the need to find common and principled ground with what we regard as the epitome of injustice. Of course that search for common ground will be distasteful. But it is precisely the point of integrity that, in a pluralistic society, each must respect the principles of justice 'instinct in the standing political arrangement of his particular community, . . . whether or not he thinks these the best principles from a utopian standpoint' (213).

Is it a mistake to push Dworkin's argument so far in this accommodationist direction? Is it, in particular, a mistake for this sort of example, where the injustice with which integrity recommends accommodation – the injustice of slavery – seems so particularly egregious? Dworkin concedes that '[a]n association of principle is not automatically a just community' (213). But could it be *this* unjust?

There are reasons the example is inapposite, and I shall go into them in a moment. From the point of view of jurisprudence and political philosophy, however, those reasons cannot turn on the egregious nature of the injustice at stake, or on how passionately anyone feels about it. (For again that will be something on which people disagree.) It is not the jurist's job or that of the political philosopher to stipulate thresholds of injustice beyond which integrity ceases to apply. Our task is not to display our own opinions about the just and the unjust, but to emphasize as one of the circumstances of integrity that people differ in what engages their passionate moral sentiments and that they are therefore likely to disagree about which injustices meet a given threshold of seriousness.

Having said that, I should emphasize that particular individuals may find that their moral feelings on some potential injustice are so intense as to outweigh any continued commitment to a political system that would require them to work out a common course of action with their opponents. If that is the case, then the circumstances of fairness and so of integrity no longer apply to them (and *pro tanto* they no longer apply to the *whole* society). For the circumstances of fairness are not only that there is disagreement, but that there is a felt need, shared by the disputants, for common action in spite of such disagreement. Such a felt need for common action may have its limits. If it does, the people in question may no longer feel themselves part of the community in which power has been shared or alternated with their opponents, and thus they may no longer feel themselves called upon to address coherence- or integrity-related problems concerning the patchwork of current standards that results.

This may happen, too, at the level of a whole society if an issue of justice proves to be one on which the usual principles of fair decision and the sharing or alternating of power are no longer politically acceptable. Either side or both may prefer the dissolution of the political community to a continued accommodation of the other view or to a continued subjection of the issue to the vicissitudes of electoral politics. Whether that produces peaceful secession or civil war, the upshot is unlikely to be one in which the normal circumstances of integrity obtain. A seceding faction or the victorious faction will seek in the wake of the conflict to purge all traces of what it repudiates as radically unjust principles from its current political arrangements. If it succeeds, there may be nothing left to accommodate – nothing left to come to terms with in a principled compromise – along the lines that integrity requires.

Something like this – or a complex and perhaps flawed version of it – seems to be true of the postbellum United States and slavery. At any rate, the possibility indicates one final advantage of our talk of 'the circumstances of' integrity. Though moderate scarcity and limited altruism are among the circumstances of justice, the logic of 'circumstances'[32] is such that a commitment to justice is not a *commitment* to scarcity and limited altruism. A partisan of justice would not (or should not) be dismayed if goods become superabundant or men's indifference and suspicion of one another gradually wither away, any more than a partisan of charity would be dismayed by the abolition of poverty or a partisan of courage by a diminution in the amount of danger in the world.[33] Similarly, partisans of fairness will not be dismayed by the emergence of unanimity on any issue. Not only that, but *qua* partisans of fairness they will have nothing to say about the desirability or undesirability of a political community's falling apart over some issue of justice. For all that fairness tells us, it may be better all round that men no longer feel the need to act in community with those whose views they despise. Or – if that is *not* better – some additional argument (such as Hobbes's argument about the horrors of the state of nature) is necessary to show why. That a felt need for common action is one of the circumstances of fairness does not show that the felt need is to be cherished nor that it is always justified.

In much the same way, setting out the circumstances of integrity enables us to grasp the conditions of *its* application, and make some theoretical sense of Dworkin's own intuitive (and by itself unsatisfactory) view that the relative weight of integrity will be less in cases where the issue of justice is particularly serious (381–97). The seriousness of the issue is not itself a reason for diminishing the weight assigned to integrity. It may be an indication, nevertheless, that some of the circumstances of integrity no longer obtain. We cannot guarantee that people will always want to persevere in community and share power with those whose views about justice they reject. It is the common sense of politics that they often do, and Dworkin is right to give this fact central place in his jurisprudence and political theory. The limits of that willingness, however, provide a better account (better than any philosopher's own intensely held sentiments) of the conditions under which integrity and fairness ought to give way to straightforward individual judgements of justice.

---

[32] In formal terms, the logic of 'circumstances' is, roughly, the logic of presupposition.
[33] Cf. Sandel, *Liberalism and the Limits of Justice*, 28–46.

III. Rights and Judicial Review

Chapter Ten

Between Rights and Bills of Rights

1. CONSTITUTIONAL REFORM

'Individuals have rights, and there are things no person or group may do to them (without violating their rights).'[1] 'Each person possesses an inviolability founded on justice that even the welfare of society as a whole cannot override.'[2] 'There would be no point in the boast that we respect individual rights unless that involved some sacrifice, and the sacrifice in question must be that we give up whatever marginal benefits our country would receive from overriding these rights when they prove inconvenient.'[3]

These are familiar and persuasive propositions of political philosophy. What do they imply about institutions? Should we embody our rights in legalistic formulas and proclaim them in a formal Bill of Rights? Or should we leave them to evolve informally in dialogue among citizens, representatives, and officials? How are we to stop rights from being violated? Should we rely on a general spirit of watchfulness in the community, attempting to raise what John Stuart Mill called 'a strong barrier of moral conviction' to protect our liberty?[4] Or should we also entrust some specific branch of government – the courts, for example – with the task of detecting violations and with the authority to overrule any other branch that commits them, including the legislature?

The advantages of this last approach continue to attract proponents of constitutional reform in the United Kingdom. Ronald Dworkin, for example, has argued that a system of judicial review of legislation would forge a decisive link between rights and legality, giving the former much greater prominence in British public life. By throwing the authority of the courts behind the idea of rights, the legal system might begin to play 'a different, more valuable role in society'. Lawyers and judges might take on roles more akin to those of their counterparts in the United States:

The courts, charged with the responsibility of creating . . . a distinctly British scheme of human rights and liberty, might think more in terms of principle and less in terms of narrow precedent. . . . Different men and women might then be tempted to the law as a career, and from their ranks a more committed and

---

[1] Nozick, *Anarchy, State and Utopia*, ix.
[3] Dworkin, *Taking Rights Seriously*, 193.
[2] Rawls, *A Theory of Justice*, 3.
[4] Mill, *On Liberty*, Ch. 1, 18.

idealistic generation of judges might emerge, encouraging a further cycle in the renaissance of liberty.[5]

If these judges used their new powers well, Dworkin concludes, governments would no longer be free, as they are now, to treat liberty as a commodity of convenience or 'to ignore rights that the nation has a solemn obligation to respect'.[6] What should we say about these proposals?[7] In discussions of constitutional reform, I find that people take it for granted that enthusiasm for Dworkin's proposal is shared by any philosopher whose moral theory or normative theory of justice is organized around the idea of rights. Surely, it is said, anyone who believes in rights will welcome a proposal to institutionalize a Bill of Rights and give the courts power to strike down legislation that encroaches on basic liberties.[8]

In this part of the book, I am going to question that assumption. I want to develop five main lines of argument. The first is a negative case: I shall show in this chapter that there is no necessary inference from a right-based position in moral or political philosophy to a commitment to a Bill of Rights as a political institution along with an American-style practice of judicial review.

Secondly, I shall argue – also in this chapter – that philosophers ought to be more aware than other proponents of constitutional reform of the difficulty, complexity, and controversy attending the idea of basic rights. I shall argue that they have reason – grounded in professional humility – to be more than usually hesitant about the enactment of any canonical list of rights, particularly if the aim is to put that canon beyond the scope of ordinary political debate and revision.

Thirdly, I shall try and persuade those who talk about rights to pay more attention than they do to the processes by which decisions are taken in a community under conditions of disagreement. That was one of the themes of Part I – particularly Chapter Five, where we focused on legislative decision-making in what I referred to as 'the circumstances of politics'. Throughout Part III, I am going argue that those circumstances – the existence of disagreement and the need, despite disagreement, to set up a common framework – apply at least as much to issues of rights as they apply to what is usually regarded as the more modest agenda of legisla-

---

[5] Dworkin, *A Bill of Rights for Britain*, 23.   [6] Ibid., 12 and 21.

[7] By the time this book appears, they may be more than 'proposals'. The Human Rights Bill currently making its way through Parliament aims at the incorporation of the European Convention on Human Rights into British law (although it is still not clear what, exactly, the judicial review of legislation in the UK will amount to).

[8] For example, Bruce Ackerman assumes in his book *We the People: Foundations* that scholars who have a philosophical commitment to fundamental rights – 'rights foundationalists', as he calls them – believe that 'the whole point of having rights is to trump decisions rendered by democratic institutions that may otherwise legislate for the collective welfare' (ibid., 11–12).

tive politics. It follows that theories of rights as much as theories of public policy need to be complemented by theories of *authority*, whose function it is to determine how decisions are to be taken when the members of a community disagree about what decision is right. Since we must assume a context of disagreement, a principle such as 'Let the right decision be made' cannot form part of an adequate principle of authority, for it will reproduce not resolve the disagreement with which we are grappling. It follows that, if people disagree about basic rights (and they do) while nevertheless needing (as they do) a common framework, an adequate theory of authority in this area can neither include nor be qualified by any simple conception of rights as 'trumps' over majoritarian forms of decision-making.[9] On the contrary, any theory of rights as institutional trumps will necessarily have to depend on the prior invocation of some method of collective decision-making to figure out which of the contestant theories of rights in society is to be regarded as society's theory of rights for these purposes.

It is on this basis, fourthly, that I shall raise questions about judicial review as a practice. It seems likely that in a constitutional regime of the sort envisaged by Dworkin, the courts will inevitably become a major, if not the main forum for the revision and adaptation of basic rights in the face of changing circumstances and social controversies. (This is an extrapolation from the experience of constitutional politics in the United States.) I shall suggest that a theorist of rights ought to have grave misgivings about this prospect. For surely, the people have a right to participate in all aspects of the democratic governance of their community, a right which is quite deeply connected to the values of autonomy and responsibility that are celebrated in our commitment to other basic liberties. That right to democratic participation is a right to participate on equal terms in social decisions on issues of high principle and not just interstitial matters of social and economic policy. What is more, to the extent that there is a difference between issues of political substance and issues of political procedure, the right to participate should surely pertain to the latter as well. I shall argue that our respect for such democratic rights is called seriously into question when proposals are made to shift decisions about the conception and revision of basic principles from the legislature to the courtroom, from the people and their admittedly imperfect representative institutions to a handful of men and women, supposedly of wisdom, learning, virtue, and high principle who, it is thought, can alone be trusted to take seriously the great issues that they raise.

Fifthly, I shall try to answer some defences of judicial review which present it as a consummation of democracy, rather than as something

---

[9] See also the discussion in s. 5 of Ch. 1, above.

inherently opposed to the principle of democratic participation. This response will be the burden of Chapters Twelve and Thirteen, below.

2. RIGHT-BASED THEORIES

My immediate purpose in this chapter is to show that there is no necessary inference from the idea of rights or from the premises of a right-based moral theory to the desirability of judicially-enforced constitutional rights as a concrete political arrangement.

What do I mean by 'a *right-based* theory'? The terminology is adapted from Ronald Dworkin's discussion in *Taking Rights Seriously*, proposing 'a tentative initial classification of political theories' into right-based, duty-based, and goal-based types.[10] The idea is that in any but the most intu-itionistic theory, it is possible to distinguish between judgements that are more or less *basic*, in the sense that the less basic judgements are derivable from or supported by the more basic ones.[11] Sometimes in a political theory we may reach a level of 'basic-ness' below which it is impossible to go – a set of judgements which support other judgements in the theory but which are not themselves supported in a similar way. These will be the *fundamental* propositions of the theory or, as Dworkin has called them else-where, its '*constitutive*' positions.[12] Utilitarians pride themselves on the fact that their moral theory is organized explicitly in this way, and Dworkin's typology assumes that a structure of that kind can be discerned in many non-utilitarian theories as well.[13]

[10] See Dworkin, *Taking Rights Seriously*, 90–6. For further discussion of this typology, see Mackie, 'Can There be a Right-Based Moral Theory?'

[11] Joseph Raz stresses that the relation is one of support not logical entailment. If we think for different reasons that there should be (i) a right to free political speech, and (ii) a right to free commercial speech, we may sum that up by saying there should be (iii) a right to free speech generally. But although (iii) entails (i), it does not support it on this account of our rea-soning. See Raz, *The Morality of Freedom*, 169.

[12] See Dworkin, *A Matter of Principle*, 186 ff.

[13] Does this commit those who use Dworkin's typology to 'foundationalism' in moral and political theory? The term has a wider and a narrower meaning. In its wider (and weaker) meaning, 'foundationalism' refers simply to the linear mode of organization that I have inti-mated: that there is some non-circular or unidirectional structure of support and justification within a theory. The alternative to foundationalism in this sense is 'holism', where theorems are considered to be supported as much by what they imply as by what more general prin-ciples imply them. There is no doubt that a classification into right-based, duty-based, and goal-based types presupposes that the theories being classified are foundationalist in this sense. When foundationalism is criticized, however, people usually have in mind a stronger position than this. It is that the truth or assertibility of the 'basic propositions' or 'axioms' of such a theory can be immediately apprehended or intuited, and that the linear structure transmits this fundamental justifiability throughout the theory. The classification in this chapter is not committed to this epistemology, and it does not presuppose any such com-mitment on the part of the theories being classified.

For my purposes here, nothing much hangs on the precise *distinction* between right-, duty-, and goal-based theories. I shall not go into the detail of Dworkin's classification.[14] What I want to work with is the idea that a concern for individual rights may lie in the foundations of a theory, leaving it an open question what those foundations entail at the level of political and constitutional construction.

Opinions differ as to whether the concerns at the basis of a theory of rights are exclusively concerns about freedom, exclusively concerns about independence, exclusively concerns about equality, or whether other material interests and needs may also be accorded basic importance in their own right. I hope to avoid that issue here as well (though it is one of the controversies whose significance I shall discuss a little later in the chapter).[15] Different theories will identify different individual rights – to freedom, independence, dignity, etc. – as having fundamental and abiding importance, and they will regard a sense of that importance as a general basis for normativity within the theory.

As premises, these concerns are liable to be fairly abstract in character. One would not expect to find propositions like the Fourth Amendment to the US Constitution in the *foundations* of a theory of rights. A right to the protection of one's home against unreasonable searches is likely to be based on the importance accorded to a deeper individual interest such as privacy. A right to privacy may in turn be based on even deeper premises about the importance of autonomy and living life on one's own terms. Derivative conclusions will then be generated by working out what is required in the circumstances of modern society if the deepest interests in this series are to be respected. That is what normative argument amounts to in right-based political philosophy.

Sometimes in the development of such an argument, we may reach intermediate conclusions which enable us to say that some relatively concrete interest must be regarded as important if some deeper interest is to be properly respected. This is where *familiar* propositions about rights will figure in a well-thought-out theory. As we move from deep abstract premises to particular concrete recommendations, we may find ourselves saying things like 'People have a right to free speech' or 'Everyone has a right to elementary education' or 'Suspects in police custody have a right not to be tortured.' Though these propositions indicate important individual interests, the importance of those interests is explained by their deeper connection to other, more abstract interests whose importance is ultimate in the theory.[16]

---

[14] For an unnecessarily protracted discussion, see Waldron, *The Right to Private Property*, 64–105.

[15] See s. 6, below.

[16] See the excellent discussion in Raz, *The Morality of Freedom*, 168–70.

However, right-based theories are not always articulated in a linear structure of this kind, moving from abstract rights through a series of derivative rights, each one supported by and more concrete than the last. Sometimes the implications of abstract premises are teased out in a different structure. John Rawls's discussion in *A Theory of Justice* is an example. It seems plausible to say, as Ronald Dworkin has argued, that Rawls's theory is premised on some very deep assumption 'that individuals have a right to equal concern and respect in the design and administration of the institutions that govern them'.[17] But in trying to see the concrete implications of that premise, Rawls develops his model-theoretic device of the 'original position' leading to the choice of two lexically ordered principles to govern the basic structure of a society. At least one of these (the 'Difference Principle') is not formulated in terms of rights at all.[18] Maybe the further process of inferring policy recommendations from the Difference Principle will involve some re-introduction of the language of rights.[19] But there is nothing inevitable about that: everything depends on how the deep concerns of the theory are best articulated in the concrete circumstances in which they are applied. The fact that there are rights in the foundations does not mean that there must be rights, so to speak, all the way up.

The point is a general one and can be applied to other types of theory as well. Utilitarianism has, in or near its foundations, a sense that the basic aim of morality is the maximization of utility. Whenever there is a choice of actions, it is better, from the theory's point of view, that that action be chosen which secures the greatest balance of utility, all things considered. But though we find this 'act-utilitarian' formula in the foundations of the theory, it does not follow that the theory's practical recommendation for men and women in the real world is to adopt an act-utilitarian decision-procedure. 'Indirect' utilitarianism suggests that the basic aim may be better served if individuals follow certain rules which they treat more or less as absolute requirements in most of the circumstances they face.[20] Indeed, if a goal-based utilitarianism is articulated realistically, it may involve a commitment to rights at the surface even though rights do not figure at all in its deeper premises.[21] This example shows that we cannot infer much

[17] Dworkin, *Taking Rights Seriously*, 180.

[18] Indeed it is important for Rawls that the principle governing economic inequalities *not* be seen as a principle of particular entitlement. See Rawls, *A Theory of Justice*, 64 and 88. I have discussed the relation between justice and rights in Rawls's and other theories in Waldron, *Liberal Rights*, 26–34.

[19] I have in mind the arguments intimated in Rawls, *A Theory of Justice*, Ch. 5. See also Martin, *Rawls and Rights* and Pogge, *Realizing Rawls*.

[20] See, e.g., Hare, *Moral Thinking*, Chs. 2–3 and 9.

[21] See the various discussions in Frey (ed.), *Utility and Rights*. However, for doubts about the utilitarian defence of rights, see Lyons, 'Utility and Rights'.

about the practical recommendations of a normative theory from the character of its fundamental premises.

So far we have considered only the relation between basic and derivative positions *within* a normative theory. The fact that in a given theory, the basic premises (or even the intermediate theorems) are best formulated as rights does not show that the derivative recommendations of the theory are best formulated as rights. But suppose, for the sake of argument, that the normative recommendations of a right-based theory *are* formulated as rights. Can we say anything about the relation between those recommendations and the actions that they call for in the real world? If someone believes in *moral* rights, does that mean he is to be taken as demanding *legal* rights?

Jeremy Bentham thought the answer was 'Yes.' Or rather, he thought this was the best we could make of what was really an oxymoron – the idea of a moral, that is, a non-legal right.[22] Maybe, he thought, we can reinterpret natural rights claims as normative claims about the legal rights that ought to be established: 'In proportion to the want of happiness resulting from the want of rights, a reason exists for wishing that there were such things as rights.'[23] However, even Bentham's most sympathetic commentators have been bewildered by this insistence that the noun 'right' must necessarily refer (either descriptively or normatively) to *legal* rights. He did not take that view of 'duty', 'obligation', or 'right' (the adjective), each of which (he was prepared to say) had a normative meaning established by the principle of utility that was quite independent of the idea of positive law.[24]

One objection to Bentham's analysis is that sometimes we talk of moral rights when we have no intention of saying anything about what the law ought to be. When my mother asks if I intend to remarry and adds 'I have a right to be told the truth', she is not saying anything about the law. She is saying I ought to tell her the truth and giving me some indication that I owe that duty *to her* in virtue of some interest she has at stake.

---

[22] Bentham, 'Supply without Burthen', 73: 'Right and law are correlative terms: as much so as son and father. Right is with me the child of law: from different operations of law result different sorts of rights. A natural right is a son that never had a father.' See also Waldron, 'Supply Without Burthen Revisited'.

[23] Bentham, 'Anarchical Fallacies', 53. The passage continues: 'But reasons for wishing there were such things as rights, are not rights; – a reason for wishing that a certain right were established, is not that right – want is not supply – hunger is not bread.'

[24] There is an excellent discussion in Hart, *Essays on Bentham*, 85 ff.

However, let us put those cases aside; let us accept H. L. A. Hart's suggestion that usually, when talk of rights is in the air, there is an implicit suggestion that the use of force (and thus the mechanisms of law) would not be inappropriate to secure what is required.[25] Even so, it does not follow that the normative claim

(1) P has a (moral) right to X

entails

(2) P (morally) ought to have a legal right to X.

If (1) entails anything about the law, it presumably entails

(3) The law ought to be such that P gets X.

There may be all sorts of ways in which X may be secured legally for P, without his having a legal *right* to it.[26]

Here, of course, a lot will depend on exactly how one defines 'legal right'. Maybe, on a very broad definition of the term, *any* legal procedure by which X is secured for P amounts to the existence of P's legal right to X. I do not want to rule out such a broad definition, except to indicate that it will not advance the argument of this part of the book one way or the other. Most jurists, however, think that the phrase 'legal right' has quite a narrow meaning. To say that P has a legal right is to indicate the existence of an articulated legal rule or principle entitling P to X. It indicates that P has standing to claim X and to bring suit for it in a court of law. And for most jurists, it indicates that officials have very limited discretion in determining who gets X and who does not. We distinguish, in other words, between (a) legal situations in which X is P's by right and he may peremptorily demand it and the law is such that his demand must be met unless there are extraordinary circumstances, and (b) legal situations in which some official has been vested with discretion to determine on a case by case basis how best to distribute a limited stock of resources like X to applicants like P. Students of public administration argue back and forth about whether it is better to have systems of rights in welfare law, for example; and these arguments presuppose that the existence of a legal right is a highly specific type of institutional arrangement along the lines of (a).[27]

As far as I can see, nothing that institutionally specific is entailed by a claim like (1) above. I can imagine an advocate for the homeless saying,

[25] Hart, 'Are There Any Natural Rights?', 79–80.

[26] A similar point is made in Shue, *Basic Rights*, 16: '[A] right has not been fulfilled until arrangements are in fact in place for people to enjoy whatever it is to which they have the right. Usually, perhaps, the arrangements will take the form of law, making the rights legal ones as well as moral ones. But in other cases, well-entrenched customs, backed by taboos, may serve better than laws – certainly better than unenforced laws.'

[27] See the discussion in Simon, 'Legality, Bureaucracy, and Class in the Welfare System'.

'The homeless have a (moral) right to shelter', and certainly meaning that *something* legal should be done about it, but leaving it an open question whether that would be best achieved by a legal arrangement of type (a) or a legal arrangement of type (b). For suppose the following facts are known. There are many homeless people and, as things stand on any given night, only a limited stock of public housing, hotel rooms, and places in shelters that can be allocated to them. The circumstances of homeless individuals vary: some are with families, some are alone; some are sick, some are healthy; some have been homeless for months, others have just become homeless; some have the strength and morale to apply for a place, others wander helplessly in the streets. I guess it is possible that an advocate who believes they all have a moral right to shelter will want to set up a rule whereby anyone who can prove he is homeless is assigned a place by a responsible official immediately, without further ado (until the available places run out). That would be clearly describable as a legal right to shelter. But it is equally possible that the homeless advocate will urge a more flexible arrangement – an arrangement that allows officials to match accommodation to need, to make quick judgements about who is sick and desperate and who is not, to hold some places in reserve for hapless folks found wandering in the rain in the early hours of the morning, and so on. And one can imagine that choice being made *on right-based grounds*: on the ground that, in the circumstances, this arrangement will better serve the moral principle that the homeless have a right to shelter.

To put the point strongly: a moral claim that people have the right to shelter is a claim about the importance of their getting shelter. It is not a claim about the importance of their being assigned shelter in accordance with a specific type of legal or bureaucratic procedure.

4. FROM LEGAL RIGHTS TO CONSTITUTIONAL RIGHTS

Suppose everything I have said so far is wrong. Suppose the assertion of a moral right *is* always a moral demand for a legal right. Should we take the further step of saying that anyone who assents to (2), above, should also be committed to

(4) P (morally) ought to have a constitutional right to X

if his support for (2) is wholehearted? Does a person who is in favour of a legal right always have a reason to demand that extra level of protection?

Not necessarily. There are practical reasons and reasons of principle to make him hesitate. To secure constitutional protection, the proponent of the right will either have to agitate for constitutional reform or, if there is already a Bill of Rights, persuade those entrusted with the task of

interpreting it to recognize the new right under the heading of some existing provision. Either way, the political difficulties are considerable. The
proponent of the right may well think that the process of securing constitutional protection would take too long or be too difficult, and that it may
distract people from the more important task of actually making the legal
provision that is called for.[28]

Those are strategic reasons for resisting the inference from (2) to (4). But
suppose a political opportunity for constitutionalization has in fact arisen
(as it has arisen now in the United Kingdom). Are there any reasons of
principle for hesitating in the face of that opportunity?

One point which is not *quite* as pragmatic as those already mentioned
has to do with apprehensions about verbal rigidity. A legal right that finds
protection in a Bill of Rights finds it under the auspices of some canonical
form of words in which the provisions of the charter are enunciated. One
lesson of American constitutional experience is that the words of each provision in the Bill of Rights tend to take on a life of their own, becoming the
obsessive catchphrase for expressing everything one might want to say
about the right in question. For example, First Amendment doctrine in
America is obsessed to the point of scholasticism with the question of
whether some problematic form of behaviour that the state has an interest
in regulating is to be regarded as 'speech' or not. ('Is pornography
speech?' 'Is burning a flag speech?' 'Is topless dancing speech?' 'Is panhandling speech?' 'Is racial abuse speech?' and so on.) Yet surely this is not
the way to argue about rights. Rights are principles of deep and pervasive
concern. We may use the phrase 'freedom of speech' to pick out the sort of
concerns we have in mind in invoking a particular right; but that is not the
same as saying that the *word* 'speech' (as opposed to 'expression' or 'communication' etc.) is the key to our concerns in the area. The same is true for
other formulas of American constitutional doctrine: 'cruel and unusual
punishment', 'free exercise' of religion', 'due process of law', etc.[29]

Of course, as we saw in Chapter Four, legislation too is embodied in
determinate phraseology: every statute has its text. The difference is that
the legislative text can readily be amended to meet our evolving sense of
how best to get at the important issues at stake. If we think that one of the
crucial tests for scrutinizing punishments is 'unusual-ness,' we can write
that into our statute. If later we see the merits of encouraging innovation
in sentencing, we may want to express the proper constraints in some
other way, and amend our criminal justice legislation accordingly. And of

---

[28] The story of the Equal Rights Amendment in the US would have been a sorrier one if all
legislative initiatives against sex discrimination had rested on the success of this particular
constitutional campaign. See Mansbridge, *Why We Lost the ERA.*

[29] I have discussed this a little more in Waldron, *The Law*, 83–4, and in *Nonsense Upon Stilts*,
177–81.

course this process of evolving phraseology is even easier if we are talking about legal recognition in the form of common law principles and precedents, and easier still if rights take the form of 'conventional' understandings subscribed to in the political community at large, as they have in Britain for many years. With that less articulate, less formulaic heritage of right-based concern, people can discuss issues of rights and limited government, issues of abortion, discrimination, punishment, and toleration in whatever terms seem appropriate to them, free from the obsessive verbalism of a particular written charter.

For these reasons, then, the proponent of a given right may be hesitant about embodying it in a constitutionally entrenched Bill of Rights. He may figure that the gain, in terms of an immunity against wrongful legislative abrogation, is more than offset by the loss in our ability to evolve a free and flexible discourse of politics.

5. RESPECT AND DISTRUST

But the deepest reasons of liberal principle for being unhappy about a Bill of Rights have yet to be addressed. When a provision is entrenched in a constitutional document, the claim-right (to liberty or provision) that it lays down is compounded with an immunity against legislative change. Those who possess the right now get the additional advantage of its being made difficult or impossible to alter their legal position. That can sound attractive; but as W. N. Hohfeld emphasized, we should always look at both sides of any legal advantage.[30] The term correlative to the claim-right is of course the duty incumbent upon officials and others to respect and uphold the right. And the term correlative to the constitutional immunity is what Hohfeld would call *a disability*: in effect, a disabling of the legislature from its normal functions of revision, reform, and innovation in the law. To think that a constitutional immunity is called for is to think oneself justified in disabling legislators in this respect (and thus, indirectly, in disabling the citizens whom they represent). It is, I think, worth pondering the attitudes that lie behind the enthusiasm for imposing such disabilities.

To embody a right in an entrenched constitutional document is to adopt a certain attitude towards one's fellow citizens. That attitude is best summed up as a combination of self-assurance and mistrust: self-assurance in the proponent's conviction that what he is putting forward really *is* a matter of fundamental right and that he has captured it adequately in the particular formulation he is propounding; and mistrust,

---

[30] Hohfeld, *Fundamental Legal Conceptions*.

implicit in his view that any alternative conception that might be concocted by elected legislators next year or in ten years' time is so likely to be wrong-headed or ill-motivated that *his own* formulation is to be elevated immediately beyond the reach of ordinary legislative revision.

This attitude of mistrust of one's fellow citizens does not sit particularly well with the aura of respect for their autonomy and responsibility that is conveyed by the substance of the rights which are being entrenched in this way. The substantive importance of a given right may well be based on a view of the individual person as essentially a thinking agent, endowed with an ability to deliberate morally and to transcend a preoccupation with his own particular or sectional interests. For example, an argument for freedom of speech may depend on a view of people as 'political animals' in Aristotle's sense, capable of evolving a shared and reliable sense of right and wrong, justice and injustice, in their conversations with one another. If *this* is why one thinks free speech important, one cannot simply turn round and announce that the products of any deliberative process are to be mistrusted.

If on the other hand, the desire for entrenchment is motivated by a predatory view of human nature and of what people will do to one another when let loose in the arena of democratic politics, it will be difficult to explain how or why people are to be viewed as essentially bearers of rights. In order to develop a theory of rights, we need some basis for distinguishing those interests which are characteristic of human dignity from those which are relatively unimportant in a person's activity and desires. If our only image of man is that of a self-seeking animal who is not to be trusted with a concern for the interests of others, we lack the conception of dignified moral autonomy on which such discriminations of interest might be based.

In general, the attribution of rights to individuals is an act of faith in the agency and capacity for moral thinking of each of those individuals. Rights involve choices; and their exercise requires the agent to select which of a number of options he would like to realize in his life and in his dealings with others. Of course, rights may be abused, and indeed a right may be exercised wrongly.[31] But if the typical upshot of an agent's exercise of a right vested in him were moral havoc or a reckless or malicious assault on the interests of others, we should quickly rethink the basis of the original rights-attribution.

Moreover, we trust agents not just with the responsible exercise of the rights assigned to them, but also with some degree of responsibility for determining exactly what are the appropriate limits of their rights, *vis-à-vis* the rights of others. In a good society, this is perhaps done by the legal

---

[31] See Waldron, 'A Right to Do Wrong', 21.

system. But legal systems do not come out of the air; in rights-based political theories they are typically founded (even if indirectly) upon popular sovereignty, so that there is a theoretical commitment to the proposition that those who are to have the rights in question are also in principle capable of thinking them properly through. We think this anyway, in liberal theory, to the extent that we are prepared to talk about *natural* rights: though there is no guarantee that the Lockean farmer will not take more than his share or that an individual punishing a natural law offence will not be moved by passion or revenge to excessive retribution, still liberal natural rights theory is predicated on the assumption that it is as safe to entrust such decisions to ordinary individuals as it is to entrust them to anyone, and that it is much safer on the whole to entrust them to ordinary people than to those whose natural virtue has been corrupted by the 'artificial Ignorance, and learned Gibberish' of legal scholasticism.[32] Natural rights theory thus embodies a certain conception of human nature. It is not just a conception of certain vulnerabilities, certain ways in which we may fall prey to one another. There is also a positive image of responsible self-assertion: the right-bearer is one who is self-aware and vigorously conscious of both the extent of and the limits on what he is entitled to demand from others.[33] Theorists of rights, then, are committed to the assumption that those to whom rights are assigned are *normally* those to whom decisions about the extent of rights can be entrusted. Or at least we assume that this is not simply out of the question – as it would be if some of the more lurid images of popular irrationality and majority tyranny were accepted.

These are not intended as knock-down arguments against constitutionalizing rights. All I have tried to show so far is that there is nothing obvious about combining a respect for rights with a profound mistrust of people in their democratic and representative capacities. Accordingly there is nothing perverse in saying: 'The reasons which make me think of the human individual as a bearer of rights are the very reasons that allow me to trust him as the bearer of political responsibilities. It is precisely because I see each person as a potential moral agent, endowed with dignity and autonomy, that I am willing to entrust the people *en masse* with the burden of self-government.' Once we see *this* as an intelligible set of attitudes, we might be more hesitant in expressing our enthusiasm for rights in terms of the disabling of representative institutions.

---

[32] See Locke, *An Essay Concerning Human Understanding*, Bk. III, Ch. x, para. 9, 495. See also Ch. 11, s. 6, below.

[33] See also Waldron, 'Rights and Needs – The Myth of Disjunction'.

The attitudes we take towards our fellow citizens will depend in part on how easy we think it is to come up with an adequate conception of the rights that deserve protection. If someone has developed such a conception and if, moreover, he thinks it a relatively easy task, he will tend to distrust anyone who comes up with a conception of rights that differs from his own. After all, he thinks of himself as acting in good faith; and since the task presents no special difficulties, it is likely that his good faith will have yielded good results. The only explanation, then, of other people's contrary results is that they must have been acting for some ulterior motive. To put it another way, if we really do hold that the truths that we have come up with are 'self-evident', our only explanation of different results being arrived at by other people must be that the others are simpletons or rogues. Either way, we have reason (on this understanding of the task) to embody our self-evident conclusions in immutable form as soon as possible, in order to insulate them from the folly and chicanery of misguided revision or reformulation.

If, on the other hand, we take the view that the whole business of thinking about rights is fraught with difficulty and that it is something on which, with the best will in the world, people of good faith may differ, we will not evince the same distrust of our opponents' suggestions nor indeed the same dogmatic confidence in our own. Those who think it possible that they are mistaken should be less inclined to cast their conclusions in stone, and more open to the possibility that subsequent debate among their fellow citizens will from time to time produce conclusions that are better than their own.

Which of these views of our task is correct? A theorist of rights has to work out what rights people have, how they are to be formulated, and how important they are in relation to other moral and political considerations. Is this an easy task or a difficult one?

There is some pressure to insist on its facility. Talk of individual rights is often supposed to be a way of registering fairly basic objections to the arcane computations of the utilitarian calculus. It is the utilitarian who is supposed to be telling us that everything is very complicated, and that whether we allow horrible things like torture, censorship, or the execution of the innocent depends on all the circumstances, long-run calculations of probability, etc. The theorist of rights, by contrast, is supposed to be the one who can produce the trump card, the peremptory argument-stopper: 'Thou shalt not kill.'[34] The idea of rights has often been seized on precisely as a way of avoiding the casuistry of trade-offs and complex moral calcu-

---

[34] Cf. Anscombe, 'Modern Moral Philosophy', 40.

lations – a way of insisting that certain basics are to be secured and certain atrocities prohibited, come what may. But if rights themselves are morally complicated, the spectre of casuistry reappears. Complicated problems presumably require complicated solutions; but it was the *simplicity* of right-based constraints that was supposed to be their main advantage over other more recondite and precarious modes of moral reasoning.[35]

The sad fact is, however, that this simplicity and moral certainty is unavailable. No one in the trade now believes that the truth about rights is self-evident or that, if two people disagree about rights, one of them at least must be either corrupt or morally blind. In the thirty years or so of the modern revival of the philosophical study of rights, there has been a proliferation of rival theories and conceptions.[36] Many of these have occasioned an outpouring of essays, articles, and symposia discussing, elaborating and criticizing their accounts.[37] In addition there are hundreds of articles devoted to particular rights or making particular points about the whole idea of rights,[38] as well as a number of important books attacking the whole idea of rights and the individualist presuppositions of that idea.[39]

To believe in rights is to believe that certain key interests of individuals, in liberty and well-being, deserve special protection, and that they should not be sacrificed for the sake of greater efficiency or prosperity or for any aggregate of lesser interests under the heading of the public good. Now some people think this very idea is misguided; but even those who propound it in political philosophy recognize its difficulty. Any theory of rights will face disagreements about the interests it identifies as rights, and the terms in which it identifies them. Those disagreements will then be vehicles for controversy about the proper balance to be struck between individual interest and countervailing social considerations, under the auspices of 'clear and present danger', 'catastrophic moral horror', and the congestion of values and principles that we find in crowded theatres that are not on fire.

In addition, theories of rights have to face up to controversies about the forms of duty that they ground and the forms of moral priority they

---

[35] I have discussed these points further in Waldron, 'Rights in Conflict'.

[36] As well as the works by Nozick, Rawls and Dworkin cited at the beginning of this chapter (see *supra*, fn. 1–3), one might also cite the following major contributions: Ackerman, *Social Justice in the Liberal State*; Finnis, *Natural Law and Natural Rights*; Gauthier, *Morals by Agreement*; Gewirth, *Human Rights*; Raz, *The Morality of Freedom*; and Wellman, *Real Rights*. This list is by no means complete.

[37] See, for example, the following collections of essays: Cohen (ed.), *Ronald Dworkin and Contemporary Jurisprudence*; Daniels (ed.), *Reading Rawls*; Paul (ed.), *Reading Nozick*; Regis (ed.), *Gewirth's Ethical Rationalism*.

[38] Two anthologies (with bibliographies) are Lyons (ed.), *Rights* and Waldron (ed.), *Theories of Rights*.

[39] See, for example, MacIntyre, *After Virtue*; Sandel, *Liberalism and the Limits of Justice*; and Glendon, *Rights Talk*.

establish: absolute duties, prima facie duties, lexical priorities, weighted priorities, agent-relative side constraints, agent-relative prerogatives, and so on.[40] Our experience with these issues in moral philosophy indicates that their prominence in the literature is directly proportional to both their difficulty and their importance.

Finally, theorists of rights must develop accounts of who they take to be right-bearers: they must develop theories of the person, and articulate those into an account of the rights (or whatever) of foetuses, infants, the elderly, the comatose, the mentally ill, and so on. They have to say something about the rights of animals, trees, groups, corporations, and works of art. Even within the terms of a given theory of rights, its development and articulation is a complex and challenging task, and it should not surprise us if this is something on which reasonable people reach strikingly different conclusions.

How should a philosopher approach these difficulties? The first and most obvious point is that, in his own work, he should recognize the possibility that he is mistaken. Robert Nozick noted in the preface to *Anarchy, State and Utopia* that each author tends to write as though mankind has been struggling for aeons with some philosophical or ethical problem, but 'he finally, thank God, has found the truth and built an impregnable fortress around it'.[41] In fact each of us is familiar with the business of argumentation, objections, answers to objections, rejoinders, and revisions. Indeed, we often use that apparatus to structure the way we write: here is my preliminary thesis; here is my account of the main objections to it; here are the answers to all but one of the objections; and here are the epicycles that are needed to accommodate the unanswerable objection. That mode of presentation and the ethic of fallibility it evinces are the staple rhetoric of modern philosophical writing.

Of course everyone thinks his own current position is correct; otherwise he would not be putting it forward. In the area of rights, where it is precisely questions of relative urgency and moral priority that are at stake, everyone will think that he has got the priorities right and that the alternative views are wrong. Though each should think it possible he is mistaken, it is not necessarily a good idea for him to incorporate that misgiving into the fabric of his theory. There is a difference between being modest about one's conclusion and modifying the conclusion to take account of that modesty. Modifying the conclusion may well diminish, rather than enhance, the proponent's conviction that it is correct. Still, though one may be convinced now that *this*, rather than some more modest formulation, is the correct one, it is part of philosophical maturity to be

[40] See, e.g., Sen, 'Rights and Agency' and the other essays in Scheffler (ed.), *Consequentialism and its Critics.*

[41] Nozick, *Anarchy, State and Utopia*, xii.

able to combine that conviction with a recollection of past occasions where similar beliefs have had to be abandoned in the face of philosophical difficulty, and to combine it therefore with an openness to counter-argument and refutation in the future.[42]

Such fallibilism can be taken in a purely Cartesian spirit: a solitary thinker's openness to his own revisions, self-criticisms, and reformulations. For most of us, however, it is an aspect of the way we do philosophy *together*, as members of a community of thinkers and critics. We accept and embrace the circumstance of a plurality of views and the trenchant disagreements they give rise to. Again, the discipline thrives on this. The interplay of arguments is expected to produce better theories that will form the basis for an even more vigorous debate, and so on. In these debates, each of us has a responsibility to take the perspective of the philosophical community from time to time, as well as the perspective of the particular view he is defending. From the latter perspective, one is a passionate partisan of a theory. From the former perspective, however, one knows that it is wrong to expect any particular theory, no matter how attractive or well argued, to survive the process of debate unscathed. One recognizes that debate has a point: collective interaction as a way of reaching towards complicated truth. Simple truths, self-evident truths may form in single minds, but complicated truths (in which category I include all propositions about individual rights) emerge, in Mill's words, only 'by the rough process of a struggle between combatants fighting under hostile banners'.[43]

7. PHILOSOPHY AND POLITICS

Our professional awareness of these theoretical difficulties ought to have some impact on how we think about substantive political controversies. In recent years, issues such as the following have had to be dealt with in the United States as matters of constitutional right: abortion, affirmative action, campaign finance reform, criminal procedure in capital cases, drug use in religious ceremonies, defamation in relation to free speech, gun control, hate speech, homelessness, immigrants' rights, land use restrictions, panhandling, pornography, reapportionment, school prayer, voter-registration, welfare, and zoning. We all know these are matters fraught

[42] The classic defence of such fallibilism is Mill, *On Liberty*, Ch. 2. See also Popper, *Conjectures and Refutations*, esp. Chs. 16–20.

[43] Mill, *On Liberty*, Ch. 2, 58. The whole sentence reads: 'Truth in the great practical concerns of life, is so much a question of the reconciling and combining of opposites that very few have minds sufficiently capacious and impartial to make the adjustment with an approach to correctness, and it has to be made by the rough process of a struggle between combatants fighting under hostile banners.'

with difficulty and moral complexity, matters on which reasonable people disagree – including reasonable citizens, reasonable legislators, and reasonable judges.

The author of this book (along with many of his readers) has firm views on most of these topics; each of us has his views which he regards as well thought through. What is more, many think that their views on topics like these are *objectively* either right or wrong and that it matters which, for these are issues about rights and justice not merely questions of preference. We all believe that fundamental values are at stake in these matters – liberty, autonomy, justice, respect for persons, human dignity, and so on. We write as though those who differ from us about these matters differ so fundamentally that there is barely any common ground for coexistence in society. We say, 'These are matters of principle, matters of *right*! These are not up for grabs in the ordinary political process. These issues are not negotiable!'

Yet none of us really believes this. Our political confidence in our own views, and our philosophical awareness of the deep and important values at stake, is matched by a reluctant recognition of the reasonableness of disagreement and a firm determination – at times (as in the American Civil War) a ferocious determination – to go on sharing a social world with those who differ from us. Thus it seems not inappropriate for legal and political philosophers to spend some time reflecting on their readiness as citizens to live and act together with those whose disagreements with them on matters like these they pretend to regard as fundamental and, in theory, non-negotiable.

The way we phrase and present our academic theories indicates that philosophers are very bad at this. But the way we deal with our colleagues suggests the opposite. Our disagreements among ourselves in the profession on issues of substantive justice – the disagreements that we air at our conferences, publish in our journals, and teach our students – are at least as fundamental as those which divide the citizenry (and our representatives and our judges). And yet we maintain not only civility with one another but a quite robust professional *esprit de corps* and even friendship with those we oppose. Nozickians and socialists schmooze at 'Liberty Fund' gatherings. Most Marxist philosophers can imagine nothing more delightful than a conversation with an opponent over dinner. Any bunch of people who find themselves in this sort of situation have a responsibility to think through how their civility and coexistence are possible in the face of such disagreement, and to bear that in mind as they formulate their positions theoretically.

I want to suggest, then, that in exercising this responsibility, we should think of the various people taking part in political disagreements out there, in the real world, as being in many ways *just like us* when we disagree about some normative issue in a seminar or a journal. Or rather they are just like us with this one proviso: we have the luxury of not having to make a decision; they have to engage not only in hard thinking about what is just and what rights people have, but also in what we in the academy may too easily dismiss as the sordid and distasteful business of actual collective decision-making in the absence of moral consensus. We pride ourselves, of course, that our thinking in books, articles, and seminars is more reasoned and more profound than the thinking engaged in by working politicians and their constituents. And so it should be: in the social division of labour, it is our task to take time and energy to think these things through as carefully as it is possible to think them. But it is a mistake, I believe, to regard our thought as different in kind from that of a citizen-participant in politics. Political philosophy – at least in the normative philosophy-and-public-affairs mode – is simply conscientious civic discussion without a deadline.

To think that such discussions are different in kind is not just an error of arrogance; it is a substantial philosophical mistake. At least since the seventeenth century, our conception of *argument* in political philosophy has been guided by the idea that social, political and legal institutions are to be, in principle, explicable and justifiable to all those who have to live under them. We have rejected the esoteric in political theory; we have rejected the idea of *arcana imperii*.[44] The model-theoretic ideas of consent and social contract, and the corresponding constraints of publicity and transparency, commit us to producing arguments that purport to be intelligible to anyone whose interests they affect, and that – in spirit, if not in idiom – are consonant with the arguments that they would find persuasive in their conversations with one another. There is, as I have argued elsewhere, an important connection between liberal argumentation and the Enlightenment conviction that everything real can in principle be explained, and everything right can in principle be justified, to everyone.[45] Modern political philosophy evinces a commitment to the idea that theoretical argument aims not merely to justify laws or political proposals, but to justify them *to* the ordinary men and women whom they will affect.

For present purposes, the implication of this democratic model of political theory is that each of us should think of his conception of rights as a particularly well-worked out opinion or position which, in outline, might be held by any citizen. Similarly, we should think of the theoretical disagreements we have among ourselves as particularly civil, thoughtful, and protracted versions of the disagreements that take place among citizens in the public realm. Conversely, when we come across a citizen or party of citizens holding a view about rights that differs from our own, we

---

[44] Cf. Donaldson, *Machiavelli and Mystery of State.*
[45] See Waldron, 'Theoretical Foundations of Liberalism', 134 ff.

should think of that along the lines that we think of a colleague's contrary conception: something to be disagreed with but respected, treated as a good faith contribution to a debate in which nothing at all is self-evident.

These considerations should be sufficient to make us pause before adopting some of the more disrespectful images of democratic decision-making that one finds in constitutionalist writings. Cynics sometimes say that legislative and electoral politics is entirely a matter of self-interest, and that representatives and voters never raise their minds above the sordid question, 'What's in it for me?' This of course is an empirical issue, but I believe the cynicism is exaggerated.[46] Certainly the idiom of self-interest is not the idiom in which citizens' views about rights are normally expressed. Consider the debate about abortion. The pro-life and pro-choice factions cannot both be correct on the issues of whether foetuses have rights and whether women have the right to choose abortion, but it is surely indisputable that both sides are engaged in good faith on exactly those general and difficult questions of ethics. Each group appears to be arguing for a particular view about what rights there are, and what sort of beings have them, in just the way (maybe a little less articulate) that we argue when we disagree in an applied ethics class.[47]

I suppose that if one were desperate to sustain one's cynicism, one might insist that even our philosophical convictions are really only a cover for self-interest. So then political deliberation will not benefit from analogy with philosophical debate. Both will be discredited as the reflex of self-interest. But then it will be hard to limit this cynicism, and impossible to draw very many interesting political or institutional conclusions. Why not be equally cynical about the opinions of judges? (Many people are.) Why not be cynical also about constitution-framers, about Madison or Jefferson? Why not say it about *anyone* who purports to think or write on such an issue – including ourselves?

If, on the other hand, we are willing (as most of us in our vanity are) to say that we and some of our friends are high-minded, or that at least when *philosophers* write about abortion or euthanasia they are not motivated by covert self-interest, that they are thinking through the issues of principle as carefully as they can, why are we not prepared to say this too about ordinary citizens and their representatives, who certainly – some of the time – look and sound as earnest and high-minded as we do when they disagree with one another? It seems to me we should ponder very carefully the implications of the sort of generalized contempt for the ordinary

46 See further Waldron, 'Rights and Majorities: Rousseau Revisited'.

47 Actually, deeper and broader issues of value and lifestyle may be at stake as well: see Luker, *Abortion and the Politics of Motherhood*. This does not undermine my point: just because a debate about abortion implicates issues of lifestyle does not mean it has become simply a clash of self-interest.

citizen which seems to pervade most people's cynicism about electoral and legislative politics.

8. THE TASK AHEAD

Those are some things to bear in mind when we think about rights, constitutional rights, and limits on legislation. What I have said in this chapter does not amount to a *theory*, let alone a full-blown *constitutional jurisprudence*. The discussion in the last few sections is intended as a note of caution, warning us against the more extravagant inferences that philosophers sometimes draw from the fact that they find themselves disagreeing with masses of ordinary citizens on questions of fundamental rights.

To reiterate: I think it is very important to bear in mind, first, that issues of rights are by all accounts (especially *our* accounts) complicated, and secondly, that they are issues on which there is disagreement even among those who understand the complications and even in the most propitious circumstances for thought and unlimited deliberation among the best intellects in our society. If we bear all that in mind, we will be better equipped to deal with the institutional question, 'Who shall decide what rights we have when we all disagree?' We will be able to approach the issue of whether to assign controversial issues of rights to courts or legislatures – to an elite of wise men or to the representatives of the people who will be affected by the determination – in a frame of mind that is philosophically more modest, legally less overbearing, and politically less panic-stricken than the current mentality of constitutionalization.

Chapter Eleven

Participation: The Right of Rights

1. INTRODUCTION

'The great right of every man,' said William Cobbett, 'the right of rights, is the right of having a share in the making of the laws, to which the good of the whole makes it his duty to submit.'[1] What sort of right is this? How is it justified? And how important is it in relation to other rights? Cobbett called it 'the right of rights', a phrase which when read carelessly might suggest that participation is more important than the other rights with which it might conflict. For example: exercising their right to political participation, the members of a majority may vote in favour of some limit on (say) the free exercise of religion. Now, if participation is the right of rights, it looks as though the right to religious freedom is going to have to give way, in cases like this, in order to vindicate the right of participation. In this chapter, however, I shall argue that talk of *conflict of rights* is inappropriate in this sort of case. I shall argue that the special role of participation in a theory of rights is not a matter of its having moral priority over other rights. Instead it is the upshot of the fact that participation is a right whose exercise seems peculiarly appropriate in situations where reasonable right-bearers disagree about what rights they have.

2. A NEGATIVE OR A POSITIVE RIGHT?

To begin with, what sort of right is this 'right of having a share in the making of the laws'? Karl Marx distinguished famously between the rights of man and the rights of the citizen. The rights of man – such as property, security and religious liberty – are 'nothing but the rights of . . . egoistic man, man separated from other men and the community'. But the rights of the citizen – voting, eligibility for office, and the freedom to discuss and criticize the conduct of public affairs – are quite unlike the traditional rights of man. The rights of the citizen, far from being atomistic, are 'political rights that are only exercised in community with other men'.[2]

---

[1] Cobbett, from *Advice to Young Men and Women, Advice to a Citizen* (1829), quoted in Macfarlane, *The Theory and Practice of Human Rights*, 142.

[2] Marx, 'On the Jewish Question', 144–6.

The point is undeniable. One cannot understand political rights in terms of the drawing of boundaries around autonomous individuals.[3] These rights are to be understood instead as establishing a basis on which large numbers of right-bearers act together to control and govern their common affairs. Certainly, it would be a mistake to regard political participation as a merely 'negative' right, protecting people from interference. The distinction between positive and negative rights – that is, between a right correlative to another's duty to actually *do something* for the right-bearer's benefit and a right correlative to another's duty to *refrain from doing something* that interferes with the right-bearer's freedom – is arguably unhelpful anyway. It has all the difficulties of the philosophers' distinction between acts and omissions. It faces the additional difficulty that a given right is usually correlative not to single duties but to arrays of duties, some of them duties of omission, others duties of action.[4] And it is particularly unhelpful in the case of political rights.

We can see this if we consider Maurice Cranston's use of the distinction in his attack on the inclusion of 'economic and social' principles in the 1948 Universal Declaration of Human Rights:

The traditional 'political and civil rights' can . . . be readily secured by legislation; and generally they can be secured by fairly simple legislation. Since those rights are for the most part rights against government interference with a man's activities, a large part of the legislation needed has to do no more than restrain the government's own executive arm. This is no longer the case when we turn to 'the right to work', 'the right to social security', and so forth.[5]

Whatever the case with civil rights such as religious freedom, *political* rights certainly cannot be secured by legislation that does 'no more than restrain the government's own executive arm'. The right to vote is not a matter of negative freedom to express a preference for one's favourite politician, and it is not secured by the individual's simply being left alone by the state to do this when he pleases. One has the right to vote only if one's vote is counted and given effect in a system of collective decision that determines policy, leadership, and authority. To vote is to exercise a Hohfeldian *power*[6] (albeit a heavily conditional power): it is to perform an action which (if enough others also perform it) alters the assignment of rights and duties in the community. (It is more like executing a power of attorney than like making a speech.) Respect for such a right is costly, in at least two ways. First, to institute an effective system of voting requires manpower and resources. Secondly, the right to vote is costly to officials

[3] Or 'hyper-planes in moral space', or whatever other nerdy jargon we use: cf. Nozick, *Anarchy, State and Utopia*, 57.
[4] See Waldron, 'Rights in Conflict'.
[5] Cranston, 'Human Rights, Real and Supposed'.
[6] For 'power', see Hohfeld, *Fundamental Legal Conceptions*, 50 ff.

inasmuch as it makes their tenure in office vulnerable to decision-making by the voters and requires them to abandon office whenever the voters render an adverse verdict.

It is wrong therefore to contrast the kinds of demands made in the name of political rights and the kinds of demands made in the name of economic and social rights. Though the latter are not Hohfeldian powers, still rights of both sorts require the institution and operation of administrative systems; both involve manpower and resources; both presuppose a relatively stable and well-organized society; and both require governments and government officials to do certain things under certain conditions, not merely refrain from doing certain things.

But perhaps this is to take too superficial a view. Someone who wanted to insist that the right to vote is *really* a negative right might argue as follows. The right to vote is important only because the exercise of political power is a matter of moral concern. And the exercise of political power is a matter of moral concern only because it restricts the (negative) liberty of individuals. We argue for the right to vote, therefore, by saying (1) that individuals have a fundamental negative right against the coercion that the exercise of political power involves, (2) that this fundamental right is respected either by limiting the exercise of political power or by securing the consent of those who are subject to it, and (3) that voting is a way of securing something like consent.[7] Although securing consent may be a costly and time-consuming activity (as it is also in other areas of negative rights), that fact alone does not make the right which the consent protects any less a negative right.

This account is ingenious; it contains a substantial element of truth; and it would be almost completely persuasive were it not for the fact that we can also offer an alternative account of what lies beneath the right to vote – an account which represents the deeper consideration as a positive rather than a negative right. People owe each other certain fundamental duties of respect and mutual aid which are better fulfilled when orchestrated by some central agency like the state than when they are left to the whims of individuals.[8] But since it is *my* duties (among others') whose performance the state is orchestrating, I have a right to a say in the decision-mechanisms which control their orchestration.

---

[7] This account is broadly Lockean in character, and one would want to invoke the complexities of a theory like Locke's to justify the claim that voting in a majoritarian system counted as individual consent. Briefly, one would have to show that the system of majoritarian voting – or the constitutional basis on which it was set up – commanded or ought to command the unanimous consent of those legitimately subject to the political power in question. See Locke, *Two Treatises of Government*, II, paras. 95–99 and 132, (330–3 and 354–5). See also Waldron, *The Dignity of Legislation*, Chs. 4 and 6.

[8] For different versions of this account, see Goodin, 'The State as Moral Agent', and Dworkin, *Law's Empire*, 195–216.

I am not saying that the account I have just given is superior to the account given in the paragraph before. It is a competitor; or maybe the two are complementary. But surely we do not have to choose between them in order to work out – formally – what sort of right the right to vote is. It seems better to give an account of what it involves, what sort of duties it imposes, whether it is a power or a claim-right, etc., and leave it as a *separate* though certainly an important question in political philosophy what opportunities or difficulties, associated with political power and political organization, the right to vote is responsive to so far as its ultimate justification is concerned.

3. SHARING POWER

Marx believed that political rights involved collective activity not only in the way in which they were established and secured but also in the way in which they were understood and exercised.[9] He was right about this too. That there is a collective element in the way in which the rights of the citizen are understood is evident from the term commonly used to describe them: the right to *participate*. To participate is 'to take a part or share in an action . . .', something which necessarily supposes that one is not the *only* person with a part or share in the activity in question.

There is an ambiguity here. Sometimes when we talk about the people participating in government, we mean that there is a place for involvement by ordinary people or their representatives alongside whatever other groups, classes, or individuals exercise power and authority in the state. Thus the Roman people participated in the governance of the republic through the *Comitia* and through the intercession of the tribunes of the plebs; but the *sharing* which this 'participation' connotes is sharing with other non-popular elements in the republic such as the (aristocratic) Senate. Participation here means the coexistence of different modes of government in a mixed regime. However, when participation in politics is demanded these days as a human right, it usually means much more than this. The demand is not merely that there should be a popular element in government, but that the popular element should be decisive. The demand is for democracy, not just the inclusion of a democratic element in a mixed regime.

[9] I will not discuss Marx's critique of political rights in a bourgeois society. Briefly, his position was that the collective character of such rights is distorted by the political system's being regarded as a means to economically individualistic ends. (Marx, 'On the Jewish Question', 147.) See also Marx, 'Critical Remarks on the King of Prussia and Social Reform', 126.

What becomes of the *sharing* connoted by 'participation' in this second more radical demand? 'Sharing' refers now to the fact that each individual claims the right to play his part, *along with the equal part played by all other individuals,* in the government of the society. As a right-bearer he demands that his voice be heard and that it count in public decision-making. But the form in which his demand is made – a right to *participation* – acknowledges on its face that his is not the only voice in the society and that his voice should count for no more in the political process than the voice of any other right-bearer. His contribution aspires, of course, to decisiveness. But the aspiration is tempered by principles of fairness and equality implied in the universalization of his claim.[10]

In this regard, the right to participate displays up front – in its *slogan* – something that most of us think about rights of all sorts but usually make evident only at the level of *theory*. When we talk about a right to liberty, for example, or even rights to certain basic liberties, we think that the extent of the right in question is determined by something like a principle of equality. Thus, John Rawls's principle of liberty embodies a commitment to equality: 'Each person is to have an equal right to the most extensive basic liberty compatible with a similar liberty for others.'[11] Because the exercise of one person's liberty may conflict with and thus limit the liberty of another, the proper extent of the right is determined by making adjustments in what is allowed to each so that the final scheme is secured for all at the highest level of individual liberty consistent with equality.

Actually, there is another constraint in the Rawlsian formula. It is important not only that liberty be equal for all, but also that the scheme of basic liberties secured for each be 'adequate' at an individual level.[12] It must be adequate, that is, for the purposes for which each individual wants and requires liberty – namely, self-development and the living of a life in accordance with his own conception of the good.[13] A concern for adequacy takes seriously the possibility that, in a crowded society, the equality requirement may squeeze the liberty of each person down to such a modicum that, at the individual level, it is scarcely worth having or fight-

---

[10] To put it another way: he demands no more than an equal share, but the logic of equality in this as in other contexts requires that it be equality at the highest level of individual effectiveness consistent with a like effectiveness for all. (See Vlastos, 'Justice and Equality', 62–8.)

[11] Rawls, *A Theory of Justice*, 60.

[12] Thus, in a more recent formulation, Rawls talks of 'a *fully adequate* scheme of equal basic liberties which is compatible with a similar scheme of liberties for all' (my emphasis). See John Rawls, 'The Basic Liberties and their Priority', 5.

[13] Berlin, *Four Essays on Liberty*, 124, states the adequacy condition in this way: '[T]here ought to exist a certain minimum area of personal freedom which must on no account be violated; for if it is overstepped, the individual will find himself in an area too narrow for even that minimum development of his natural faculties which alone makes it possible to pursue, and even to conceive, the various ends which men hold good or right or sacred.'

ing for. The algebra of modern liberalism rests on the hope that this will turn out not to be the case, and that the two constraints of equality and adequacy can be satisfied together.[14]

A similar issue may be posed for political participation. As we saw in Chapter Five, the modern voter is sometimes afflicted by an anxiety that his individual voice and vote will be lost among the millions of others who participate with him in elections and referendums.[15] If each person's voice is so insignificant, it may be questioned whether the right of participation is actually a right worth having. This concern loomed large in Benjamin Constant's argument for preferring what he called the liberty of the moderns to the liberty of the ancients. In the ancient Greek and Roman republics, '[t]he share which . . . everyone held in national sovereignty was by no means an abstract presumption as it is in our own day. The will of each individual had real influence: the exercise of his will was a vivid and repeated pleasure.'[16] The same is not true, Constant said, of the individual in the modern political community. Even in 1819 the size of the community dwarfed the participatory contribution of each citizen:

His personal influence is an imperceptible part of the social will which impresses on the government its direction. . . . Lost in the multitude, the individual can almost never perceive the influence he exercises. Never does his will impress itself upon the whole; nothing confirms in his eyes his own cooperation.[17]

So long as each person's share of political authority is this small, it seems difficult to make a case for its adequacy. Accordingly it is hard to argue for it as a matter of right – hard, that is, to show the importance of its not being qualified, complemented or undermined by other non-democratic mechanisms of political decision-making.[18]

Some say the diminution of each vote is more than made up for by the corresponding scale of the issues it addresses. I am only one voice among millions, but the social decision in which I participate is a decision affecting millions. The voter's choice therefore is still something that should be taken seriously when such momentous outcomes are in question.[19]

---

[14] To put it in more distinctively Rawlsian language, the hope is that the rational can be reconciled with the reasonable: see Rawls, *Political Liberalism*, 48 ff.

[15] See above, Ch. 5, s. 11.

[16] Constant, 'The Liberty of the Ancients Compared with that of the Moderns', 314 and 316.

[17] Ibid., 316.

[18] For a use of this argument to defend judicial review, see Dworkin, *Freedom's Law*, 21.

[19] See Parfit, *Reasons and Persons*, 73–5. Parfit argues that familiar puzzles about why people vote when their vote has such a small chance of determining the result rest on the assumption that people only vote for the sake of the difference outcomes may make to their personal well-being. If we suppose, however, that each person is concerned by the difference outcomes may make to the general welfare, then the decision to vote may look more rational. If the cost to me of voting is $10 but the difference between the outcome I favour and the outcome I oppose is worth (I think) $2,000 to each American, then as an altruist I will certainly

However, it may be wrong to think that adequacy is best understood as a function of power – that is, power in the crude sense of *scale of consequences diminished by improbability of decisiveness*. Perhaps the adequacy condition for the right to participate has less to do with a certain minimum prospect of decisive impact and more to do with avoiding the insult, dishonour,[20] or denigration that is involved when one person's views are treated as of less account than the views of others on a matter that affects him as well as the others. Some rights involve what Joel Feinberg has called 'comparative justice', meaning that what justice requires in the distribution of certain goods is not any particular amount, or any amount adequate to a particular purpose, but an amount determined primarily by the need to avoid inequality (or some other form of quantitative unfairness, like disproportionality) in the amounts awarded to different persons.[21] Feinberg argues, persuasively, that the key to comparative justice is avoiding the arbitrariness and insult that unequal or disproportionate treatment involves (no matter what absolute level of treatment we are talking about).[22] I suspect this too is primary in the resentment people feel when they are excluded from participation in public affairs in which other members of their society are involved. If this is correct, it may be impossible and inappropriate to distinguish adequacy and equality as separate constraints in the case of the right to participate in politics.

The position has to be understood carefully. A comparative justice account of participatory rights still needs to be supplemented by an account of what is at stake in the exercise of political power. Comparative injustice with regard to political authority is not the same as comparative injustice in regard, say, to criminal punishment: both may involve elements of insult, but the character of the insult differs as between the two cases.

So what is the appropriate account, in the case of participation? The peculiar insult to an individual, A, of A's being excluded from political power has to do, first, with the impact of political decisions on A's own rights and interests, and, second, with A's possession of the capacity to decide responsibly[23] about those issues (even granted that A's own rights

---

vote whenever I think the chance of my vote being decisive is greater than 1 in 52 billion. As Parfit notes, political scientists who bother with these calculations believe that the chance is in fact an order of magnitude greater than this (i.e. more like one in several hundred million).

[20] Cf. Aristotle, *The Politics*, Bk. III, Ch. 10, 65–6 (1281a29–32): 'Then ought the good to rule and have supreme power? But in that case everybody else, being excluded from power, will be dishonored. For the offices of a state are posts of honor; and if one set of men always hold them, the rest must be deprived.'

[21] See Feinberg, 'Noncomparative Justice', 266–7.

[22] Ibid., 286–7.

[23] Gaus, *Justificatory Liberalism*, 248–57 misleadingly suggests that a concern for equality is necessarily a concern for the vote as a personal good, rather than a concern about one's status as an equal.

and interests are not the *only* rights and interests involved). Because A is affected (along with B, C, D, . . .), A can think of himself as having standing in the matter. (This, I take it, is the force of Colonel Rainsborough's insistence at Putney that '. . . the poorest he that is in England has a life to live as the greatest he . . .'.)[24] And because A has a sense of justice, A may think of himself as having what it takes to participate in decisions where others' rights are also involved. If A is nevertheless excluded from the decision (for example, because the final decision has been assigned to an aristocratic elite), A will feel slighted: he will feel that his own sense of justice has been denigrated as inadequate to the task of deciding not only something important, but something important in which he, A, has a stake as well as others. To feel this insult does not require him to think that his vote – if he had it – would give him substantial and palpable power. He knows that if he has the right to participate, so do millions of others. All he asks – so far as his participation is concerned – is that he and all others be treated as equals in matters affecting their interests, their rights, and their duties.

4. DOES PARTICIPATION HAVE AN INSTRUMENTAL JUSTIFICATION?

Although the influence of an individual vote is small, the effects of voting by large numbers of individuals are not. Politics is a serious business. In modern societies, political decisions determine, by action or default, things like the distribution of food, housing, medical and educational services. Through legislation, they determine the details of respect for the individual, the pursuit of justice, and the parameters of civil and political freedom. And (in interaction with other states) political decisions by elected officials govern war and peace, co-operation and hostility, not to mention the control and unleashing of weapons of mass destruction.[25]

Jon Elster has suggested, on the basis of considerations like these, that ultimately any defence of the right to participate – indeed any defence of *any* system of political authority – must be an *instrumental* defence.[26] After all, political decisions are decisions *about* something which we all acknowledge to be important; so surely that sense of the important stakes for which the political game is played should govern our thinking about the appropriate rules for the game. Elster intends this as a criticism of what are

---

[24] 'The Putney Debates: the Debate on the Franchise' (1647) in Wootton (ed.), *Divine Right and Democracy*, 286.

[25] Cf. Barry, 'Comment', 47; quoted in Elster, *Sour Grapes*, 99.

[26] See Elster, 99. See also Macfarlane, *The Theory and Practice of Human Rights*, 141: 'It is important to stress that all political rights are instrumental rights, whose importance lies in the ends which the right concerned may be used to secure.'

sometimes called 'expressivist' theories of voting – theories which hold that voting is best understood and valued as a mode of self-expression, and that the point of giving everyone the vote is to provide them with an opportunity to identify themselves publicly with some view on a matter of common concern.[27] He is right to make this criticism. If voting determines outcomes as serious as war and peace, liberty and oppression, poverty and equality, surely it is irresponsible to regard individual votes as a form of flamboyant self-expression. Expressivist accounts of the importance of participation convey the misleading impression that the substance of politics – the decisions to be made and their implications for real people – matters less than the catharsis, the righteous sense of commitment, and the agonistic flair involved in publicly identifying a particular view as one's own.

Defenders of the expressivist view may respond by appealing once again to Constant: they will say that since the actual influence of my individual vote is vanishingly small anyway, I might as well use it as an occasion for self-expression, rather than worry my head about outcomes, probabilities, or consequences. But this is no more plausible in participatory politics than in any other case of collective action involving millions of individuals. Consider, for example, roadside pollution due to traffic: I may not be able to identify the contribution *I* make to the health problems of poor families living near freeways, but I am well aware that their health is imperilled by hundreds of thousands of drivers including me. I know too that it is only the fitting of emissions control devices to automobiles by most of these drivers that can possibly abate that threat. If I drive without such a device, I am doing something wrong despite the indiscernibility of the harm occasioned by the emissions from my car in particular: I am failing to play my part in the collective enterprise of averting great harm in circumstances in which only a collective enterprise will do. Though it is true that the enterprise does not require the participation of absolutely everyone (and so it does not require *my* participation, provided enough others take part), still there is no reason of fairness for me in particular to relieve myself of the burden of participation, given that the participation of most drivers is required.[28] So – to return to the point about expressivism – even though the emissions of an individual automobile may have only a tiny impact on the environment, it surely does not follow that individual drivers are entitled to regard the decision whether or not to fit anti-

---

[27] Elster cites the following from Stanley Benn, 'The Problematic Rationality of Political Participation', 19, as an example of an expressivist theory: '[P]olitical activity may be a form of moral self-expression, necessary not for achieving any objective beyond itself (for the cause may be lost), nor yet for the satisfaction of knowing that one had let everyone else know that one was on the side of the right, but because one could not seriously claim, even to oneself, to be on that side without expressing the attitude by the actions most appropriate to it in the paradigm case.'

[28] I owe this last point to Griffin, *Well-Being*, 206–19.

emission devices as an occasion for flamboyant self-expression. The stakes are too high, and even though there are millions of us involved, nothing but millions of drivers making the right decision will avert the very great harm of pollution.

Something similar is true of the moral importance of voting. When a government is elected or a plebiscite takes place, millions of voters act together to secure something (which they regard as) important, something that in our political system cannot be secured save by our acting together in very large numbers. The particular form this collective enterprise takes is for us to match our numbers against the large number of those we expect to engage – wrongfully, we think – in a similar collective enterprise on the other side. If I fail to vote (for the candidate or measure that deserves to win), I have done a wrong comparable to that involved in the emissions example: I have failed to play my part in the collective action that is required in our political system in order to secure an important good or avoid a grave harm. And I have done so in circumstances where there is no reason in fairness for me in particular to relieve myself of the burden of participation, given that the participation of most (right-minded) citizens is required. In these circumstances, it is irresponsible for me to regard my vote simply as an occasion for self-expression; instead I should reflect responsibly on the difference it is actually likely to make (along with millions of other votes) to life-and-death issues that affect everyone.

So: each individual should participate in a way that pays attention to the consequences of his participation. But does it follow, as Elster suggests, that therefore the justification of the system of participation must be instrumental or consequentialist? I think not. The argument of the last few paragraphs concerns the attitude a voter should take to his exercise of the franchise. He should exercise it responsibly, on the basis of what his vote (along with large numbers of others) may cause to happen in the world. But from the fact that considerations of a certain kind ought to guide a right-bearer in the exercise of a given right, we are not entitled to infer that his actually having the right is justified by considerations of that sort.

We can infer *something* from the gravity of the considerations mentioned at the beginning of this section. If the decision as to *how* to vote should be taken seriously because of the high stakes involved, it certainly follows that the question as to whether there *is* a right to vote is to be taken seriously also. Because of what is at stake in politics, the principle of participation requires a strong and robust defence – one that can be presented, for example, as a credible response to perennial worries about the risks that losers run in submitting to majority decisions. In the context of this sort of concern, the argument that they must accept such risks so that people can enjoy the indulgence of *expressing* themselves at the ballot box does seem seriously out of its league.

We can put the same point in a slightly different way. Voting is a way of deciding among important social options. Those who urge one option or the other will put forward serious justificatory arguments designed to show, first, that the stakes in the decision are very high, and secondly, why it is important that those stakes should play out in a particular way. No defence of voting or of the right to vote can succeed if it denigrates these arguments or if it relies on their being treated as unimportant. Since an affirmation of the right to participate addresses the issue of *who is to make social decisions when the stakes are this high*, it requires a justification that is, so to speak, in the same league of moral seriousness as the justifications associated with the substantive options that compete in the political forum. Elster is right, then, to condemn the frivolity of the expressivist accounts. But it is a mistake to think that only instrumental considerations can have the requisite degree of seriousness. Particularly since it is a *right* we are considering – the right to participate (in decisions affecting one, on equal terms with others) – we should ask whether there is not a defence available, with the requisite level of seriousness, that is not itself an instrumentalist account.

In general, theorists of rights are uneasy about instrumental justifications. Inasmuch as they present rights as a means to a social end, instrumental justifications leave the rights hostage to contingent calculations of utilitarian advantage.[29] A right with an instrumental justification is always liable to managerial manipulation, limiting the right or modifying its exercise in order to fine-tune the generation of socially desirable consequences.[30] And this seems to be at odds with the 'trumping' function of rights, which is precisely to set limits on the pursuit of social utility.[31]

I do not mean this, however, as a knock-down argument against instrumental justifications. It is not enough simply to *repeat* 'Rights as Trumps', as though that were some sort of mantra. Surely we do not have a trumping right to harm other people or to participate in harming them. And if, as seems to be the case, the exercise of voting rights is capable of causing grave harm as well as doing great good, the instrumentalist is entitled to ask what exactly is wrong with governing their scope or distribution in a way that is calculated to minimize the harm and maximize the good? And he is entitled to press for an answer, not an incantation.

---

[29] See Lyons, 'Utility and Rights'.

[30] If we accept an instrumental theory of participation, we must accept (as Macfarlane points out, *The Theory and Practice of Human Rights*, 141) that 'arguments about the nature and requirements of political rights will, when used in debates about the desirability of restricting or extending political rights, be colored by the expectations of political consequences which will follow from the changes projected'.

[31] For rights as trumps, see Dworkin, *Taking Rights Seriously*, xi. See also Dworkin, 'Rights as Trumps'.

The real answer that we should give him has to do with the difficulty of specifying the goals of such instrumental management.[32] The specification of social goals – to which participatory rights are supposed (on his account) to be instrumental – is not only intensely controversial in modern society; it is of course the primary subject matter of the very politics that participatory rights are supposed to constitute. Those who claim participatory rights are demanding the right to participate *in resolving controversies of exactly this sort*. They want to be among those who determine the social goals and conceptions of the common good relative to which political management and political instrumentality will be defined. That is why the point made earlier – about not simply *inferring* the need for an instrumental justification of the right from the instrumental responsibility associated with its exercise – is so important. In deciding how to vote, the individual citizen must figure out what is important in politics, and how his vote along with millions of others can best promote it. This instrumental responsibility requires judgement among ends as well as means; and it involves choice among intensely controversial alternatives. The whole point of voting is that, in the teeth of these controversies, social ends are to be determined collectively by millions of individual judgements. But that can hardly be so if the process of enfranchising, counting, and implementing these judgements is governed and modified by some prior and entrenched selection among the alternatives.

5. PRINCIPLE AND AUTHORITY

Politics is about principle as well as policy. What happens in the political process determines not only what our social goals are, but also the content and distribution of individuals' rights. Of course the political process cannot control anyone's critical sense of what rights we have or ought to have, nor can it affect the truth about that issue (if talk of truth is appropriate here). But since people disagree about what rights we have or ought to have, the specification of our legal rights has to be accomplished through some political process.

Rights, in other words, are no exception to the general need for authority in politics. Since people hold different views about rights and since we have to settle upon and enforce a common view about this, we must ask:

---

[32] In a discussion of similar managerial approaches to free speech, Robert Post remarks that '[m]anagerial structures necessarily presuppose objectives that are unproblematic and hence that can be used instrumentally to regulate domains of social life. The enterprise of public discourse, by contrast, . . . requires that all possible objectives, all possible versions of national identity, be rendered problematic and open to inquiry.' (Post, *Constitutional Domains*, 275.)

'Who is to have the power to make social decisions, or by what processes are social decisions to be made, on the practical issues that competing theories of rights purport to address?' As political philosophers, our task is to inquire into the principles and criteria by which this question of authority is to be answered? The claim we have been examining – the claim that political participation is a right – constitutes an answer, or at least part of an answer, to the question of authority. When someone asks, 'Who shall decide what rights we have?', one answer (*my* answer) is: 'The people whose rights are in question have the right to participate on equal terms in that decision.' But it is not the only possible answer. Instead of empowering the people on the grounds that it is after all their rights that are at stake, we might instead entrust final authority to a scholarly or judicial elite, on the ground that they are more likely to get the matter right.

As we begin our discussion of these proposals, it may be worth making a few general observations about the problem of authority in politics.

(1) First, a point about disagreement and objectivity. That we disagree and therefore need to invoke an authority is not necessarily a concession to moral subjectivism or conventionalism or relativism. One can recognize the existence of disagreement on matters of rights and justice – one can even acknowledge that such disagreements are, for practical political purposes, irresolvable – without staking the meta-ethical claim that there is no fact of the matter about the issue that the participants are disputing.[33] The need for authority in the area of rights is not a consequence of the rejection of objectivity in that area; it is a response to the fact that, even if there is an objective right answer to the question of what rights we have, still people disagree implacably about what that right answer is. (This was our argument in Chapter Eight.)

(2) Thus, secondly, we are not to *despair* of substantive thought or deliberation about rights. What one needs to do is *complement* one's theory of rights with a theory of authority, not *replace* the former with the latter. The issue of what counts as the right decision about rights does not disappear the moment we answer the question 'Who decides?' On the contrary, substantive theorizing about rights is what we expect the designated authority (for example the participants in a democracy) to do. As we saw at the beginning of Chapter Two, each competing theory of rights can be understood as a well-thought-out piece of advice offered to whomever has been identified (by the theory of authority) as the person to take the decision or as one of the persons who is to provide an input into the public choice

[33] For the contrary view, see Barber, *Strong Democracy*, 129: 'Where there is certain knowledge, true science, or absolute right, there is no conflict that cannot be resolved by reference to the unity of truth, and thus there is no necessity for politics.' See also Estlund, 'Making Truth Safe for Democracy'.

mechanisms that will yield a collective decision. The mechanism needs inputs or the authority needs advice (or a theory of its own), and so *someone* (or, preferably, many people) should be thinking through the substantive issues, undeterred in this by the existence of disagreement and opposing alternatives.

(3) But, thirdly, a substantive theory of rights is not itself the theory of authority that is needed in the face of disagreement about rights. An adequate answer to the question of authority must really settle the issue. It is no good saying that when people disagree about rights, the view which should prevail is *the truth about rights* or *the best account of the rights we have.* Each theorist regards his own view as better than any of the others (otherwise he would abandon his theory and adopt one of the others). So this way of settling on a social choice in the face of disagreement would reproduce exactly the disagreement that called for an authority-rule in the first place. The theory of authority must identify some view as the one to prevail on criteria other than those which are the source of the original disagreement. This is one of Thomas Hobbes's contributions to political philosophy: any theory that makes authority depend on the goodness of political outcomes is self-defeating, for it is precisely because people *disagree* about the goodness of outcomes that they need to set up and recognize an authority.[34]

I find that people are very unhappy about this third point. Because the liberties and interests that rights protect are so important, they are uncomfortable with any political procedure that leaves open the possibility of our being saddled with (objectively) wrong answers about rights. This discomfort sometimes leads them to qualify their views about authority with a rider that is supposed to protect individual rights against that possibility. For example, they may say, 'If the members of a society disagree about some issue, then a social decision should be reached by majority voting, *provided individual rights are not violated thereby.*' But the emphasized rider will not work as part of a theory of authority for a society in which rights themselves are a subject of political disagreement. People who disagree *inter alia* about rights will disagree about what this theory of authority requires, and that latter disagreement will be nothing but a reproduction of the problem about rights which indicated the need for a theory of authority in the first place.

Similarly, as I stressed at the end of Chapter One, we cannot say that the whole *point* of rights is to 'trump' or override majority decisions.[35] Rights

---

[34] See Hobbes, *Leviathan*, Ch. 18 and *De Cive*, VI, 6.

[35] Dworkin, *Taking Rights Seriously*, 199–200. Notice that this use of the 'rights-as-trumps' idea is slightly different from that discussed above at fn. 31 and accompanying text. Rights as trumps over social utility is a different idea from rights as trumps over majority-decision: see Waldron, 'Rights as Majorities: Rousseau Revisited'.

may be the very thing that the members of the society are disagreeing about, the very issue they are using a system of voting to settle. If we say, in a situation in which people disagree about rights, that rights may 'trump' a majority decision, it is incumbent on us to announce which of the competing conceptions of rights is to do the trumping, and how that is to be determined. But to make such an announcement in the name of the whole society is of course to beg the very question at issue.[36]

(4) It follows from what has been said that, unless one is very lucky, there will often be a dissonance between what one takes to be the right choice and what one takes to be the authoritative choice in political decision-making. A person who holds a complete political theory – one that includes a theory of authority as well as theories of justice, rights, and policy – may find himself committed to the view that the wrong decision ought to prevail. His theory of justice may condemn policy B and prefer policy A on right-based grounds, but his theory of authority may support a decision procedure (designed to yield a social choice in the face of disagreement about, for example, the justice of A or B) which, when followed, requires that B be implemented.

This prospect is simply unavoidable. Richard Wollheim called it 'a paradox in the theory of democracy'.[37] He imagined citizens feeding their individual evaluations of policies into a democratic machine which would always choose the policy with the greatest number of supporters. The paradox arises from the fact that each citizen, if he is a democrat, will have an allegiance to the machine and its output, as well as to the evaluation which counts as his own whole-hearted input. It is the paradox that allows 'one and the same citizen to assert that A ought to be enacted, where A is the policy of his choice, and B ought to be enacted, where B is the policy chosen by the democratic machine'.[38] But Wollheim was wrong to describe it as a paradox of *democracy*. It is a general paradox in the theory of authority – a paradox affecting *any* political theory which complements its account of what ought to be done with an account of how decisions ought to be made when there is disagreement about what ought to be done.

It is general in another way as well – general as opposed to exceptional. In modern societies, disagreement (including disagreement about principles) is one of the basic circumstances of political life, in roughly the way

---

[36] Hence the motto of this book: 'And when men that think themselves wiser than all others, clamor and demand right Reason for judge; yet seek no more, but that things should be determined, by no other mens reason but their own, it is as intolerable in the society of men, as it is in play after trump is turned, to use for trump on every occasion, that suite whereof they have most in their hand.' (Hobbes, *Leviathan*, Ch. 5, 33.)

[37] Wollheim, 'A Paradox in the Theory of Democracy'.   [38] Ibid., 84.

that moderate scarcity is one of the circumstances of justice.[39] When we think about distributive justice, we must be ready for situations in which *not everybody gets what he wants*: the circumstance of moderate scarcity tells us that this is not exceptional, but normal, in the conditions of human life. We must not construct a conception of justice that laments this as an unfortunate aberration or as a distasteful aspect of second-best theory: we must rather construct a theory that places this prospect firmly in the core of our thinking about justice. The same is true of disagreement and disappointment in politics. In the circumstances of politics, a person must expect (unless he is very lucky) to find himself from time to time bound by social arrangements he regards as unjust. That is almost bound to happen, seeing that it is the function of law to lay down rules in circumstances where people disagree about justice. Wollheim's paradox therefore should not be regarded as an anomaly. It is a normal predicament for most people at least some of the time and for many people most of the time, in the circumstances of politics.

These points about Wollheim's Paradox are quite important for modern debates about rights, courts, and constitutionalism. Rights-based judicial review of legislation is often defended by pointing to the possibility that democratic majoritarian procedures may yield unjust or tyrannical outcomes. And so they may. But so may *any* procedure that purports to solve the problem of social choice in the face of disagreements about what counts as injustice or what counts as tyranny. The American practice of allowing the Supreme Court to make the final decision (by majority voting among its members) on issues of fundamental rights has on occasion yielded egregiously unjust decisions (certainly decisions opposed, on grounds of justice, by me and many of my friends).[40] Anyone whose theory of authority gives the Supreme Court power to make decisions must – as much as any democrat – face up to the paradox that the option he thinks just may sometimes not be the option which, according to his theory of authority, should be followed.

Of course, as Wollheim argued at the end of his essay, the paradox does not really involve a contradiction. A person who believes that A is the right decision but B the decision that should be implemented, is offering answers to two different, though complementary questions. That B should be implemented is his answer to the question, 'What are *we* to do, given that we disagree about whether A or B is just?' That A is the right

---

[39] For 'the circumstances of justice', see Rawls, *A Theory of Justice*, 126–30.

[40] For an uncontroversial example of an egregiously unjust decision, see the *'Dred Scott'* decision, *Scott* v. *Sandford* 60 US (19 How) 393 (1857). See also *Lochner* v. *New York* 198 US 45 (1905), and the more than 150 cases in which fine pieces of labour and factory legislation were struck down by state and federal courts in the period 1880–1930. (There is a list in Forbath, *Law and the Shaping of the American Labor Movement*, 177–92.)

decision is his own contribution to the disagreement that called forth that question.

(5) A fifth point follows in connection with Wollheim's 'Paradox'. (This is the first of the two points which, I said at the very beginning of the chapter, it was my overall aim to establish.) We sometimes say that a principle of authority (such as participatory majoritarianism) *conflicts* with other rights, for example in situations in which popular majorities vote to impose restrictions on some right (call it the target right); and we say that in this situation one of the rights must give way. Either the target right prevails, in which case the members of the majority do not have the participatory right to make whatever laws they like; or participation prevails, in which case the target right must give way to the popular will. I believe, however – and I argued this in detail in Chapter Nine – that this is a misleading characterization and that 'conflict' is the wrong word to describe what is happening in cases like this. Principles of authority such as participatory majoritarianism are principles for governing social decision-making in circumstances where some members of the society think that rights require one thing and other members of the society think that rights require something else. When majority voting indicates that one of these factions has prevailed politically, the result will seem to the members of that faction to be congruent with what is required by rights, even as it seems to the members of the other faction to be at odds with what is required by rights. This disparity – as to whether there is actually a conflict with rights or not – should alert us to the danger in treating the right to participate and the target right as co-ordinate principles, competing on the same level. If we talk about a conflict between target rights and participatory majoritarianism, we seem to imply that sometimes the target right may weigh more heavily, and sometimes participation may weigh more heavily. But the problem is not about weighing and balancing; the problem is that we disagree in these cases about what exactly rights require, and thus we disagree about what ought to go into one side of the balance.

The point of the last paragraph is not to convince the reader that we ought to invoke participatory majoritarianism in order to settle disagreements about rights. (That will be the burden of sections 6 and 7 of this chapter.) There are other principles of authority available, such as monarchy (one supreme ruler decides), judicial aristocracy (the final decision is assigned to the members of a Supreme Court), or various forms of mixed regime. All I am showing is that *if* we choose participatory majoritarianism (indeed, if we choose *any* of these principles of authority), it makes no sense to talk of a conflict between the principle of authority that we choose and the rights about which the authority has to decide. Since we disagree about whether these rights exist or not and about what they entail if they do, there is no neutral way of stating what exactly it is that is supposed to be competing with participatory majoritarianism (or whatever the principle of authority is).

(6) One last point. Like all rights, the one that we are considering – participation – is also an appropriate target or subject matter for authority. In politics, the right to participate (its nature and limits) is one of the things on which we disagree and about which we have to decide. But, unlike other rights, the right to participate also presents itself as a possible answer (or part of an answer) to the question of authority. That participation can be both the subject matter of authority as well as part of a theory of authority might seem to pose some threat of circularity: it seems circular to use a principle of authority to settle disagreements *about* authority, or to use majoritarian methods to settle disagreements *about* majoritarianism. I do not think this appearance of circularity can be sustained; but I will not argue that here. The matter is dealt with at some length in the final chapter – Chapter Thirteen – of the book.[41]

6. A RIGHTS-BASED SOLUTION

Participation, I said, is about principle as much as policy. Those who fought for the vote (whether for working people, the propertyless, women, former slaves, or others disenfranchised on grounds of race) had in mind the right to participate not only on policy issues but also on the great issues of principle facing their society. I suspect also that most them fought for participation in the second or radical sense I mentioned in section 3 of this chapter – participation of each individual along with all others in the society as equals, not simply the participation of a democratic element, along with non-democratic elements, in a mixed regime. These two points go together. Those who demanded the right to vote were not seeking radically democratic participation only on issues of policy, as though they would be satisfied by participation in the other sense – the mixed-regime sense – on issues of principle. They believed that the issues of principle affecting them – the people – should be settled, ultimately, by them and them only on a basis that paid tribute to their fundamental equality.[42]

[41] See below, Ch. 13en, ss. 6–9.

[42] Now, as I have stated it here, this sounds like an exaggeration of their claim, as though it were a demand for direct democracy, whereas most often what was wanted was a vote in the election of representatives. But the underlying point remains. To the extent that a system of representation was thought necessary (on practical grounds), the challenge was to show that such structures were (in the circumstances) the best way of respecting the principle of individuals' political equality. To show that a given structure of representation respected the

Understood in this way, the demand for equal suffrage amounted to the claim that issues of right should be determined by the whole community of right-bearers in the society – that is, by all of those whose rights were at stake. As a principle of authority, it was the claim that disagreements about rights should be settled by those who were the subjects of that disagreement. People who make this claim are aware that it is controversial. But they think it wrong and offensive *to them as right-bearers* to reject the claim out of hand.

Let me explain that last point in detail, because it goes to the heart of the issues about participation and rights that I am trying to set out.

I have argued elsewhere[43] that the idea of rights is based on a view of the human individual as essentially a thinking agent, endowed with an ability to deliberate morally, to see things from others' points of view, and to transcend a preoccupation with his own particular or sectional interests. The attribution of any right, I said, is typically an act of faith in the agency and capacity for moral thinking of each of the individuals concerned.[44] This is partly reflected in the fact that rights typically provide an individual with a protected choice on an issue which remains morally significant: the right-bearer must choose between options which are right or wrong, considerate or inconsiderate, noble or depraved.[45] The faith in the right-bearer's choice evinced by the attribution of the right is certainly not confidence that he will unerringly make the right choice; nevertheless it is borne of a conviction that he has the wherewithal to ponder responsibly whatever moral issues the choice involves.

Beyond that, the way in which the idea of rights emerged in early modern thought should remind us that right-bearers were conceived in the first instance as appropriate rights-*thinkers* (not merely as potential victims whose interests needed protection). The emergent idea of natural rights connoted not just that ordinary individuals were the proper focus of moral and political concern, but also that ordinary individuals were naturally competent judges of issues of right. Rights were attributed to individuals in the state of nature, a circumstance in which each person had nothing but his own resources – his own intellect, his own reason – to indicate to him the rights that he and others had. Theorists such as John Locke were happy to embrace this idea – again, not on account of any great confidence that individual reasoners in the state of nature could be relied on to come up

---

combination of ideals in a mixed regime (equality, perhaps, but also respect for the experience and upbringing of a clerisy or aristocracy) would be a different and probably easier challenge.

[43] See Waldron, 'A Right-Based Critique of Constitutional Rights'. See also Ch. 10, above.

[44] Again, this is the equivalent for a theory of rights of Rawls's emphasis of the importance of attributing to people 'a sense of justice' in a theory of justice. See Rawls, *A Theory of Justice*, Ch. VIII, esp. 505–10.

[45] See Waldron, 'A Right to do Wrong'.

with conclusions that were exactly and unerringly correct,[46] but on account of their confidence that the *type* of reasoning in which ordinary individuals could be expected to engage was not inappropriate to the questions that they necessarily had to pose for themselves. Certainly Locke rejected out of hand the view – very common today – that on issues of rights the reasoning of judicial officials (Supreme Court justices and their clerks) is to be preferred to the reason and judgement of ordinary men and women.[47] The reasoning of legal scholars on matters of rights Locke regarded as 'artificial Ignorance, and learned Gibberish' – contemptible and mischievous in comparison to the straightforward and 'unscholastick' reasoning of 'the illiterate and contemned Mechanick' pondering his own rights.[48] The point is that the idea of natural rights – rights in the state of nature – was predicated precisely on the *absence* of lawyerly thinking. It involved instead a tight conjunction of concern for each individual as a creature of God[49] and respect for the reason with which God had endowed him:

The Freedom then of Man and Liberty of acting according to his own Will, is grounded on his having Reason, which is able to instruct him in that Law he is to govern himself by, and make him know how far he is left to the freedom of his own will.[50]

It is impossible, on this account, to think of a person as a right-bearer and not think of him as someone who has the sort of capacity that is required to figure out what rights he has.

This means that arguing about a person's rights is not like arguing about the rights of animals or about the preservation of a building. When we argue about someone's rights, the subject of the conversation is likely to have a considered view on the matter. And since the point of any argument about rights has to do with the respect that is owed to this person as an active, thinking being, we are hardly in a position to say that our conversation takes *his* rights seriously if at the same time we ignore or slight anything *he* has to say about the matter. Yet again, I emphasize that this does not mean a person has whatever rights he thinks he has or that he cannot be wrong in what he thinks. But it does show that there is *something* appropriate about the position we are considering – that the right-bearers

[46] See Waldron, 'Locke's Legislature'.

[47] Cf. Locke, *Two Treatises*, II, para. 12, 275: '[F]or though it would be besides my present purpose, to enter here into the particulars of the law of Nature, or its measures of punishment; yet it is certain that there is such a Law, and that too, as intelligible and plain to a rational Creature, and a Studier of the Law, as the positive Laws of Common-wealths, nay possibly plainer; As much as Reason is easier to be understood, than the Phansies and intricate Contrivances of Men, following contrary and hidden interests put into Words.'

[48] See Locke, *An Essay Concerning Human Understanding*, Bk. III, Ch. X, 495.

[49] Locke, *Two Treatises*, II, para. 6, 271.   [50] Ibid., II, para. 63, 309.

should be the ones to decide what rights they have, if there is disagreement about that issue – and something unpleasantly inappropriate and disrespectful about the view that questions about rights are too hard or too important to be left to the right-bearers themselves to determine, on a basis of equality.

7. THE TROUBLE WITH RIGHTS-INSTRUMENTALISM

From all of this, we may conclude that the attractiveness of democratic participation consists largely in the fact that it is a *rights-based*[51] solution to the problem of disagreement about rights. It calls upon the very capacities that rights *as such* connote, and it evinces a form of respect in the resolution of political disagreement which is continuous with the respect that rights as such evoke.

It is not the only rights-based approach. It is possible to approach the problem of disagreement and authority in regard to rights on the basis of a sort of rights-instrumentalism: one chooses whatever decision-procedures are most likely to answer the question 'What rights do we have?' correctly.[52] If the people or their representatives can be relied on to come up with the right answer through majority-voting in a legislature, then we set up a right to participation. But if we think judges, bishops, or scholars might do a better job, then we should forgo or qualify popular participation and entrust the final decision to the courts, to a synod, or to a clerisy. I do not want to deny that this is an honourable approach. It takes very seriously the prospect that a given procedure may yield the wrong answer. It says: wrong answers may be tolerable in matters of policy; but on matters of principle, if the wrong answer is given, then *rights will be violated*, and it is important to avoid this outcome if at all possible or at least to minimize it (to the extent we can). The rights-instrumentalist thinks that the participatory approach, which I defended in the previous section, simply gestures towards right-bearers' capacities and hopes for the best. This, the instrumentalist says, is irresponsible: instead we should be doing everything in our power to reduce the rights-violations that will result from our political processes, and that means adopting the minimization of wrong answers as our explicit criterion of authority in this area.

Rights-instrumentalism is of course heir to the difficulty we discussed at the end of section 4. Though I do not believe there is anything *intrinsically* repugnant about an instrumentalism or consequentialism of rights,[53]

---

[51] For the idea of rights-based, duty-based, and goal-based theories, see Dworkin, *Taking Rights Seriously*, 171 ff. See also Ch. 10, above.

[52] See Dworkin, *Freedom's Law*, 34. See also the discussion of this in Ch. 13, below.

[53] For criticism of the idea of rights-violations as something to be minimized, see Nozick, *Anarchy, State and Utopia*, 28 ff. For the contrary view, see Sen, 'Rights and Agency'.

rights-instrumentalism seems to face the difficulty that it presupposes our possession of the truth about rights in designing an authoritative procedure whose point it is to settle that very issue. Consider, for example, the question whether people have rights to socio-economic assistance and, if so, whether these rights impose limits on property rights. A person who thinks that the answer to either question is 'No' will probably respond differently to the instruction 'Design a set of political procedures most likely to yield the truth about rights' than a person who believes that there *are* socio-economic rights and that they *do* place limits on property. Indeed, disparate views on this and similar issues explain most of the differences in constitutional-design proposals among rights-instrumentalists.[54] There seems, then, something question-begging about using rights-instrumentalism as a basis for the design of political procedures among people who disagree on issues such as this.

Maybe a more modest rights-instrumentalism is available. Instead of saying (in a question-begging way) that we should choose those political procedures that are most likely to yield the rights specified in a particular controversial conception, we might say instead that we should choose or design political procedures that are most likely to get at the truth about rights, *whatever* that truth turns out to be.

But this is not straightforward either. Consider some familiar moves in this more modest rights-instrumentalism. If we think that deliberation about rights is distorted by self-interest, we will try to design institutions that insulate rights-authorities from any immediate concern with the impact of their decisions on their own interests. But if we do this we should do it in full awareness that we are flying in the face of other epistemic precepts: that decisions about rights are best taken by those who have a sufficient stake in the matter to decide responsibly (an argument often used to justify a property franchise), or that the very idea of natural rights celebrates the ability of ordinary people to reason responsibly about the relation between their own interests and those of others (the argument we considered in section 6). We find similar antinomies with other epistemic approaches. If we think the truth about rights requires training and wisdom to discern, we might endow scholars, even moral philosophers, with political authority. If we think, on the other hand, as Locke did, that academic casuistry distorts clear thinking on these matters, we might incline instead to entrust the decision to ordinary voters. Indeed if we accept anything like Jean-Jacques Rousseau's conception of epistemic virtue on the matters that are supposed to be governed by the general will of the people, we might even set up democratic procedures

---

[54] For a discussion of the way this affected American constitutional design, see Nedelsky, *Private Property and the Limits of American Constitutionalism*.

that minimize public deliberation and the opportunity for rhetoric and factionalism.[55]

A quick review of such antinomies should be enough to assure us that it is almost as difficult to defend an impartial account of what the modest version of rights-instrumentalism requires as it is to find a non-question-begging version of direct instrumentalism. In the midst of moral disagreement we are not in possession of any uncontroversial moral epistemology. Most theories of moral knowledge (and thus also most theories of moral expertise and epistemic pathology in moral reasoning) are associated directly with a particular set of substantive moral claims: naturalism with utilitarianism, intuitionism with deontology, feminist epistemology with particular equality-claims, and so on. Even among professional epistemologists, there is not the sort of consensus about *paths* to moral truth that would be required for a non-question-begging instrumental defence of political procedures for use among those who disagree, fundamentally, about which moral claims are true and which are not.[56]

It seems then that, as a basis for addressing the issue of authority, rights-instrumentalism faces difficulties which have to do, not just with contingent practicalities, but with a failure ultimately to take seriously the problem of disagreement which poses the issue of authority in the first place. People disagree about rights; they also disagree about the best way to reason about rights; so they simply cannot in their collective capacity follow the instruction 'Confer the authority to resolve these disagreements on those persons and procedures most likely to yield the right answer' in a non-question-begging way.[57]

It follows, I think, that the theory which rejects rights-instrumentalism, and which maintains instead that right-bearers have the right to resolve disagreements about what rights they have among themselves and on roughly equal terms, is the only plausible rights-based theory of authority left in the field. Not only does it not face the question-begging difficulties of rights-instrumentalism, it also has the advantage over the latter that it does not consecrate forms of authority which are radically at odds with those entrusted to ordinary right-bearers in the ordinary exercise and contemplation of their rights. In this sense, we can plausibly say that participation is the rights-theorist's most natural answer to the problem of authority and the disagreements about rights that give rise to that problem. In short, the right to participate is indeed, as William Cobbett suggested, 'the right of rights'.

---

[55] See Rousseau, *The Social Contract*, Bk. II, Ch. 3 and Bk. IV, Chs. 1–3.
[56] See also the excellent discussion in Gaus, *Justificatory Liberalism*, 185.
[57] See also Ch. 9, above.

Chapter Twelve

Disagreement and Precommitment

The constitutional structures we are considering in this part of the book – a Bill of Rights with judicial review of legislation – need not be thought of as undemocratically imposed upon the people. If by now a Bill of Rights has been incorporated into British law, for example, it will have been because Parliament or perhaps the people in a referendum have voted for incorporation.

Ronald Dworkin once argued that this alone is sufficient to dispose of the objection that such constraints are contrary to the spirit of democracy. On his view, the democratic objection is self-defeating because polls reveal that more than 71 per cent of people believe that British democracy would be improved by the incorporation of a Bill of Rights.[1]

The objection cannot be disposed of quite so easily. The fact that there is popular support, even overwhelming popular support, for an alteration in the constitution does not show that such an alteration would make things more democratic. Certainly, my arguments in this part of the book entail that if the people want a regime of constitutional rights, that is what they should have: that is what the principle of participation requires, so far as constitutional change is concerned. But we must not confuse the reason for carrying out a proposal with the character of the proposal itself. If the people voted to experiment with dictatorship, democratic principles might give us a reason to allow them to do so. But it would not follow that dictatorship is democratic.

Let me put the matter more theoretically. There is a distinction between democracy and popular sovereignty. The principle of popular sovereignty – basic to liberal thought – requires that the people should have whatever constitution, whatever form of government they want. But popular sovereignty does not remove or blur the differences that exist among the various forms of government on the menu from which the people are supposed to choose. John Locke and Thomas Hobbes both believed in popular sovereignty. They argued that the people – acting by majority-decision – had the right to vest legislative authority in a single individual or small group of individuals (thus constituting a monarchy or an aristocracy) or alternatively in an assembly comprising the whole people or in a

[1] Dworkin, *A Bill of Rights for Britain*, 36–7.

large representative institution (thus constituting a direct or an indirect democracy).[2] But although this decision was to be popular and majoritarian, and in that sense democratic, it was at the same time a significant choice between democratic and undemocratic options. Hobbes believed that the people would be making a mistake if they vested sovereignty in a democratic assembly;[3] Locke, on the other hand, credited the people with thinking that they 'could never be safe . . . till the Legislature was placed in collective bodies of Men, call them Senate, Parliament, or what you please', and he thought it important for that collective body to be the 'Supream Power' of the commonwealth.[4] Neither of them thought a constitution became more democratic simply by being the upshot of popular choice.

There may be a connection the other way. It may be easier to establish that a polity is based on popular sovereignty if it is in fact democratically organized. We can see this if we reflect a little on the artificiality of the Hobbes/Locke model. The distinction between a democratic method of constitutional choice and the democratic character of the constitution that is chosen is clearest when we can point to a founding moment in the life of a political society (a moment of constitutional choice) and distinguish between the decision-procedures used at that moment and the decision-procedures which, at that moment, it was decided to employ in all subsequent political decision-making. But in the real world, the formation of a new political order is seldom so tidy.

Often the decisions which determine the shape of a society's constitution are entangled with or woven into the fabric of ordinary political life.[5] As they occur they may be indistinguishable – in time, solemnity, or any other respect – from the ordinary run of political decision-making. Often, for example, we will not know whether a new way of doing things (in some run-of-the-mill case or even in some crisis which is not evidently or on its face a *constitutional* crisis) is going to 'stick' – that is, whether it is going to become established as a rule or practice governing the conduct of political life, or whether it will turn out to be just an aberration, consigned to the minutiae of history. Even in the United States where there is a full written constitution and an established tradition of interpreting it, an event which has fundamental significance for the basis on which political life is conducted may not advertise itself as 'constitutional'.[6] Certainly in the United Kingdom and elsewhere, understanding the formation and

---

[2] Hobbes, *Leviathan*, Ch. 19, 129 ff.; Locke, *Two Treatises of Government*, II, para. 132, 354.
[3] Hobbes, *De Cive*, Ch. X, 129–40.
[4] Locke, *Two Treatises of Government*, II, para. 94, 329–30 and para 149, 366–7. I have discussed this view of Locke's at some length in Waldron, 'Locke's Legislature'.
[5] See Brest, 'Further Beyond the Republican Revival'.
[6] See Tiedeman, *The Unwritten Constitution of the United States*.

growth of the constitution is often a matter of studying apparently routine political events, to discern which of them have and which of them have not acquired normative significance so far as the conduct and organization of other political events are concerned.[7]

An attribution of popular sovereignty to a political system is therefore a matter of judgement. It requires us to figure out which decisions count as constitutive of the political system in question and to venture a certain explanatory hypothesis to account for the constitutional significance of those decisions – a hypothesis to the effect that they 'stuck' or became established as constitutional practices because they were acceptable as such to most of the ordinary members of the society. Obviously this will be easiest to justify in a society whose ordinary workings are democratic, because the events we adjudge 'constitutional' will be part of that ordinary working.

The argument is not cast iron, however. It is one thing for a particular decision to be made democratically; it is another thing for it to sustain the same popular support under the description that it is setting a constitutional precedent. The American people may support the ratification of an important treaty in a referendum; but some of them might have voted 'No' if they had thought their support was going to be regarded as effecting a change in the constitutional rule requiring that treaties be ratified by a vote in the Senate not by a vote among the people.[8] Thus the events which amount over time to a change in the constitution may be democratic events without its being proper to describe that constitutional change as democratic.

2. PRECOMMITMENT

Still, suppose that a Bill of Rights together with an American-style mechanism of judicial review of legislation has been chosen by the people and supported by a majority in full awareness that this amounts to a constitutional reform. Then – it may be said – even if we cannot infer that judicial review is democratic, we have surely nevertheless answered the democratic objection. The existence of written constitutional constraints and the courts' power to interpret and apply them – these would not be products of judicial usurpation. Rather they would be mechanisms of restraint that the people have deliberately and for good reasons chosen to impose on themselves.

---

[7] See Marshall, *Constitutional Conventions*. There is also an accessible account of this aspect of the British Constitution in Waldron, *The Law*, 56–87.

[8] This example is adapted from Ackerman and Golove, 'Is NAFTA Constitutional?'

Why would they do this? What makes this sort of self-restraint intelligible? The answer is that everyone knows that majoritarian legislation can be unjust; everyone knows that popular majorities can sometimes be panicked or tempted into passing measures that harm or discriminate against minorities who are powerless politically to resist them. Is this knowledge consistent with what I said in Chapters Ten and Eleven?[9] There I argued that respect for individual rights is not compatible with a purely predatory image of legislative majorities, for majorities are made up of individual right-bearers and part of what we respect in individuals is their ability as right-bearers to figure out responsibly what they owe to others. Now the argument in Chapters Ten and Eleven does not require us to think of right-bearers as angels or to deny that, acting individually or *en masse*, they are sometimes capable of rights-violations. It does require us to say, however, that although right-bearers may on occasion be rights-violators, they are not themselves indifferent to that possibility. To the extent that they foresee it, they have as right-bearers the moral capacity to condemn it in advance and take precautions against the temptations that may trigger it. So if constitutional constraints and mechanisms of judicial review are set up by popular decision, they may be viewed as precautions which responsible right-holders have taken against their own imperfections. Such precautions do not therefore involve any fundamental disrespect for the people or their capacities of self-government. On the contrary they represent the epitome of those capacities in a troubled and complicated world.

I shall call this the 'precommitment' view of constitutional constraints, and much of the rest of this chapter will be devoted to a critique of it. For the moment, however, let us consider it in the best possible light. In the words of one of its most persuasive proponents, the view presents the constitutional arrangements which we have been discussing as 'a kind of rational and shared precommitment among free and equal sovereign citizens at the level of constitutional choice'.[10] Its effect may be summed up as follows:

By the exercise of their rights of equal participation [the people] agree to a safeguard that prevents them, in the future exercise of their equal political rights, from later changing their minds and deviating from their agreement and commitment to a just constitution. . . . By granting to a non-legislative body that is not electorally accountable the power to review democratically enacted legislation, citizens provide themselves with a means for protecting their sovereignty and independence from the unreasonable exercise of their political rights in legislative processes. . . . By agreeing to judicial review, they in effect tie themselves into their unanimous

---

[9] See above Ch. 10, s. 5 and Ch. 11, s. 6.

[10] Freeman, 'Constitutional Democracy and the Legitimacy of Judicial Review'. See also Waldron, 'Freeman's Defense of Judicial Review'.

agreement on the equal basic rights that specify their sovereignty. Judicial review is then one way to protect their status as equal citizens.[11]

As I said, the precommitment view is an attractive one. We are familiar with it from personal ethics: an individual may have reason to impose upon himself certain constraints so far as his future decision-making is concerned. Ulysses decided that he should be bound to the mast in order to resist the charms of the sirens, and he instructed his crew that 'if I beg you to release me, you must tighten and add to my bonds'.[12] A smoker trying to quit may hide his own cigarettes, a chronic over-sleeper with a weakness for the 'Snooze' button may place his alarm clock out of reach on the other side of the bedroom, and a heavy drinker may give his car keys to a friend at the beginning of a party with strict instructions not to return them when they are requested at midnight.

These arrangements strike us not as derogations from individual freedom, but as the epitome of self-government. Freedom, after all, is not just moving hither and yon with the play of appetites: it is a matter of *taking control* of the basis on which one acts; it is a matter of the self being in charge of its desires and not vice versa.[13] The idea is sometimes explicated in terms of the related concept of *autonomy*: 'Autonomy of the will is the property that the will has of being a law to itself.'[14] Aware now of a way in which it might be determined by various forces in the future, the autonomous will seeks to limit such determination by responding to certain considerations of principle in advance.

So, similarly, it may be said, an electorate may resolve collectively to bind itself in advance to resist the siren charms of rights-violations. Aware, as much as the smoker or the drinker, of the temptations of wrong or irrational action, the people as a whole in a lucid moment may put themselves under certain constitutional disabilities – disabilities which serve the same function in relation to democratic values as are served by strategies like hiding the cigarettes or handing the car keys to a friend in relation to the smoker's or the drinker's autonomy. The smoker really desires to stop smoking, the drinker does not really want to drive under the influence; the mechanisms they adopt enable them to secure the good that they really want and avoid the evil which, occasionally despite themselves, they really want to avoid. Similarly, the people really do not want to discriminate on grounds of race, to restrict free speech, or to allow the police to search people's homes without a warrant. They are aware, however, that on occasion they may be panicked into this. And so they have

---

[11] Freeman, 'Constitutional Democracy and the Legitimacy of Judicial Review', 353–4.

[12] Quoted in Elster, *Ulysses and the Sirens*, 36.

[13] See also the discussion of *strong evaluation* and *second-order desires* in Frankfurt, 'Freedom of the Will and the Concept of a Person', and Taylor, 'What is Human Agency?'

[14] Kant, *Grounding for the Metaphysics of Morals*, 44.

taken precautions, instituting legal constraints as safeguards to prevent them from doing in a moment of panic what in their more thoughtful moments they are sure they do not want to do. As Stephen Holmes states the view (though this is not quite Holmes's *own* account of constitutional precommitment):[15]

A constitution is Peter sober while the electorate is Peter drunk. Citizens need a constitution, just as Ulysses needed to be bound to his mast. If voters were allowed to get what they wanted, they would inevitably shipwreck themselves. By binding themselves to rigid rules, they can better achieve their solid and long-term collective aims.[16]

Constitutional constraint, in other words, is a means by which the will of the people secures its own responsible exercise.

3. CAUSAL MECHANISMS VERSUS EXTERNAL JUDGEMENT

In a seminal study of precommitment, Jon Elster has suggested that a decision at t_1 counts as a way of 'binding oneself' *vis-à-vis* some decision at t_2 only if '[t]he effect of carrying out the decision at t_1 [is] to set up some *causal* process in the external world'.[17] He means to exclude purely internal strategies like deciding to decide: 'our intuitive notion of what it is to bind oneself seems to require that we temporarily deposit our will in some external structure'.[18]

In the political case, we may want to ask: what counts as an *external* structure? Elster himself has doubts about the application of his analysis to constitutional constraints:

[T]he analogy between individual and political self-binding is severely limited. An individual can bind himself to certain actions, or at least make deviations from them more costly and hence less likely, by having recourse to a legal framework that is external to and independent of himself. *But nothing is external to society.* With the exception of a few special cases, like the abdication of powers to the International Monetary Fund, societies cannot deposit their will in structures outside their control; they can always undo their ties should they want to.[19]

His point is well taken so far as popular sovereignty is concerned: what the people can do, constitutionally, they can always *in some sense* undo.[20] Yet

---

[15] We shall consider Holmes's somewhat more subtle view in ss. 6 and 7, below.

[16] Holmes, *Passions and Constraint*, 135.

[17] Elster, *Ulysses and the Sirens*, 42 (my emphasis).

[18] Ibid., 43. In general, says Elster, decisions to decide have very little impact. 'I decide that I shall decide that p' has the same ritual and redundant sound as 'if someone were to buy several copies of the morning paper to assure himself that what it said was true' – *idem*, quoting Wittgenstein, *Philosophical Investigations*, para. 265.

[19] Elster, *Solomonic Judgements*, 196 (emphasis in original).

[20] See Rawls, *Political Liberalism*, 234–5.

there is a sense nevertheless that constitutional provisions can be binding, a sense that has to do with institutional structure *within* the framework controlled overall by 'the people' as popular sovereign. Even though the constraints are not external to that framework, they are in the relevant sense external to the particular agencies in which 'the will of the people' is embodied for purposes of ordinary political decision. I shall return to these issues towards the end of this chapter.[21]

A separate set of issues is raised by Elster's reference to causal mechanisms. A decision at t_1 counts, he said, as a precommitment only if its effect is 'to set up some causal process in the external world'.[22] Does this include or exclude strategies like the drinker giving his car keys to a friend? The friend's possession of the car keys is not really a *causal* mechanism ensuring or increasing the probability that the drinker will not drive home at midnight. Instead it operates by virtue of the friend's undertaking at t_1 not to give back the car keys at t_2 together of course with the friend's willingness at t_2 to actually honour that undertaking. My point is not that the friend may prove unreliable; for so may a causal mechanism. It is rather that the precommitment operates via the friend's judgement and decision, and to that extent its operation at t_2 is not entirely under the drinkers's *ex ante* control at t_1.

An advantage of using a non-causal mechanism such as the judgement of a friend is that it enables the agent to bind himself to a principle that does not operate deontologically or rigidly. Most people who condemn drink-driving (in themselves and others) do so without considering that there may be circumstances in which driving with an elevated blood-alcohol level is the right thing to do. Suppose I design a mechanism that prevents me from ever starting my car when my blood-alcohol level exceeds 0.05 per cent. Then I may be dismayed to find that I cannot drive my baby to the hospital if the child becomes desperately ill while I am hosting a cocktail party at my home (and no one else has a car, and no one else can drive, etc., etc.). I discover, in other words, the need for exceptions to the rule. Now if the exceptions are clear-cut then perhaps a sophisticated mechanism can embody them as well: I install a device that also measures the body temperature of my baby and allows me to drive drunk whenever that temperature exceeds 102 degrees Fahrenheit. But if the exceptions are complicated or numerous, or if delicate judgement is required in order to establish whether or not exceptional conditions obtain, then of course it will be better to abandon causal mechanisms altogether and instead entrust the car keys to a sober friend, hoping that the friend will make what is in the circumstances an ethically appropriate decision.

---

[21] See the discussion at the end of s. 5, *infra*.   [22] Elster, *Ulysses and the Sirens*, 42.

Clearly, if constitutional constraints are regarded as forms of democratic precommitment, they operate more on the model of the friend's judgement than on the model of a causal mechanism. Except in rare cases (like 'dual key' controls of nuclear weapons) constitutional constraints do not operate mechanically, but work instead by vesting a power of decision in some person or body of persons (a court), whose job it is to determine *as a matter of judgment* whether conduct that is contemplated (say, by the legislature) at t_2 violates a constraint adopted at t_1.

As I said, the advantage of such forms of constraint is that they do not operate rigidly, but leave some room for judgement. The disadvantage is that they then become capable of operating in ways that do *not* represent the intentions of the agent who instituted them at t_1. Provided one's intention is sufficiently simple-minded, a causal mechanism can embody it perfectly: the physical rigidity of the mechanism represents, as it were, the strength and single-mindedness of the agent's resolve. Though the machine is a mindless thing, its operation may for that very reason enhance rather than undermine the agent's autonomy, because it works to bind him to exactly the decision *he* intended. But if agent A has vested a power of decision in someone else, B, with room for the exercise of judgement by B, then one may wonder whether this is really an instance of autonomous precommitment by A. Binding oneself to do at t_2 exactly what one intends at t_1 to do at t_2 is one thing; delivering one's power of decision as to what to do at t_2 over to the judgement of another person is something quite different. Person A may have good reason to do that of course (i.e. surrender his judgement to B) – and *in a sense* that would be a form of precommitment. That is, the *act* of precommitment may be autonomous; but its operation may be something less than a consummation of the agent's autonomy inasmuch as it is subject to the judgement of another. In other words, it would not be a form of precommitment that enabled one to rebut an objection based on the importance of A's hanging on to his autonomy or, in the case of constitutional constraints, an objection on democratic grounds. It would be more like the vote to vest power in a dictator which we discussed in section 1: when the people vote for dictatorship, then maybe dictatorship is what they need, and maybe dictatorship is what they should have, but let us not kid ourselves that dictatorship is therefore a form of democracy.

I believe this point is *not* rebutted by showing that an independent power of judgement is necessary for the sort of constraint that the agent (or the people) want to set up. In *Freedom's Law* and elsewhere Ronald Dworkin has presented an attractive picture of the US Constitution in which many of the provisions of the Bill of Rights are taken to embody abstract moral principles. Dworkin argues that an accurate historical understanding of the Equal Protection clause, for example, precludes any interpretation which does not represent it as a moral principle framed at a very high level of generality.[23] Since it is obvious (and was obvious in 1868) that abstract moral principles cannot be interpreted and applied without the exercise of human judgement, Dworkin is able to show that the Framers of the Fourteenth Amendment intended members of the judiciary to employ their powers of moral judgement to determine how exactly the actions of state legislatures should be constrained in the name of equal protection. Since this is what the states voted for when the Amendment was ratified, the arrangement amounts to a deliberate decision by various agents, not to constrain themselves by mechanical means as in Ulysses' case, but to have themselves constrained by others' judgement.

Furthermore, in cases like this the necessity for judgement cannot be understood except on the assumption that it will sometimes be exercised – and exercised properly – in ways that were not foreseen by those who set up the constraint. After all, if its proper exercise could always be foreseen in advance, then no exercise of judgement would ever really be required; constitutional jurisprudence would become, as we say, 'mechanical'. Dworkin is quite right to insist therefore that, once one accepts the abstract-principle interpretation of the Bill of Rights[24] and the analytic connection between abstraction and judgement, it is a mistake to accuse modern judges of violating the Framers' intentions simply because the Framers did not contemplate or would have been surprised by some particular modern application of their principle.

But there is yet another point about the link between abstraction and judgement that *does* pose difficulties for the precommitment idea. Not only should we not expect particular applications of the principles embodied in the Bill of Rights to be *ex ante* foreseeable and unsurprising; we should also not expect them to be uncontroversial. The inference of particular applications from a complex principle is something on which people are likely to disagree, particularly if – as Dworkin rightly argues – the inference in every case should be made from the whole array of abstract principles embodied in the constitution, not just the principle embodied in the particular provision appealed to.[25] Again, if we value judgement in relation to our constitutional commitments, we should not flinch at this conclusion. But it does eat away at any claim that precommitment is a form of self-government – that is, government not only of the people but *by* the people – or that it preserves the democratic or self-governing character of a regime. The argument to that effect goes as follows.

[23] Dworkin, *Freedom's Law*, 7–15.
[24] Not of all its provisions of course: Dworkin argues that the Third Amendment, for example, does not on its face amount to a commitment of principle. Ibid., 8–9.
[25] Ibid., 150. See also Dworkin, *Law's Empire*, 250–4.

Early in our tradition, political theorists developed a taxonomy of various forms of constitution, of which the most familiar is the Aristotelian distinction between government by one man, government by a few men, and government by the many. The distinction was not necessarily a matter of whose *will* was to prevail in a society. According to Aristotle, the distinction was needed even in a society ruled by law, since the application of law required judgement and there was a question about who should apply the laws.[26] Judgement foreshadows disagreement, and in politics the question is always how disagreements among the citizens are to be resolved. As I have argued throughout the book, this includes disagreements about rights and justice and thus disagreements about the things covered by the abstract moral principles to which the people have committed themselves in their constitution. Different forms of government amount to different answers to the question: whose judgement is to prevail when citizens disagree in their judgements?

Now there may be good reasons for the people to offer as their answer to this question: 'Not us, or our representatives, but the judiciary.' If so, that amounts *pro tanto* to a refusal of self-government.[27] It amounts to an embrace of what Aristotle would call 'aristocracy' – the rule of the few best.

Of course it is not wholly aristocratic, for the few best are to exercise their judgement on the interpretation and application of principles which, initially at any rate and in their most general form, are chosen by the people. The fact that authority is accorded to the people's choice as to which abstract principles are to be adopted for interpretation by the judges makes this a mixed constitution.

But the aristocratic nature of the arrangement is not diminished by the mere fact that the aristocrats are exercising judgement rather than will. For in our best understanding, politics is *always* a matter of judgement, even at the most abstract level: even the framing of the Fourteenth Amendment is an act of judgement – by the people – as to what a good republic now requires (in light of its history etc.). The democratic claim has always been that the people are entitled to govern themselves by their own judgements. So, to the extent that they invest the judiciary with an overriding power of judgement as to how something as basic as equal protection is to be understood, allowing that judgement to override the judgement of the people or their representatives *on this very issue*, it is undeniable that (in terms of the Aristotelian taxonomy) they have set up what would traditionally be described as a non-democratic arrangement.

---

[26] See Aristotle, *The Politics*, Bk. III, Ch. 15, 76 (1286a25–30).

[27] This is Abraham Lincoln's position in the 'First Inaugural Address', at 221, suggesting that if such questions were to be settled by the Supreme Court, in ordinary cases, 'the people will have ceased, to be their own rulers, having, to that extent, practically resigned their government, into the hands of that eminent tribunal'.

In Chapter Thirteen we will consider whether this way of characterizing regimes is adequate. Ronald Dworkin has argued that democracy should be understood not simply in terms of 'Whose judgements prevail?' but more generally in terms of 'Are the people treated respectfully as equals?'[28] There is, as we shall see, a lot to be said for that conception. What I have been labouring here is the more modest point that the constitutional arrangements we have been discussing cannot really be regarded as a form of precommitment by an agent A at time t_1 to a decision (for time t_2) which A himself has chosen. Instead it is a form of submission by A at t_1 to whatever judgement is made at t_2 by another agent, B, in the application of very general principles which A has instructed B to take into account.

One final observation to clarify the point that I am making. It is sometimes said that what justifies judicial review is that it would be inappropriate for the representatives of the people (acting by majority-decision) to be 'judge in their own case',[29] in determining whether or not a piece of legislation violates the rights of a minority. But if a constitutional provision (protecting minority rights) is really a precommitment of the people or their representatives, then there is in principle nothing whatever inappropriate about asking them: was this the precommitment you intended? If a dispute arises among the crew whether Ulysses should continue to be bound to the mast long after the sirens' song has become inaudible because some of the crew believe he wanted also to resist the attractions of the *next* island they sailed past, then there is nothing to do but *ask Ulysses*. To refrain from doing so on the ground that this would make him judge in his own case would be absurd – that is, if the name of the game really is *precommitment*. Precommitment cannot preserve the aura of autonomy (or democracy in the constitutional case) unless the person bound really is the judge of the point and extent of his being bound. Ulysses of course may not be able to give us a rational answer if we do not get round to asking him until he is already under the influence of the sirens' song. Then there is nothing we can do but make *our own decision* about whether to blindfold him or not. At *that* stage we should stop justifying our decision by calling it a consummation of Ulysses' autonomy. The best we can now say on autonomy grounds is that we are acting, paternalistically, as Ulysses *would have acted* had he been lucid and in possession of full information etc., not that we are acting in the way he clearly wanted us to act in defence of his autonomy. So, similarly, if we follow the logic of precommitment in the political case, the people are presumably authorities – not judges in their own cause, but *authorities* – on what they have precommitted themselves

[28] Dworkin, *Freedom's Law*, 17 ff.
[29] See for example, ibid., 16. See also the discussion of *'nemo iudex in sua causa'*, below, in Ch. 13, s. 8.

to. If that authority is challenged – for example, because the people are now thought to be in the very state (of panic or anger, etc.) that they wanted their precommitment to counteract – then all we can say is that the notion of precommitment is now no longer useful in relation to the controversy. Once it becomes unclear or controversial what the people have committed themselves to, there is no longer any basis in the idea of precommitment for defending a particular interpretation against democratic objections.

4. DISAGREEMENTS OR WEAKNESS OF WILL?

We have concentrated for a while on the implementation of a precommitment: is it a causal mechanism, or does it consist rather in entrusting a decision to someone else's judgement? There are also things to be said about the reasons that motivate precommitment in the first place.

In cases of individual precommitment, the agent is imagined to be quite certain, in his lucid moments, about the actions he wants to avoid, the reasons for their undesirability, and the basis on which he might be tempted nevertheless to perform them. The smoker knows that smoking is damaging his health and he can furnish an explanation in terms of the pathology of nicotine addiction of why he craves a cigarette notwithstanding his possession of that knowledge. The drinker knows the statistics about drink-driving and he knows too how intoxication works. He knows at the beginning of the evening that at midnight his ability to drive safely and his judgement about his ability to drive safely will both be seriously impaired.

These cases fall into recognized categories of decisional pathology or *akrasia*.[30] Responsible individuals are aware of their own vulnerability to things like lust, laziness, impulse, anger, panic, passion, and intoxication. They are aware that these conditions can lead them to behave in ways they themselves believe to be undesirable. Though that belief may actually accompany the behaviour in question, it is often referred to in the literature as a belief held and acted upon 'in a calm moment' – a moment when the agent foresees the conditions of *akrasia* but is not actually afflicted by them, and so is able to make arrangements which lessen the probability that he will behave akratically in the future.

Much of this may be thought to apply in the political realm also. Constitutional constraints may be seen as prophylactics against political *akrasia* – that is, against the pathology of anger, panic, or greed that is often thought to be endemic in democratic politics. The history of political

---

[30] This is Elster's description: *Ulysses and the Sirens*, 36–7. The classic discussion of weakness of the will is Aristotle, *Nichomachean Ethics*, Bk. VII, Chs. 1–10.

thought in the West is largely the history of warnings about the hasty, greedy, and intemperate courses on which the masses are likely to embark, if they ever get power in their hands. If we are worried about a majority falling upon the property of the rich or the rights of a minority in a moment of greed, panic or anger, then perhaps constitutional precommitment makes sense.[31] But it is questionable whether we should take *akrasia* as our model for the circumstances in which Bills of Rights and the judicial review of legislation actually operate. Let me explain.

In most cases in which judicial review is contemplated by the defenders of constitutional constraints – certainly in most of the high-profile American cases – the situation looks something like this:

(1) The people commit themselves in their constitution (by a supermajority) to some fairly abstract formula about rights. Some of them (the minority) have misgivings about the principle – they think its adoption is wrong or unwise – while even among those who support its ratification, opinions differ as to what in detail it amounts to.

(2) A legislature passes a measure, which arguably violates the constitutional provision. The measure is supported by a majority of representatives, some because they do not believe it falls under the constitutional principle, others because they oppose the constitutional principle and always did.

(3) A court, deciding by a simple majority, holds that the legislature's enactment is unconstitutional. Four out of the nine justices argue, however, in dissent, that the legislation should not be struck down. They maintain that the interpretation of the Bill of Rights that would be required to sustain a finding of unconstitutionality is implausible, mainly on the ground that such interpretation would make the relevant constitutional provision quite unattractive from a moral point of view. Needless to say their brethren on the bench do not agree with this.

Now consider these three decisions, and the background of disagreement that they presuppose. The disagreement among the justices in (3) is in part a disagreement about *what makes a constitutional provision morally unattractive*. That of course is exactly what the members of the legislature were disagreeing about when they voted on the bill. And it was also one of the focuses of disagreement among the people when the constitutional provision was originally adopted. It is the same disagreement all the way through, though the weight of opinion has shifted back and forth: a supermajority of the people on one side in decision (1); a simple majority of their

---

[31] We should note, however, that such precommitments have been singularly ineffective in the US, at least so far as moments of national panic are concerned: see, e.g., *Debs* v. *United States* 249 US 211 (1919) and *Korematsu* v. *United States* 323 US 214 (1944).

legislative representatives on the other side in decision (2); and a simple majority of justices back in the other direction again in decision (3). And this of course is what we should expect when a complex and highly charged moral issue is put in slightly different forms to different constituencies for decision at different times.

My theme in all this is reasonable disagreement, but I cannot restrain myself from saying that anyone who thinks a narrative like this is appropriately modelled by the story of Ulysses and the sirens is an idiot. Ulysses is sure that he wants to listen but not respond to the sirens' song; the people in our example are torn. If Ulysses were somehow to untie himself and get ready to dive over the side of the boat and swim to the sirens, it would be clear to his crew that this was exactly the action he commanded them to restrain; but in most constitutional cases, opinions differ among the citizens as to whether the legislation in question is the sort of thing they wanted (or would or should have wanted) in a founding moment to pre-empt. What's more, all the judges and all the legislators know in our example that the issue they are facing is one on which reasonable people disagree, whereas in the *Odyssey* the crew members can be assured that Ulysses' straining at or breaking his bonds is the product of a decisional pathology that is well understood by everyone involved, including Ulysses.

In other words, in the constitutional case we are almost always dealing with a society whose members disagree in principle and in detail, even in their 'calm' or 'lucid' moments, about what rights they have, how those rights are to be conceived, and what weight they are to be given in relation to other values. They need not appeal to aberrations in rationality to explain or characterize these disagreements. As I have argued throughout the book, disagreements about rights are sufficiently explained by the difficulty of the subject matter and by what Rawls refers to as 'the burdens of judgment'.[32] A constitutional 'precommitment' in these circumstances is therefore not the triumph of pre-emptive rationality that it appears to be in the cases of Ulysses and the smoker and the drinker. It is rather the artificially sustained ascendancy of one view in the polity over other views whilst the complex moral issues between them remain unresolved. Imposing the template of precommitment on this situation smacks more of Procrustes than Ulysses.

A better individual analogy – better, that is, than the case of Ulysses or the drinker or the smoker – might be the following. Imagine a person – call her Bridget – who is torn between competing conceptions of religious belief. One day she opts decisively for traditional faith in a personal God. She commits herself utterly to that view and abjures forever the private

---

[32] Rawls, *Political Liberalism*, 54–8.

library of theological books in her house that, in the past, had excited and sustained her uncertainty. Though she is no book-burner, still she locks the door of her library and gives the keys to a friend, with strict instructions never to return them, not even on demand.

But new issues and old doubts start to creep into Bridget's mind after a while ('Maybe Tillich was right after all . . .'), and a few months later she asks for the keys. Should the friend return them? Clearly, this is quite a different case from (say) withholding car keys from the drinker at midnight. Both involve forms of precommitment. But in Bridget's case, for the friend to sustain the precommitment would be for the friend to take sides, as it were, in a dispute between two or more conflicting selves or two or more conflicting aspects of the same self within Bridget, each with a claim to rational authority. It would be to take sides in a way that is simply not determined by any recognizable criteria of pathology or other mental aberration. To uphold the precommitment would be to sustain the temporary ascendancy of one aspect of the self at the time the library keys were given away, and to neglect the fact that the self that demands them back has an equal claim to respect for *its* way of dealing with the vicissitudes of theological uncertainty.

Upholding another's precommitment may be regarded as a way of respecting that person's autonomy only if a clear line can be drawn between the aberrant mental phenomena the precommitment was supposed to override, on the one hand, and genuine uncertainty, changes of mind, conversions, etc., on the other hand.[33] In Ulysses' case and in the case of the potential drunk-driver, we can draw such a line. In Bridget's case, we have much more difficulty, and that is why respecting the precommitment seems more like taking sides in an internal dispute between two factions warring on roughly equal terms.

As if that were not bad enough, if we were really looking for an analogy to the judicial review example, we should imagine the theological case with this difference – that Bridget hands the keys of the library to a *group* of friends, who then decide by majority voting when it is appropriate to return them to her. They find they *have* to decide by majority-voting since they disagree about the issue along the very lines of the uncertainty that is torturing Bridget herself.

Clearly there are dangers in *any* simplistic analogy between the rational autonomy of individuals and the democratic governance of a community. The idea of a society binding itself against certain legislative acts in the future is problematic in cases where members disagree with one another about the need for such bonds, or if they agree abstractly about the need but disagree about their content or character. It is particularly problematic

[33] For an excellent discussion, see Schelling, *Choice and Consequences*, Ch. 4. See also Schelling, 'Ethics, Law and the Exercise of Self-Command'.

where such disagreements can be expected to persist and to develop and change in unpredictable ways. And it becomes ludicrously problematic in cases where the form of precommitment is to assign the decision, procedurally to another body, whose members are just as torn and just as conflicted about the issues as the members of the first body were.

If, moreover, the best explanation of these persisting disagreements is that the issues the society is addressing are themselves *very difficult issues*, then we have no justification whatever for regarding the temporary ascendancy of one or other party to the disagreement as an instance of full and rational precommitment on the part of the entire society. In these circumstances – which, as I have said, are the circumstances of politics – the logic of precommitment must be simply put aside, and we must leave the members of the society to work out their differences and to change their minds in collective decision-making over time, the best way they can.

5. ULYSSES, THE PEOPLE

It may be thought that the model of Ulysses or the potential drunk-driver cannot be extended *anyway* to constitutional issues because in constitutional cases we are dealing not with one individual binding himself, but with a complex collective agent – consisting of millions of people – binding itself by setting certain of its own agencies at odds with one another. Moreover, if we apply this to instances like American constitutional law, we have to contemplate 'the people' not just as millions of disparate individuals but as an entity that is continuous over several centuries, so that our being bound today by formulas laid down by a group of white-supremacist revolutionaries in 1791 is represented as a form of autonomous precommitment *by us*. It might be thought that this strains the credibility of the elements of self, agency, and autonomy involved in the precommitment idea.

What difference does it make, then, when we move from decisional strategies by individuals, intended to last for a few hours or a few days, to the constitutional commitments of a whole people intended to endure over centuries?

The main difference is the one we have just finished discussing. In almost every case, a decision at t_1 by a whole people (comprising millions of individuals) to preclude a certain decision, D, by them at t_2 will be a subject of disagreement. At t_1, opinions will differ both as to whether D is undesirable, and even if it is, as to whether it is properly the subject of constitutional constraint. Nevertheless a precommitment will not be entered into at t_1 unless many more people think D is undesirable than favour D. What's more, those who vote for a constraint will do so, presumably, because they fear that among the present opponents of D are some who may be driven at a future time t_2 by panic, greed, or anger to vote in its favour; that is, they fear an akratic shift in the balance of opinion. But suppose now that we have reached t_2 and that despite the constitutional constraint, D has somehow found itself on the political agenda and it turns out that a majority of the people are in favour of D. If the desirability of D was controversial at t_1, then the akratic explanation is not the only possible explanation of the shift in opinion. An alternative and more charitable (more respectful) explanation is that, as public debate has gone on, many people have become convinced by the arguments in favour of D that were put forward originally by the minority at t_1 or by new arguments that have been put forward since.

The plurality of a political community, the inevitable existence of diversity of opinion and reasonable disagreement among them on all matters of rights and justice, and the dynamics of both formal and informal deliberation over time – these three things mean that we are seldom in a position to say, with any assurance, that majority support for a given position at t_2 represents the weakness or panic that opponents of the position thought at t_1 they had reason to fear. It *may* represent the *akrasia* that they feared. But equally it may represent nothing more insidious than the sort of shift in the balance of opinion that we associate naturally with ongoing deliberation, particularly as circumstances change and one generation succeeds another in the body politic.

We saw in section 4 that it is possible to construct an individual analogue of this: Bridget was genuinely torn over theological issues, and she resolved one way at t_1 but changed her mind at t_2.[34] This sort of thing is perfectly familiar. But although changes of mind are as familiar as constancy in the case of individuals, we are not familiar with anything remotely approaching Ulysses-like steadfastness and unanimity in the case of large political communities. Unanimous agreement, as John Locke has pointed out, 'is next impossible ever to be had'.[35] So there is something spectacularly inappropriate about using the unequivocal precommitment of an individual as a model for constitutional constraint. The plurality of politics, the reasonableness of disagreement, and the dynamics of debate mean that Bridget should be our model, not Ulysses. And as we have seen it is not possible to construct in Bridget's case the sort of account of precommitment that would allow us, in the political case, to finesse the democratic objection.

[34] Schelling argues in 'Ethics, Law and the Exercise of Self-Command', that the political case can illuminate the individual case (as opposed to, or as well as, vice versa): he says that in all instances of individual precommitment, we are dealing in effect with the politics of two or more 'selves' within a single person. This of course does not make the political cases any easier.

[35] Locke, *Two Treatises*, II, para. 98, 332–3.

I mentioned a moment ago that one of the circumstances contributing to the dynamics of public debate and the corresponding shifts in public opinion is that the membership of the political community is constantly changing. Stephen Holmes cites Thomas Jefferson's calculation that actuarially (at the end of the eighteenth century) 'half of those of 21 years and upwards living at any one instant will be dead in 18 years 8 months'.[36] Why, then, said Jefferson, should a subsequent generation be bound by constitutional commitments entered into not by them but by their ancestors?

If political precommitments are understood primarily as individual strategies then this objection succeeds. Suppose Tom votes for a law requiring the use of seat belts in automobiles because he wants to overcome his lazy and akratic neglect of his own safety.[37] And suppose the law passes. What Tom has done then is band together with a large number of others, each hoping to make use of this collective mechanism in order to bind himself. Though the law is a coercive one, it can be defended against autonomy-based critiques inasmuch as each of the coerced individuals deliberately sought it as a mechanism of enhancing their responsible individual autonomy. But once Tom and his original band of fellow citizens pass away, it will not be possible to offer *this defence* of the seat-belt law to their children and grandchildren. Of course Tom's descendants may renew the law or allow it to remain on the books unrepealed for the very reasons that led Tom to vote in its favour. Then again, they may not. If they do not, we cannot defend the law *to them* as a precommitment, for it was at best a precommitment by the individuals of Tom's generation, not theirs.

However, when the precommitment idea is deployed in a political context, it is usually deployed in terms of a precommitment by the people as a collective entity, rather than as a series of particular precommitments by individual voters taking advantage of collective mechanisms such as laws. In cases where the precommitment is conceived to be collective, the intergenerational objection is not by itself decisive. After all, if citizens may *ever* be bound by legislation with anything less than unanimous support – and opponents of constitutional constraint of course believe that they may – then it must be because they have constituted themselves as a political entity, a community which is not simply the aggregate of its individual members. Ronald Dworkin asks:

Why am I *free* – how could I be thought to be governing *myself* – when I must obey what other people decide even if I think it wrong or unwise or unfair to me or my family? What difference can it make how many people must think the decision

---

[36] Holmes, *Passions and Constraint*, 142, citing Jefferson, *Writings*, 961.
[37] I am grateful to Amy Gutmann for this way of understanding precommitment.

right and wise and fair if it is not necessary that *I* do? . . . The answer to these enormously difficult questions begins in the communal conception of collective action. If I am a genuine member of a political community, its act is in some pertinent sense my act, even when I argued and voted against it . . .[38]

Opinions differ of course as to what this communal conception requires, and we will explore some of the issues in Chapter Thirteen. But at the very least, citizens must share some sense that they are 'all in this together'. They must share the sense – which we associated in Chapter Five with 'the circumstances of politics' – that there are common problems which are worth their while solving together despite their divergent views as to what the solution ought to be. And they must articulate this shared sense onto their support for mechanisms of collective decision that allow them to precipitate out of their disagreements a single course of action that they accept as binding on all.

Their sense of sharing these concerns and commitments with others will involve some view – probably tacit – as to who these 'others' are. That view will have a temporal as well as a geographic dimension. People will ask themselves, 'How widely is it necessary that a common view be taken on these issues?' and their answers will yield theories of borders, federalism, and the territorial separation of national and state jurisdictions. And they will also ask themselves, 'How important is it for our shared solution to a common problem to extend and remain in force over time?' Just as their answers to the first question will indicate why a person one side of a border is conceived to be bound by a certain law while someone a few miles away is not, so their answer to the second question will yield a theory as to why individuals may sometimes be bound, not only by laws they voted against, but also by laws adopted decades before they were born. I am not saying what their answers ought to be, and I am certainly not saying that there is no political community unless its laws are taken to bind future generations in perpetuity. But it is more than likely that the requisite sense of membership and community will extend across generations, so that in principle there should be no difficulty about being bound by the decision of one's ancestors. So, if our forefathers deemed certain precommitments necessary, the mere fact that those precommitments are supposed to extend over time, and outlast those who enacted them, should not in itself be a reason for not honouring them or for condemning them as incompatible with the idea of self-government.

That said, however, the inter-generational dimension might bear on our discussion in the following way. It is natural, when these possibilities are being considered prospectively (as they are, presently, in the United Kingdom) to focus on the *ex ante* rationality and autonomy of

---

[38] Dworkin, *Freedom's Law*, 22.

precommitment. It seems like a good idea *now* for us to commit ourselves pre-emptively against *future* violations of rights. But it is important that those who embark upon constitutional change have the capacity to look upon what they are presently doing with the eyes of years, even centuries to come.[39] We have to have in mind that at some future date a large number of people, favouring a change in some law or in the understanding of some right, will experience the force of the constraint which we are setting up as a restriction on their autonomy.

They want to reform laws regarding electoral campaign finance, for example, but they find that their efforts are constrained by a free speech provision in their constitution. Opponents of campaign finance reform may seek to mollify the anger that this constraint generates among the majority by defending it as a precommitment entered into by a previous generation. Now it is possible that the majority will be deaf to this characterization, and deaf to it for the very reason that the precommitment was set up: the majority is in precisely the pathological state that the precommitment was designed to counteract. But it is also possible that the majority will resist the precommitment characterization, not because they are overwhelmed by passion or anger, but because they disagree with the ideas about free speech that seemed plausible to their ancestors. *Ex ante* the precommitment seemed like a good idea; *ex post*, it might seem silly given what we know about democracies, mass media, and electoral campaigns. And if the majority now know that even at the time the precommitment was entered into, there were voices warning against attempting to bind future generations in matters as complex as this, they will be particularly inclined to regard the constraint as unreasonable. Now of course that's hindsight; that's a view of the precommitment *ex post*. But it's a view which, imaginatively, the framers of the precommitment ought to take very seriously *ex ante*. They should ask themselves: is there a reason now to doubt that this provision will seem reasonable as a precommitment to those whom it constrains in the future? It seems to me that the existence of good faith disagreement about the content of the precommitment at the time that it is proposed is *always* a reason for answering that question in the affirmative. Disagreement *ex ante* portends unreasonableness *ex post*.

So although the inter-generational dimension is not necessarily conclusive against the precommitment characterization of constitutional constraints, it is likely to be conclusive in fact inasmuch as the future has a disconcerting tendency to vindicate the wisdom of those whose views or apprehensions might have been in the minority at the time the constraint was originally imposed.

[39] See Arendt, *On Revolution*, 198.

I guess it follows from this that a constitutional constraint is less unreasonable *qua* precommitment, the greater the opportunity for altering it by
processes of constitutional amendment.[40] We need to bear in mind, however, that such processes are usually made very difficult; indeed their difficulty – the difference, for example, between the majority required for
constitutional amendment and the majority required for routine legislative change – is precisely definitive of the constraint in question. So if there
is an objection to a certain constitutional constraint, that objection is not
rebutted by pointing to a formal opportunity for amendment or change;
the nature and extent of that opportunity is precisely what is being
objected to. All we can say is that the objection would have been even
stronger, if the opportunity for amendment had not existed. Certainly, the
opportunity for constitutional amendment adds nothing to the case for
considering a constitutional constraint as a *precommitment*: at best, all it
does is alter our understanding of what it is that we are trying to defend
by presenting it in this light.

6. CONSTITUTIVE RULES

I noted earlier that Jon Elster had some doubts about whether constitutional constraints could really be described as precommitments, since they
were not 'external' to the people who set them up.[41] We said that the
answer to this is that the constraints are external to some of the institutions
set up by the people to act in their name, even though they are not external to the people themselves, considered as 'popular sovereign'. I now
want to return to this point, for it raises interesting questions about the
relation between constitutional constraints and the constitutive rules of
political institutions.

A bunch of individuals must constitute themselves as a people – that is,
as a political community – even in order to frame a constitution. But
mostly what they do in their framing is to construct what they hope will
be an enduring set of institutions which can embody decision procedures
and mechanisms of collective action. In his recent book *Passions and
Constraint*, Stephen Holmes has argued that constitutional constraints
have important *constitutive* functions in this regard:

[C]onstitutions may be usefully compared to the rules of a game and even to the
rules of grammar. While *regulative* rules (for instance, 'no smoking') govern preexistent activities, *constitutive* rules (for instance, 'bishops move diagonally') make a
practice possible for the first time. . . . Constitutions do not merely limit power;

[40] This point was made by Ronald Dworkin, in discussion at the New York University
Law School Program for the Study of Law, Philosophy and Social Theory, Fall 1996.
[41] Elster, *Solomonic Judgements*, 196. See the beginning of s. 3 above.

they can create and organize power as well as give it direction. . . . When a constituent assembly establishes a decision procedure, rather than restricting a preexistent will, it actually creates a framework in which the nation can for the first time, have a will.[42]

The point is clearest in the case of political procedures. We saw in Chapter Four that a deliberative assembly needs procedural rules in order to facilitate and focus its debates. If these rules are themselves up for grabs in the very sessions they are supposed to structure, then it will be hard for a large group of diverse deliberators to proceed with any assurance that they are not talking at cross purposes or going round in circles. Like the rules of grammar, procedural rules cannot be regarded simply as a way of handcuffing or restraining participants.[43] Instead they make participation possible, by setting out a matrix of interaction in which particular contributions can take their place and 'register', so to speak. Of course the rules of grammar are not really something we *decide* upon in order to facilitate speech. They just emerge: we find ourselves with them as part and parcel of our ability to communicate.[44] But in the context of an enacted constitution, procedural rules are the product of decisions made in order to constitute public decision-making. As Holmes puts it, 'Decisions are made on the basis of predecisions. Electoral choices are made on the basis of constitutional choices. When they enter the voting-booth, for instance, voters decide who shall be president, but not how many presidents there shall be.'[45]

All this is very important. It is equally important, however, to notice the differences between this form of procedural 'predecision' and precommitment properly so-called. Let me explain.

Ulysses ties himself to the mast so that when the question arises as to whether he should leave the ship in response to the sirens' song, any decision he makes to leave will be ineffective. Similarly, the drinker hands his car keys to a friend, to make it that much less likely that he will decide in favour of driving when the question about getting home from the party arises at midnight. Those are examples of precommitment: to adapt our definition from Jon Elster,[46] an agent carries out a certain decision at time t_1 in order to decrease the probability that he will carry out another decision at time t_2.

But in Holmes's example, the procedural rule ('Only one President') adopted at t_1 is not supposed to operate when (or if) the people are deciding at a later time how many presidents to have; it is not intended to constrain any decision on that occasion. Instead it is designed to oper-

---

[42] Holmes, *Passions and Constraint*, 163–4.   [43] Ibid., 163.
[44] Cf. David Hume's observation about promises, conventions, and the emergence of language, in Hume, *A Treatise of Human Nature*, Bk. III, Part II, s. ii, 490.
[45] Holmes, *Passions and Constraint*, 167–8.   [46] Elster, *Ulysses and the Sirens*, 39.

ate at a time when people are choosing who is to be the president. Unlike Ulysses' tying himself to the mast or the drinker's giving his car keys to a friend, setting up a procedural rule is not designed to increase the probability of any particular decision at t_2; the point of it is simply to frame and constitute a type of decision-making procedure. Its importance in structuring that procedure does not allow us to infer anything about its precluding any later rethinking about the number of chief executives to have. (Likewise the constitutive importance of the rules of baseball or the conventions of English spelling does not show that it is wrong or unwise to vary these rules; all it shows is that, however much we vary the rules, they need to be settled on any occasion in which someone wants to engage in the practice or play the game that the rules constitute.)

Sure, there may be *other* arguments for not constantly revising the constitutive rules of various activities. If we change the rules of baseball too often, the fans will be confused and the players unable to develop a consistent set of skills. Change the conventions of spelling, and the Vice-President may be unable to keep up. There are well-known conservative arguments in politics as well, of which the best known are those of Edmund Burke:

By this unprincipled facility of changing the state as often, and as much, and as in many ways as there are floating fancies or fashions, the whole chain and continuity of the commonwealth would be broken. No one generation could link with another. Men would become little better than the flies of a summer.[47]

Now this Burkean argument may well motivate constitutional precommitments, as a precaution against hasty alteration in the constitutive procedures of our politics. We entrench our present procedures at t_1 against change at t_2 because we fear that if we were to indulge our half-baked reformist impulses at t_2 we would become little more than the flies of a summer. And if we do this, our precommitment will be liable to all the difficulties about pluralism and disagreement which we have already considered – for nothing is surer than that Burke's arguments about the dangers of constitutional change are matters on which reasonable people disagree.

My present point, however, is that it would be a mistake to confuse those Burkean precommitments with the constitutive procedures themselves. Accordingly, it is misleading to suggest – as Stephen Holmes suggests – that constitutional constraints have the facilitating and enabling character of constitutive rules of procedure.

---

[47] Burke, *Reflections on the Revolution in France*, 192–3.

7. PRECOMMITMENT AND ASSURANCE

So far, we have established that constitutive procedures should not be assimilated to precommitments. But precommitments of other sorts may be practically or politically necessary in the constitution of a people.

In a purely formal sense, a political community may be constituted by a rule about voting; but such procedural rules constitute a meaningful political reality only in relation to the legal and social context which conditions the character of public debate. Government by popular majority is one thing if votes are taken after lengthy periods of argument back and forth among the citizens and their representatives; it is quite another thing if votes are taken without any deliberative interaction at all or if the political culture is such that most people are afraid to voice their opposition as soon as any hint of majority consensus begins to emerge. Indeed, these conditions concerning deliberation are arguably so important that majority-decision may amount, in effect, to something quite different – to a different form of government, to the constitution of a quite different sort of 'we, the people' – depending on the conditions. Holmes argues that, of all the different forms of government that may result, only some are entitled to be called 'democracy':

Democracy is government by rational and free public discussion among legally equal citizens, not simply the enforcement of the will of the majority. . . . Not any 'will,' but only a will formed in vigorous and wide-open debate should be given sovereign authority. The legally guaranteed right of opposition is therefore a fundamental norm of democratic government; it provides an essential precondition for the formation of democratic public opinion.[48]

We will consider this (and a similar claim by Ronald Dworkin) as a general proposition about the true meaning of 'democracy' in Chapter Thirteen. For now, we must try to understand it in relation to the logic of precommitment.

The idea is that in setting up democratic institutions, in constituting the very possibility of 'the will of the people', the members of a society intend to commit themselves not just to any old form of majoritarianism but to a particular form of majority-decision, namely the sovereignty of a popular 'will formed in vigorous and wide-open debate'.[49] This they cannot do, without at the same time doing their best to create an open and tolerant climate for the effective expression of political opposition and dissent. And that in turn requires them to establish certain guarantees that minority opposition and dissent will not evoke any backlash from either temporary or permanent majorities. Such guarantees – the argument goes – are not

---

[48] Holmes, *Passions and Constraint,*171.   [49] *Idem.*

credible unless the people have put in place constitutional mechanisms to restrain their own natural repressive response to the irritation of minority criticism. A precommitment of this kind may look negative, and members of the majority may feel that its immediate effect is to prevent them from doing things that they want to do. But in the medium and long term, constitutional guarantees of free speech and loyal opposition are indispensable for meaningful political debate. They are conditions for the very thing which the members of the majority want from their constitution: the emergence, through majoritarian procedures, of an informed and effective basis for popular decision. That – as I understand it – is Holmes's argument.

It is an attractive argument. And I believe it would amount to a compelling case for the enactment of constitutional constraints immune to subsequent legislative revision if either of two conditions were met. It would be compelling if the people were constant and unanimous in their conception of majority-decision and of the conditions necessary for its effective realization. Or – even if they did not agree about those issues – it would be a compelling argument for constitutional constraints if minorities had reason to fear that any legislative rethinking of the rules about free speech and loyal opposition would be a way of crushing or silencing dissent.

In fact, neither condition is satisfied. Though almost every defender of majority-decision is committed to *some* form of deliberative democracy, opinions vary widely as to what deliberation should amount to and as to the legal, political and social conditions that should surround it. I should not need to labour the point, but here are a few of the issues about which reasonable democrats disagree: proportional representation, referendums, the frequency of elections, term limits, the basis of electoral districting, state-funded access to television airtime for candidates, and campaign finance generally. People disagree about the publication of opinion polls, about free speech in shopping malls, about the influence of special interest groups and political action committees, and about the public's interest in the internal workings of political parties. They disagree too about such topics as heckling, hate speech, ethnic representation, criminal defamation, and the concepts of sedition, insurrection, and subversion.

We are blessed with a rich and thoughtful literature on all of this, from the *Federalist* papers to such modern tomes as Charles Beitz's *Political Equality*, Lani Guinier's *The Tyranny of the Majority*, and Cass Sunstein's *The Partial Constitution*. The various opposing accounts put forward by these and other thinkers amount to diverse attempts to work out in detail the nature of the political system to which we have committed ourselves – or (more correctly) to which we are, in our ongoing political and constitutional practices, in the process of committing ourselves.

The persistence of these disagreements is characteristic of all modern democracies, and in most societies there is a natural connection between this sort of discussion among intellectuals, constitutionalists, and political scientists and the more formal processes by which the people and their representatives debate and vote on proposals for constitutional reform. Voters in New Zealand recently adopted and made use of a system of proportional representation; voters in the United Kingdom will soon have the opportunity to decide among various proposals for reform of the second chamber of their legislature; and electoral campaign finance is on the legislative agenda almost everywhere. Each country studies the constitutional experience of the others; in every one of these debates, citizens weigh complex arrays of pros and cons; and though people and their professors may plead passionately for one option or another, debates about constitutional structure are by and large conducted in a spirit of mutual respect and in common acknowledgement that this is not an area of life where the truth is well known and self-evident.

In some countries, effective decisions on constitutional structure may be made by parliaments, and of course the parliamentarians disagree among themselves as to what is desirable. (The House of Commons debate in 1998 on the Human Rights Bill is a fine example.) In other countries, they are made by popular voting in referendums, and it turns out, predictably, that the people disagree as well. Even in countries like the United States where the political culture entrusts these issues largely to the courts, the justices are seldom unanimous. It turns out that the judges disagree as much as anyone else – and disagree reasonably and in good faith – about the nature of their constitutional stewardship and the commitments of principle which that stewardship is supposed to embody.

All this is surely healthy; it is exactly what we should expect; and we may describe it – for the purposes of legal and political philosophy – in any number of ways. But one thing, it seems to me, we cannot say: we cannot describe this process in terms of a set of unequivocal popular precommitments to a particular form of political decision-making. How to make collective decisions in politics? – all we can say is that this is something we are continuing to work on.

I said that the argument we have been considering in this section would amount to a compelling case for constitutional constraints immune from legislative revision if either of two conditions were satisfied – that is, if either the people's commitments in this respect were settled, constant, and unequivocal, or if revisiting such issues threatened grave danger to dissidents or minorities. We have just seen that the first of these conditions is not satisfied. The second is not satisfied either.

Dissidents do need an assurance that their opposition will not elicit a repressive or murderous response. In some countries (even in some that call themselves democracies) that assurance is tenuous or non-existent. This is a matter of great concern, but it is not what interests us here; in those countries, constitutional structures have failed altogether. There may, however, be one or two countries where the assurance dissidents need actually does exist by virtue of constitutional structure, but where it is so fragile that any attempt by the people or their representatives to revisit and vote upon issues of political structure would reasonably be seen by minorities as a way of attacking and undermining their guarantee of freedom and loyal opposition. Perhaps some of the new democracies of Eastern Europe and the former Soviet Union fall into this category. Arguably, however, these are the countries that can *least* afford the constitutional rigidity that the precommitment idea involves;[50] their people need to be able to experiment with a variety of detailed procedural forms as, slowly, over the *decades*, they attempt to elaborate their own constitutional traditions. At any rate, the specifications I have given – opposition freedoms guaranteed in fact by constitutional constraints but in a way that is so fragile that they would be threatened by *any* legislative attempt to revisit or restructure those constraints – these specifications do not apply to the United States and they do not apply to the United Kingdom. In both countries there are robust and established traditions of political liberty (which have flourished often *despite* the best efforts of the judiciary);[51] and in both countries there are vigorous debates about political structure that seem able to proceed without threatening minority freedoms.

For that reason, then, and because these background issues of political structure, political procedure, and political culture remain the subject of ongoing, healthy, and benign disagreement, the panic-stricken model of Odyssean precommitment seems singularly inappropriate as a basis or template for constitutional theory.

[50] See Holmes and Sunstein, 'The Politics of Constitutional Revision in Eastern Europe'. The observations with which Holmes and Sunstein conclude their discussion (ibid., 305–6) are worth quoting at length: 'The basic issues with which contemporary politicians in Eastern Europe must grapple concern territorial boundaries, the question of political membership, the assignment of first property rights and the sudden redistribution of private wealth (including *nomenklatura* privatization), settling scores or closing books on the past. These problems, faced by no Western democracy today, cannot be easily resolved by invoking liberal principles. And they cannot be addressed judicially, by a nonaccountable body of knowledgeable men and women. They will also not be imposed by a conquering army and accepted by a defeated and morally chastened people. They can be resolved only politically. Crucial decisions must be made with all the messiness of parliamentary bargaining and ad hoc compromise, carried out to some extent under the public eye. . . . It is futile and even illegitimate to attempt at the outset to entrench certain answers in a constitutional framework immunized against change. Attempts to depoliticize or juridify constitution making are unreasonable in societies where the future is so open and the choices so basic and so large.'
[51] See fn. 31 above.

Chapter Thirteen

The Constitutional Conception of Democracy

1. DEMOCRATIC RIGHTS

The idea of democracy is not incompatible with the idea of individual rights. On the contrary, there cannot be a democracy unless individuals possess and regularly exercise what we called in Chapter Eleven 'the right of rights' – the right to participate in the making of the laws. Not only that but, as I argued at the end of Chapter Ten, there is a natural congruence between rights and democracy. The identification of someone as a right-bearer expresses a measure of confidence in that person's moral capacities – in particular his capacity to think responsibly about the moral relation between his interests and the interests of others. The possession of this capacity – a sense of justice, if you like[1] – is the primary basis of democratic competence. Our conviction that ordinary men and women have what it takes to participate responsibly in the government of their society is, in fact, the same conviction as that on which the attribution of rights is based.

In Chapters Ten and Eleven, I invoked this connection in order to embarrass theorists of rights who professed apprehensions about or indifference towards the ideal of democratic decision-making. But the congruence between rights and democracy is a two-way street. A theorist of rights should not be in the business of portraying the ordinary members of a democratic majority as selfish and irresponsible predators. But equally a theorist of democracy should not affect a pure proceduralist's nonchalance about the fate of individual rights under a system of majority-decision, for many of these rights (even those not directly implicated in the democratic ideal) are based on the respect for individual moral agency that democracy itself involves.

Constitutional theorists like Ronald Dworkin are therefore quite correct when they say we are not entitled to appeal to any fundamental opposition between the idea of democracy and the idea of individual rights as a basis for criticizing a practice like American-style judicial review of legislation. There is no such fundamental opposition. If there is a democratic objection to judicial review, it must also be a rights-based objection. And that objection cannot be sustained unless we are prepared to answer some

[1] See Rawls, *Political Liberalism*, 19.

hard questions about how rights are supposed to be protected in a system of democratic decision-making.

The rights I want to emphasize in this chapter fall into two main categories: (a) rights that are actually constitutive of the democratic process, and (b) rights which, even if they are not formally constitutive of democracy, nevertheless embody conditions necessary for its legitimacy.

Consider first the rights required for the constitution of a democracy – (a). Theorists disagree about whether democracy is anything more than a procedural ideal,[2] but certainly it is *at least* the idea of a political procedure constituted in part by certain rights. Democracy requires that when there is disagreement in a society about a matter on which a common decision is needed, every man and woman in the society has the right to participate on equal terms in the resolution of that disagreement. The processes that this involves may be complex and indirect; there may be convoluted structures of election and representation. But they are all oriented in the end towards the same ideal: participation by the people – somehow, through some mechanism – on basically equal terms. This means that there cannot be a democracy unless the right to participate is upheld, and unless the complex rules of the representative political process are governed, fundamentally, by that right. If some are excluded from the process, or if the process itself is unequal or inadequate, then both rights and democracy are compromised.

A second set of rights – (b) – we have to consider takes us beyond issues of formal procedure. Apart from those that constitute the democratic process, there are many rights that may plausibly be represented as conditions for the legitimacy or moral respectability of democratic decision-making. No one thinks that any old bunch of people is entitled to impose a decision on others, simply on the ground that there are more individuals in favour of the decision than against it. Democracy and majority-decision make moral sense only under certain conditions. The most obvious of these conditions are free speech and freedom of association – rights which establish a broader deliberative context in civil society for formal political decision-making. But I have in mind also claims about rights that have little or no procedural aspect. In *Freedom's Law*, Dworkin argues that a person is not bound by the decisions of a democracy unless he is in some satisfactorily substantive sense a member of the community whose democracy it is. Membership is not just a matter of formal participation: it is also a matter of a person's interests being treated with appropriate concern. Even if he has a vote, he can hardly be expected to accept majority decisions as legitimate if he knows that other members of the community do not take his interests seriously or if the established institutions of the

---

[2] See, e.g., Beitz, *Political Equality*, Ch. 4. See also Ch. 5, s. 14, above.

community evince contempt or indifference towards him or his kind (25).[3] And Dworkin makes a similar case for the importance of the community respecting the moral independence of its members. He thinks I cannot be a member of a community, in the suitably robust sense that generates legitimacy and political obligation, unless I can reconcile my membership with self-respect; and I can do that only if the community does not purport to dictate my fundamental ethical convictions (25–6).

I am not sure whether we should accept this last argument of Dworkin's. But no doubt *some* arguments work along these lines. There are surely some rights such that, if they were not respected in a community, no political legitimacy could possibly be accorded to any majoritarian decision-procedure. Is it not appropriate, then, for majority decision-making to be constrained by rights which satisfy this formula? One could hardly complain about such constraints in the name of democracy, for a democracy unconstrained by such rights would be scarcely worthy of the name. Such an objection would be directed against the establishment or protection of the very conditions that made democracy an ideal worth appealing to.

The relation between democracy and the conditions of its legitimacy may be represented as a relation between rights: that is, the rights under class (a) *presuppose* the rights under class (b). Sometimes when we talk about one set of rights presupposing another, it is because we think the rights in the second set are preconditions for the meaningful or effective exercise of the first. Thus, Henry Shue argues that the meaningful exercise of any right presupposes that the right-bearers have rights to subsistence and security and that these latter rights have been satisfied.[4] No doubt this applies to political rights as well: one cannot meaningfully exercise the right to vote in conditions of terror or starvation. But the relation I discussed in the previous paragraph is slightly different. It represents one set of rights as the conditions of the *legitimate* exercise of another. (It is a bit like saying that the right to sell an object presupposes that the seller owns the object.) Legitimacy is an issue because the exercise of participatory rights is not just a matter of freedom. When one votes, one exercises a Hohfeldian power[5] which (together with the exercise of that power by enough others) may alter the legal position of certain other people, perhaps against their wishes, perhaps to their disadvantage. Having this impact on others is permissible only under certain conditions, and those conditions may be represented as rights held by anyone who is liable to be subject to such impact.

Rights in classes (a) and (b) I shall call 'rights associated with democracy'. In a broader sense all rights are associated with democracy because,

---

[3] In this chapter, numbers in parentheses are page references to Dworkin, *Freedom's Law*.
[4] See Shue, *Basic Rights*, Ch. 1.

as I said at the beginning of this section, all rights require the same sort of respect for individuals which democracy also requires. Many theorists have sought to confine their argument for constitutional rights to those rights that are related directly or indirectly to the democratic process.[6] They imagine – wrongly, as we shall see – that no democratic objection can be sustained against right-based constraints concerned with the procedural integrity of democracy. And they believe – again, I think, wrongly – that the concerns a democrat ought to have about rights do not apply to what they call 'substantive rights' unrelated to the democratic process. In fact, the right-based argument for democracy cannot be separated off from other rights in this way. Based as it is on respect for persons as moral agents and moral reasoners, the premises of that argument will certainly yield substantive conclusions about what people are entitled to so far as personal freedom is concerned and it may well yield conclusions about affirmative entitlements in the realm of social and economic well-being. Sure, some of these conclusions are also related to the democratic process as constitutive elements or as conditions of its legitimacy. But the premises of the right-based case for democracy may provide a direct argument for substantive rights that bypasses the case for democracy. These rights, then, are associated with democracy not in the sense of being constitutive of it or presupposed by it, but in the sense of being other conclusions of the very premises that ground the rights-based case for democracy.

For most of this chapter, however, I shall confine my attention to classes (a) and (b). Rights in class (a) have been the focus of a well-known argument by John Hart Ely to the effect that no democratic objection can be sustained against judicial review to vindicate rights that are procedurally constitutive of democracy.[7] Dworkin thinks Ely is wrong to confine his attention to class (a), however, and I agree with him on that.[8] The argument I want to examine in the body of the chapter deals with both categories. Then, towards the very end, in sections 11 and 12, I shall return to the broader issue of democratic protection for rights in general

2. DOES JUDICIAL REVIEW IMPROVE DEMOCRACY?

In the United States and in the United Kingdom, Ronald Dworkin has been a firm defender of the compatibility of democracy with constitutional rights and judicial review.[9] His recent book, *Freedom's Law* articulates a

---

[5] See Hohfeld, *Fundamental Legal Conceptions*, 50 ff.
[6] The best known example is Ely, *Democracy and Distrust*.   [7] *Idem.*
[8] See Dworkin, *A Matter of Principle*, 59–69. See also Waldron, 'A Right-Based Critique of Constitutional Rights', 39–41.
[9] See Dworkin, *A Matter of Principle*, 9–71, Dworkin, *A Bill of Rights for Britain*, and Dworkin, *Law's Empire*, Ch. 10.

new version of that defence. Dworkin believes it is no accident that new democracies – in South Africa, for example, or in Central and Eastern Europe – turn almost instinctively to some version of the constitutional arrangements we are considering. They do so, he thinks, not because they are nervous or ambivalent about democracy, but because a system combining popular legislation, constitutional guarantees, and judicial review seems like the form of democracy that, in their circumstances, will offer the best assurance that the rights associated with democracy will continue to be respected. America chose a particularly attractive form of democracy at its birth, Dworkin argues (70–71). Its Founding Fathers invented the idea that the very *constitution* of a country -the document that establishes, empowers, and shapes the structures of government – should also be the guarantor of human rights.[10] This idea that government should be bound to the rights associated with democracy by the very authority that structures and empowers its democratic procedures is in Dworkin's view 'the most important contribution our [i.e. United States] history has given to political theory' (6). It would be a 'historic shame', he says, if Americans were to lose faith in this practice just as it is beginning to inspire the world (71).

In *Freedom's Law*, Dworkin does not merely defend the familiar claim that judicial review on the basis of constitutional principle makes a society more *just* than it would be without it. Sure, he does accept that familiar claim (at least so far as the United States is concerned), and he has defended it elsewhere.[11] The challenging thing about the *Freedom's Law* position is that Dworkin actually insists, without any qualification, that '[a] constitution of principle, enforced by independent judges, is not undemocratic' (123). There is no trade-off between rights and democracy, he insists. Instead he thinks that the practice of allowing a handful of unelected and unaccountable judges to strike down laws passed by a representative legislature helps constitute a distinctive and excellent form of democracy in the United States (15). What's more, his reason for believing this remarkable claim is no longer the reason we criticized at the beginning of Chapter Twelve – namely, that the practice is something the American people have chosen.[12] He now maintains that whoever chose it chose *an option favourable to democracy*.

In one or two places Dworkin goes beyond this, and gives the impression that he thinks a political system which allows ordinary majorities to make decisions about rights should not be regarded as genuinely democratic. He says any version of democracy that requires 'deference to tem-

[10] See also Black, *A New Birth of Freedom*, 5 and 89.

[11] Dworkin, *Law's Empire*, 356.

[12] See above, Ch. 12, fn. 1 and accompanying text. (Professor Dworkin has indicated in conversation that he does not now hold the view attributed to him in that passage.)

porary majorities on matters of individual right is . . . brutal and alien, and many other nations with firm democratic traditions now reject it as fake' (71). Mostly, however, his position is less strident than that. The argument I want to criticize in this chapter is the argument intended to show that American-style constitutional arrangements are no less democratic on account of judicial review, not the argument that judicial review is actually *required* by democracy. In his most careful formulation, Dworkin says:

I do not mean that there is no democracy unless judges have the power to set aside what a majority thinks is right and just. Many institutional arrangements are compatible with the moral reading, including some that do not give judges the power they have in the American structure. But none of these varied arrangements is in principle more democratic than others. Democracy does not insist on judges having the last word, but it does not insist that they must not have it. [7]

So, although Ronald Dworkin is among those who urge the introduction of American-style arrangements into the United Kingdom, I do not think he really wants to say that the Westminster system as it stands is brutally undemocratic or less democratic because it lacks a system of judicial review. Mostly what he wants to say is that if judicial review were introduced, Britain would be *no less democratic* in consequence. That's what I want to consider in this chapter: I want to ask one more time, in the light of Dworkin's arguments, whether there is in fact a loss to democracy when the elected legislature of a society is subjected to judicial power. Dworkin thinks there is not. I shall try to show that this is not established by his arguments in *Freedom's Law*.

3. JUDICIAL REVIEW AND JUSTICE

I want to begin this discussion with a word about the more familiar claim I mentioned – namely, that judicial review may make a society more just (whether or not it is compatible with democracy). As I said, Dworkin believes this too, certainly as far as America is concerned. 'The United States', he says, 'is a more just society than it would have been had its constitutional rights been left to the conscience of majoritarian institutions.'[13]

Should we accept this as a starting point? I have my doubts. Like any claim involving a counterfactual ('more just than it would have been if . . .'), it is an extraordinarily difficult proposition to assess. As we consider it, we think naturally of landmark decisions like *Brown* v. *Board of Education*,[14] and the impact of such decisions on desegregation and the promotion of racial equality. But it is not enough to celebrate *Brown*. Verifying the counterfactual would involve not only an assessment of the

---

¹³ Dworkin, *Law's Empire*, 356.   ¹⁴ *Brown* v. *Board of Education* 347 US 483 (1954).

impact of that and similar decisions but also a consideration of the way in which the struggle against segregation and similar injustices might have proceeded in the United States if there had been no Bill of Rights or no practice of judicial review.[15] About the only evidence we have in this regard is the struggle against injustice in other societies which lacked these institutions. Many such societies seem to be at least as free and as just as the United States,[16] though of course it is arguable such comparisons underestimate the peculiarities of American politics and society. In addition, a proper assessment of the claim would require us to consider the injustice that judicial review has caused as well as the injustice it has prevented. It would require us to consider, for example, the injustice occasioned by the striking down by state and federal courts of some 150 pieces of legislation concerning labour relations and labour conditions in the period (now referred to as the *Lochner* era) from 1885 to 1930.[17] Not only that, but it would also require us to consider the longer term effects of the discrediting of parliamentary socialism within the American labour movement that resulted from repeated judicial obstruction of otherwise successful legislative initiatives.[18] One would have to balance all that against the good that the courts have done. Dworkin is aware that the record on judicial review is far from perfect, and he has very little positive to say about the jurisprudence of the *Lochner* era. I cannot help feeling however that he underestimates the damage done in this period when he says that '[i]n fact, the most serious mistakes the Supreme Court has made, over its history, have been not in striking down laws it ought to have upheld, but in upholding laws it ought to have struck down' (388).[19]

The claim about justice may in the end be impossible to verify. And even were it true, it would still involve a problematic trade-off between justice and democratic ideals, unless the more ambitious claim of *Freedom's Law* could be sustained. For Dworkin acknowledges that democracy *would* be eroded if we were to give a bunch of unelected philosopher-kings the power to overrule legislation simply on the ground that they thought it unjust: 'Even if the experts always improved the legislation they rejected – always stipulated fairer income taxes than the legislature had enacted, for example – there would be a loss in self-government which the merits of their decision could not extinguish' (32). To reach the distinctive conclusions of *Freedom's Law*, Dworkin must therefore show that in some circumstances judicial review of legislation does not detract at all from, and

---

[15] Though see also Rosenberg, *The Hollow Hope*, 39–169.

[16] See Dahl, *Democracy and its Critics*, 189.

[17] For a list, see Forbath, *Law and the Shaping of the American Labor Movement*, Appendices A and C.

[18] Ibid., 37–58.

[19] For examples of the kinds of case Dworkin is referring to here, see those cited above in Ch. 12, fn. 31.

maybe even enhances, the democratic character of the political system of which it is a part.

4. IMPROVING PUBLIC DEBATE

One way he tries to show this is by considering the effect of constitutional adjudication on the character of public debate. Modern civic republicans and participatory democrats emphasize the importance of citizens engaging actively in political deliberation, and some of them have misgivings about judicial review because they think it tends to undermine this engagement by removing important decisions of principle from the democratic forum. Dworkin believes, however, that the quality of public debate may actually be better on this account:

When an issue is seen as constitutional, . . . and as one that will ultimately be resolved by courts applying general constitutional principles, the quality of public argument is often improved, because the argument concentrates from the start on questions of political morality. . . . When a constitutional issue has been decided by the Supreme Court, and is important enough so that it can be expected to be elaborated, expanded, contracted, or even reversed by future decisions, a sustained national debate begins, in newspapers and other media, in law schools and classrooms, in public meetings and around dinner tables. That debate better matches [the] conception of republican government, in its emphasis on matters of principle, than almost anything the legislative process on its own is likely to produce. [345]

He cites as an example the great debate about abortion surrounding the Supreme Court's decision in *Roe* v. *Wade*,[20] saying it has involved many more people and has led to a more subtle appreciation of the complexities involved than in other countries where the final decision about abortion was assigned to elected legislatures. As a result of entrusting it to the courts:

Americans better understand, for instance, the distinction between the question whether abortion is morally and ethically permissible, on the one hand, and the question whether government has the right to prohibit it, on the other; they also better understand the more general and constitutionally crucial idea on which that distinction rests: that individuals have rights that may work against the general will or the collective interest or good. [345]

In this way, Dworkin thinks, a system of final decision by judges on certain great issues of principle may actually enhance the participatory character of our politics.[21]

---

[20] *Roe* v. *Wade*, 410 US 113 (1973).
[21] This, Dworkin says, is particularly the case if the debate is oriented towards what he calls a 'moral reading' of the Constitution (7–15).

I am afraid I do not agree with any of this. Consider first what is said about political discussion. Dworkin acknowledges that he is making tentative empirical claims about the quality of public debate. My experience is that national debates about abortion are as robust and well-informed in countries like the United Kingdom and New Zealand, where they are not constitutionalized, as they are in the United States – the more so perhaps because they are uncontaminated by quibbling about how to interpret the text of an eighteenth century document. It is sometimes liberating to be able to discuss issues like abortion directly, on the principles that ought to be engaged, rather than having to scramble around constructing those principles out of the scraps of some sacred text, in a tendentious exercise of constitutional calligraphy. Think of how much more wisely capital punishment has been discussed (and disposed of) in countries where the debate has not had to centre around the moral reading of the phrase 'cruel and unusual punishment', but could focus instead on broader aims of penal policy and on dangers more morally pressing than 'unusualness', such as the execution of the innocent.[22] It is simply a myth that the public requires a moral debate to be, first of all, an interpretive debate before it can be conducted with any dignity or sophistication.

Or consider the debate about homosexual law reform initiated by the 1957 Wolfenden Report in Great Britain,[23] and sustained in the famous exchange between Lord Devlin and H. L. A. Hart in the 1960s.[24] Despite their focus on the decisions of a legislature (the British Parliament), these authors seemed to evince a perfectly adequate grasp of the distinction between whether something is morally permissible and whether government has the right to prohibit it. They did not need to be taught that by a court. Indeed, if the US Supreme Court's intervention on a similar issue is anything to go by, the American debate is actually impoverished by its constitutionalization. As Mary Ann Glendon has remarked, the decision in *Bowers* v. *Hardwick*[25] is remarkable for the 'lack of depth and seriousness of the analysis contained in its majority and dissenting opinions', compared with the discussion that has taken place in other countries.[26] If the debate that actually takes place in American society and American legislatures is as good as that in other countries, it is so *despite* the Supreme Court's framing of the issues, not because of it.

Still, suppose Dworkin is right that the quality of public discussion may be improved by citizens' awareness that the final disposition of some issue of principle is to be taken out of the hands of their elected rep-

---

[22] See also the discussion in Ch. 10, s. 4.
[23] *Report of the Committee on Homosexual Offences and Prostitution*, Cmd. no. 247 (1957).
[24] See Hart, *Law, Liberty and Morality* and Devlin, *The Enforcement of Morals*.
[25] *Bowers* v. *Hardwick* 478 US 186 (1986).   [26] Glendon, *Rights Talk*, 151.

resentatives and assigned instead to a court. The idea that civic republicans and participatory democrats should count this as a gain is a travesty. Civic republicans and participatory democrats are interested in *practical political deliberation*, which is not just any old debating exercise, but a form of discussion among those who are about to participate in a binding collective decision. A star-struck people may speculate about what the Supreme Court will do next on abortion or some similar issue; they may even amuse each other, as we law professors do, with stories of how *we* would decide, in the unlikely event that we were elevated to that eminent tribunal. The exercise of power by a few black-robed celebrities can certainly be expected to *fascinate* an articulate population. But that is hardly the essence of active citizenship. Perhaps such impotent debating is nevertheless morally improving: Dworkin may be right that 'there is no necessary connection between a citizen's political impact or influence and the ethical benefit he secures through participating in public discussion' (30). But independent ethical benefits of this kind are at best desirable side effects, not the primary point of civic participation in republican political theory.

5. DEMOCRATIC ENDS AND DEMOCRATIC MEANS

As I said, Dworkin acknowledges the tentativeness of his response to the civic republicans. His main argument for the claim that judicial review involves no cost in terms of democracy is somewhat different. It goes as follows.

Suppose a piece of legislation is enacted by an elected assembly and then challenged by a citizen on the ground that it undermines one of the rights associated with democracy. (The example Dworkin gives (32) is a statute prohibiting flag-burning.) And suppose the issue is assigned to a court for decision, and the court strikes down the statute, accepting the citizen's challenge. Is there a loss to democracy? The answer, Dworkin says, depends entirely on whether the court makes the right decision. If it does – that is, if the statute really was incompatible with the rights required for a democracy – then democracy is surely improved by what the court has done. For the community is now more democratic than it would have been if the anti-democratic statute had been allowed to stand. Of course, Dworkin adds,

if we assume the court's decision was wrong, then none of this is true. Certainly it impairs democracy when an authoritative court makes the wrong decision about what the democratic conditions require – but no more than it does when a majoritarian legislature makes a wrong constitutional decision that is allowed to stand. The possibility of error is symmetrical. [32–3]

It follows, says Dworkin, that democratic constitutional theory ought to be oriented primarily to results (34). In every society, there will be questions whether enacted legislation conflicts with the fundamental principles of democracy. These questions should be assigned to whatever institution is likely to answer them correctly. In some countries, for all we know, this may be the legislature. But often there is reason to think the legislature is not the safest vehicle for protecting the rights associated with democracy (34). In that case, we should assign the issue to the courts, if we think they are a safer bet. We should not be deterred, says Dworkin, by the fact that courts are not constituted in a way that makes them democratically accountable. Accountability does not matter, he says. The crucial thing is that courts are reliable at making good decisions about democracy. That is all a partisan of democracy should care about.

That is the argument. Notice how it turns on an elision between a decision *about democracy* and a decision *made by democratic means*. Dworkin seems to be suggesting that if a political decision is about democracy, or about the rights associated with democracy, then there is no interesting or interestingly distinct question to be raised about the way in which (i.e., the institutional process by which) the decision is made. All that matters is that the decision be right, from a democratic point of view. In the case of social justice, that is not so: the right decision about social justice may have been reached, but – as Dworkin concedes (32) – it still matters whether it was reached democratically. In the case of a decision about democracy, however, he thinks the distinction collapses.

I wonder whether, on reflection, Dworkin really means to collapse content and legitimacy in this way. Suppose the United Kingdom became embroiled in a debate about the democratic merits of proportional representation (PR), and that in a moment of national exasperation with the inability of elected politicians to resolve this issue, the Queen were to announce that henceforth the electoral system would be organized on the basis of 'Single Transferable Vote'. Suppose also, for the sake of argument, that the Queen's decision was the right one: that the version of PR she chose really does make an electoral system more democratic than the old-fashioned 'first-past-the-post' system. Could this possibly be regarded as an exercise of democratic power on the ground that it confined itself to a question about the nature of the democratic process and answered that question correctly? In New Zealand a few years ago, the issue which we are imagining being settled in Britain by the Queen was settled in fact by two popular referendums, separated by a year or so of public education and careful debate. Is it really Dworkin's position that the Queen's intervention (in our imagined example) would be no less democratic a way of settling this issue than the popular referendums in New Zealand? Should we not rather say – would it not be much clearer to say – that in the imaginary British case a democratic issue was settled *undemocratically*? And that there *was* therefore a loss in self-government, *even though the Queen got the answer right*?

Of course there is an additional difference: we are imagining the Queen intervening in a sort of unconstitutional *putsch*. A system of judicial review would presumably not have that character.[27] Actually that's not quite true: at the birth of judicial review in the United States, some jurists did regard it as constitutionally irregular; and certainly, if it were introduced into the UK, various English pedants could be relied on to make the point that any abrogation of parliamentary sovereignty was both unconstitutional and illogical. Anyway, whether something is constitutionally irregular is a separate question from whether it is undemocratic (though sometimes the latter is a ground for the former). If someone were to ask (in our hypothetical case) why the Queen's intervention was an *important* as opposed to a trivial irregularity, we would surely say that it was important because it compromised democracy, because she had usurped a decision that should properly have been taken by the people or their representatives. And that's the point I want to make: concerns about the democratic or non-democratic character of a political procedure do not evaporate when the procedure in question is being used to address an issue about the nature of democracy.

The same argument may be put more concisely. If a question comes up for political decision in a community, a member of the community might reasonably ask to participate in it on equal terms with his fellow citizens. Now there may be all sorts of reasons for denying his request, but it would surely be absurd to deny it on the ground that the question was one about democracy. That would be absurd because it would fail to address his concern that a question about democracy, as much as any political question, should be settled by democratic means.

So I do not think we should accept Dworkin's claim to have created 'a level playing field on which the contest between different institutional structures for interpreting the democratic conditions must take place' (33). The playing field is not level. There *is* something lost, from a democratic point of view, when an unelected and unaccountable individual or institution makes a binding decision about what democracy requires. If it makes the right decision, then – sure – there is something democratic to set against that loss; but that is not the same as there being no loss in the first place. On the other hand, if an institution which *is* elected and accountable makes the wrong decision about what democracy requires, then although there is a loss to democracy in the substance of the decision, it is not silly for citizens to comfort themselves with the thought that at least they made

---

[27] I am grateful to Stephen Perry for this point.

their *own* mistake about democracy rather than having someone else's mistake foisted upon them. Process may not be all that there is to democratic decision-making; but we should not say that, since the decision is *about* democracy, process is therefore irrelevant.

6. DISAGREEMENT, AGAIN

Dworkin acknowledges that reasonable citizens may disagree about what democracy requires and about the rights that it involves or presupposes.[28] They disagree about details like the voting age, electoral laws, and campaign finance. And they disagree also about some of the fundamentals: the basis of representation and the connection between political and social equality. They certainly disagree about what democracy presupposes as conditions of legitimacy. For example: What are the issues on which we require a common decision? How much concern must different sections of the community have for one another, before minorities may reasonably be expected to trust the majority? How much moral independence for its members does an attractive conception of community presuppose? Even if they agree that democracy implicates certain rights, citizens will surely disagree what these rights are and what in detail they commit us to.

The persistence of these disagreements makes a difference to the way we are able to proceed in constitutional design. The suggestion in *Freedom's Law* is that we should use a results-driven criterion for choosing the institutions to which decisions about democratic rights should be entrusted:

I see no alternative but to use a result-driven rather than a procedure-driven standard. . . . The best institutional structure is the one best calculated to produce the best answers to the essentially moral question of what the democratic conditions actually are, and to secure stable compliance with those conditions. [34]

But a citizenry who disagree about what would count as the right results are not in a position to construct their constitution on this basis. (That is why, as I argued in Chapter Seven, John Rawls's approach to constitutional design, in *A Theory of Justice*, is so misconceived.) Using a result-driven approach, different citizens will attempt to design the constitution on a different basis. A libertarian will seek participatory procedures that maximize the prospect of legislation that is just by his own free market standards, while a social democrat will seek participatory procedures that

---

[28] See Dworkin, *Freedom's Law*, 34: 'People can be expected to disagree about which structure is overall best, and so in certain circumstances they need a decision procedure for deciding that question, which is exactly what a theory of democracy cannot provide. That is why the initial making of a political constitution is such a mysterious matter . . .'

maximize the prospects for legislation embodying collective and egalitarian concern. How can they together design a political framework to structure and accommodate the political and ideological differences between
them? The only way they can do that is if they have managed already to
adopt a view that can stand in the name of them all about the results they
should be aiming at. But if they have managed that, from a baseline of disagreement, they must have been in possession of decision-procedures that
enable them to get to that result. And presumably their possession of *those*
decision-procedures can be explained only on the basis of their use of
something other than a results-driven test (for choosing procedures) in the
past.

We seem, then, to be in a bind. It looks as though it is disagreement all
the way down, so far as constitutional choice is concerned. On the one
hand, we cannot use a results-driven test, because we disagree about
which results should count in favour of and which against a given decision-procedure. On the other hand, it seems we cannot appeal to any procedural criterion either, since procedural questions are at the very nub of
the disagreements we are talking about.

7. THE CAPACITY TO THINK PROCEDURALLY

Someone may say, 'Well, what did you expect? Even if we buy the view
that right-based respect for persons is also respect for their sense of justice
and thus respect for their political capacity, it does not follow that the
people are to be entrusted with procedural questions of constitutional
design. Ordinary political competence cannot be expected to extend to the
building and care of the framework within which ordinary political competence is to be exercised.' Something along these lines is at back of what
I perceive as the very considerable popularity of the John Hart Ely view
mentioned earlier: namely, that even if there is an affront to democracy
when substantive issues are taken away from the people, there is no
affront when *procedural* issues are taken away.[29]

But that will not do. I said earlier that there is a theoretical connection
between respect for people's rights and respect for their capacities as
political participators. Now there is no reason to suppose that the moral
capacities respected in the idea of rights are only capacities to think substantively, as opposed to capacities to think reflectively about procedures.
On the contrary, the emergence of rights-theories in the modern era was
associated not just with the substantive self-confidence of individual
reason, but also with a certain *epistemological* self-confidence, that is, a

[29] Ely, *Democracy and Distrust*.

confidence on the part of individuals in their ability to reflect systematically on the procedures that knowledge and rational deliberation
involved.[30] Whether in the form of Descartes's self-imposed strictures of
method in the *Discourse on the Method*, or in John Locke's patient enquiry
in the *Essay* into 'what objects our understandings were, or were not, fitted to deal with',[31] enlightenment optimism on behalf of the individual
mind was optimism at least as much in regard to its reflections upon
methodology as in regard to its achievements of substance. This optimism
was mirrored, in early modern political philosophy, in the assumption
that the one decision that did have to be made by the people – deliberating and voting together, unaided by authority or tradition – was the choice
of a political procedure for the civil society they were inventing.[32]
Government might not end up being democratic; some theorists, like
Hobbes, advised strongly against democracy.[33] But they had no doubt that
the choice of a constitution – and thus the pondering of the very issues
about what different political processes involved or presupposed – was
one that could only be made by the people.[34]

So, working in this tradition of political thought, we will not get very far
with any argument that limits the competence of popular self-government
to issues of substance and stops it short at the threshold of political procedure, assigning questions about forms of government to a body of a different sort altogether. Democracy is in part *about* democracy: one of the
first things on which the people demand a voice about, and concerning
which they claim a competence, is the procedural character of their own
political arrangements.

8. JUDGES IN OUR OWN CASE?

Still, the problem we face may not be one of capacity. We have to consider
the suggestion – implicit in Dworkin's argument – that allowing the
majority to decide upon the conditions under which majority-decisions
are to be accepted may be objectionable because it makes them judge in
their own case. Those who invoke the principle of *nemo iudex in sua causa*

---

[30] For the connection between liberal political theory and enlightenment optimism in epistemology, see Waldron, 'Theoretical Foundations of Liberalism'.

[31] Locke, *An Essay Concerning Human Understanding*, Epistle to the Reader.

[32] See Hobbes, *Leviathan*, Chapter 17, 120–1; Locke, *Two Treatises of Government*, II, paras.
95–8 and 132–3, 330–3 and 354–5.

[33] Hobbes, *Leviathan*, Ch. 19.

[34] See Hobbes, *The Elements of Law*, Part II, Ch. XXI: 'The first in order of time of these three
sorts [of commonwealth] is democracy, and it must be so of necessity, because an aristocracy
and a monarchy, require nomination of persons agreed upon; which agreement in a great
multitude of men must consist in the consent of the major part; and where the votes of the
major part involve the votes of the rest, there is actually a democracy.'

in this context say that it requires that a final decision about rights should *not* be left in the hands of the people: it should be passed on to an independent and impartial institution such as the US Supreme Court.[35]

It is hard to see the force of this argument. Almost any conceivable decision-rule will eventually involve *someone* deciding in his own case, in one or maybe two different ways. First, unless it is seriously imagined that issues of right should be decided by an outsider – by a Rousseauian 'lawgiver' perhaps,[36] or by some neo-colonial institution that stands in relation to a given community as (say) the British Privy Council stands in relation to New Zealand – such decisions will inevitably be made by persons whose own rights are affected by the decision. Even a Supreme Court justice gets to have the rights that he determines American citizens to have. We too often forget this: often our scholarly talk about when 'the people' or 'the majority' may be entrusted (by us?) with decisions about rights has something of the haughty air of a John Stuart Mill talking *de haut en bas* about native self-government in India.

It is sometimes said that what *nemo iudex* implies is that a democratic majority should not have the final say as to whether its decision about rights is acceptable. If there is a question about whether the majority's decision is acceptable, then the majority should not adjudicate that question. This will not do either. Unless we envisage a literally endless chain of appeals, there will always be some person or institution whose decision is final. And of that person or institution, we can always say that since it has the last word, its members are *ipso facto* ruling on the acceptability of their own view. Facile invocations of *nemo iudex in sua causa* are no excuse for forgetting the elementary logic of authority: people disagree and there is need for a final decision and a final decision-procedure.

Invoking *nemo iudex* may be appropriate when one individual or faction purports to adjudicate an issue concerning its own interests, as opposed to those of another individual or faction or as opposed to the rest of the community. (Historically, those who have invoked it against democratic government have often tried to portray democracy as class rule, i.e., self-interested rule by the lower classes.) The objection in such cases to A being judge in his (or its) own case is that B (the other party in the dispute) is excluded from the process. But it seems quite inappropriate to invoke this principle in a situation where the community as a whole is attempting to resolve some issue concerning the rights of *all* the members of the community and attempting to resolve it on a basis of equal participation. There, it seems not just unobjectionable but *right* that all those who are

---

[35] I am grateful to George Kateb for insisting that I confront this point.
[36] See Rousseau, *The Social Contract*, Bk. II, Ch. 7, 76–9.

affected by an issue of rights should participate in the decision (and if we want a Latin tag to answer *nemo iudex*, we can say, '*Quod omnes tangit ab omnibus decidentur*').

9. BEGGING THE QUESTION

Still, the impression of some sort of logical difficulty remains. Surely there is something question-begging in the idea of a democratic decision about democracy? Is there not something circular in assigning to the majority decisions about the nature and limits of majority decision-making? And if it is circular or question-begging, is that not a reason for assigning decisions of this sort to some other individual or institution?

I am not so sure. Let us think it through. Suppose the citizens of a country do not have the legal right to X and that some among them believe that a system of majority decision-making can have no legitimacy in a community whose members do not have that right. Others in the society, who are opposed to the right to X, deny this. If the issue between the pro-X and anti-X factions is dealt with by a majority vote in the legislature, confirming that people are not to have the right to X, the pro-X faction may reasonably refuse to accept the legitimacy of this result. I do not mean they are necessarily right about the relation between X and democracy. I mean that, given the disagreement about this between them and their opponents, any claim that the issue about the right to X was settled legitimately by the vote would indeed be question-begging.

Notice two things about this conclusion, however. First: if, in the absence of a right to X, a majority decision confirming that citizens do not have the right to X is problematic so far as its legitimacy is concerned, the same would have to be said of the opposite decision in these circumstances. So even if the majority had voted the other way – that is, even if they had voted to institute the right to X – that decision too would be tainted by the fact that it was taken among a citizenry who, as things stood, lacked this right thought by one faction to be so essential for legitimate majority decision-making. Pragmatically, of course, the pro-X faction might be expected to take its victories where it found them, and not worry too much about their legitimacy. But that does not make the process any the less tainted, on their own account of democracy.

Secondly, and much more importantly: the fact that a majoritarian process is arguably tainted by the absence of a right to X does not mean that other processes (such as judicial decision-making) are therefore preferable or legitimate. In most cases, the claim that the right to X is one of the conditions of legitimate democracy is unlikely to be true unless X is also one of the conditions of the legitimacy of *any* political system.

Dworkin argues that 'a society in which the majority shows contempt for the needs and prospects of some minority is illegitimate as well as unjust' (25). But surely it follows from this, not only that majority decisions lack political legitimacy in that society, but that legitimacy cannot be accorded to *any* political decisions, made by *any* procedure, under the circumstances he mentions. The majority contempt Dworkin describes is liable to destroy the entire basis of political community for the society, depriving any group in it of the right to speak for the society as a whole. The legitimate basis for rule by a monarch would be undermined by the divisions and hatred he imagines, as would rule by an aristocratic elite or, for that matter, rule by the courts. If the circumstances are such as to warrant minority distrust of a dominant majority, they will certainly arouse misgivings about the basis on which judges are selected and the social and political culture that is likely to inform their decisions.

There is an important general point here. Sometimes we talk carelessly as though there were a *special* problem for the legitimacy of popular majority decision-making, a problem that does not exist for other forms of political organization such as aristocracy or judicial rule. Because the phrase 'tyranny of the majority' trips so easily off the tongue, we tend to forget about other forms of tyranny; we tend to forget that legitimacy is an issue that pertains to *all* political authority. Indeed it would be very odd if there were a *graver* problem of legitimacy for popular majoritarian decision-making. Other political systems have all the legitimacy-related dangers of popular majoritarianism: they may get things wrong; they may have an unjust impact on particular individuals or groups; in short, they may act tyrannically. But they have in addition one legitimacy-related defect that popular majoritarianism does not have: they do not allow a voice and a vote in a final decision-procedure to every citizen of the society; instead they proceed to make final decisions about the rights of millions on the basis of the voices and votes of a few.

Of the categories of rights I set out in section 1 of this chapter – (a) rights constitutive of democracy and (b) rights presupposed by democracy – I have concentrated in this section on rights in group (b). I did so because this group seemed most promising for Dworkin's claim that there is something question-begging about using majority procedures to determine what rights we have. But a similar conclusion can be reached concerning rights in group (a).

Suppose citizens disagree about the basis of suffrage, about campaign finance, or about proportional representation. In extreme cases, one side to the disagreement may claim that a majority-decision made in the absence of the constitutive right that they are arguing about has no legitimacy whatsoever. They may say, for example – quite plausibly – that a majority of men has no moral right to decide in the name of the whole community whether women shall have the right to vote. As before, it does not follow that some other body – the monarch or the courts – has the right to decide this issue simply because the male citizenry does not. What follows is that we are left in a legitimacy-free zone in which the best that we can hope for is that a legitimate democratic system emerges somehow or other. This is not the same as saying we are now using a results-driven test of legitimacy. It is rather a pragmatic expression of hope in circumstances where it is not open to us to use any communal criterion of legitimacy at all.

To repeat, then: the situation may be such that the legitimacy of *any* political decision about a right associated with democracy, by any procedure or institution, is thrown in doubt. That, I think, is undeniable. Does it not follow, then, that in these circumstances we *have* to appeal to a results-driven approach? It does not, for two reasons.

First, as we have already seen, the existence of controversy about the rights associated with democracy means that a results-driven approach is unavailable too, or unavailable to us as a political community. Individuals and factions may have their own result-based opinions of course, but then they will also have their own opinions about procedures (for example, their own opinions about the relation between democracy and the right in question). There is thus no advantage either way for a results-driven as opposed to a proceduralist approach.

Secondly, it is possible, as a matter of practical politics, to use an ordinary and familiar procedure like majority-decision to settle one of these questions, while leaving open the issue of legitimacy. Suppose, for example, that we use majoritarian procedure A to decide whether to continue with a procedure of that kind in our politics or to replace it with a somewhat different political procedure B. And suppose we vote to retain procedure A. We may accept that vote as a pragmatic matter, without investing it with democratic legitimacy in any particularly question-begging way. In other words, the fact that, pragmatically, we have to find some way of resolving disagreements about the rights associated with democracy does not mean that we have no choice but to adopt a results-driven test. The pragmatics may drive us instead to an informal and unfreighted use of some familiar decision-procedure, a use that does not beg the questions of legitimacy that are at issue. (Notice, of course, that all this can also be said about a results-driven test. If we can get away with using a partisan results-driven test such as the Rawlsian one, that too can be a purely pragmatic basis for constitutional design. In other words, the pragmatic possibility I am outlining in this paragraph is open to both sides. All I am insisting on in this section is that we are not *required* to adopt a results-driven approach: pragmatism, in this regard, is not necessarily the same as orientation to results.)

Sure, to a careless eye, it may look as though we are privileging one of the possible outcomes – namely, procedure A – by using *it* as the procedure for deciding among the possible outcomes. And – I have heard people say – if it makes sense to privilege one of the outcomes in this case, why does it not also make sense to privilege one of the outcomes in an ordinary case where substantive rather than procedural questions are at stake? But to decide among procedures A and B by using procedure A as our method is not to *privilege* procedure A; it is simply to use it. If we choose one of the procedures which are up for decision as the procedure for making that very decision, we do so simply because *we need a procedure* on this occasion and this is the one we are stuck with for the time being.

Remember, finally, that the fact that an issue concerns a right associated with democracy does not mean that we are necessarily brought to the impasse I have been discussing. For one thing, the right in question may be incidental rather than central to democratic legitimacy. Democracy is a complex and variegated ideal, and some of the rights associated with it in one type of system may be called in question without anyone thinking that therefore democracy as such is called in question. For another thing, even if the right in question is thought by one side to be essential to democracy, it does not follow that a majority-decision is question-begging. Suppose that the right to X is in question among the members of a community all of whom currently *do* have the right to X, and that some think, as before, that X is one of the conditions of legitimate democracy while others deny this. And suppose the people (or their representatives) vote by a majority for a bill that narrows or abrogates the right to X. Can *this* majority decision be criticized by the pro-X faction as illegitimate? Is any claim about the legitimacy of *this* decision question-begging as between the proponents and the opponents of the right to X? Surely not. Unless there is some other problem with democracy in the society (a problem undisclosed in the terms of our hypothetical), the decision about X has been made under what the pro-X faction regard as the optimal conditions of legitimacy. People had their right to X and they made a collective decision (about that right). Certainly the pro-X faction will have their doubts about political decisions *subsequent* to this one, for they will think the abrogation of X has undermined the prospective legitimacy of majoritarianism in that community. But these doubts will affect *all* subsequent political decisions – on substantive as well as procedural matters – and (as before) decisions made by courts as much as decisions made by popular majorities. They will even affect the legitimacy of a future decision to restore the right to X. So we see once again there is nothing necessarily circular about majority decision-making on an issue concerning the rights associated with democracy.

10. SUMMA CONTRA DWORKIN

The conclusions of this chapter so far may be summarized as follows. We examined Ronald Dworkin's arguments in *Freedom's Law* in favour of judicial review on the American model, and we accepted the following positions he defended: (1) there is an important connection between rights and democracy; (2) some individual rights must be regarded as conditions on the legitimacy of majority-decision, and (3) if people disagree about the conditions of democracy, an appeal to the legitimacy of majority-decision to settle that disagreement may be question-begging.

However, we also argued for the following claims, which contradict the inferences that Dworkin wanted to draw from (3). We argued (4) that if an appeal to the legitimacy of majority-decision to settle a disagreement about the conditions of democracy is question-begging, then an appeal to the legitimacy of judicial review (or any political procedure) to settle that disagreement is *also* likely to be question-begging; (5) the fact that an appeal to the legitimacy of majority-decision to settle a disagreement about the conditions of democracy is question-begging does not mean that we have no choice but to use a decision-procedure selected according to a results-driven test; and (6) in cases where an appeal to the legitimacy of majority-decision to settle a disagreement about the conditions of democracy is not question-begging, there is no reason to disparage majority-decision on the basis of *nemo iudex in sua causa*.

Against Dworkin's central argument in *Freedom's Law*, we argued (7) that there is always a loss to democracy when a view about the conditions of democracy is imposed by a non-democratic institution, even when the view is correct and its imposition improves the democracy. We also argued, near the beginning of the chapter, against a couple of incidental positions that Dworkin maintains. We argued (8) that there is no reason to think that judicial review improves the quality of participatory political debate in a society, and (9) that it is an open question whether judicial review has made the United States (or would make any society) more just than it would have been without that practice.

11. IS EVERYTHING UP FOR GRABS?

I have argued that there is nothing particularly question-begging about assigning issues about democracy to popular participatory procedures. There is nothing logically inappropriate about invoking the right to participate to determine issues about rights, including issues about participation itself. There is no reason, therefore, why each individual's claim to participate in the making of the laws by which he is governed should be arrested at the threshold of procedure. Logic does not require us to assign questions about political and constitutional arrangements for final decision to a non-participatory institution. On the contrary, there is something democratically incomplete – certainly something unpleasantly condescending – about a constitution that empowers a small group of judges or other officials to veto what the people or their representatives have settled on as their answers to disputed questions about what democracy involves.

Still, none of this assuages the worries with which we began. Granted there is nothing illogical in assigning disputes about the rights associated with democracy to a majoritarian procedure, what guarantee do we have that such rights would be respected? How can rights be secure if they are at the mercy of majority decision? How is respect for rights consistent with a process that appears to place no a priori limits on political outcomes? Do the conclusions to which we have been driven not leave everything up for grabs?

The most straightforward answer is 'Yes – everything *is* up for grabs in a democracy, including the rights associated with democracy itself.' Or, certainly, everything is up for grabs which is the subject of good-faith disagreement. That's the key to the matter, for to say that something which was the subject of good faith disagreement was nevertheless *not* up for grabs would be to imagine ourselves, as a community, in a position to take sides in such a disagreement without ever appearing to have done so. Suppose again that the members of a community disagree about whether people ought to have the right to X. To say that, nevertheless, the right to X should not be up for grabs in this community, is to say that the community has already taken a side in this disagreement. And one is entitled to wonder how exactly *that* came about (given the disagreement) without at some earlier stage the right to X having indeed been up for grabs in a decision procedure addressing the question of whether this right was something to which the community ought to commit itself.

The panic about everything being 'up for grabs' is of course in part a panic about self-government in the political realm. We are not sure of each other in the way we purport to be sure of ourselves. We want to govern ourselves – I mean govern ourselves politically, acting together, acting in the company of others – but we know we disagree about the principles on which such government should be conducted. Each of us therefore must face the prospect that the values *he* takes seriously, the priorities *he* has, the principles to which *he* has a strong attachment, may not be the values, priorities, and principles held by the voter in the next booth. We can try if we like to suppress these disagreements, to denigrate the other's views as selfish or irrational and exclude them as far as possible from our politics. But, as I have argued, we can hardly do this in the name of *rights*, if it is part of the idea of rights that a right-bearer is to be respected as a separate moral agent with his own sense of justice. If, on the other hand, we resolve to treat each other's views with respect, if we do not seek to hide the fact of our differences or to suppress dissent, then we have no choice but to adopt procedures for settling political disagreements which do not themselves specify what the outcome is to be.[37] In that sense, politics does leave things up for grabs in a way that is bound to be disconcerting from each individual's point of view. Respect for the opinions and consciences of others means that a single individual does not have the sort of control over political outcomes that his conscience or his own principles appear to dictate. That bullet, I think, simply has to be bitten.

'Up for grabs', however, may indicate a couple of other things, neither of which is entailed by the position that I have been arguing for.

'Grabs' can connote selfish pork-barrelling – a feeding frenzy of interest rather than a good faith disagreement of principle. Reasonable men and women will quite properly be alarmed by the prospects for rights in a society where each citizen and interest group is attempting to grab as much as it can. Rights generally would be in peril in such a situation, including of course the rights that are constitutive of democracy. My argument has proceeded on the premise that democratic politics need not be like that, and that it is in fact much less like that than the denigrators of popular majoritarianism tend to claim. I have insisted too that we should resist the temptation to say that it *is* like that simply because we find ourselves contradicted or outvoted on some matter of principle. We do not need to invoke self-interest to explain disagreement about rights, for it is sufficiently explained by the difficulty of the subject-matter and by what John Rawls called 'the burdens of judgment'.[38] If we ascribe someone's political difference with us to the influence of self-interest, that must be justified as a *special* explanation, over and above the normal explanation of human disagreement about complex questions.

I may be wrong about all this, of course: perhaps politics just is a clash of interests. (There is a danger, too, that this is what it is becoming around the world, as a sort of self-fulfilling prophecy evoked by the contempt for legislative politics exported triumphantly as the American contribution to democratic theory.) But if so, we should recognize that it is not just the reputation of popular majoritarianism that is in danger. If democratic politics is just an unholy scramble for personal advantage, then individual men and women are not the creatures that theorists of rights have taken them to be. If we think nevertheless that certain interests of theirs require special protection (against majorities and other kinds of tyrant), we shall have

---

[37] See above Ch. 5, ss. 2 and 9.
[38] Rawls, *Political Liberalism*, 54–8. For a discussion of 'the burdens of judgment', see above Ch. 5, s. 12 and Ch. 7, s. 2.

to develop a theory of justice and a theory of politics that does not associate the call for such protection with the active respect for moral capacity
that the idea of rights has traditionally involved.

Mostly, however, what I want to insist on is this. The alternative to a
self-interest model of politics is not a scenario in which individuals, as
responsible moral agents, converge on a single set of principles which add
up to *the truth* about justice, rights and the common good. That would not
be a credible alternative from a social science point of view. The proper
alternative to the self-interest model is a model of opinionated disagreement – a noisy scenario in which men and women of high spirit argue
passionately and vociferously about what rights we have, what justice
requires, and what the common good amounts to, motivated in their disagreement not by what's in it for them but by a desire to get it right. If we
take *that* as our alternative model, we may be more inclined to recognize
that real world politics are not necessarily governed by self-interest than if
we think the only alternative to the self-interest model is one which has
high-minded citizens converging on the truth. I have tried to show that we
can construct a theory of politics for the model of opinionated disagreement – a theory of legitimate decision-procedures which works on the
assumption that people who really care about justice and rights may
nevertheless disagree about what they entail. Of course any political
theory is bound to be something of an ideal-type in relation to the messiness of the real world.[39] A full and faithful account may require us to blend
in elements from a variety of theories. What I am suggesting, however, is
that if we want to do justice to that part of our political experience which
involves people sometimes being prepared to consult their ideals as well
as their utilities, then it is the model of disagreement, not the model of
moral convergence, that we should reach for to blend with or qualify the
more cynical model of interest.

The second sense of 'up for grabs' that I want to disown has to do with
hasty, volatile, and impetuous 'grabbing'. That a certain right is 'up for
grabs' in majoritarian politics may mean that it is respected today, abro-
gated tomorrow, and reinstated in an amended form on Monday morning.
We alluded briefly in Chapter Five to Thomas Hobbes's suggestion that
one of the most distinctive features of democratic politics is its inconstancy.[40] There are a variety of ways in which a democratic constitution
may mitigate this inconstancy. The legislative process may be made more
complex and laborious, and in various ways it may be made difficult to
revisit questions of principle for a certain time after they have been settled.
(Such 'slowing-down' devices may also be supported in the political

---

[39] For this notion of ideal-type, see Weber, *Economy and Society*, Vol. I, 20–2.
[40] Hobbes, *De Cive*, Ch. X, 137–8.

community by values associated with 'the rule of law'.) None of this need be regarded as an affront to democracy; certainly a 'slowing-down' device of this sort is not like the affront to democracy involved in removing issues from a vote altogether and assigning them to a separate non-representative forum like a court. However, as I argued in Chapter Twelve, democracy *would* be affronted by any attempt to associate such 'slowing down' with the idea that there is something pathological about one side or the other in a disagreement of principle. In that chapter, I argued against the 'Ulysses and the Sirens' model of precommitment, which presents constitutional constraints as a form of immunization against madness. We are not entitled to secure stability at the cost of silencing dissent or disenfranchising those who express it. And we should not use the ideas of constitutional caution or constitutional commitment as a way of precluding effective deliberation on a matter on which the citizens are still developing and debating their various views.

12. DISAGREEMENT ABOUT LIMITS

We know that if rights are entrusted to the people for protection they will be entrusted to men and women who disagree about what they amount to. It is tempting to infer, from the fact of such disagreement and from the processes (like voting) which will be necessary to resolve it, that this sort of protection in politics is as good as no protection at all. It is tempting to think that people who are prepared to countenance voting on matters of fundamental right, and to accept the view of the majority, simply do not take rights seriously.

Actually that is a temptation which is awfully *easy* to resist in certain contexts. For nobody thinks this about a tribunal like the United States Supreme Court. Surely the Justices on the Supreme Court take rights seriously if anybody does. Yet the Justices disagree about rights as much as anyone, and they resolve those disagreements by simple majority-voting. The established practice in America is that the people are to accept as authoritative a determination by the Court as to what rights they have, even when that determination is based on a knife-edge 5-to-4 vote among the Justices. We count heads on the court, we call for the appointment of a conservative or a liberal Justice, we talk about a particular Justice being the 'swing vote' on the court – and none of this seems to shake our confidence that rights are being addressed in the only way they could be addressed among articulate and opinionated individuals. We cannot therefore argue that rights are not being taken seriously in a political system simply on the ground that the system allows majority voting to settle disagreements as to what rights there are. On the contrary, a political culture – such as that which pervades and surrounds the US Supreme Court – may be a culture of rights, a culture in which rights are taken with the utmost seriousness, even though it is at the same time a culture of disagreement and a culture oriented to the idea that at the end of the day there may be nothing to do about a disagreement except count up the ayes and the noes.

Equally, I think we should not underestimate the extent to which the idea of rights may pervade legislative or electoral politics. The idea of rights is the idea that there are limits on what we may do to each other, or demand from each other, for the sake of the common good. A political culture in which citizens and legislators share this idea but disagree about what the limits are is quite different from a political culture uncontaminated by the idea of limits, and I think we sell ourselves terribly short in our constitutional thinking if we say that the fact of disagreement means we might as well not have the idea of rights or limits at all.

I want to end with two examples from the classics of liberal political philosophy, which will help to explain what I mean.

The first is the example of John Locke, well known as the founder of modern liberalism, and well known too for his insistence that the authority of the legislature is limited by respect for the natural rights – the lives, liberties, and property – of the people.[41] Legislators, said Locke, are not entitled to do just as they like. If they 'endeavour to invade the Property of the Subject, and to make themselves . . . Masters, or Arbitrary Disposers of the Lives, Liberties, or Fortunes of the People', they forfeit their authority. 'These are the bounds which the trust that is put in them by the Society, and the Law of God and Nature, have set to the Legislative Power of every Commonwealth.'[42] Yet Locke conjoined this classic liberal doctrine of the limited legislature with an insistence that '[i]n all Cases, whilst the Government subsists, the Legislative is the Supream Power . . . and all other Powers in any Members or parts of the Society [are] derived from and subordinate to it'.[43] The conjunction sounds curious to our jaded ears: how can he possibly mean what he says about a limited legislature, if he is not prepared to countenance any superior institution (like a court) to do the limiting? Is a theory of limits without institutional enforcement not the same as no theory of limits at all?

---

[41] The paragraphs that follow are adapted from the first of my 1996 Seeley Lectures, 'Locke's Legislature'. (See Waldron, *The Dignity of Legislation*, Ch. 4.)

[42] Locke, *Two Treatises of Government*, II, para. 142, 363.

[43] Ibid., II, para. 150, 367–8. The conjunction is not inadvertent on Locke's part: it's not a matter of *our* juxtaposing two disparate parts of a patchwork manuscript. On the contrary, Locke makes it explicit in a single passage: 'Though the Legislative, whether placed in one or more, whether it be always in being, or only by intervals, tho' it be the Supream Power in every Commonwealth; yet, First, It is not, nor can possibly be absolutely Arbitrary over the Lives and fortunes of the People.' (Ibid., II, para. 135, 357.)

The question ignores the importance of political culture and public political understanding. 'To *understand* Political Power right' is the aim of the *Second Treatise;*[44] and the assumption on which Locke proceeds is that a polity pervaded by a right understanding will differ remarkably in its character and operations from a polity whose members are under wilful or negligent misapprehensions about the rights and basis of government.[45]

The idea of right-based limits is thus, in the first instance, a matter of political self-understanding. It seemed important to Locke that legislators should go about their task imbued with a moral and philosophical sense that there are limits to what they may do, and that they should commit themselves (as a matter of virtue or duty associated with their office) to ascertain what those limits are and whether or not they are contravened by the legislative proposals that come before them. It seemed to him also important for citizens to imbue their deference to the authority of the legislature with an exactly similar sense. They should act and respond to its dictates with an awareness that they are not required (by social contract etc.) to do *whatever* the legislature says, but that they are entitled to disobey or *in extremis* rebel when it goes beyond its limits. Accordingly citizens should understand that they, too, must try as hard as *they* can to understand what those limits are and whether or not the laws that are presented to them contravene those limits. Moreover, Locke wants to encourage a political culture in which people accompany these convictions with a sense that the matters in question are objective, and that they may get it wrong, and that if they do, they are answerable to God for their mistakes and for whatever havoc results.

Still – someone may respond – political culture and self-understanding are all very well; but why was Locke unwilling to countenance some arrangement like a supreme court to make a final determination about whether the legislature has betrayed its trust? Why would he not consider the option of the judicial review of legislation?

Scholars have noted that Locke says very little about the judiciary as a distinct branch of government. Peter Laslett argues that on Locke's account the judiciary was not a separate power at all: '[I]t was the general attribute of the state.'[46] To govern, on Locke's account, is to make a public judgement as to what natural law requires – both in general and in detail – and to set that judgement up as a basis for social coordination and enforcement. And that is what the Lockean legislature does. Unless one is

---

[44] Locke, *Two Treatises of Government*, II, para. 4, 269 (my emphasis).

[45] See ibid., II, para. 111, 343. See also Locke's insistence in the 'Preface' to the *Two Treatises of Government* that 'there cannot be done a greater Mischief to Prince and People, than the propagating wrong Notions concerning Government' (ibid., 138).

[46] Laslett, 'Introduction' to Locke, *Two Treatises of Government*, 120.

proposing a bicameral legislature (something with which Locke had no difficulty),[47] there is no need for an *additional* institution to test whether the legislature's enactments are in accordance with natural law. That is what legislating *is*; that is the function that legislators are supposed to perform as they deliberate and vote. To the extent that members of the society disagree about this – to the extent that the natural law limits are controversial – legislation just *is* the adjudication of those controversies.

In theory, that function might be performed by a nine man junta clad in black robes and surrounded by law clerks. They might be the ones who deliberate and judge and vote on these issues. Locke's point here is more or less the same as Hobbes's:[48] whatever is the supreme power is in effect the legislature. But Locke puts it more carefully and democratically than Hobbes does. His position seems to be that, if there are controversies among us about natural law, it is important that a *representative* assembly resolve them.[49] He thinks it important that the institution which, by its representative character, embodies our 'mutual Influence, Sympathy, and Connexion'[50] should also be the one which determines our disagreements about justice, rights, the common good, and natural law. The institution which comprises our representatives and the institution which resolves our ultimate differences in moral principle should be one and the same. It is by combining these functions that the legislature embodies our deliberative virtue and our sense of mutual responsibility. 'This', as Locke says, 'is the Soul that gives Form, Life, and Unity to the Commonwealth', and this is why an assault on the integrity or position of the legislature (whether from inside or outside its ranks) is the most heinous attack on 'the Essence and Union of the Society'.[51]

I find this a powerful and appealing position. It embodies a conviction that these issues of principle are *ours* to deal with, so that even if they must be dealt with by some institution which comprises fewer than all of us, it should nevertheless be an institution that is diverse and plural and which, through something like electoral accountability, embodies the spirit of self-government, a body in which we can discern the manifest footprints of our own original consent.[52] It connects the themes we have been pursuing in this part of the book with the themes we pursued in Chapters Two through Five – the importance of matters on which there are different views and variegated opinions being settled by institutions which in their size and diversity pay tribute to the essential plurality of politics.

---

[47] See Locke, *Two Treatises of Government*, II, para. 213, 408.
[48] Hobbes, *Leviathan*, Ch. XXVI, 184.
[49] See especially Locke, *Two Treatises of Government*, II, para. 94, 329–30 and para. 143, 364.
[50] Ibid., II, para. 212, 407.   [51] *Idem*.
[52] The phrase is from Pangle, *The Spirit of Modern Republicanism*, 254.

The second of the two examples I said I would invoke from the canon of political theory is the example of John Stuart Mill, in the argument about individual freedom that he presented in the essay *On Liberty*. When my students read *On Liberty*, they assume almost without thinking that it is a defence of the First Amendment, and a call for the institution of some similar constitutional constraint in Victorian England. It does not occur to them to take seriously Mill's insistence that he is not talking about laws and constitutions at all, that he is addressing himself to public opinion, that he is seeking to raise 'a strong barrier of *moral* conviction'[53] against 'an increasing inclination to stretch unduly the powers of society over the individual both by the force of opinion and even by that of legislation'.[54] In our modern preoccupation with mechanisms of enforcement, we tend to lose sight of the possibility that freedom of thought and discussion might be respected more on account of the prevalence of a spirit of liberty among the people and their representatives – a political culture of mutual respect – than as a result of formal declarations or other institutional arrangements.[55] That I think is serious short-sightedness. As the fate of scores of 'constitutions' around the world shows, paper declarations are worth little if not accompanied by the appropriate political culture of liberty. And political philosophy, if it has any effect in the world at all, is likely to have much more effect on political culture than it has on political institutions *per se*, even if that effect is more diffuse and less flattering to ourselves as would-be counsellors to the powerful.[56] In other words, I think that in political philosophy we should be as interested in the condition of political culture – the array of current understandings – as we are in having our own cherished principles institutionalized.

Certainly that was Mill's view. Individual liberty cannot be expected to hold its ground, said Mill, 'unless the intelligent part of the public can be made to feel its value'.[57] If we are concerned about individual liberty, then, the first thing we should do is not call for a Bill of Rights to be enforced by a court, but develop among ourselves a culture of liberty in which the idea is appreciated and taken seriously among those who will be participating in major social and political decisions. And – as I suggested in Chapters Ten and Eleven – this is what we should want to do anyway, if we really take liberty seriously. For we cannot seriously think that liberty in general is safe in a society in which it is an accepted political tactic to regard ordi-

---

[53] Mill, *On Liberty*, Ch. 1, 18 (my emphasis).   [54] *Idem.*
[55] Cf. Alexander Hamilton in *The Federalist Papers* LXXXIV, 476–7: The security of a right like freedom of the press, 'whatever fine declarations may be inserted in any constitution respecting it, must altogether depend on public opinion, and on the general spirit of the people and of the government. And here, after all, . . . must we seek for the only solid basis of all our rights.'
[56] See Waldron, 'What Plato Would Allow' and also Waldron, 'Dirty Little Secret'.
[57] Mill, *On Liberty*, Ch. 3, 90.

nary citizens as nothing but selfish and irresponsible members of preda-tory political majorities. Taking liberty seriously means taking each other seriously as holders of views about liberty.

But here's the twist. We cannot expect any idea – let alone the idea of lib-erty – to be taken seriously in society, we cannot expect the intelligent part of the public to feel its value, if it is not itself subject to vigorous debate and contestation. That is the argument put forward in defence of freedom of thought and discussion in Chapter Two of Mill's essay – the argument about the importance of disagreement in a vigorous and progressive cul-ture. And obviously it applies reflexively to liberty itself. The principle of liberty and the principles underlying other rights are no exception to Mill's argument that, without genuine debate and disagreement, a creed adopted among the people tends

to be received passively, not actively, . . . incrusting and petrifying [the mind] against all other influences addressed to the higher parts of our nature; manifest-ing its power by not suffering any fresh and living conviction to get in, but itself doing nothing for the mind or heart except standing sentinel over them to keep them vacant.[58]

Mill is notorious for the suggestion that it might even be necessary some-times to actually manufacture disagreement, if dissent is not available to perform this invigorating function. If people did not disagree about an issue of right, we might have to provide 'some contrivance for making the difficulties of the question as present to [each person's] consciousness as if they were pressed upon him by a dissentient champion, eager for his con-version'.[59] Fortunately we are not in that situation. Since there *are* people who disagree about any given proposition of right, and who will voice that disagreement 'if law or opinion will let them, let us thank them for it, open our minds to listen to them, and rejoice that there is someone to do for us what we otherwise ought, if we have any regard for either the cer-tainty or vitality of our convictions, to do with much greater labor for our-selves'.[60]

That, I think, is as good a place as any to finish. We *do* disagree about rights, and it is understandable that we do. We should neither fear nor be ashamed of such disagreement, nor hush and hustle it away from the forums in which important decisions of principle are made in our society. We should welcome it. Such disagreement is a sign – the best possible sign in modern circumstances – that people *take rights seriously*. Of course, as I have said a million times, a person who finds himself in disagreement with others is not for that reason disqualified from regarding his own view as correct. We must, each of us, keep faith with our own convictions. But taking rights seriously is also a matter of how we respond to contradiction

---

[58] Ibid., Ch. 2, 49–50.   [59] Ibid., Ch. 2, 53–4.   [60] Ibid., Ch. 2, 55.

by others, even on an issue of rights. Though each of us reasonably regards his own views as important, we must also (each of us) respect the elementary condition of *being with others*, which is both the essence of politics and the principle of recognition that lies at the heart of the idea of rights. When one confronts a right-bearer, one is not just dealing with a person entitled to liberty, sustenance, or protection. One is confronting above all a particular *intelligence* – a mind and consciousness which is not one's own, which is not under one's intellectual control, which has its own view of the world and its own account of the proper basis of relations with those whom it too sees as other. To take rights seriously, then, is to respond respectfully to this aspect of otherness and then to be willing to participate vigorously – but as an equal – in the determination of how we are to live together in the circumstances and the society that we share.

Bibliography

ACKERMAN, BRUCE, *Social Justice in the Liberal State* (New Haven: Yale University Press, 1980).
—— *We the People: Foundations* (Cambridge: Harvard University Press, 1991).
ALLEN, ANITA and REGAN, MILTON (eds.), *Debating Democracy's Discontents* (Oxford: Oxford University Press, forthcoming).
ANSCOMBE, G. E. M., 'Modern Moral Philosophy', in Anscombe, *Ethics, Religion, and Politics*.
—— *Ethics, Religion, and Politics: Collected Philosophical Papers*, Volume III (Oxford: Basil Blackwell, 1981).
—— and GEACH, PETER THOMAS (eds.), *Descartes: Philosophical Writings* (London: Nelson, 1964).
AQUINAS, THOMAS, *On Princely Government* in Aquinas, *Selected Political Writings*.
—— *Selected Political Writings*, edited by A. P. d'Entreves (Oxford: Basil Blackwell, 1959).
ARENDT, HANNAH, *The Human Condition* (Chicago: University of Chicago Press, 1958).
—— *On Revolution* (Harmondsworth: Penguin Books, 1973).
ARISTOTLE, *Nichomachean Ethics*, translated by Sir David Ross (London: Oxford University Press, 1954).
—— *The Politics*, edited by Stephen Everson (Cambridge: Cambridge University Press, 1988).
ARNESON, RICHARD, 'Democratic Rights and National and Workplace Levels', in Copp et al. (eds.), *The Idea of Democracy*.
ATIYAH, P. S. and SUMMERS, ROBERT S., *Form and Substance in Anglo-American Law: A Comparative Study of Legal Reasoning, Legal Theory, and Legal Institutions* (Oxford: Clarendon Press, 1987).
AUSTIN, JOHN, *Lectures on Jurisprudence*, Fifth edition, edited by R. Campbell (Edinburgh: John Murray, 1885).
—— *The Province of Jurisprudence Determined*, edited by Wilfrid E. Rumble. (Cambridge: Cambridge University Press, 1995).
BAGEHOT, WALTER, *The English Constitution* (London: Oxford University Press, 1928).
BAKER, KEITH MICHAEL (ed.), *Condorcet: Selected Writings* (Indianapolis: Bobbs Merrill, 1976)
BALDWIN, S. E., *Two Centuries' Growth of American Law 1701–1901* (New York: C. Scribner's sons, 1901).
BARBER, BENJAMIN, *Strong Democracy: Participatory Politics for a New Age* (Berkeley: University of California Press, 1984).
BARRY, BRIAN, 'Comment', in Stanley Benn et al., *Political Participation*.
—— *Justice as Impartiality* (Oxford: Clarendon Press, 1995).
BEITZ, CHARLES, *Political Equality* (Princeton: Princeton University Press, 1989).

BENHABIB, SEYLA (ed.), *Democracy and Difference: Contesting the Boundaries of the Political* (Princeton: Princeton University Press, 1996).

BENN, STANLEY, 'The Problematic Rationality of Political Participation', in Benn at al., *Political Participation*.

—— et al., *Political Participation* (Canberra: Australian National University Press, 1978).

BENTHAM, JEREMY, *An Introduction to the Principles of Morals and Legislation*, edited by J. H. Burns and H. L. A. Hart (London: Methuen, 1970).

—— *Of Laws in General*, edited by H. L. A. Hart (London: Athlone Press, 1970).

—— *A Comment on the Commentaries and A Fragment on Government*, edited by J. H. Burns and H. L. A. Hart (London: Athlone Press, 1977)

—— 'Anarchical Fallacies', in Waldron (ed.), *Nonsense Upon Stilts*.

—— 'Supply without Burthern, *or* Escheat *vice* Taxation', in Waldron (ed.), *Nonsense Upon Stilts*.

BERLIN, ISAIAH, *Four Essays on Liberty* (Oxford: Oxford University Press, 1969).

BICKEL, ALEXANDER, *The Least Dangerous Branch: The Supreme Court at the Bar of Politics*, Second Edition (New Haven: Yale University Press, 1986).

BLACK, CHARLES L., Jun., *A New Birth of Freedom* (New York: Grosset/Putnam, 1997).

BLACKBURN, SIMON, 'Rule-Following and Moral Realism', in S. Holtzman and C. Leich (eds.), *Wittgenstein: To Follow a Rule* (London: Routledge, 1981).

—— *Spreading the Word: Groundings in the Philosophy of Language* (Oxford: Clarendon Press, 1984).

—— 'Errors and the Phenomenology of Value', in Honderich (ed.), *Morality and Objectivity*.

BLACKSTONE, WILLIAM, *Commentaries on the Laws of England*, (Philadelphia: J. B. Lippincott & Co., 1864).

BORK, ROBERT, 'Neutral Principles and Some First Amendment Problems', *Indiana Law Journal*, 47 (1971).

BOSANQUET, BERNARD, *The Philosophical Theory of the State*, Second Edition (London: Macmillan & Co., 1910).

BRENNAN, WILLIAM, 'Why Have a Bill of Rights?', *Oxford Journal of Legal Studies*, 9 (1989).

BREST, PAUL, 'The Misconceived Quest for the Original Understanding', *Boston University Law Review*, 60 (1980).

BRINK, DAVID, *Moral Realism and the Foundations of Ethics* (Cambridge: Cambridge University Press, 1989).

BURKE, EDMUND, *Reflections on the Revolution in France* (Harmondsworth: Penguin Books, 1969).

CALABRESI, GUIDO, *A Common Law for the Age of Statutes* (Cambridge: Harvard University Press, 1982).

CANE, PETER and STAPLETON, JANE (eds.), *Essays for Patrick Atiyah* (Oxford: Clarendon Press, 1991).

CANNING, JOSEPH, *The Political Thought of Baldus de Ubaldis* (Cambridge: Cambridge University Press, 1987).

—— *A History of Medieval Political Thought 300–1450* (London: Routledge, 1996).

CARTER, LIEF, *Contemporary Constitutional Law-making: The Supreme Court and the Art of Politics* (New York: Pergamon Books, 1985).

CHAPMAN, JOHN and WERTHEIMER, ALAN (eds.), *Nomos XXXII: Majorities and Minorities* (New York: New York University Press, 1990).

CHEYETTE, FREDRIC L. (ed.) *Lordship and Community in Medieval Europe: Selected Readings* (Huntingdon, NY: Robert E. Krieger, 1975) .

COBBETT, WILLIAM, *Advice to Young Men and Women, Advice to a Citizen* (1829).

COHEN, JOSHUA, 'Deliberation and Democratic Legitimacy', in Hamlin and Pettit (eds.), *The Good Polity*.

COHEN, MARSHALL (ed.), *Ronald Dworkin and Contemporary Jurisprudence* (Totowa: Rowman and Allenheld, 1983).

COLEMAN, JULES, 'Negative and Positive Positivism', in Coleman, *Markets, Morals and the Law*.

—— *Markets, Morals and the Law* (Cambridge: Cambridge University Press, 1988).

—— *Risks and Wrongs* (Cambridge: Cambridge University Press, 1992).

CONDORCET, MARQUIS DE, 'Essay on the Application of Mathematics to the Theory of Decision-making', in Baker (ed.), *Condorcet: Selected Writings*.

CONSTANT, BENJAMIN, 'The Liberty of the Ancients Compared with that of the Moderns', in Fontana (trans. & ed.) *Constant: Political Writings*.

COPP, DAVID, 'Could Political Truth Be a Hazard for Democracy?', in Copp et al. (eds.), *The Idea of Democracy*.

COPP, D., HAMPTON, J., AND ROEMER, J. (eds.), *The Idea of Democracy* (Cambridge: Cambridge University Press, 1993).

CRANSTON, MAURICE, 'Human Rights, Real and Supposed', in Raphael (ed.), *Political Theory and the Rights of Man*.

CROSLAND, SUSAN, *Anthony Crosland* (London: Jonathan Cape, 1982).

DAHL, ROBERT A., *Democracy and Its Critics* (New Haven: Yale University Press, 1989).

DANIELS, NORMAN (ed.), *Reading Rawls: Critical Studies on Rawls' A Theory of Justice*, Second Edition (Stanford: Stanford University Press, 1989).

DENNETT, DANIEL, 'Intentional Systems', *Journal of Philosophy*, 68 (1971).

DESCARTES, RENE, *Discourse on the Method of Rightly Directing One's Reason and of Seeking Truth in the Sciences*, in Anscombe and Geach (eds.), *Descartes: Philosophical Writings*.

DEVLIN, PATRICK, *The Enforcement of Morals* (Oxford: Oxford University Press, 1965).

DONALDSON, PETER, *Machiavelli and Mystery of State* (Cambridge: Cambridge University Press, 1988).

DWORKIN, RONALD, *Taking Rights Seriously*, Revised Edition (London: Duckworth, 1977).

—— 'Rights as Trumps', in Waldron (ed.), *Theories of Rights*.

—— *A Matter of Principle* (Cambridge: Harvard University Press, 1985).

—— *Law's Empire* (Cambridge: Harvard University Press, 1986).

—— *A Bill of Rights for Britain* (London: Chatto and Windus, 1990).

—— 'Objectivity and Truth: You'd Better Believe It', *Philosophy and Public Affairs*, 25 (1996).

DWORKIN, RONALD, *Freedom's Law: The Moral Reading of the American Constitution* (Cambridge: Harvard University Press, 1996).

ELSTER, JON, *Sour Grapes: Studies in the Subversion of Rationality* (Cambridge: Cambridge University Press, 1983).

—— *Ulysses and the Sirens: Studies in Rationality and Irrationality* (Cambridge: Cambridge University Press, 1984).

—— *Solomonic Judgements: Studies in the Limits of Rationality* (Cambridge: Cambridge University Press, 1989).

ELY, JOHN HART, *Democracy and Distrust: A Theory of Judicial Review* (Cambridge: Harvard University Press, 1980).

ESKRIDGE, WILLIAM N., *Dynamic Statutory Interpretation* (Cambridge: Harvard University Press, 1994).

ESTLUND, DAVID, 'Making Truth Safe for Democracy,' in Copp et al. (eds.), *The Idea of Democracy.*

ESTLUND, DAVID M., WALDRON, JEREMY, GROFMAN, BERNARD, and FELD, SCOTT L., 'Democratic Theory and the Public Interest: Condorcet and Rousseau Revisited', *American Political Science Review*, 83 (1989).

FARBER, DANIEL A. and FRICKEY, PHILIP P., *Law and Public Choice: A Critical Introduction* (Chicago: University of Chicago Press, 1991).

FEINBERG, JOEL, 'Noncomparative Justice,' in his collection Feinberg, *Rights, Justice and the Bounds of Liberty: Essays in Social Philosophy.*

—— *Rights, Justice and the Bounds of Liberty: Essays in Social Philosophy* (Princeton: Princeton University Press, 1980).

FINNIS, JOHN, *Natural Law and Natural Rights* (Oxford: Clarendon Press, 1980).

FISH, STANLEY, *Doing What Comes Naturally: Change, Rhetoric and the Practice of Theory in Literary and Legal Studies* (Durham: Duke University Press, 1989).

—— 'Play of Surfaces: Theory and Law', in Leyh (ed.), *Legal Hermeneutics.*

FONTANA, BIANCAMARIA (trans. & ed.), *Constant: Political Writings* (Cambridge: Cambridge University Press, 1988).

FORBATH, WILLIAM E., *Law and the Shaping of the American Labor Movement* (Cambridge: Harvard University Press, 1991).

FREEMAN, SAMUEL, 'Constitutional Democracy and the Legitimacy of Judicial Review', *Law and Philosophy*, 9 (1990).

FREY, R. G.(ed.), *Utility and Rights* (Oxford: Basil Blackwell, 1984).

FRIEDMAN, BARRY, 'The History of the Countermajoritarian Difficulty, Part One: The Road to Judicial Supremacy', *New York University Law Review*, 73 (1998).

FRIEDMAN, MILTON, *Capitalism and Freedom* (Chicago: University of Chicago Press, 1962).

FULLER, LON, 'Positivism and Fidelity to Law: A Reply to Professor Hart', *Harvard Law Review*, 71 (1958).

—— *The Morality of Law* (New Haven: Yale University Press, 1964).

GALLIE, W. G., 'Essentially Contested Concepts', *Proceedings of the Aristotlean Society*, 56 (1955–56).

GAUS, GERALD, *Justificatory Liberalism: An Essay in Epistemology and Political Theory* (New York: Oxford University Press, 1996).

GAUTHIER, DAVID, *Morals by Agreement* (Oxford: Clarendon Press, 1986).

—— 'Constituting Democracy', in Copp et al. (eds.), *The Idea of Democracy*.

GEWIRTH, ALAN, 'Positive Ethics and Normative Science', *Philosophical Review*, 69 (1960).

—— *Human Rights: Essays on Justification and Applications* (Chicago: University of Chicago Press, 1982).

GLENDON, MARY ANN, *Rights Talk: The Impoverishment of Political Discourse* (New York: Free Press, 1991).

GOODIN, ROBERT E., 'The State as Moral Agent', in Hamlin & Pettit (eds.), *The Good Polity*.

GRAY, JOHN CHIPMAN, *The Nature and Sources of the Law*, Second Edition (New York: Macmillan, 1927).

GREEN, LESLIE, 'Law, Coordination and the Common Good', *Oxford Journal of Legal Studies*, 3 (1983).

—— 'The Concept of Law Revisited', *Michigan Law Review*, 94 (1996).

GREENAWALT, KENT, *Law and Objectivity* (New York: Oxford University Press, 1992).

GRICE, PAUL, *Studies in the Way of Words* (Cambridge: Harvard University Press, 1989).

GRIFFIN, JAMES, *Well-Being: Its Meaning, Measurement and Moral Importance* (Oxford: Clarendon Press, 1986).

GROFMAN, BERNARD and FELD, SCOTT, 'Rousseau's General Will: A Condorcetian Perspective', *American Political Science Review*, 82 (1988).

GUINIER, LANI, *The Tyranny of the Majority: Fundamental Fairness in Representative Democrcay* (New York: Free Press, 1995).

GUTMANN, AMY, 'Democracy and its Discontents', in Sarat and Villa (eds.), *Liberal Modernism and Democratic Individuality*.

—— and THOMPSON, DENNIS, *Democracy and Disagreement* (Cambridge: Harvard University Press, 1996).

HABERMAS, JURGEN, *Moral Consciousness and Communicative Action*, translated by Christian Lenhardt and Shierry Weber Nicholsen (Cambridge: MIT Press, 1990).

—— *Between Facts and Norms: Contributions to a Discourse Theory of Law and Democracy*, translated by William Rehg (Cambridge: MIT Press, 1996).

HAMLIN, ALAN and PETTIT, PHILIP (eds.), *The Good Polity: Normative Analysis of the State* (Oxford: Basil Blackwell, 1989).

HAMPTON, JEAN, *Hobbes and the Social Contract Tradition* (Cambridge: Cambridge University Press, 1986).

HAND, LEARNED, *The Spirit of Liberty* (New York: Knopf, 1952).

—— *The Bill of Rights* (Cambridge: Harvard University Press, 1958).

HARDIN, RUSSELL, *Morality Within the Limits of Reason* (Chicago: University of Chicago Press, 1988).

—— 'Public Choice versus Democracy', in Copp et al. (eds.), *The Idea of Democracy*.

HARE, R. M., *The Language of Morals* (Oxford: Clarendon Press, 1952).

—— *Moral Thinking: Its Levels, Method and Point* (Oxford: Clarendon Press, 1981).

HART, H. L. A., *Law, Liberty and Morality* (Oxford: Oxford University Press, 1963).

—— *Essays on Bentham: Jurisprudence and Political Theory* (Oxford: Clarendon Press, 1982).

HART, H. L. A., 'Positivism and the Separation of Law and Morals', reprinted in Hart, *Essays in Jurisprudence and Philosophy*.

—— *Essays in Jurisprudence and Philosophy* (Oxford: Clarendon Press, 1983).

—— 'Are There Any Natural Rights?', in Waldron (ed.), *Theories of Rights*.

—— *The Concept of Law*, Second Edition, edited by Penelope Bulloch and Joseph Raz (Oxford: Clarendon Press, 1994).

HAYEK, F. A., *The Constitution of Liberty* (London: Routledge and Kegan Paul, 1960).

—— *Rules and Order* (London: Routledge and Kegan Paul, 1973).

HOBBES, THOMAS, *De Cive: The English Version*, edited by Howard Warrender (Oxford: Clarendon Press, 1983).

—— *Leviathan*, edited by Richard Tuck (Cambridge: Cambridge University Press, 1988).

—— *Behemoth* or *The Long Parliament*, edited by Stephen Holmes (Chicago: University of Chicago Press, 1990).

—— *De Corpore Politico*, edited by J. C. A. Gaskin (Oxford: Oxford University Press, 1994).

HOHFELD, WESLEY N., *Fundamental Legal Conceptions* (New Haven: Yale University Press, 1923).

HOLMES, STEPHEN, *Passions and Constraint: On the Theory of Liberal Democracy* (Chicago: University of Chicago Press, 1995).

—— and SUNSTEIN, CASS, 'The Politics of Constitutional Revision in Eastern Europe', in Levinson (ed.), *Responding to Imperfection*.

HOLT, J. C., *Magna Carta*, Second Edition (Cambridge: Cambridge University Press, 1992).

HONDERICH, TED (ed.), *Morality and Objectivity: a Tribute to J. L. Mackie* (London: Routledge, 1985).

HONIG, BONNIE, *Political Theory and the Displacement of Politics* (Ithaca: Cornell University Press, 1993).

HUME, DAVID, *A Treatise of Human Nature*, edited by L. A. Selby-Bigge (Oxford: Clarendon Press, 1888).

—— *An Enquiry Concerning the Principles of Morals*, edited by L. A. Selby-Bigge (Oxford: Clarendon Press, 1902).

JEFFERSON, THOMAS, *Writings*, edited by Merrill Peterson (New York: Library of America, 1984).

KANT, IMMANUEL, *Grounding for the Metaphysics of Morals*, translated by J. Ellington (Indianapolis: Hackett Books, 1981).

—— *The Metaphysics of Morals*, translated by Mary Gregor (Cambridge: Cambridge University Press, 1991).

KELLEY, DONALD R., *The Human Measure: Social Thought in the Western Legal Tradition* (Cambridge: Harvard University Press, 1990).

KELSEN, HANS, *The Pure Theory of Law*, translated by Max Knight (Berkeley: University of California Press, 1970).

KNAPP, STEVEN and MICHAELS, WALTER BENN, 'Against Theory', *Critical Inquiry*, 8 (1982).

KNAPP, STEVEN and MICHAELS, WALTER BENN, 'Intention, Identity and the Constitution: A Response to David Hoy', in Leyh (ed.), *Legal Hermeneutics*.

KNIGHT, JACK and JOHNSON, JAMES, 'Aggregation and Deliberation: On the Possibility of Democratic Legitimacy', *Political Theory*, 22 (1994).

LANDES, WILLIAM and POSNER, RICHARD, 'The Independent Judiciary in an Interest-Group Perspective', *Journal of Law and Economics* 18 (1975).

LASLETT, PETER and FISHKIN, JAMES (eds.), *Philosophy, Politics and Society*, Fifth Series (Oxford: Basil Blackwell, 1979).

LASLETT, PETER and RUNCIMAN, W. G. (eds.), *Philosophy, Politics and Society*, Second Series (Oxford: Basil Blackwell, 1969).

LAUNDY, PHILIP D., *Parliaments in the Modern World* (Brookfield, Vt.: Gower Publishing, 1989).

LEVINSON, SANFORD, *Constitutional Faith* (Princeton: Princeton University Press, 1988).

—— (ed.), *Responding to Imperfection: The Theory and Practice of Constitutional Amendment* (Princeton: Princeton University Press, 1995).

LEYH, GREGORY (ed.), *Legal Hermeneutics: History, Theory and Practice* (Berkeley: University of California Press, 1992).

LIEBERMAN, DAVID, *The Province of Legislation Determined: Legal Theory in Eighteenth Century Britain* (Cambridge: Cambridge University Press, 1989).

LINCOLN, ABRAHAM, 'First Inaugural Address', in Lincoln, *Great Speeches*.

—— *Great Speeches* (New York: Dover Publications, 1991).

LOCKE, JOHN, *An Essay Concerning Human Understanding*, edited by P. Nidditch (Oxford: Clarendon Press, 1975).

—— *Two Treatises of Government*, edited by Peter Laslett (Cambridge: Cambridge University Press, 1988).

LOVIBOND, SABINA, *Realism and the Imagination* (Minneapolis: University of Minnesota Press, 1983).

LUHMANN, NIKLAS, *A Sociological Theory of Law*, translated by Elizabeth King and Martin Albrow (London: Routledge and Kegan Paul, 1985).

LUKER, KRISTEN, *Abortion and the Politics of Motherhood* (Berkeley: University of California Press, 1984).

LYONS, DAVID (ed.), *Rights* (Belmont: Wadsworth, 1979).

—— 'Utility and Rights', in Waldron (ed.), *Theories of Rights*.

MACCORMICK, NEIL, *Legal Reasoning and Legal Theory* (Oxford: Clarendon Press, 1978).

—— *H. L. A. Hart* (London: Edward Arnold, 1981).

MCDOWELL, JOHN, 'Values and Secondary Qualities', in Honderich (ed.), *Morality and Objectivity*.

MACEY, JONATHAN R., 'Promoting Public-Regarding Legislation through Statutory Interpretation: An Interest Group Model', *Columbia Law Review*, 86 (1986).

MACFARLANE, L. J., *The Theory and Practice of Human Rights* (London: St. Martin's, 1985).

MACINTYRE, ALASDAIR, *After Virtue: A Study in Moral Theory* (London: Duckworth, 1981).

MACKIE, J. L., *Ethics: Inventing Right and Wrong* (Harmondsworth: Penguin Books, 1977).

—— 'Can There be a Right-Based Moral Theory?', in Waldron (ed.), *Theories of Rights*.

MCMURRIN, S. (ed.), *Liberty, Equality and Law: Selected Tanner Lectures on Moral Philosophy* (Salt Lake City: University of Utah Press, 1987).

MADISON, JAMES, 'Speech of August 7, 1787', in Meyers (ed.), *The Mind of the Founder.*

—— HAMILTON, ALEXANDER, and JAY, JOHN, *The Federalist Papers* edited by Isaac Kramnick (Harmondsworth: Penguin Books, 1987).

MANSBRIDGE, JANE, *Why We Lost the ERA* (Chicago: University of Chicago Press, 1986).

MARMOR, ANDREI, *Interpretation and Legal Theory* (Oxford: Clarendon Press, 1992).

—— 'Authorities and Persons: A Reply to Jeremy Waldron', *Legal Theory*, 1 (1995).

MARONGIU, ANTONIO, 'The Theory of Democracy and Consent in the Fourteenth Century', in Cheyette (ed.), *Lordship and Community in Medieval Europe.*

MARSHALL, GEOFFREY, *Constitutional Conventions: The Rules and Forms of Political Accountability* (Oxford: Clarendon Press, 1984).

MARSIGLIO OF PADUA, *Defensor Pacis*, trans. Alan Gewirth (Toronto: University of Toronto Press, 1980).

—— *Defensor Minor and De Translatione Imperii*, ed. Cary J. Nederman (Cambridge: Cambridge University Press, 1991).

MARTIN, REX, *Rawls and Rights* (Lawrence: University Press of Kansas, 1985).

MARX, KARL, 'Critical Remarks on the Article "The King of Prussia and Social Reform" ' in McLellan (ed.) *Karl Marx: Selected Writings.*

—— *Karl Marx: Selected Writings*, David McLellan (ed.) (Oxford: Oxford University Press, 1977).

—— 'On the Jewish Question', in Waldron (ed.), *Nonsense Upon Stilts.*

MAY, KENNETH, 'A Set of Independent Necessary and Sufficient Conditions for Simple Majority Decision', *Econometrica*, 20 (1952).

MEESE, EDWIN, 'Interpreting the Constitution', in Rakove (ed.), *Interpreting the Constitution.*

MEYERS, MARVIN (ed.), *The Mind of the Founder: Sources of the Political Thought of James Madison* (Hanover: Brandeis University Press, 1973).

MICHELMAN, FRANK, 'Law's Republic', *Yale Law Journal*, 97 (1988).

MILL, JOHN STUART, *On Liberty* (Indianapolis: Bobbs Merrill, 1955).

—— *Collected Works of John Stuart Mill*, edited by John Robson (Toronto: University of Toronto Press, 1984).

—— *Essays on Equality, Law and Education*, in Mill, *Collected Works of John Stuart Mill*, edited by John Robson (Toronto: University of Toronto Press, 1984).

—— *Considerations on Representative Government* (Prometheus Books, 1991).

MITCHELL, AUSTIN, 'Clay Cross', *Political Quarterly*, 45 (1974).

MOORE, MICHAEL, 'Moral Reality', *Wisconsin Law Review* [1982].

—— 'A Natural Law Theory of Interpretation', *Southern California Law Review*, 58 (1985).

NAGEL, THOMAS, *The Possibility of Altruism* (Princeton: Princeton University Press, 1970).

—— *The View from Nowhere* (New York: Oxford University Press, 1986).

NEDELSKY, JENNIFER, *Private Property and the Limits of American Constitutionalism: The Madisonian Framework and its Legacy* (Chicago: University of Chicago Press, 1990).

NORTON, PHILIP (ed.), *Legislatures* (New York: Oxford University Press, 1990).

NOZICK, ROBERT, *Anarchy, State and Utopia* (Oxford: Basil Blackwell, 1984).

OKIN, SUSAN MOLLER, *Justice, Gender and the Family* (New York: Basic Books, 1989).

O'ROURKE, P. J., *Parliament of Whores: A Lone Humorist Attempts to Explain the Entire U.S. Government* (New York: Atlantic Monthly Press, 1991).

PANGLE, THOMAS, *The Spirit of Modern Republicanism.* (Chicago: University of Chicago Press, 1988).

PARFIT, DEREK, *Reasons and Persons* (Oxford: Clarendon Press, 1984).

PAUL, JEFFREY (ed.), *Reading Nozick: Essays on 'Anarchy, State and Utopia'* (Oxford: Basil Blackwell, 1982).

PENNOCK, J. ROLAND and CHAPMAN, JOHN W. (eds.), *Nomos XXV: Liberal Democracy* (New York: New York University Press, 1983).

PLATTS, MARK, 'Moral Reality', in Sayre-McCord (ed.), *Essays in Moral Realism.*

POGGE, THOMAS, *Realizing Rawls* (Ithaca: Cornell University Press, 1989).

POLSBY, NELSON W., *Congress and the Presidency*, Third Edition (Englewood Cliffs, NJ: Prentice Hall, 1976).

—— 'Restoration Comedy', *Yale Law Journal*, 84 (1993).

POPPER, KARL, *Conjectures and Refutations: The Growth of Scientific Knowledge* (London: Routledge and Kegan Paul, 1969).

POSNER, RICHARD, A., 'Statutory Interpretation – in the Classroom and in the Courtroom', *University of Chicago Law Review*, 50 (1983).

—— *Overcoming Law* (Cambridge: Harvard University Press, 1995).

POST, GAINES, *Studies in Medieval Legal Thought: Public Law and the State, 1100–1322* (Princeton: Princeton University Press, 1964).

POST, ROBERT, 'Theories of Constitutional Interpretation', in Post (ed.), *Law and the Order of Culture.*

—— *Constitutional Domains: Democracy, Community, Management* (Cambridge: Harvard University Press, 1995).

—— (ed.), *Law and the Order of Culture* (Berkeley: University of California Press, 1991).

POSTEMA, GERALD J., *Bentham and the Common Law Tradition* (Oxford: Clarendon Press, 1986).

POUND, ROSCOE, 'Common Law and Legislation', *Harvard Law Review*, 21 (1908).

QUINE, W. V. O., *Word and Object* (Cambridge: MIT Press, 1960).

RADIN, MAX, 'Statutory Interpretation', *Harvard Law Review*, 43 (1930).

RAKOVE, JACK (ed.), *Interpreting the Constitution: The Debate Over Original Intent* (Boston: Northeastern University Press, 1990).

RAKOWSKI, ERIC, *Equal Justice* (Oxford: Clarendon Press, 1991).

RAPHAEL, D. D. (ed.), *Political Theory and the Rights of Man* (London: Macmillan, 1967).

RAWLS, JOHN, *A Theory of Justice* (Cambridge: Harvard University Press, 1971).

—— 'The Basic Liberties and their Priority' (1981), in McMurrin (ed.), *Liberty, Equality and Law.*

RAWLS, JOHN, *Political Liberalism* (New York: Columbia University Press, 1993).

—— 'The Domain of the Political and Overlapping Consensus', in Copp et al. (eds.), *The Idea of Democracy*.

RAZ, JOSEPH, *The Authority of Law: Essays on Law and Morality* (Oxford: Clarendon Press, 1979).

—— *The Concept of a Legal System*, Second Edition (Oxford: Clarendon Press, 1980).

—— 'Authority, Law and Morality', *The Monist*, 68 (1985).

—— *The Morality of Freedom* (Oxford: Clarendon Press, 1986).

—— *Practical Reason and Norms*, Second Edition (Princeton: Princeton University Press, 1990).

—— 'The Relevance of Coherence', *Boston University Law Review*, 72 (1992).

—— *Ethics in the Public Domain* (Oxford: Clarendon Press, 1994).

REDMAN, ERIC, *The Dance of Legislation* (New York: Simon and Schuster, 1973).

REGIS, EDWARD (ed.), *Gewirth's Ethical Rationalism: Critical Essays* (Chicago: University of Chicago Press, 1984).

RIKER, WILLIAM H., *Liberalism Against Populism* (San Francisco: Witt Freeman, 1982).

—— and WEINGAST, BARRY R., 'Constitutional Regulation of Legislative Choice: The Political Consequences of Judicial Deference to Legislatures', *Virginia Law Review*, 74 (1988).

ROSENBERG, GERALD N., *The Hollow Hope: Can Courts Bring About Social Change?* (Chicago: University of Chicago Press, 1991).

ROUSSEAU, JEAN-JACQUES, *The Social Contract*, translated by G. D. H. Cole (London: Everyman, 1973).

RUBIN, EDWARD, 'Law and Legislation in the Administrative State', *Columbia Law Review*, 89 (1989).

RUSHDIE, SALMAN, *Imaginary Homelands: Essays and Criticism 1981–1991* (London: Granta Books, 1991).

SANDEL, MICHAEL, *Liberalism and the Limits of Justice* (Cambridge: Cambridge University Press, 1982).

SARAT, AUSTIN and KEARNS, THOMAS R. (eds.), *Law's Violence* (Ann Arbor: University of Michigan Press, 1992).

—— —— (eds.), *Legal Rights: Historical and Philosophical Perspectives* (Ann Arbor: University of Michigan Press, 1996).

—— and VILLA, DANA (eds.), *Liberal Modernism and Democratic Individuality* (Princeton: Princeton University Press, 1996).

SAYRE-McCORD, GEOFFREY (ed.), *Essays in Moral Realism* (Ithaca: Cornell University Press, 1988).

SCALIA, ANTONIN, *A Matter of Interpretation: Federal Courts and the Law* (Princeton: Princeton University Press, 1997).

SCHEFFLER, SAMUEL (ed.), *Consequentialism and its Critics* (Oxford: Oxford University Press, 1988).

SCHELLING THOMAS C., *Choice and Consequences: Perspectives of an Errant Economist* (Cambridge: Harvard University Press, 1984).

—— 'Ethics, Law and the Exercise of Self-Command', in McMurrin (ed.) *Liberty, Equality and Law*.

SCHWARTZ, BERNARD, *The Bill of Rights: A Documentary History* (New York: Chelsea House, 1971).

—— 'Curiouser and Curiouser: The Supreme Court's Separation of Powers Wonderland', *Notre Dame Law Review*, 65 (1990).

SEELEY, JOHN, *Introduction to Political Science: Two Series of Lectures* (London: Macmillan, 1896).

SELZNICK, PHILIP, *The Moral Commonwealth* (Berkeley: University of California Press, 1994).

SEN, AMARTYA, *Collective Choice and Social Welfare* (San Francisco: 1970).

—— 'Rights and Agency', in Scheffler (ed.), *Consequentialism and its Critics*.

SHAPIRO, IAN and DECEW, JUDITH WAGNER (eds.), *Nomos XXXVII: Theory and Practice* (New York: New York University Press, 1995).

SHUE, HENRY, *Basic Rights: Subsistence, Affluence and U.S. Foreign Policy* (Princeton: Princeton University Press, 1980).

SIMON, WILLIAM, 'Legality, Bureaucracy, and Class in the Welfare System', *Yale Law Journal*, 92 (1983).

SKINNER, DAVID and LANGDON, JULIA, *The Story of Clay Cross* (London: Spokesman Books, 1974).

SKINNER, QUENTIN, *The Foundations of Modern Political Thought*, Volume One: *The Renaissance* (Cambridge: Cambridge University Press, 1978).

SMITH, WILLIAM, *Remarks on Law Reform* (London: Sweet and Maxwell, 1840).

STRACHEY, LYTTON, *Eminent Victorians* (New York: Harcourt Brace and Company, 1918).

STURGEON, NICHOLAS, 'Moral Explanations', in Geoffrey Sayre-McCord (ed.), *Essays on Moral Realism*.

SUMMERS, ROBERT S., 'Statutes and Contracts as Founts of Formal Reasoning', in Cane and Stapleton (eds.), *Essays for Patrick Atiyah*.

SUNSTEIN, CASS R., *The Partial Constitution* (Cambridge: Harvard University Press, 1993).

—— *Legal Reasoning and Political Conflict* (New York: Oxford University Press, 1996).

THOMPSON, E. P., *Whigs and Hunters: The Origin of the Black Act* (Harmondsworth: Penguin Books, 1977).

THOREAU, HENRY DAVID, 'Civil Disobedience', in Thoreau, *Walden & Other Writings*.

—— *Walden & Other Writings of Henry David Thoreau*, ed. Brooks Atkinson (New York: Modern Library, 1937).

TIEDEMAN, C. G., *The Unwritten Constitution of the United States* (New York: G.P. Putnam's Sons, 1890).

TIERNEY, BRIAN, *Religion, Law, and the Growth of Constitutional Thought: 1150–1650* (Cambridge: Cambridge University Press, 1982).

TOCQUEVILLE, ALEXIS DE, *Democracy in America*, Henry Reeve translation (New Rochelle, NY: Arlington House, n.d.).

TWINING, WILLIAM and MIERS, D., *How to do Things With Rules* (London: Wiedenfeld and Nicholson, 1976).

ULLMANN, WALTER, *Principles of Government and Politics in the Middle Ages* (London: Methuen, 1961).

ULLMANN, WALTER, *A History of Political Thought in the Middle Ages* (Harmondsworth: Penguin Books, 1965).

—— *Jurisprudence in the Middle Ages* (London: Variorum Reprints, 1980).

UNGER, ROBERTO MANGABEIRA, *What Should Legal Analysis Become?* (London: Verso, 1996).

VIROLI, MAURIZIO, *From Politics to Reason of State: The Acquisition and Transformation of the Language of Politics 1250–1600* (Cambridge: Cambridge University Press, 1992).

VLASTOS, GREGORY, 'Justice and Equality', in Waldron (ed.), *Theories of Rights.*

WALDRON, JEREMY, 'A Right to Do Wrong', *Ethics*, 92 (1981); reprinted in Waldron, *Liberal Rights.*

—— 'Theoretical Foundations of Liberalism', *Philosophical Quarterly*, 37 (1987); reprinted in Waldron, *Liberal Rights..*

—— *The Right to Private Property* (Oxford: Clarendon Press, 1988).

—— 'Rights in Conflict', *Ethics*, 99 (1989); reprinted in Waldron, *Liberal Rights.*

—— *The Law* (London: Routledge, 1990) .

—— 'Rights and Majorities: Rousseau Revisited', in Chapman and Wertheimer (eds.), *Nomos XXXII: Majorities and Minorities*; reprinted in Waldron, *Liberal Rights.*

—— 'Minority Cultures and the Cosmopolitan Alternative', *University of Michigan Journal of Law Reform*, 25 (1992).

—— *Liberal Rights: Collected Papers 1981–91* (Cambridge: Cambridge University Press, 1993).

—— 'A Right-Based Critique of Constitutional Rights', *Oxford Journal of Legal Studies*, 13 (1993).

—— 'Assurances of Objectivity', *Yale Journal of Law and Humanities*, 5 (1993).

—— 'Religious Contributions to Political Deliberation', *San Diego Law Review*, 30 (1993).

—— 'Vagueness in Law and Language – Some Philosophical Perspectives', *California Law Review*, 82 (1994).

—— 'Freeman's Defense of Judicial Review', *Law and Philosophy*, 13 (1994).

—— 'What Plato Would Allow', in Shapiro and Decew (eds.), *Nomos XXXVII: Theory and Practice.*

—— 'The Wisdom of the Multitude: Some Reflections on Bk. III, Ch. 11 of Aristotle's *Politics*', *Political Theory*, 23 (1995).

—— 'Rights and Needs – The Myth of Disjunction', in Sarat and Kearns (eds.), *Legal Rights: Historical and Philosophical Perspectives.*

—— 'Kant's Legal Positivism', *Harvard Law Review*, 109 (1996).

—— 'Supply Without Burthern Revisited', *Iowa Law Review*, 82 (1997).

—— 'Dirty Little Secret', *Columbia Law Review*, 98 (1998).

—— 'Locke's Legislature', in Waldron, *The Dignity of Legislation.*

—— 'All We Like Sheep', forthcoming in *Canadian Journal of Law and Philosophy* (1999).

—— 'Virtue *en Masse*', in Allen and Regan (eds.), *Debating Democracy's Discontents.*

—— *The Dignity of Legislation* (Cambridge: Cambridge University Press, forthcoming).

—— (ed.), *Theories of Rights* (Oxford: Oxford University Press, 1984).

—— (ed.), *Nonsense Upon Stilts: Bentham, Burke and Marx on the Rights of Man* (London: Methuen, 1987).

WALKER, RALPH, *The Coherence Theory of Truth: Realism, Anti-Realism, Idealism* (London: Routledge, 1989).

WALZER, MICHAEL, *Spheres of Justice* (New York: Basic Books, 1983).

WEBER, MAX, *Economy and Society*, edited by G. Roth and C. Wittich (Berkeley: University of California Press, 1968).

WELLMAN, CARL, *Real Rights* (New York: Oxford University Press, 1995).

WHEARE, K. C., *Legislatures*, Second Edition (Oxford: Oxford University Press, 1968).

WINCH, PETER, *The Idea of a Social Science and its Relation to Philosophy* (London: Routledge and Kegan Paul, 1958).

WINSTON, KENNETH, 'Toward a Liberal Conception of Legislation', in Pennock and Chapman (eds.), *Nomos XXV: Liberal Democracy*.

WITTGENSTEIN, LUDWIG, *Philosophical Investigations*, trans. G. E. M. Anscombe (Oxford: Basil Blackwell, 1984).

WOLLHEIM, RICHARD, 'A Paradox in the Theory of Democracy', in Laslett and Runciman (eds.), *Philosophy, Politics and Society*.

WOOLF, CECIL N. SIDNEY, *Bartolus of Sassoferrato: His Position in the History of Medieval Political Thought* (Cambridge: Cambridge University Press, 1913).

WOOTTON, DAVID (ed.), *Divine Right and Democracy: An Anthology of Political Writing in Stuart England* (Harmondsworth: Penguin Books, 1986).

YOUNG, IRIS MARION, 'Communication and the Other: Beyond Deliberative Democracy', in Benhabib (ed.), *Democracy and Difference*.

Index